READINGS OF THE *GATELESS BARRIER*

COLUMBIA READINGS OF BUDDHIST LITERATURE

COLUMBIA READINGS OF
BUDDHIST LITERATURE

SERIES EDITOR: STEPHEN F. TEISER

The series Columbia Readings of Buddhist Literature is intended to offer students and teachers the best scholarship, in a pedagogically useful form, concerning the whole range of Buddhist literature. Each book in the series is crafted to provide for each Buddhist text the essential background knowledge, a series of close readings of the text, and introductions to the ways the text has been interpreted throughout the history of Buddhism. The Dharma Drum Foundation for Research in the Humanities and Social Sciences is delighted to sponsor the series. The foundation supports a wide range of scholarly research, academic exchange, publications, and social work. The present work is one of the finest exemplary East Asian texts for this series, and we look forward to future volumes that will further the understanding of Buddhist literature.

—Sheng Yen (1931–2009), Founder of Dharma Drum Foundation

This series is published with the sponsorship of the Dharma Drum Foundation for Humanities and Social Science Research.

Readings of Dōgen's Treasury of the True Dharma Eye, Steven Heine

Readings of Śāntideva's Guide to Bodhisattva Practice, Jonathan C. Gold and Douglas S. Duckworth, editors

Readings of the Vessantara Jātaka, Steven Collins, editor

Readings of the Platform Sūtra, Morten Schlütter and Stephen F. Teiser, editors

Readings of the Lotus Sūtra, Stephen F. Teiser and Jacqueline I. Stone, editors

READINGS OF THE
GATELESS BARRIER

Edited by Jimmy Yu

COLUMBIA UNIVERSITY PRESS   NEW YORK

Columbia University Press
Publishers Since 1893
New York   Chichester, West Sussex

Library of Congress Cataloging-in-Publication Data
Names: Huikai, 1183–1260. Wumen guan. English. | Yu, Jimmy, 1968– editor.
Title: Readings of the Gateless barrier / edited by Jimmy Yu.
Description: New York : Columbia University Press, 2024. | Series: Columbia readings of
Buddhist literature | Includes bibliographical references and index.
Identifiers: LCCN 2023059386 (print) | LCCN 2023059387 (ebook) | ISBN 9780231207362
(hardback) | ISBN 9780231207379 (trade paperback) | ISBN 9780231556958 (ebook)
Subjects: LCSH: Huikai, 1183–1260. Wumen guan. | Koan. | Spiritual life—Zen Buddhism.
Classification: LCC BQ9289.H843 R43 2024 (print) | LCC BQ9289.H843 (ebook) |
DC 294.3/443—dc23/eng/20240108

Cover design: Milenda Nan Ok Lee
Cover calligraphy: Kun Tianshi
Cover art: elic / Shutterstock

CONTENTS

ACKNOWLEDGMENTS

I WISH TO express my gratitude to the Dharma Drum Foundation for their dedication to the series Columbia Readings of Buddhist Literature, and to the series editor, Stephen F. Teiser, for his kind and clear guidance. I am grateful also to Columbia University Press, especially to our executive editor, Wendy Lochner, and to our copyeditor and production editor, Leslie Kriesel. I also want to voice my thanks to Ashley Messenger, whose meticulous work as my editor was crucial in the preparation of the manuscript. Many thanks also to Özüm Üçok-Sayrak, who prepared the index with care and expertise. I also extend my thanks to our contributors for their generosity in sharing their insights and experience. To our families we remain grateful, as always, for their patience and support.

A NOTE TO THE READER

ALTHOUGH THERE are many English translations of the *Gateless Barrier*, we have provided an authoritative annotated translation at the end of this volume that each contributor cites in their chapter. The back matter also includes a review of the strengths and weaknesses of all major English translations of the *Gateless Barrier* and a cross-reference between our translation and three selected English translations, with page numbers for different cases. In the character glossary, Chinese pronunciations of personal names in the *Gateless Barrier* are provided first, followed by their Japanese pronunciation for those more familiar with the Japanese Zen tradition. All Asian personal names, technical terms, and title of texts are indicated by S, C, K, and J for Sanskrit, Chinese, Korean, and Japanese throughout this volume.

READINGS OF THE *GATELESS BARRIER*

INTRODUCTION

THE *GATELESS BARRIER* IN CONTEXT

Jimmy Yu

THE *GATELESS Barrier* (C. *Wumen guan*; J. *Mumonkan*; K. *Mumun'gwan*) is one of the most innovative, beloved, yet enigmatic texts of East Asian Buddhism. Compiled by the Chinese Chan master Wumen Huikai (1183–1260) in 1228, this work contains forty-eight "public cases" or *gong'ans* (J. *kōans*; K. *kongans*)—dialogues or stories of spiritual awakening—that arguably represent the best examples of the *gong'an* genre. Modern scholars have written extensively about the general history of this literature, but there is no single volume dedicated to examining the innovation, use, and influence of the *Gateless Barrier gong'an* collection from the past to the present. This book fills that void and introduces the various ways this seminal work has been read, contemplated, transmitted, and experienced in the history of East Asian Buddhism and in modern times. In doing so, it opens up new ways of appreciating the text from philosophical, literary, cultural, gendered, and experiential perspectives.

One of the unique features of this volume consists in its effort to bring together both scholarly studies and experiential insight on *Gateless Barrier gong'ans*. The past few decades, particularly in North America, have witnessed a scholarly shift in Buddhist and Chan/Zen studies from philological and philosophical analyses to historical and culturally embodied approaches. This has resulted in a more nuanced appreciation of the development of Buddhist thought and enriched our understanding of the ever-evolving ways of reading Buddhist teachings. The *Gateless Barrier* is a text that people have contemplated and worked with in meditation for centuries, right up to the present. One might therefore consider the *Gateless Barrier* as a site of social rift, insight, and personal meaning that has orchestrated how people saw and continue to experience the world.

The *Gateless Barrier*'s significance has also changed through time. It had faded into obscurity as an independently circulating work during the latter part of the imperial period in China but became central in Japan because Wumen had a Japanese dharma heir, Muhon Kakushin (1207–1298), who brought it back to Japan. The work soon became an object of study for both Sōtō and Rinzai traditions of Japanese Zen, and even part of the curriculum for Zen monastics. It became so popular that some cases in modified form would show up in theatrical plays for the general public. In the modern West, it was translated into English well over a dozen times, and people have appreciated it from multiple perspectives as a source of authority, inspiration, and spiritual insight. With a life of its own, the *Gateless Barrier* is anything but an antiquarian, fossilized text of scholarly inquiry.

In attempting to work toward a more balanced approach by providing a grounded and three-dimensional picture of how the *Gateless Barrier* was—and continues to be—practiced and lived, this volume situates the text intimately in its historical, social, cultural, and literary contexts across the past and present. The overall aim is to provide a range of perspectives on the spectrum between objectivity and normativity, offering both outsider and insider, etic and emic appreciations of the text.

The contributors to this volume have already substantially studied the *gong'an* literature or the *Gateless Barrier* specifically in previously published monographs or articles. Drawing from their earlier studies, they have streamlined and updated their perspectives to bring new insights and interpretations, with the goal of helping beginners through the process of close reading. Each of them approaches the *Gateless Barrier* from a particular angle, offering insights on its historical relevance, literary structure, and philosophical implications, as well as on the embodied practice and contemporary experience of *gong'ans*.

To introduce first-time readers to the rich world of the *Gateless Barrier*, the following provides a broad overview of the central doctrinal and historical tenets of Buddhism, the evolution of Buddhist thought as it traveled from India to East Asia, the various approaches to Buddhist meditation, and the unique contributions of Chan "public cases," or *gong'ans*, in the world of the *Gateless Barrier*. This overview concludes with chapter summaries.

THE BUDDHA AND HIS MESSAGE

Any reference to Buddhism or Chan should begin with the historical Buddha and his significance to the rest of the Buddhist tradition. The person we normally refer to as the Buddha was a man who was born as Siddhartha Gautama, the son of a king from the Śākya clan near what is today southern Nepal. While the exact date of his birth is unknown, many scholars have set it at 563 BCE; other sources suggest that he may have been born as much as a century later, around 480. It is said that when he came to the age to succeed his father as ruler, he took an excursion outside of the palace walls. After that trip, shocked by the sufferings of sickness, old age, and death, he became an ascetic and renounced his hitherto sheltered princely life to be a spiritual seeker, following the mendicant tradition of men who lived a contemplative life in the wilderness. He resolved to find liberation from cyclic, *saṃsāric* existence, the belief that sentient beings are bound to continual transmigration in different realms of existence without end until spiritual liberation is reached. After six years of meditation and asceticism, practicing with various teachers of the day, he went off to practice by himself and finally realized awakening, the truth of existence, and *nirvāṇa*, which is the cessation of suffering and its causes. He was liberated from *saṃsāra*. Subsequently, people referred to him as Śākyamuni, the sage from the Śākya clan. He taught for forty-five years—traveling with a group of disciples from city to city, village to village, across northeastern India—to those who would listen, occasionally debating with (and according to the Buddhist sources, always defeating) teachers from other mendicant traditions, gaining followers from all social classes. After his passing, his teachings continued to spread across all of Asia and eventually into the West, and find adherents up to the present.

The ultimate significance of Śākyamuni is his title, "Buddha," which means "awakened one," the past participle of the Sanskrit root *budh*, meaning "to awaken" or "awakening." This title embodies the core message of Buddhism. All the different traditions and teachings point to "awakening." The various regional developments in the teachings may differ, but the aim is basically the same: to wake up from the slumber of *saṃsāra*, as Śākyamuni had done, by realizing the truth of existence, the wisdom of nonself (S. *anātman*).

In contradistinction to many of the other philosophical and mendicant traditions at the time—which espoused the existence of an eternal self (S. *ātman*) that transmigrates from lifetime to lifetime, taking on and leaving behind a body, much as we don and doff our clothes each day—the

Buddha realized that beings are enslaved in the *saṃsāric* cycle of rebirths precisely because they fail to recognize that the "self" to which they cling so dearly is a collection of impermanent phenomena that "exists" entirely due to causes and conditions. In other words, there is no reified *thing* as self. Instead, self is made up of nonself—that is, made up of relationships and connections. He taught that grasping a false conception of self is a delusion that perpetuates karmic actions (of body, speech, and thought) and vexations (S. *kleśa*), the conditions for suffering.

The Buddha deconstructed the self into five groups, or aggregates (S. *skandhas*), to refute the notion of a permanent reified self. The first aggregate is form, which includes not only the sense faculties (eye, ear, nose, tongue, and body) but also their corresponding sense objects (sight, sound, smell, taste, and touch), however subtle and imperceptible they may be. The rest of the four aggregates are mental. The second is feeling, the factor that accompanies every moment of consciousness, of which there can be three types: pleasurable, painful, and neutral. Pleasure is defined as that which one wishes to encounter again when it ceases. Pain is that which one wishes to avoid when it arises. Neutrality is the feeling of indifference. All feelings are the effects of past actions, the fruition of karmic seeds planted in the past by virtuous and nonvirtuous deeds of body, speech, and mind. In other words, there's a causally generated history to why we like or dislike something. In this sense, we can simply understand karma as history. The third aggregate is perception, the innate mental ability to distinguish between objects. Like feeling, it accompanies all moments of consciousness, allowing the mind to differentiate one object from another and to recognize an object seen in the past. Unlike feeling, perception depends on words, language, and concepts to distinguish between objects, categorizing, discriminating, reifying, and comparing everything. The fourth aggregate, called volition or conditioning factors, is the action taken on the basis of the previous aggregates. Volition manifests as physical, verbal, and mental actions, encompassing a disparate set of factors, including what we would call emotions, both positive (such as nonattachment, effort, and humility) and negative (such as the vexations of greed, hatred, ignorance, pride, and jealousy). There are also factors that can be either virtuous or nonvirtuous, depending on one's intention (sleep, inquiry and analysis, etc.). The fifth aggregate is consciousness, a mental continuum that underlies the previous three aggregates of feeling, perception, and volition. In Buddhism, there are six forms of consciousness based on the six senses. The eye consciousness processes colors and shapes, the ear consciousness processes sounds, the nose consciousness processes smells, the taste consciousness processes flavors, the body consciousness processes tangible objects, and the mental consciousness processes mental phenomena, that is, anything we perceive or conceptualize. Within the sixth mental consciousness there is also the self-referential consciousness and an underlying repository consciousness for all karmic impressions or seeds. All these consciousnesses originate or arise in dependence on their corresponding sense faculties and sense objects, in a tripodic relationship.

In short, these five aggregates constitute what we call a "self" and exist interdependently, moment to moment, as a complex flow of psychosomatic events (S. *dharmas*). The analogy given in the scriptures compares this process to the flowing of water in a river. We all recognize what a river is, but when examined closely, there is no discrete *thing*. Just as a river is made up of nonriver—because it is made up of droplets of water—our sense of self is made up of nonself. Even though the flow of water makes the river seem solitary, permanent, and continuous, in truth there is nothing substantial that can be grasped. Similarly, searching exhaustively through all the aggregates, one will not be able to find any discrete thing that endures. Each aspect of experience disintegrates the moment it comes into existence.

The most important takeaway from this observation is that there is nothing graspable that can be assumed to be "self." All the aggregates of body and mind function perfectly without a doer of deeds or a thinker of thoughts. Buddhism teaches that we are simply a complex psychosomatic process, a flow of causes and effects, driven by karma or the history of habitual conditioning. To perceive a self amid this process, to posit an owner whose possessions extend to the mind and the body and then out into the world, driven by desire and protected by hatred, is how we suffer in life.

The ending of suffering is the direct, personal awakening to the absence of self, experiencing that this "me, I, mine"—which once seemed so real and solid—is never actually truly present as a reified thing in the first place. Such an experience is actually the most natural and ordinary functioning—when unhindered by deluded imaginations or habitual tendencies of grasping—of what Buddhists call *prajñā* or wisdom.

After the Buddha died, several schools of Buddhist thought developed, each with its own specific theories. Many of the sects have died out, but historians can point to a division between so-called "Early Buddhist" schools (Theravāda being the most prominent surviving sect) and Mahāyāna schools, which led to the Chan/Zen traditions. A prominent Mahāyāna school within Indian Buddhism that further elaborated on the teaching of *prajñā* was the Madhyamaka or "Middle Way" tradition. Nāgārjuna (second to third century CE), the principal thinker of this tradition, elaborated on the teaching of nonself in terms of *śūnyatā*, or emptiness, in his *Mūlamadhyamaka-kārikā* (*Fundamental Verses on the Middle Way*). Another Indian Mahāyāna tradition that became prominent was Yogācāra, founded by Asaṅga and Vasubandhu, brothers who lived around the fourth century CE. This tradition examined the practical ways of understanding emptiness to lead to liberation, detailing an intricate path that transforms the different layers of consciousness into the appropriate functions of *prajñā*.

The brief account above represents the most basic Buddhist teachings focused on awakening. The history of how Buddhists lived this truth is much more complicated and creative. Although prescriptive teaching of nonself was central, the descriptive historical reality of how practitioners actually understood this teaching varied considerably.

The Buddha purportedly taught in a direct and straightforward way about the truth he discovered, but later Indian traditions have complicated it through various interpretations and philosophical treatises. Within a hundred years after the Buddha passed away, numerous traditions arose with unique approaches to his teaching. Historians have counted approximately eighteen to twenty traditions of Buddhism practiced in different regions of India and what is now Central Asia during the BCE period. Some have persisted and evolved into the common era. According to scholars, one of those traditions, the Pudgalavādins, "those who affirm the existence of the person," for example, posited an ontological "self" as neither the same as nor different from—but inseparable from—the five aggregates. While other schools predictably accused them of having smuggled in an *ātman* or "self," they vigorously denied that their person was a self; rather, they argued that this self is not susceptible to annihilation, nor is it eternal—in fact, it is simply ineffable (S. *avaktavya*).[1] Sarvāstivādins, another conservative branch, in contrast, posited that while all things are impermanent, *dharmas*—the constituents that make up all phenomenal reality—are truly existent. The conservative Sautrāntika school's theory of karmic "seeds" evolved into two extremely important concepts: "store consciousness" (S. *ālayavijñāna*), which is the part of the consciousness where karmic impressions are supposedly "stored" until fruition, and the notion of "the embryo of the Buddha" (S. *tathāgatagarbha*), or buddha nature, the innate capacity in all beings to realize awakening. The idea of store consciousness was further developed by Yogācāra Buddhism, and the buddha nature idea was adopted by a relatively minor corpus of Mahāyāna texts centering on the *tathāgatagarbha*, the buddha within. Buddhists from different traditions have historically criticized these concepts as bordering on positing the notion of self.

As these disparate teachings were committed to written form beginning sometime around the first century BCE, they spread widely to different parts of Asia and entered China around that time via the Silk Route through Central Asia. From China, Buddhism spread to the Korean peninsula around the fourth century CE, and then to Japan around the sixth century CE. In these East Asian regions, the dominant form was Mahāyāna. The two most prominent Chinese schools of Buddhism during the sixth and seventh centuries were Tiantai and Huayan. Tiantai was named after a mountain where Zhiyi (538–597), the founder of the tradition, resided. This school absorbed the Indian Madhyamaka teachings and further elaborated on them, based on the *Saddharma-puṇḍarīka*, or *Lotus Sūtra*, to suit the Chinese mind. The Huayan school was founded by Dushun (557–640) and developed by later thinkers such as Fazang (643–712). Its name comes from a translation of the *Avataṃsaka Sūtra*, or *Flower Ornament Scripture*, from which the school developed its central tenet of interpenetration of multiple realities, absorbing and furthering the Yogācāra and *tathāgatagarbha* teachings of Indian Buddhism. These two scripturally based doctrinal schools formed the basis of all East Asian Buddhist traditions. Moreover, adapting to indigenous Chinese Confucian and Daoist sensibilities, the Chinese ultimately synthesized and developed the practice-oriented tradition of Chan, which later became Sŏn in Korean and Zen in Japan.

Chan is often historicized as a Sinicized or Chinese form of Buddhism that arose in interaction with Confucianism and Daoism. But one shouldn't think of these three traditions (Confucianism, Daoism, and Buddhism) as disparate and independent. Doing so would mask the fluid boundaries and the shared linguistic-philosophical-religious ideas that pervade the larger Chinese religious landscape. For example, Chan masters used and adapted expressions that reflected Daoist terminology, such as "attaining the *dao*" ("the way") for Buddhist realization of the path (S. *mārga*), or *wu* ("nonexistence") for Buddhist ideas about the ungraspable truth of emptiness (S. *śūnyatā*). Even the Chan axiom that the truth is "not established on words and letters," pointing to the limitation of words, has deep resonance with the Daoist principle that "The way that can be spoken of is not the constant way; the name that can be named is not the constant name."[2] Many of these ideas permeated the culture socially, intellectually, and religiously, such that they would be instantly recognizable to people of different inclinations. These terms were part of the shared repertoire of Chinese language (and by extension the whole East Asian context) that had no equivalent in the original Sanskrit. But it is precisely because of these linguistic and cultural associations that Chan Buddhism would arise as the indigenous Chinese fulfillment of the Buddha's teachings on awakening. There are many good introductory books on the history of Indian Buddhism and its transformations in China and East Asia that provide further elaboration.[3]

THE CHAN PATH TO PRACTICE AND AWAKENING

Over the centuries, Buddhists in Asia have developed creative approaches or paths to awakening. Every Buddhist tradition claims its own path as the most efficacious. Some argue that delusion and defilement stem from self-grasping and that it must be eradicated for liberation to occur (proposed by so-called Early Buddhist schools). The Mahāyāna ("Great Vehicle") schools propose that even the dismantling of self must be dismantled, including all reified notions and phenomena (S. *dharma*), in order to truly realize emptiness or *śūnyatā* (proposed by the Madhyamaka tradition). Some schools set forth a detailed process of the bodhisattva path that transforms the different layers of deluded consciousness into the necessary wisdom that leads to full buddhahood (proposed by Yogācāra teachings). Some taught that all beings possess buddha nature, the potential for buddhahood, and from that perspective, all are already awakened, already free—they just need to recognize it (espoused in *tathāgatagarbha* texts). The whole East Asian tradition tried to harmonize these teachings as interrelated and not mutually exclusive through a strategy called "doctrinal classification" (C. *panjiao*; K. *pangyo*; J. *hankyō*). This system harmonized competing Buddhist teachings based on theme, time periods, and scriptures. For the purposes of this volume, the various approaches to awakening can be viewed as three distinct paths: *path of renunciation*, *path of transformation*, and *path of recognition*. This way of understanding the various strands of Buddhism avoids sectarianism and privileging the language of any specific approach. It also recognizes that aspects of these three paths can be found in all traditions of Buddhism. The reader will quickly understand where most Chan/Sŏn/Zen teachings fit within the scope of Buddhist teachings.

The *path of renunciation* corresponds to an apophatic approach of abandoning the vexations (S. *kleśas*, that is, greed, hatred, and ignorance) that fuel the cyclic existence of *saṃsāra* to awaken to the ineffable state of *nirvāṇa.* In this path, *saṃsāra* and *nirvāṇa* are perceived as opposite, wholly separate. Relatedly, the language of dismantling all the vexations that stem from self-attachment is characterized by the systematic taxonomy of defilements, the elaborate analysis of stages of their abandonment, and the gradual cultivation of concentration and insights that culminate in final liberation. In this scheme, awakening is not seen as a sudden realization of nonself; it is instead about the fruit of renunciatory practice, a systematic abandoning of defilements.

The *path of transformation* corresponds to practice-based approaches that fundamentally perceive *saṃsāra* as inseparable from *nirvāṇa*, maintaining that the former already provides all the necessary opportunities to realize the latter. Thus, the soteriological path is not abandoning *saṃsāra* in order to realize *nirvāṇa* but transforming *saṃsāra* into *nirvāṇa*—and furthermore, not only for oneself, but for all beings. Its core doctrine of *śūnyatā* (emptiness) as interdependence allows for the transformation from delusion to wisdom, from obstacles to opportunities, from consciousness to wisdom, and from *saṃsāra* to *nirvāṇa*. Since everything is interrelated and interdependent, salvation simply for oneself is seen as contrary to the nature of how things are. Thus, following this path, by working together with other living beings, the goal is shifted away from "*nirvāṇa*" per se to buddhahood, the complete fulfillment of wisdom and compassion.

The *path of recognition* builds on the nonduality of *saṃsāra* and *nirvāṇa* and espouses the mutual inclusivity of sentient beings and buddhas by teaching that awakening is already within all beings—in other words, that the mind's true nature is already free. Even vexations and deluded thinking have emptiness and freedom as their true nature. Awakened to this nature, one becomes a buddha. Deluded and unaware of it, one is an ordinary being. The perspective here is that if the true nature of all beings is originally free, naturally pure, then it cannot be hopelessly or irredeemably polluted. Consider, for example, a room's spacious nature. The nature of spaciousness is unaffected by clutter or cleanliness.

The Chan/Sŏn/Zen teachings belong to this path of recognition, where the practice is not about renouncing or transforming anything. Indeed, the very tendency to try to get rid of something (e.g., *saṃsāra*) in order to attain something else (e.g., *nirvāṇa*) is itself a delusion. One can't use delusion to cultivate *prajñā* or wisdom. This position is articulated most clearly in the *Platform Sūtra*, attributed to the sixth lineage master of Chan, Huineng (638–713).[4] Therefore, Chan master Mazu Daoyi (709–788) famously posited that "everyday mind is itself the Way" (*pingchang xin shi dao*).[5] This approach is fundamentally about recognizing what has always been true beyond the constructs of words, language, and labels. From this perspective, you are already free; the path is already present, everywhere; and contrived effort to practice is seen as extraneous. Ironically, however, various methods of Chan/Sŏn/Zen practice have been developed to provoke this awakening to selfless wisdom.

Mazu and other Chan masters' conception of the *dao* or the Way is readily seen in their discourse records (C. *yulu*). For example, a monk once asked Yunmen, "I want to be free. How do I attain freedom?" The master replied, "Who's binding you?!" Elsewhere, Linji gave this instruction to his students: "Followers of the way, as to buddhadharma, no effort is necessary. You only have to be ordinary, with nothing to do—defecating, urinating, wearing clothes, eating food, and lying down when tired."[6] In the discourse records attributed to these masters, and in the genealogical literature, or lamp records (C. *denglu*), that detailed the many interactions between a master and their disciples or interlocutors, awakening is often described as a pathless, dramatic, and sudden experience of wisdom.

Scholars argue that what became important in the Chan literature appears not to have been some abstracted Indian Buddhist depiction of liberation but the actual interaction with an awakened person, as exemplified by Chan masters who were considered the living buddhas of their time, those who had attained the *dao* or the Way. This performative soteriology, in which the drama of the practitioner's approach to and realization of awakening unfolded, later became known as "encounter dialogues," the demonstration and expression of awakening through actions.[7]

This is not to say that Chan monastics didn't meditate or cultivate the ability to work with vexations; we have descriptive accounts of their meditative practices. However, on a rhetorical and literary level, there developed a very distinct Chinese approach of articulating practice and awakening that ultimately led to the emergence of collections of master-disciple "encounters" and "public cases" of awakening stories known in Chinese as *gong'an* (K. *kongan*; J. *kōan*). The *Gateless Barrier* is a prime example of such a *gong'an* collection. These awakening stories evolved over time into literary compilations with prose and verse commentaries, and they became objects of contemplation in meditation.

One device used in these stories is paradox—the apparently nonsensical remarks or actions that jolt the mind to suddenly drop self-attachment, aware of a truth outside of ordinary logic. Another device commonly used is pseudological discussion or debate that appears completely ordinary and sober at first but ends by reducing language to gibbering inanity. Both devices are found in the *Gateless Barrier*, and they constitute one of the fiercest and most dazzling assaults ever made, not only on the conventional system of words and language but also on conventional concepts of time, space, reality, and causation. Finally, Chan *gong'ans* employ the deadliest of weapons against all that is pompous, staid, and holy: humor. Most philosophical traditions employ humor sparingly—a wise decision, no doubt, in view of the serious tone they seek to maintain—and some seem never to use it at all. Chan, on the contrary, makes it the very core of its pedagogical style, apparently knowing that one good laugh can do more than ten pages of harangue to shake people's confidence in the validity of their self-referential assumptions.

Before discussing the nature of these awakening stories, or *gong'ans*, it is useful to introduce the form, function, and history of *gong'an* collections.

WHAT IS A *GONG'AN*?

Gong'an literally means "public case." The term comes from Tang dynasty (618–907) civil court documents, referring to legal cases that must be resolved by a magistrate. Chan masters drew on this judicial metaphor to refer to the "cases" of certain past Chan masters and practitioners who had realized awakening. Just like magistrates who reviewed, scrutinized, and passed judgment on legal cases, Chan masters started to compile and comment on the short sayings and encounters of earlier masters and practitioners. Their commentary, like the magistrate's verdict, evaluated the most salient point of or catalyst for those awakening experiences, giving readers pointers of insight and inspiring them to take up these cases as their own objects of meditative investigation. The compilations of the cases together with the comments are called *gong'an* collections.[8]

Gong'an collections emerged during the Northern Song dynasty (960–1279), specifically around the twelfth century, but the literary form is complicated and can be traced back to the tenth century. The circumstances that led Chan writers to collect and collate anecdotes and sermons of past practitioners may have something to do with the collapse of the great Chinese Tang dynasty, in order to preserve the teachings of important masters and to identify a particular pattern of their awakening experiences or encounters to the Buddhist truth.

In this sense, *gong'an* collections are really anthologies of excerpted "encounters," of recorded interactions between Chan masters and their students found in discourse records and genealogical literature.

These two genres included sermons and conversations about Chan. By the tenth century, many Chan masters' discourse records already included a subgenre of texts called "verses on old [cases]" (C. *songgu*), which can be seen as a direct precursor to the *gong'an* collections of the twelfth century. This suggests that by the tenth century, the practice of commenting on earlier Chan masters' stories was already recognized as important. History has consistently shown that by the time ideas are committed to written texts, they have typically been circulating orally for a long time. The likelihood of an early phase of oral tradition within Chan cannot be overlooked.

THE STRUCTURE OF *GONG'AN* COLLECTIONS

As a literary phenomenon, *gong'an* collections are complicated, with multiple layers of comments sometimes by different masters—suggesting that their readers, who would have been Chan adepts, were expected to know the contexts of these stories, master a core repertoire of Chan texts, and display their mastery by being able to refer to them and perhaps by writing commentaries on them. This means that *gong'an* collections were part and parcel of an educated elite tradition in Chan, as some of the chapters in this volume show, akin to secular learning. For reasons that are detailed in chapter 2, the *Gateless Barrier* is an exception to this multilayer commentarial structure; it is straightforward, containing the root cases and one set of comments on them by Chan master Wumen Huikai (1184–1260).

Most other *gong'an* collections produced during the Northern Song period were quite complicated. For example, the *Blue Cliff Record* (C. *Biyan lu*; J. *Hekigan roku*), published in 1128 by Yuanwu Keqin (1063–1135), consists of root prose and verse commentary on a collection of 100 stories originally compiled by Chan master Xuedou Chongxian (980–1052). On top of this original material, Yuanwu provided a set of secondary prose and verse commentaries on Xuedou's prose and verse comments. In this sense, the *Blue Cliff Record* resembles a collaborative work of commentaries.

To each of Xuedou's original root cases, which are simple and short, a prelude by Yuanwu serves as a pointer for the reader. After each root case, Yuanwu provides a prose commentary and then the verse commentary, as well as a subcommentary on his own verse commentary. Moreover, interspersed with Xuedou's root cases, in both his prose and verse comments, are additional interlinear notes by Yuanwu. These notes, or annotations, are known as "capping phrases." Thus, the *Blue Cliff Record* consists of a complex of multilayered comments. Resembling a scriptural exegesis, this and other similarly intricate *gong'an* collections—such as the *Record of Serenity* (C. *Congrong lu*; J. *Shōyō roku*), published several years earlier in 1224 and consisting of 100 root cases by Chan master Hongzhi Zhengjue (1091–1157) with comments on them by Wansong Xingxiu (1166–1246)—invites readers to treat these works as objects of literary study.

Unlike a typical Chinese scriptural exegesis, *gong'an* comments, in both prose and verse form, do not explicitly explain or reify any Buddhist concepts. Instead, they read more like transcripts of vernacular, layered conversations. In the more complex *gong'an* collections such as the *Blue Cliff Record*, the initial conversation is between Xuedou, the compiler of the root cases, and Yuanwu, the commentator on Xuedou's root cases. A second discursive layer is added involving Yuanwu in a conversation with himself via his own comments! Finally, a third conversational layer is between Yuanwu and the audience, as he provides pointers to insights.

GONG'AN COMMENTS AS SOURCE OF AUTHORITY

Gong'an collections are taken by Chan practitioners to be equally as authoritative as traditional Buddhist scriptures and commentaries because they embody stories of awakening experiences. This authority is also forged through its production in literary, institutional, and ritual dimensions that are built into the *gong'an*.

The literary structure of *gong'an* comments, for example, always positions the Chan master compiler as the voice of awakening, equal to (and sometimes surpassing) the authority of the Buddha, passing magisterial judgment on the anecdotes of earlier masters.[9] That is to say, it is the compiler who always has the last word, commenting on the words and actions of former worthies. Consider case 6 in the *Gateless Barrier*, wherein Wumen comments on Śākyamuni Buddha holding up a flower and Mahākāśyapa smiles in response:

> He turned the noble into the lowly and sold dog meat and advertised it as mutton, proclaiming it marvelous. If the whole assembly had smiled, how would the Buddha have passed on the treasury of the true dharma eye? If Mahākāśyapa had not smiled, how would the Buddha have transmitted the treasury of the true dharma eye? If you say that the treasury of the true dharma eye can be transmitted, then the old golden-faced man would just

be deceiving villagers. If you say that it cannot be transmitted, then why did he approve of Mahākāśyapa? (see p. 255)

In this story, Wumen draws a simile between transmitting the "true dharma eye" to Mahākāśyapa, acknowledging the latter's awakened perception of the deeper significance of the Buddha's holding up a flower, to selling dog meat as mutton. Essentially, Wumen makes the Buddha out to be a charlatan, selling something as one thing despite it really being another. What's so marvelous about mutton? In fact, there is nothing special about dog meat or mutton—both are just meat. The point is not to declare which meat is better, but to eat one's fill. It is only in delusion that one sees mutton as better than dog meat. If one attaches to the expedient means of Śākyamuni or Wumen, then one misses the point, mistaking the finger pointing as the moon.

Wumen says, "If Mahākāśyapa had not smiled, how would the Buddha have transmitted the treasury of the true dharma eye?" Smile or no smile, what does it matter? How can any gesture definitively express the truth of awakening? In truth, awakening as freedom is already present; it is nothing special—like dog meat or mutton. However, awakening needs to be recognized. If one realizes awakening, something that is already present and available to all, would one make a thing out of it? From that awakened perspective, would one privilege awakening as a special experience over other experiences? Would awakening be unique and apart from delusion, if delusion is not real? Would there still be a need to "have passed on the treasury of the true dharma eye"?

Gong'an commentary pushes the practitioner to question and deconstruct conventional values people place on experiences and things. Awakening is a source of authority in the *gong'an* commentary. The Chan masters' authority comes from their position as commentators.

The Northern Song period was a time when many Chan masters and students engaged in reading, studying, commenting, and passing judgment on *gong'an* collections. It was part of the institution of Chan monasticism. The commenting itself occurred ritually as part of the Chan master's instructions to the monastics. The compilation and production of *gong'an* collections secured the Chan master commentator's special status. The widespread circulation of their comments through *gong'an* collections, and the practitioners' study of them, further affirmed their authority. All of this contributed to instituting the Chan master as the living truth of awakening.

THE *GATELESS BARRIER*

The *Gateless Barrier* by Wumen is the third of the three most famous Chinese *gong'an* collections. Different from the two described above, it arguably became one of the most influential and beloved *gong'an* collections because of its terseness and simplicity. Its aim and function appear to be very different. It does not include the elaborate literary features found in the *Blue Cliff Record*, and it does not contain expanded or interlinear commentaries on various aspects of the original cases. Instead, the *Gateless Barrier* is geared toward meditation practice.

The *Gateless Barrier* consists of forty-eight original cases of past Chan masters' sayings, compiled by Chan master Wumen himself, followed by his own instructions for how to engage with them. The instructions come in both prose and verse form, but the articulation is quite different from that found in the *Blue Cliff Record* and the *Record of Serenity* insofar as Wumen's comments intentionally aim to arouse a strong sense of existential wonderment and questioning in the reader, as he suggests in his comments on the first case.

Some modern scholars believe that Wumen first collected forty-eight old cases and then attached verses to them, and only later added the prose comments, thereby creating a *gong'an* collection. If that was indeed the process by which the text as we now have it came into existence, then we could perhaps view it as structurally similar to the original *songgu* "old cases" literature, having at its core a collection of old cases with attached verses, and the further addition of a prose comment—e.g., such as master Xuedou's root cases and verses or Hongzhi's root cases and verses, which later became the *Blue Cliff Record* and the *Record of Serenity*, respectively. However, Wumen states in his preface that he used these cases during a monastic retreat that he led at the Longxiang Monastery in the Dongjia region (present-day Wenzhou) in 1228. If we take this to be true, then the function and nature of these forty-eight cases, with his comments, are very different than the literary production of *songgu*, the *Blue Cliff Record*, and the *Record of Serenity*.

There is no explicit record of how Wumen used these *gong'ans* to teach his disciples, but there are indications in his preface and prose comments that he expected them to focus their minds with meditative effort on the *gong'ans* or specific passages therein. According to Wumen, the *gong'an* cases are meant to be engaged with through one's "whole being" as an embodied practice, and particular phrases ought to be at the front and center of one's attention "day and night" without interruption. This suggests that the *Gateless Barrier*, unlike the *Blue Cliff Record* and *Record of Serenity*, was conceived from the start as an aid to meditative practice. In this sense, perhaps the *Gateless Barrier* cases are not meant to be read or studied at all. Rather, they are meant to be engaged with, embodied, and realized.

THE PRACTICE OF WONDERMENT

The *Gateless Barrier* is unique and different from the Northern Song literary *gong'an* collections because of its emphasis on contemplative meditation. As Wumen's comments indicate, the specific *gong'ans* operate as "barriers" that must be passed through; practitioners must "arouse a mass of wonderment throughout their whole being, extending through the 360 bones and the 84,000 pores, as you come to grips" with each (see p. 251). This performative dimension of the *Gateless Barrier* points to how it was used normatively and still is being used today by Chan/Zen practitioners. As a method or meditative device, the practice of working with *gong'ans* is unique in the whole development of Buddhism. There is really nothing else quite like it.

Gong'an practice is engaging in this kind of embodied contemplation without becoming entangled in the search for its conceptual meaning; such an investigation engages with "live words" (C. *huoju*), whereas searching for a fixed meaning would only leave one bound by "dead words" (C. *siju*). At the center of the *gong'an* is the practice of "critical phrase," or *huatou* (J. *wato*; K. *hwadu*), that generates a sense of wonderment or uncertainty.

In the twelfth century, the Southern Song Chan master Dahui Zong'gao (1089–1163) shifted students away from the *gong'an* by encouraging students to meditate on the "critical phrase" or the *huatou*, which literally means the "source of spoken words." Scholars have coined a term for Dahui's meditative approach: "observing the critical phrase" (C. *kanhua*; K. *kanhwa*; J. *kanna*). The critical phrase is most often drawn from a key episode of a *gong'an*, though not all *gong'ans* supplied "critical phrases" that could be used in this way. In this sense, pivoting on a short, simple phrase, *huatous* are turning points or kernels that have the potential to spark an awakening experience. An example is the first *gong'an* in the *Gateless Barrier*: "One day a monk asked Chan master Zhaozhou Congshen, 'Does a dog have buddha nature?' Zhaozhou replied, 'No!'" The *huatou* of this *gong'an* is, "What is this 'No' (C. *Wu*; J. *Mu*)?"

The dilemma posed by this *gong'an* is that the Buddha said that all beings have buddha nature, the potential to become awakened. So why did Zhaozhou say "No"? To arouse a strong sense of wonderment or uncertainty, Wumen, in his prose comment on this *gong'an*, says that this "No" is not synonymous with the no that is the opposite of yes. This means that one cannot understand it in terms of yes or no, having or lacking, existing or not existing. In fact, to drive the sense of not knowing further, he says that this "No" is completely impenetrable and unfathomable. What is it, then? What does it mean? What is this "No"? It would be useless to come up with more concepts about it, much less study it. There's nothing to study; it's just impenetrable.

Faced with this impenetrability, Chan practitioners simply meditate on the *huatou*, or critical phrase, "What is *Wu*?" In Japan, Zen practitioners would ask, "What is *Mu*?" and stay with this sense of not knowing or wonderment until the whole world collapses into it. When this unified state of wonderment is shattered, due to some catalyst (from hearing a sound or seeing some form), one's sense of self-referencing or grasping would also be shattered. The experience of being without the filtering of self is considered awakening. However, when practitioners work on this *huatou*, they may come up with all kinds of "answers." One may even think the answer is to mimic a dog and bark, or give some other nonverbal performance. This is all wrong.

This sense of "wonderment," not knowing, or uncertainty is the key in *huatou* practice. Literally, wonderment is usually rendered as "doubt sensation" (C. *yiqing*). Many people translate it this way. However, this traditional translation leads to more problems than it clarifies. "Wonderment" is a better rendering because it conveys the sense of "not knowing" and "uncertainty," as opposed to the sense of "suspicion" and "distrust" that the word "doubt" conveys, which is also how *Webster's* dictionary defines it. In fact, in Buddhist doctrine, doubt, in the sense of suspicion (S. *vicikitsā*), is one of the six unwholesome mental factors, or *kleśas*, that hinder access to a concentrated or unified state. In Chan/Sŏn/Zen, wonderment is not this negative factor; it functions more like the indeterminate mental factor of "inquiry" or wanting to know something (S. *vitarka*), which is the basis for *huatou* practice.

Thus, *yiqing* has nothing to do with "doubt." *Yi* entails wondering and not knowing. It is used as an adjective to modify *qing*, which is the noun in this context, and it conveys the sense of feeling tone. Together, *yiqing* refers to the experiencing of wonder and not knowing, and this experience must be established on confidence and faith, as premodern Chan texts assure us.

Practitioners must absorb themselves in the *huatou* and be completely engulfed by the irresolvable impasse it presents. This experience of impenetrability and irresolvability is the experience of wonderment. The aim of the *huatou* practice is to generate that sense of not knowing, uncertainty that reaches a concentrated crescendo, priming the mind for awakening. Wonderment is the great questioning mind. When it engulfs the practitioner and continues for a long time, permeating every aspect of their life, then a catalyst, such as a sound or a form, will suddenly shatter this wonderment and along with this shattering, the practitioner's self-attachment may suddenly drop away.

The concentration developed through this wonderment from working with a *huatou* or *gong'an* is unlike the one-pointed concentration derived from traditional meditation methods, such as meditation on the breath. The sense of wonderment is an undivided and engulfing tension from the impenetrability and irresolvability of the *huatou*—it is alive and potent, free from distracting concepts, permeating everything in the daily activities of life. In this state of nonconceptuality, the discriminating mind comes to a dead end, and the practitioner remains totally open. This unified state of oneness, where attachment is at its weakest, is a state that the normal cognitive function of self-referencing or orientation falls away. It is what Chan masters call the great death (*dasi*). This eventual dropping away of self-referencing where even the *huatou* is shattered through some catalyst is called the great life (*dahuo*). Seeing the world with new eyes, free from the filtering of self, practitioners experience everything as coming to life for the first time. This is awakening. Practice, however, is not yet complete. Practitioners' self-grasping may come back, so they must continue to practice.

THE *GATELESS BARRIER* IN POST-SONG CHINA

Historical sources tell us that the *Gateless Barrier* continued to be widely read into the subsequent dynasties, particularly in Japan, but in China there appears to have been a hiatus after its publication until it was excerpted and transformed into a new kind of literary work.

In the tenth and eleventh centuries of the Northern Song dynasty, the "discourse records" and the genealogical records of "lamp histories" had become distinct genres within Chan. By the end of the Northern Song period, these genres essentially gave rise to the *gong'an* collections of the twelfth and thirteenth centuries, culminating in the *Gateless Barrier*. But simultaneously, another Chan literary genre began to emerge: the "categorized" or "classified" books, or *leishu*. To properly situate what happened to the *Gateless Barrier* after its publication in China, we must appreciate this historical and literary genre.

The "classified books," or *leishu*, are encyclopedic anthologies of excerpts from previous books. The origin of this genre can be traced back to the third century, but it only began to be widely produced during the Song, when printing became popular, and ultimately peaked during the Qing dynasty (1644–1912). Classified books were often compiled at the start of a dynasty, when it was important to establish a reputation for literary accomplishments. They served many purposes; some were intended as elementary primers or as the summum bonum of knowledge necessary to pass the examinations to become an official; some covered a particular branch of learning (history or literature, for example, which has the largest number by far); others covered a specific aspect of religion.

This genre ultimately started to influence the production of various Chan collectanea that synthesized elements of each of the prior works of the *gong'an* collection. The first Chan work within this genre was the *Essence of Succession in the Chan School* (C. *Zongmen tongyao ji*) published in 1093; another prime example is the massive fourteenth-century collection entitled *Comprehensive Anthology of the String of Pearls Verse Commentaries on Old Cases of the Chan Lineage* (C. *Chanzong songku lianzhu tongji*).[10] This work is genealogically organized around important figures: from Śākyamuni Buddha to important Mahāyāna bodhisattvas, to select Indian arhats, ending with the various Chan masters featured in previously published *gong'ans*. However, rather than providing narrative genealogy, it is composed solely of stories of these figures and their poetic verses on old cases (*songgu*) written by Chan masters, both monastic and lay, about them. In other words, it is a collection of *gong'an* verses or capping phrases organized by figures. Thus, all of the verse commentaries in the *Gateless Barrier* written by Wumen (along with verses in other *gong'an* collections like the *Blue Cliff Record* and the *Record of Serenity*) were extracted (yet properly labeled as drawn from particular *gong'an* collections) and reorganized by Chan masters. The impact of the *Gateless Barrier* therefore persisted in the form of this "classified book" of verses, which continued to be reprinted throughout the Ming period[11] for Chan practitioners to study. Thus, the impression that the text was not being read at all in China is simply untrue. Chan masters and practitioners obviously were aware of the *Gateless Barrier*, as Wumen's name and his poetic verses continued to be reprinted in the *Comprehensive Anthology of the String of Pearls Verse Commentary of the Chan Lineage.*

The classified books genre essentially replaced independently circulated *gong'an* collections in China, which explains the scant historical references to the *Gateless Barrier* as a discrete, independent work. One could argue that the times had changed in China, and the fad of compiling *gong'an* collections had simply faded out in favor of classified books.

For these reasons, we have very little information about whether there was a strong practice that centered around the *Gateless Barrier* in China after its publication. Apart from brief references by Yuan dynasty Chan masters[12] and its literary aftermath in the Chan classified anthologies, there appears to have been a pause in the independent circulation of the *Gateless Barrier*. This is certainly not true in Japan, where it was preserved from the thirteenth century onward as a sacred Zen text from China.[13] This volume addresses how the *Gateless Barrier* was preserved and studied in Japan at greater length in chapter 9 by Marta Sanvido.

CHAPTER SUMMARIES

The multiple ways of reading the *Gateless Barrier* presented here are determined, at least in part, by the unique questions each contributor brings to the text. How did the *Gateless Barrier* evolve in the context of *gong'an* literature? What ends do the *gong'ans* in it serve? How are the characters introduced and portrayed? How did Wumen use literary devices in this text? How do modern Zen practitioners work with the text? There is no single way to read the *Gateless Barrier*, and this volume likewise encourages the reader to maximize and broaden the potential interpretations. The chapters provide a model for doing so, frequently showing different ways of reading some of the very same *gong'an* cases.

In this introduction, I have provided some basic doctrines of Buddhism, a history of its transmission from India to China, and details of its development into Chan. I have also tried to encapsulate Chan's unique contribution to literature, spirituality, and human ingenuity in the *gong'an* and the *huatou* practice. The *Gateless Barrier* is a unique kind of performative text that generations of Chan practitioners used as a source of learning and a device for awakening.

In chapter 1, Albert Welter unpacks the intricate history behind case 6 of the *Gateless Barrier*, which centers on the smile of Śākyamuni Buddha's disciple Mahākāśyapa in response to the Buddha's holding up a flower on Vulture Peak. He argues that this story was both the starting and ending point in Chan's claim to the silent transmission of Buddhist truth between master and disciple as "a special transmission outside the teaching" (C. *jiaowai biechuan*, J. *kyōge betsuden*). Although the story purports to date from the life of the historical Buddha, Welter demonstrates how the historical context and the contentious claim of silent transmission are Song dynasty innovations. This chapter presents the Song period as the critical time in which the Chan identity crystalized, as the most significant innovations in the Śākyamuni-Mahākāśyapa story demonstrate. The chapter offers a detailed textual history of how Chan came to be understood in the *Gateless Barrier* and the way that we know it today.

In chapter 2, I situate the *Gateless Barrier* in the sociopolitical contexts of the literati culture and the text's relationship with Chan Buddhist clerics of the Northern and Southern Song dynasty transition. I explain the shifts that took place within Chan textual culture and spiritual practice through an examination of the unusual reaction to *gong'an* collections by one of the most celebrated Chan masters of the Southern Song dynasty, Dahui Zong'gao. At a time when so many Chan masters and practitioners of the Northern Song dynasty (960–1127) were producing *gong'an* collections as a literary endeavor, part of the rising interest in the "Chan of belles lettres," Dahui vehemently criticized it and burned the xylograph woodblocks for printing his own teacher's *gong'an* collection, the *Blue Cliff Record*. Instead, Dahui promoted the practice of observing the critical phrase or *huatou* "What is 'No'?" or *Wu*, which became the first case in the *Gateless Barrier*. In doing so, Dahui began a revolution of sorts in the Southern Song dynasty (1127–1279) that led to the widespread shift away from *gong'an* study to *huatou* practice in both monastic and literati circles—forever changing the religious landscape of Chan in China and Sŏn in Korea.

The previous two chapters provide the historical context to appreciate the development of Chan Buddhism and its flowering during Song China and elsewhere in East Asia. The next two chapters examine the *Gateless Barrier* philosophically, offering new ways of understanding Buddhist notions of truth and the nature of paradox. In chapter 3, Jin Y. Park takes a philosophical approach to the *Gateless Barrier* by questioning the ways awakening in Chan is experienced. She argues that in Chan Buddhism, and especially with the cases in the *Gateless Barrier* (cases 1, 2, 7, 14, and 46), it is not the "whatness" of truth that is important but "how" truth is encountered. This "how" is distinctive from a teleological method in which one finds truth at some final stage, as a conclusion of a search. Truth in the *Gateless Barrier* is a process, that of everyday life itself. If everyday activities are truth, why are we not aware of it? This chapter investigates these issues by exploring the locus of truth as suggested by various cases, considering its nature and encounters with it as well as the multilayered implications of such an understanding of truth in our lives.

In chapter 4, Robert Sharf takes another philosophical approach by challenging the received understanding of *gong'ans* as enigmatic stories, which include reports of startling behaviors, words, or gestures that appear to be non sequiturs or to defy logic or common sense. Instead, he shows how *gong'ans* can be seen as Chan's way of grappling with the paradoxes that sit at the very core of Mahāyāna doctrine: the identity of form and emptiness, conventional truth and ultimate truth, and delusion and awakening. Probing the nature and import of the paradoxes with philosophical rigor and subtlety, he shows how cases 2, 3, 5, 6, 11, 26, and 41 of the *Gateless Barrier* are far from literary ephemera, antiphilosophy, or incoherent mystical utterances. They are in fact critical and cogent treatments of issues that preoccupied Buddhist philosophers in China and beyond.

The following two chapters highlight the cultural, literary, and gender sensitivities in the *Gateless Barrier*. In chapter 5, Steven Heine explores several of the main cases and shows interesting connections and disconnections involving case 31, wherein Chan master Zhaozhou interacts with an irregular and inscrutable woman, who seems to outsmart him. Heine explores the role of ambiguity in this and other *gong'ans* such as case 11, in which Zhaozhou has another unconventional encounter with two mysterious hermits. In addition, he compares the pithy commentarial approach of the *Gateless Barrier* with the elaborate literary forms of the *Record of Serenity*, especially since both works present some of the same *gong'an* cases.

In chapter 6, Natasha Heller explores the role of women in four main cases. It is not surprising that cases featuring women are fewer in number than those featuring men, but such cases are also marginal with regard to the types of women depicted. Two are elderly women met along the road in cases 28 and 31; they are outside the traditional feminine domains of house and family and beyond their reproductive years. Case 35 depicts a young woman whose spirit leaves her body, and in case 42, a little girl is distinguished from the Buddha's disciples by both her age and her gender. Unlike the men, who are all in the prime of their life, the women are doubly marked by their marginality—revealing that the *Gateless Barrier* may reflect the social realities of the times. Yet, these stories can also affirm the spiritual potential of women in Chan during the Song period. Heller brings to the foreground the women's marginality and ambivalence, and questions the preponderance of misogyny in the Chan tradition in the past.

The next two chapters discuss the *Gateless Barrier* in Korea and Japan. In chapter 7, Juhn Ahn historicizes the unique development of Sŏn (C. Chan; J. Zen) Buddhism in Korea, situating it in its sociopolitical contexts that resulted in a de-emphasis of *gong'an* (K. *kongan*) practice. Using the *Sŏnmun yŏmsong chip* (*Collection of Prose and Verse Comments on Cases of the Sŏn School*) in Korea as a case in point, Ahn shows how the changing government policies shaped the focus of Sŏn practice. While the *Gateless Barrier* and the *Sŏnmun yŏmsong chip* are both influential *gong'an* collections, they were produced under different circumstances for different purposes. The *Gateless Barrier* contains a relatively small number of forty-eight old cases and provides only one master's pithy commentaries in prose and verse form. The *Sŏnmun yŏmsong chip* was collated and published to provide a comprehensive guide for Sŏn monastics in their education. Featuring over a thousand old cases, including many relevant stories as well as prose and verse commentaries for every case, this collection was meant to serve as an authoritative, encyclopedic reference for all Sŏn monks to use. The governmental policy that caused the production of this work and Chan master Dahui's influence on certain Korean Sŏn masters' privileging of the *hwadu* method (C. *huatou*; J. *wato*) ultimately led to the absence of the *Gateless Barrier* in Korea.

In chapter 8, Marta Sanvido traces the cultural and intellectual history of the *Gateless Barrier* in Japan, beginning with its propagation in the thirteenth century and culminating in its broad dissemination during the early modern period. She shows how the evolution and adaptation of the *Gateless Barrier* is an arena to investigate key turning points in the history of Japanese Zen. The chapter begins with an investigation of the *Gateless Barrier* in the context of the medieval culture of secrecy, particularly the secret *kōan* commentaries, that showcases the process of localization, wherein *kōans* were interpreted in light of influential covert notions such as embryological theories of Japanese esoteric Buddhism. The *Gateless Barrier* and its *kōans* eventually found their way into Japanese comic theater (*kyōgen*). In this setting, the enigmatic language of *kōans* was used to generate a humorous effect, implying the audience's familiarity with Zen themes. The last section delves into the story of Tachibana no Someko (1667–1705), a laywoman of the seventeenth century who authored an extensive commentary on the *Gateless Barrier*. This section not only uncovers the dissemination of *kōans* among women but also provides insights into how women perceived and used *kōans* to express their life experiences and interpretations of Buddhist teachings.

The last two chapters take a turn from scholarly analysis of the *Gateless Barrier* to its role in Zen in the West, providing a glimpse into how Buddhism is practiced in the modern time writ large. In chapter 9, Meido Moore discusses the modern practice of Rinzai Zen in the West and the place of the *Gateless Barrier* in it. Rinzai Zen teachers in Japan had refined the *kōan* method to a high degree through the work of the great Japanese Zen master Hakuin (1686–1769) and his heirs, who composed the "curricula of practice" (J. *kōan shitsunai*), which are still passed down today in Rinzai lineages. Within all of these, the *Gateless Barrier* figures prominently as a practice text. He explains not only the form and function of Rinzai Zen *kōan* practice but also the distinctively creative manner of grappling with *kōans* within meditative absorption, encompassing the practitioner's body, breath, subtle energetics, and mind—that is, harnessing the whole psychophysical being, rather than mind alone. This is *kōan kufu*, a way of going beyond intellectual examination of the cases to penetrate their very essence, as laid out in Wumen's commentary to case 1 in *Gateless Barrier*.

In chapter 10, Jan Chozen Bays discusses how Western Zen practitioners in her lineage work with the *Gateless Barrier*, centering on the breakthrough *kōans* (C. *gong'ans*; K. *kongan*) such as case 1, "*Mu*" (C. *Wu*; K. *Mu*), and case 28, "Long Have We Heard of Longtan." She describes how once some insight develops, Zen students go through several miscellaneous checking *kōans*, eventually working through the whole *Gateless Barrier* and other *kōan* collections. Chozen also discusses how she prepares students for *kōan* practice; the different ways of exploring and navigating the pitfalls of *kōans*; the difficult-to-pass *kōans* or *nantō kōans*; and how to use *kōans* in training and in daily life. She ends with a discussion of cases in the *Gateless Barrier* that deal with contradictions and karma, showing how they reveal distinct aspects of a Zen student's training.

All the chapters afford an opportunity to integrate the study of Chan, Sŏn, and Zen Buddhism more fully within East Asian studies as a whole. This volume also consciously tries to soften the hard line frequently but questionably drawn between etic and emic, insider and outsider perspectives, charting a middle ground between these forced polarities. The array of perspectives is varied, complex, and more extensive than both the academic presentation of Chan, Sŏn, and Zen Buddhism and the popular portrayals promulgated by Buddhists themselves. This richness enables readers to appreciate a broader range of concerns that go beyond the traditional emphasis on texts and doctrine typical of research on pre-modern East Asian Buddhism; it also widens the scope for the general public and Buddhist practitioners, allowing for a more historically embodied and nuanced appreciation of what the *Gateless Barrier* meant for people of the past and present. The reader will be able to locate the *Gateless Barrier* within its historical, cultural, philosophical, and spiritual contexts in a way that is not possible via other studies.

NOTES

1. This observation was attested by Xuanzang (602–664), the Chinese pilgrim who visited India in the seventh century, who stated in his journal that around a quarter of the monks in India belonged to this school; see Rupert Gethin, *Foundations of Buddhism* (Oxford; New York: Oxford University Press, 1998), 223.

2. This phrase is the first line of the Daoist classic, *Daode jing*; see D. C. Lau, *Lao Tzu Tao Te Ching* (London: Penguin, 1963), 5. For a good introduction to Daoist philosophy, see Livia Kohn, *Introducing Daoism* (London; New York: Routledge, 2008). For a systematic analysis of the linguistic strategies of Daoism and Chan, see Youru Wang, *Linguistic Strategies in Daoist Zhuangzi and Chan Buddhism: The Other Way of Speaking* (London; New York: Routledge, 2003).

3. In my recent book, I discuss in great detail how Indian Buddhism evolved in China and how one modern Chan cleric integrated the various forms of Indian and Chinese Tiantai and Huayan Buddhisms into Chan; see Jimmy Yu, *Reimagining Chan Buddhism: Sheng Yen and the Creation of the Dharma Drum Lineage of Chan* (London; New York: Routledge, 2022). Standard textbooks that provide general overviews of Buddhism's transmission are Rupert Gethin, *Foundations of Buddhism* (Oxford; New York: Oxford University Press, 1998), and Donald S. Lopez Jr., *The Story of Buddhism: A Concise Guide to Its History and Teachings* (San Francisco: HarperCollins, 2001).

4. See Morten Schlütter and Stephen F. Teiser, eds., *Readings of the Platform Sūtra* (New York: Columbia University Press, 2012).

5. See *Jiangxi Mazu Daoyi chanshi yulu*, X. no. 1321, 69:3a13.

6. See Thomas Yuho Kirchner, ed., *The Record of Linji*, trans. Ruth Fuller Sasaki (Honolulu: University of Hawaii Press, 2008), 11–12.

7. For a detailed discussion of the encounter dialogue, see John McRae, "The Antecedents of Encounter Dialogue in Chinese Ch'an Buddhism," in *The Kōan: Texts and Contexts in Zen Buddhism*, ed. Steven Heine and Dale S. Wright (New York: Oxford University Press, 2000), 46–74.

8. For a detailed discussion of what a *gong'an* is and its form and function, see T. Griffith Foulk, "The Form and Function of Koan Literature: A Historical Overview," in *The Kōan: Texts and Contexts in Zen Buddhism*, ed. Steven Heine and Dale S. Wright (New York: Oxford University Press, 2000), 15–45.

9. For a detailed discussion of the authority of the Chan master and the power dynamics at play in *gong'ans*, see Foulk, "The Form and Function of Koan Literature," 33–37.

10. The *Chanzong songku lianzhu tongji* (*Comprehensive Anthology of the String of Pearls Verse Commentaries on Old Cases of the Chan Lineage*), in 40 fascicles, was

expanded and completed in 1318 by Puhui (ca. fourteenth century) as a continuation of Faying's (ca. thirteenth century) original project in 1175, entitled *Chanzong songku lianzhu ji* (*Anthology of the String of Pearls Verse Commentaries on Old Cases of the Chan Lineage*). For the former, see X. no. 1295, 65. The latter is absorbed into the former, so is not listed in the bibliography. My dating of 1318 is based on Puhui's own preface and the postscript by a Linji Chan master Jingshan Xiling (1247–1322) in 1318. There are two other postscripts: one by Chan master Chunpeng Dugu (1259–1336) dates to 1317, which suggests the work might have been completed, perhaps in draft form, by this time; the other is by the Caodong master Tiantong Yunxiu (1242–1324) during the early 1320s (without a specific year).

11. For example, there are three versions of this work, two of which are extant: the *Comprehensive Anthology of the String of Pearls Verse Commentary of the Chan Lineage* in 40 fascicles and the 21-fascicle version, which was reprinted by Jingjie (d. 1418) in the *Hongwu nanzang* (*Southern Cannon of [Emperor] Hongwu*); see Zhang Changhong, "Chanzong songgu lianzhu tongji xulu," in *Xin shiji tushuguan* 1 (2013): 58–59. In Korean, the famous *Sŏnmun yŏmsong chip* (*Collection of Prose and Verse Comments on Cases of the Sŏn School*) published in 1226 should also be understood as belonging to this same genre. In chapter 8 of this volume, Juhn Ahn discusses this work in depth.

12. Natasha Heller, however, has found that Chan masters Gaofeng Yuanmiao (1238–1295) and Zhongfeng Mingben (1263–1323) make references to not just the verses but the *gong'an* cases themselves; see her *Illusory Abiding: The Cultural Construction of the Chan Monk Zhongfeng Mingben* (Cambridge, MA: Harvard University Asia Center, Harvard East Asian Monographs, 2014), 245–248. This suggests that the *Gateless Barrier* was in circulation at least during the Yuan period.

13. For a history of the *Gateless Barrier*, see Ishii Shūdo, "The Wu-men kuan (J. Mumonkan): The Formation, Propagation, and Characteristics of a Classic Zen Kōan Text," tr. Albert Welter, in *The Zen Canon: Understanding the Classic Texts*, ed. Steven Heine and Dale S. Wright (Oxford; New York: Oxford University Press, 2004), 207–244.

{ 1 }

THE *GONG'AN* TRADITION IN THE *GATELESS BARRIER* AS A "SPECIAL TRANSMISSION OUTSIDE THE TEACHING"

Albert Welter

O NE OF most famous *gong'ans* in the Chan tradition, *Gateless Barrier* case 6, relates how the Buddha's disciple, Mahākāśyapa, broke into a smile when the Buddha held up a flower to an assembly of the clergy on Vulture Peak, a well-known venue where Buddha allegedly preached many Mahāyāna *sūtras*.

> At an assembly on Vulture Peak, the World-Honored One held up a flower and showed it to the assembly. At that moment, everyone in the assembly was silent except Mahākāśyapa, who broke into a smile.
> The World-Honored One said, "I have the treasury of the true dharma eye, the wondrous mind of *nirvāṇa*, the true form of no-form, the subtle and wondrous gate to the dharma, the special transmission outside the teaching, not established on words and language. I now entrust it to Mahākāśyapa." (see p. 255)

This episode exemplifies and openly affirms one of the cardinal features of the Chinese Chan and Japanese Zen traditions: the silent transmission of Buddhist truth between master and disciple as "a special transmission outside the teaching" (C. *jiaowai biechuan*, J. *kyōge betsuden*). The story suggests that it originated with none other than Śākyamuni Buddha himself. According to Zen lore, this "special transmission" was then passed down from master to disciple through twenty-eight patriarchs in India, then was brought to China by the monk Bodhidharma, whose descendants flourished and eventually formed several lineages. The story thus plays a remarkably important role. Indeed, the entire tradition is predicated on this episode. The identity and credibility of every Chan and Zen master and practitioner who believes in Chan as "a special transmission" accepts it as authoritative.

The significance of this silent "special transmission" is especially evident in *gong'an* collections like the *Gateless Barrier*. The *Gateless Barrier* opens with "Zhaozhou's Dog," which illustrates this basic principle of the Chan *gong'an* tradition.

A monk asked Zhaozhou, "Does a dog have buddha nature or not?"
Zhaozhou said, "Wu!" (see p. 251)

The commentary by Wumen Huikai (1183–1260) asserts that Zhaozhou's answer "Wu!" or "No!" constitutes the first barrier of Chan. Those able to pass through it will attain the same realization as Zhaozhou and the patriarchs. Wumen compares this awakening experience to the experience of a deaf-mute who has a dream. It cannot be effectively communicated to anyone else.

This analogy underscores the degree to which the Chan *gong'an* tradition was predicated on the notion of an incommunicable, silent transmission. Awakening is an inherently individual experience that cannot be communicated conceptually through rational language or verbal means. Rather than a "statement," Zhaozhou's "Wu!" amounts to a categorical renunciation of the possibility of giving meaningful propositional form to this experience.

Although Chan tradition maintains that the principle of a "special transmission" originated with Śākyamuni and was brought to China by Bodhidharma, the development of the Mahākāśyapa silent transmission story actually parallels the growth of Chan identity much later, during the Song dynasty (960–1279). *Gong'an* collections produced during the Song, like the *Gateless Barrier* and the *Blue Cliff Records* (*Biyanlu*), represent the culmination of this search for identity as "a special transmission outside the teaching." They were compiled as testimony to the validity of this interpretation of Chan. What is of interest to me is not the mechanisms of *gong'an* practice but the developments that made *gong'an* study viable as a technique for communicating the status of Chan awakening as "a special transmission outside the teaching." Although Chan traditions often assume silent transmission as their leitmotif without question, the aim of this chapter is to chart the growth of the idea of silent transmission through documented sources, to show it was actually the product of Song dynasty revisionism.

TANG CHAN AND THE MYTH OF BODHIDHARMA

The figure of Bodhidharma casts a large shadow over Chan and Zen studies as the founding patriarch and instigator of Chan teaching in China. The fact that little is known about him is hardly unusual in the history of religions, where historical obscurity often serves to foster posthumous claims regarding religious identity, functioning as a blank slate upon which to project the hopes and aspirations of the faithful. Indeed, one learns much about the nature and character of Chan through Bodhidharma, an obscure meditation master from India, around whose image a successful challenge to Chinese Buddhist scholasticism was mounted.

History written from a Chan perspective posits Bodhidharma as a champion of "mind-to-mind transmission," focusing on the awakening experience occurring within the context of the master-disciple relationship, thereby posing an alternative to the exegetical teachings of the scholastic tradition. According to this perspective, the true, nontextual transmission of Buddhist teaching originated in China with the arrival of Bodhidharma, and in one grand stroke, the long and well-established traditions and conventions of Buddhist scholasticism in China were turned on their head. Throughout the Tang period, while Buddhist scholastics constructed ever more refined doctrinal systems, the alleged true teaching of the Buddha was secretly being transmitted among the beleaguered and isolated descendants of Bodhidharma, battling the forces of establishment Buddhism, holding steadfastly to the truth.

So pervasive is this reconstruction that virtually all Chan/Sŏn/Zen Buddhist proponents have fallen under its spell. With all the appeal of a convenient narrative of self-legitimation, the Chan version of events replaces and obscures the complex syncretistic background of Chan history with a simple and straightforward message summarized through four expressions:

1. A special transmission outside the teaching (C. *jiaowai biechuan*, J. *kyōge betsuden*)
2. Do not establish words and letters (C. *buli wenzi*, J. *furyū monji*)
3. Directly point to the human mind (C. *zhizhi renxin*, J. *jikishi ninshin*)
4. See one's nature and become a buddha (C. *jianxing chengfo*, J. *kenshō jobutsu*)

These four slogans are known even to those with otherwise limited acquaintance with Chan and serve as a common starting point for the modern study of Zen, especially in the West. The traditional position of Chan/Sŏn/Zen has been that they originated with Bodhidharma and represent the implicit message of Chan teaching from its very outset. Historians for a long time followed contemporary Japanese Rinzai Zen orthodoxy, regarding the slogans as products of the Tang period, reflecting the rise to prominence of the Chan movement in the eighth and ninth centuries during its so-called "golden age."[1] The slogans were taken as normative statements for a Chan identity fully developed by the end of the Tang. Chan *gong'an* collections compiled in the Song dynasty, like the *Gateless Barrier*, expressed the principles contained in them through dramatic encounters and riddle-like exchanges. But what are the origins of these four slogans, and how did they come to represent the normative Chan tradition of Bodhidharma?

Taken individually, the slogans are found in works dating before the Song. However, they do not appear together as a four-part series of expressions until well into the Song, when they are attributed to Bodhidharma in a collection of the recorded sayings of Chan master Huai (992–1064) contained in the *Collection of Topics from the Garden of the Patriarchs* (*Zuting shiyuan*), compiled in 1108.[2] Three of the slogans—"do not establish words and letters," "directly point to the human mind," and "see one's nature and become a buddha"—were already well established as normative Chan teaching by the beginning of the Song. But the status of the fourth slogan—"a special transmission outside the teaching"—as a valid interpretation of the true meaning of "do not establish words and letters" was the subject of great controversy throughout the Song. The reason is not hard to fathom. This slogan sharply contradicted the textual basis upon which the Buddhist scholastic tradition in China was based. It was met with great resistance from Buddhist and Chan circles.

Nevertheless, without the acceptance of this first slogan, the *Gateless Barrier* and the Chan *gong'an* tradition more generally would not have taken the form that they did and might not have developed at all. The *gong'an* tradition thereby serves as vivid illustration of the principles expressed in "a special transmission outside the teaching."

CHAN SLOGANS AND THE FORMATION
OF CHAN IDENTITY

The notion that Chan represented a teaching within the Buddhist tradition advocating "do not establish words and letters," "directly point to the human mind," and "see one's nature and become a buddha" was widely acknowledged by the ninth century. These three slogans are all documented in Chan works dating from the Tang period.

"Do not establish words and letters" is recorded in the work of Zongmi (780–841) and became a set phrase (along with "mind-to-mind transmission") during the latter half of the eighth century and the first half of the ninth.[3] According to Yanagida Seizan, the first recorded instance where the slogan "directly point to the human mind" appears is in Huangbo's (d. 850) *Essential Teachings on the Transmission of the Mind* (*Chuanxin fayao*), compiled in 849.[4] "Seeing one's nature" was an old idea in China promoted by Daosheng (355–434), a disciple of Kumārajīva. Drawing from Mahāyāna doctrine, Daosheng advocated the notion of an inherent buddha nature in everyone, including *icchantika*, deluded beings who otherwise often are said to never be able to achieve buddhahood. The full phrase *jianxing chengfo* (see one's nature and become a buddha) first appeared in a commentary to the *Nirvāṇa Sūtra*, in a statement attributed to Sengliang (502–557): "To see one's nature and become a buddha means that our own nature is buddha."[5] In the *Essential Teachings on the Transmission of the Mind*, the three slogans are even documented together, two—"directly point to the human mind" and "see one's nature and become a buddha"—in the exact same language with which they would later be appropriated, with the third—"do not rely on spoken words"—as a conceptually implicit form of the slogan "do not establish words and letters" (*buli wenzi*).[6] By the end of the Tang period, therefore, Chan had an undisputed identity encapsulated by and represented through these three slogans. This was the universally accepted image of Chan in the early Song.

The first use of the phrase "a special transmission outside the teaching" that can be documented with historical certainty is in the *Patriarch's Hall Collection* (*Zutang ji*). This is regarded as the oldest extant Chan transmission history to include multibranched lineages, dating back to 952.[7] But even here, the lone and seemingly insignificant appearance of the phrase is overshadowed by the repeated use of the other three slogans. The phrase is also included in a "tomb inscription" of Linji Yixuan (d. 866), the founder of the Linji (J. Rinzai) lineage, appended to the end of the *Record of Linji* (*Linji lu*), the compilation of his biography and teachings.

According to this inscription, Linji's use of the phrase was prompted by frustration after he had mastered the monastic disciplines (*vinaya*) and studied a wide range of the scriptures and commentaries (*sūtras* and *śāstras*): "These are prescriptions for the salvation of the world, not the principle of a special transmission outside the teaching."[8] The historical authenticity of this inscription as the work of Linji's disciple is highly dubious, but the connection of "a special transmission outside the teaching" with the *Record of Linji* is highly suggestive of a Chan identity that had developed in the Linji lineage during the Song dynasty.

Although the *Record of Linji* professes to be the discourse of Linji as recorded by his disciples, the current form of the text dates from an edition issued in 1120, accompanied by a new preface by a reputedly high-ranking (but otherwise unknown) Song bureaucrat, Ma Fang. This same edition is also the oldest extant source for Linji's purported "tomb inscription," claiming Linji's explicit use of the phrase. This all suggests that sometime around the beginning of the twelfth century or before, Linji became associated with the Song image of Chan as "a special transmission outside the teaching." This is also around the same time when the phrase was added to the list of Chan slogans attributed to the Chan patriarch Bodhidharma in the *Collection of Topics from the Garden of the Patriarchs*. The association with Linji and Bodhidharma was thus the culmination of a process through which the identity of Chan as "a special transmission outside the teaching" was transformed by members of the lineage, casting a strong shadow of influence over the Tang Chan tradition as well as stamping the image of Chan and Zen down to the present day.

Song dynasty *gong'an* collections like the *Gateless Barrier* memorialized the contributions made by Linji and his teachers, associates, disciples, and heirs by making them prominent subjects of *gong'an* episodes. According to the oldest extant record of Linji's teachings and activities, he was a viable candidate for association with the new slogan. For example, in one of his sermons he is recorded as saying: "In bygone days I devoted myself to the *vinaya* and also delved into the *sūtras* and *śastras*. Later, when I realized that they were medicines for salvation and displays of doctrines in written words, I once and for all threw them away and, searching for the Way, I practiced meditation."[9] The source of the *Record of Linji* first appeared in the *Expanded Lamp Record of the Tiansheng Era* (*Tiansheng guangdeng lu*). Compiled in 1029, it is the primary source documenting a new Chan identity as "a special transmission outside the teaching" in the early Song.

CHAN IDENTITY AS
"A SPECIAL TRANSMISSION"

The *Expanded Lamp Record* is one of a number of important Chan transmission records, literally "lamp records" (*denglu*), compiled in the Song dynasty. As their name implies, the purpose of these texts is to record the transmission lineages of important Chan masters. Using a biographical format, lines of descent were traced and links established between masters. Previous transmission records compiled in the Tang dynasty had already succeeded in tracing the lineage back to Śākyamuni through a line of Indian patriarchs (conventionally established as twenty-eight in number). A major innovation of the Song dynasty records was to establish lineal transmission with multiple branches. This became the basis for the so-called "five houses" of Chan.

Among the Song Chan transmission records, the *Transmission of the Lamp Record in the Jingde Era* (*Jingde chuandeng lu*), compiled by Daoyuan in 1004, is regarded as the most important. It was the first to be accepted in official Song circles, even by the emperor himself. Prior to this official recognition, Chan was regarded as outside the Buddhist mainstream. When the *Transmission of the Lamp Record* was admitted into the Buddhist canon of sacred scriptures, it was a major turning point for the Chan movement and set standards that all subsequent transmission records would follow. It helped establish a number of well-known Chan conventions: "great awakening" (*dawu*), the awakening experience as the culmination of Chan practice; confirmation of one's realization by a recognized master as the legitimate criterion for succession; and the transmission verse as a poetic representation of one's awakening. Many incidents involving Chan masters and Chan-style dialogues and encounters between practitioners later memorialized in *gong'an* collections like the *Gateless Barrier* were first recorded in the *Transmission of the Lamp Record*. Of the forty-eight cases in the *Gateless Barrier*, for example, twenty-five are found in the *Transmission of the Lamp Record* and another four are found in the *Expanded Lamp Record*.

The *Expanded Lamp Record* and other Song dynasty Chan transmission records are usually accorded little importance alongside the *Transmission of the Lamp Record*, and their contribution has frequently been ignored or minimized. In the present context, however, the *Expanded Lamp Record* surpasses even the *Transmission of the Lamp Record*. As an "expanded record" (*guangdeng*) of Chan transmission, it was clearly intended to supplement and revise the claims of the previous text. The need for a new transmission record, a mere twenty-five years after the *Transmission of the Lamp Record* was compiled, suggests that the earlier version was found lacking. In short, Chan masters associated with new lineages ascendant in the early Song dynasty were transforming Chan, remaking it to fit their own aspirations. The *Expanded Lamp Record* was a tribute to the contributions of and the novel styles being promoted by these new masters, many of whom were still alive or only recently deceased when the *Expanded Lamp Record* was compiled.

One of the most important contributions that this "new breed" of Chan masters made was to establish Chan as "a special transmission outside the teaching"; this phrase appears in the *Transmission of the Lamp Record* in an altered form in the preface (considered below) and appears several times in the *Expanded Lamp Record* as one of its most prominent features. The new breed also created important "discourse records," many for the first time, of masters associated with the Chan lineage whom they wished to promote. According to the *Expanded Lamp Record*, the interpretation of Chan as a "special transmission outside the teaching" was not the innovation of Bodhidharma or any of a number of likely candidates associated with the Tang Chan tradition. The first mention of it is in the biography of Chan master Guisheng (d.u.), recipient of a Purple Robe, from the Guangjiao Cloister in Ruzhou, active in the early Song period, in the last decades of the tenth century and the first decades of the eleventh. Guisheng uses the phrase in connection with a sermon in which he attempts to explain the meaning of Bodhidharma's coming from the West: "When Bodhidharma came from the West and transmitted the dharma in the lands of the East (i.e., China), he directly pointed to the human mind, to see one's nature and become a buddha ... What is the meaning of his coming from the West? A special transmission outside the teaching."[10] In this way, Guisheng's reference was directly connected to previously established slogans of the collective Chan identity, the image of Bodhidharma, and the implicit meaning of Bodhidharma's message.

This same link between Bodhidharma's message and the interpretation of Chan is also established in the biography of Chan master Shishuang Chuyuan (987–1040) of Mount Nanyuan in Yuanzhou, active in the early decades of the eleventh century.[11] As Chuyuan was the teacher of both Yangqi Fanghui (992–1049) and Huanglong Huinan (1002–1069), heads of the two branches that dominated the Linji lineage during the Song, the influence of his interpretation was considerable. The question regarding the meaning of "a special transmission outside the teaching" even acquired its own *gong'an*-like status in Song Chan circles. As the phrase became one of the central features of Bodhidharma's teaching (along with "directly point to the human mind" and "see one's nature and become a buddha"), the question "What is [the meaning of] the one saying: 'a special transmission outside the teaching'?" came to be asked in the same manner as "What is the meaning of Bodhidharma coming from the West?" as a test of a Chan master's understanding.

In spite of this association between Bodhidharma and the interpretation of Chan as "a special transmission outside the teaching" by many masters in the *Expanded Lamp Record*, there is no evidence for such a connection in the record's biography of Bodhidharma.[12] Here he is more aptly characterized as the conveyor of the "seal of the Dharma" (*fayin*), or as transmitter of the "Buddha mind seal" (*foxin yin*). In the biographies of Bodhidharma's descendants—i.e., the second Chinese patriarch, Huike (487–593); the third patriarch, Sengcan (d. 606); and the fourth patriarch, Daoxin (580–651)—the transmission is characterized primarily in terms of "the treasury of the true dharma eye" (*zheng fayan zang*) (familiar to many in its Japanese pronunciation, *shōbōgenzō*); it is confirmed also in the *Expanded Lamp Record* biographies of Śākyamuni and Mahākāśyapa, which make a point of stipulating that the "content" of the transmission between them was "the treasury of the true dharma eye." This constitutes the content of transmission from patriarch to patriarch through all the subsequent biographies of the Indian patriarchs in the *Expanded Lamp Record*.[13] It is inscribed as the essential teaching passed to Mahākāśyapa from Śākyamuni in *Gateless Barrier* case 6, the so-called "Flower Sermon." The *Expanded Lamp Record* suggests that the depiction of Bodhidharma's message in terms of "a special transmission outside the teaching" was the product of early Song interpretation. The *Expanded Lamp Record* also alludes to the fact that this new interpretation was not universally accepted.

Other Chan masters with biographies recorded in the *Expanded Lamp Record*, contemporaries of Guisheng and Chuyuan, retained a more traditional interpretation of Bodhidharma. Chan master Xingming (932–1001) of the Kaihua Monastery of Dragon Mountain in Hangzhou continued to maintain "the patriarch [Bodhidharma] came from the West claiming 'directly point to the human mind, see one's nature and become a Buddha, and do not exert one iota of mental energy,'"[14] thereby invoking standard Chan slogans without recourse to the new interpretation of Bodhidharma's message as "a special transmission outside the teaching." In doing so, Xingming was confirming another accepted view of Chan in the early Song, based on interpretations of Chan in the Tang dynasty that emphasized "harmony between Chan and the teaching."

TWO INTERPRETATIONS OF CHAN

Until the *Transmission of the Lamp Record* and *Expanded Lamp Record*, the prevailing view of Chan accepted in official circles was one of harmony between Chan and the Buddhist scriptural tradition. The phrase "a special transmission outside the teaching" had not gained standard currency when it was affirmed in the *Expanded Lamp Record*. The situation began to change in the latter half of the tenth century, when some Chan monks began promulgating their claim that Chan was "a special transmission outside the teaching"—viz., fundamentally independent of the scholastic tradition of Buddhism that preceded them. This precipitated a conflict within the Chan movement over its proper identity. Advocates of Chan as a special transmission within the teaching—that is, as the culmination of the Buddhist scriptural tradition—began to defend themselves against what they deemed to be pernicious, self-defeating claims. The story of this conflict is embedded in the rise of the Fayan lineage, one of the Five Houses, in the Wuyue region and in their affirmation of Chan Buddhism in the early Song dynasty.

In the tenth-century period of the so-called Five Dynasties and Ten Kingdoms, China was without effective central control and politically and geographically divided into several autonomous regions. The fate of Buddhism fell into the hands of warlords who controlled these regions. Given the recent experience of dynastic collapse and the perception of Buddhist culpability for the fall of the Tang empire (based on an alleged Buddhist drain on precious resources and a turn away from social responsibilities), most warlords in the north, the so-called Five Dynasties, continued policies established in the late Tang designed to restrict Buddhist influence over Chinese society. As a result, support for Buddhism during this period was confined to a few regions, mostly in the south, that figured prominently among the Ten Kingdoms. Chan lineages emerged as the principal beneficiaries. The established schools of the Tang, viz., Huayan and Tiantai, had been highly dependent on imperial support and were left vulnerable when it was withdrawn. Campaigns against Buddhism during the Tang were generally directed at obvious targets: the large, wealthy Huayan and Tiantai monasteries. Equally debilitating for Buddhism was the collapse of Tang society, which deprived the aristocratic classes of wealth and position and Buddhism of its source of extragovernmental patronage. Chan lineages (such as the "Northern school" of Shenxiu and the "Southern school" of Shenhui) located near the capital and dependent on imperial allies suffered a similar fate.

Partly as a result of these changing political and socioeconomic circumstances, Chan emerged as the dominant movement within Chinese Buddhism. At the same time, support for Buddhism varied from region to region, and this environment naturally produced different conceptions regarding the normative identity of the Chan school. These regionally based variations became best remembered in the heightened debate over whether it represented "a special transmission outside the teaching" (*jiaowai biechuan*) or "the harmony between Chan and the teaching" (*jiaochan yi zhi*). In other words, it was a controversy between the notion of Chan as an independent tradition and an interpretation of Chan in terms of continuity with the mainline Buddhist scriptural tradition. The debate is already implicit in the thought of Zongmi, the ninth-century Buddhist syncretic thinker who interpreted Chan positions in terms of the doctrines of Buddhist scholasticism, intentionally merging Chan ideologies with traditional Chinese Buddhist schools. To understand the emergence of the slogan "a special transmission outside the teaching," one needs to review the partisan reactions this debate generated in the early Song dynasty.

The Buddhist revival in tenth-century China was dominated by the Fayan lineage. Fayan Wenyi's (885–958) teachings attracted numerous students, many of whom achieved considerable fame. The influence of his disciples was especially strong in two kingdoms in the south, Southern Tang (Jiangxi) and Wuyue (Zhejiang), which provided the strongest support for Buddhism during this period. The normative definition of Chan in Fayan circles, later summarized as the "harmony between Chan and the teaching," directly countered the alternative notion of "a special transmission outside the teaching."

Broadly conceived, the promotion of Buddhism in Wuyue envisioned solutions to the social and political turmoil plaguing China through the revival of past Buddhist traditions. In short, Chinese culture in Wuyue was Chinese Buddhist culture, informed heavily by Tang Buddhist traditions, rooted in a vision where Buddhism was an indispensable force in the creation of a civilized society. As a result, the Wuyue revival of Buddhism was broad and far-reaching. Wuyue rulers made a concentrated effort to build temples and pilgrimage sites, restoring the numerous Buddhist monuments and institutions in their region. Historically important centers such as Mount Tiantai were reclaimed. New Buddhist centers like the Yongming Monastery in Qiantang (Hangzhou) were established. Ambassadors were sent to Japan and Korea to collect copies of important scriptures no longer available in China. After several decades of constant dedication to these activities, the monks and monasteries of Wuyue acquired considerable reputations. Monks throughout China, fleeing hardship and persecution, flocked to the protection and prosperity that Wuyue monasteries offered. Rulers of non-Chinese kingdoms sought to enhance their reputations by sending monks from their countries to study under famous Wuyue masters.

The Buddhist revival in Wuyue was largely carried out under the Chan banner, and the nature of the revival determined the traditional qualities of Wuyue Chan. In addition to embracing innovations, Wuyue Chan identified with old Tang traditions, and this became a standard feature in its collective memory. The distinguishing character of the Fayan lineage within Chan is typically recalled through the syncretic proclivities of its masters. The reconciliation of Wuyue Chan with the larger tradition of Chinese Buddhism was coupled with undisputed normative aspects of Tang Chan self-identity. This is readily apparent in the Wuyue Buddhist definition of itself in distinctly Chan terms. Even the writings of Zanning (919–1001), a Wuyue *vinaya* master who became the leading Buddhist scholar-bureaucrat at the Song dynasty court, reveal a definition of Buddhism in terms of a Chan identity that was compatible with conventional Buddhist teaching. In a section of his work on monastic administration, the *Topical Compendium of the Buddhist Clergy*, where he describes "The Transmission of Meditation and Contemplation Techniques to China," Zanning praises Bodhidharma for having first proclaimed in China the following: "directly point to the human mind; see one's nature and become a buddha; do not establish words and letters"; this is the "official" view in Wuyue Chan, along with a characterization of Chan as the quintessential teaching of Buddhism ("the Chan of the Supreme Vehicle").[15]

The fact that the fourth slogan, "a special transmission outside the teaching," was omitted was not an accident. The above definition is closely connected to the view of Chan as quintessential, which presupposes harmony between Chan and Buddhist teaching. Rather than "a special transmission outside the teaching," Zanning considered Bodhidharma's teaching a branch of the larger tradition of Buddhism stemming from Śākyamuni:

> The dharma preached by the buddhas of the three ages [past, present, and future] is always the same, and the learning imparted by the sacred ones of the ten directions is textually uniform. The teachings of Śākyamuni are the root [fundamental teaching]; the words of Bodhidharma are a branch [supplementary teaching]. How truly lamentable to turn one's back on the root to chase after the branches![16]

Zanning's definition of Chan explicitly criticizes practitioners who denigrated Śākyamuni's teachings in favor of Bodhidharma's. Using language that his audience of Confucian-trained bureaucrats could easily identify with, Zanning leveled harsh words at those who viewed Chan as some kind of "special transmission outside the teaching:" "[The government minister] who does not follow the virtuous influence of his sovereign is referred to as a rebellious minister. [The son] who does not carry on the legacy of his father is referred to as a disobedient son. Anyone daring to defy the teachings of the Buddha is referred to as a follower of demonic heterodoxies."[17] His aim was to validate an orthodox interpretation of Chan following the conventional understanding of Wuyue masters: "Based on an examination of the records and writings of those who have sought [meditation] techniques from the past down to the present, Chan meditation in India is taught along with the vehicle of Buddhist teaching [and not independently]." Those who conceive of a Chan identity independent of Buddhist teaching do not understand that "the scriptures are the words of the Buddha, and meditation is the mind of the Buddha; there is no discrepancy whatsoever between what the Buddha conceives in his mind and what he utters with his mouth."[18]

The Wuyue perspective on the harmony between Chan and the scriptures was not unprecedented. A century earlier Zongmi had promoted harmony or correspondence, arguing that Chan teachings are in full accord with the Buddhist canon as well as with the doctrinal positions of Buddhist schools.[19] His views provided the model for Wuyue Chan, both for Zanning and for the teachings of Yongming Yanshou (904–975), Wuyue Chan's well-known representative. Yanshou's commitment to the principle of "harmony between Chan and the teaching" is evident throughout his writings, as is his opposition to rival notions of Chan that isolate it from Buddhist teachings and practices (i.e., as a special transmission outside the teachings). This view did not go unchallenged.

By the mid- to late Tang dynasty, Chan factions had arisen that took a radical, antinomian stance to Buddhist scriptures and practices. Believing that "everything that comes into contact with one's eyes is in the state of bodhi—whatever comes into contact with one's feet is the Way [to awakening],"[20] expressions linked with the radical vision of the Hongzhou Chan of Mazu Daoyi (709–788) and Huangbo Xiyun (d. 850) and inherited by Linji Yixuan, became a pretext for licentious behavior. In this iteration, breaking the bounds of conventional morality was viewed as an expression of an enlightened nature.

In contrast, Yanshou viewed Chan as a teaching supportive of Buddhist ritual and conventional practices firmly based on the theoretical assumptions of Tang Buddhist scholasticism. Yanshou drew from such standard Buddhist premises as "the myriad phenomena are mind only" and the "interpenetration of *li* [noumenon] and *shi* [phenomena]" a radical phenomenalism different from that of his radical Chan adversaries. Believing it "unreasonable to assume that [any phenomenon] is deprived of the essence of *li* [noumenon]"[21] and taking the interpenetration of *li* and *shi* as a reasonable proposition, Yanshou recommended the plurality of Buddhist practices as the guiding principle. Doctrinally, this meant that the entire scriptural canon became united in a great, all-encompassing harmony. From the perspective of practice, all actions affirmed in Buddhist teachings, without exception, were the actions of a buddha.

Yanshou's view was in marked contrast to the rhetorical pronouncement of radical Chan that characterized conventional teaching and practice as an enslavement of one's enlightened nature and a sign of one's delusion. According to Yanshou, "increasing cultivation with myriad practices [is required to] make the mind clear and lucid; . . . if the myriad dharmas (i.e., practices) are none other than mind, how can the mind be obstructed by cultivating them?"[22] The Chan experience, in his eyes, does not culminate in an undifferentiated mystical union of the sacred and profane where one defies moral and principled behavior in favor of licentious expression. Rather, Chan incorporated a concrete program of activities sanctioned by the mainline Buddhist tradition: prayers and rituals in devotional rites aimed at enlisting the blessings of the buddhas, participation in Buddhist assemblies, and so on.

Yanshou thus clearly distinguishes his style of Chan from the style of Chan practitioners who "have become attached to emptiness, and [whose practice] is not compatible with the teaching."[23] Rather than "enslaving one's thought and wearing out one's body," as critics charged, conventional Buddhist activities (the myriad good deeds) are viewed positively: they are "provisions with which bodhisattvas enter sainthood . . . gradual steps with which buddhas assist [others] on the way [to awakening]."[24]

In the end, much was at stake over the two competing interpretations of Chan. The syncretic conception of a "harmony between Chan and the teaching" and the alternative conception of "a special transmission outside the teaching" reflect different religious epistemologies. In essence, the distinction is between a form of doctrinal reasoning, a view that explanations can communicate the truth coupled with the belief that the vehicle of this reasoned explanation is Buddhist scripture, and conversely, a type of mysticism, a more radical view that the experience of awakening is beyond reification, verbal explanation, or rational categories, and relatedly, that even Buddhist scripture is ultimately incapable of conveying that experience. In sum, the debate in early Song Chan was whether Chan is acquiescent with the tradition of Buddhist rationalism or belongs to an independent mystical tradition.

The history of Chan/Sŏn/Zen is generally presented as denying Buddhist rationalism in favor of a mysticism that in principle transcends every context, including even the Buddhist one. The "orthodox" Chan position maintains that the phrase "do not establish words and letters" is consistent with "a special transmission outside the teaching," treating the two slogans as a pair. In this interpretation, both phrases are said to point to the common principle that true awakening, as experienced by the Buddha and transmitted through the patriarchs, is independent of verbal explanations, including the record of the Buddha's teachings (i.e., scriptures) and later doctrinal elaborations (i.e., commentaries). This interpretation was not acknowledged in Wuyue Chan, which distinguished the phrase "do not establish words and letters" from the principle of an independent transmission apart from the teaching and treated the two as antithetical, opposing ideas. Wuyue Chan acknowledged the validity of Bodhidharma's warning against attachment to scriptures and doctrines but did not accept that it amounted to a categorical denial. The scriptures and doctrines were useful adjuncts on the path toward awakening and provided legitimate guides in working to attain it. However, as Chan became established in the Song, monks and officials rose to challenge the Wuyue interpretation and to insist on an independent tradition apart from the teaching.

A TALE OF TWO PREFACES

The view of harmony between Chan and the teaching exhibited in the writings of Yanshou and Zanning is oddly inconsistent with the influential *Transmission of the Lamp Record* promoting the Fayan lineage, compiled by the Wuyue monk Daoyuan. The *Transmission of the Lamp Record* was innovative in ways that signaled a departure from Wuyue Chan. It became the model for the new style of Buddhist biography prevalent in Song dynasty Chan, emphasizing lineage as the basis for sectarian identity. Moreover, through the prominence that this text gave to transmission verses and "encounter dialogues," it represented a style of Chan that seemed at odds with conventional Buddhism and the ideal of "harmony between Chan and the teaching."

Other evidence, however, supports the Wuyue view of a harmonious relationship, based on a comparison of the two prefaces for the work that became known as the *Transmission of the Lamp Record:* the "standard" preface by Yang Yi (974–1020) included in all editions and an original, largely forgotten preface, also by Yang Yi, compiled for the work under a different title, *Anthology of the Common Practice of Buddhas and Patriarchs (Fozu tongcan ji)*. The latter reveals, among other things, that Daoyuan's compilation was subjected to an editing process by leading Song officials, headed by Yang Yi himself. Since that original compilation is no longer extant, it is difficult to assess the extent to which editorial changes were made to the text during this process. However, the two prefaces indicate that, at the very least, the conception of the work was significantly altered. Daoyuan's original title, *Fozu tongcan ji*, as a "common practice of the buddhas and patriarchs," suggests harmony between Chan and the Buddhist tradition. The disparity between Daoyuan's conception of an *Anthology of the Common Practice of Buddhas and Patriarchs* and Yang Yi's conception of the revised work as the *Transmission of the Lamp Record* is reflected in the content of Yang Yi's two prefaces, revealing the two different ways that Chan was perceived. One concerns the view of the relation of Chan to Buddhist practices in terms of compatibility (i.e., the common practice); the other relates how the teaching of Bodhidharma is expressed in the Chan slogan as a "special transmission." The first preface, which we may assume concurs more directly with Daoyuan's intention for the work, conceives of Chan practice in a way consistent with Wuyue Chan. It states: "The best way of release from birth and death [i.e., *saṃsāra*] is to realize *nirvāṇa*; to instruct those who are confused, myriad practices are employed according to the differences among practitioners."[25] Yang Yi's second preface, issued after revising the work under the title *Transmission of the Lamp Record*, cast the meaning of Chan practice in an entirely different light. In contrast to an interpretation of Chan as a teaching where "myriad practices [*wanxing*] are employed according to the differences among practitioners," the second preface insists that the teachings of Chan masters be viewed in terms of "a special practice outside the teaching" (*jiaowai biexing*). Not only did Yang Yi's new conception promote Chan exclusivity and implicitly undermine Chan pluralism, it also paralleled the expression "a special transmission outside the teaching" (*jiaowai biechuan*), which was coming into vogue around the same time and was expressly asserted in the *Expanded Lamp Record*.

Yang Yi's presence in the reinterpretation of Chan is a sure indication of the important role Chan played in the Song as well as the role played by Song literati in determining the shape of Chan ideology. The biography of Yang Yi in the *Expanded Lamp Record* compiled by Li Zunxu (988–1038), a son-in-law of one emperor and brother-in-law of another—which consolidated the position of Chan as a "special transmission outside the teaching"—describes how Yang Yi's reinterpretation was closely linked to the Chan masters with whom he associated.[26] Initially these were Master An and Master Liang (both otherwise unknown), described as descendants of Fayan Wenyi. Later he developed close relations with Zhenhui Yuanlian (951–1036) of the Linji lineage. Moreover, Yang Yi's adoption of a new perspective on Chan intensified under the influence of Li Wei, a close cohort at the Song court who was an avid follower of Linji lineage masters. In this way, Yang Yi's own biography parallels the changes occurring in early Song Chan, changes that are reflected in his two prefaces. Yang Yi, more than any other figure, was ultimately responsible for establishing Chan as "a special transmission outside the teaching" in official circles.

THE ORIGINS OF MAHāKāśYAPA'S SMILE

The surge of recognition for Chan as "a special transmission outside the teaching" stimulated a number of ancillary developments to help give credence to this unique claim. As reviewed at the beginning of this chapter, the most important of these was the story recounted in the *Gateless Barrier* about how the "special transmission" was first conceived in the interchange between Śākyamuni and Mahākāśyapa. The credibility and legitimacy of the Chan tradition, as it took shape and began to assume a comprehensive form, necessitated this. Chan claimed the awakening of Śākyamuni as its unique possession, transmitted from mind to mind (*yixin chuanxin*) between master and disciple, not via written texts. Ironically, however, official acknowledgment of this tradition of secret, unwritten lore relied on written documents to substantiate the claim.

For a credible sequence to be maintained, the genesis of a mind transmission had to originate with none other than the Buddha himself. This made the alleged transmission from Śākyamuni to Mahākāśyapa the first and crucial link in the chain, the prototype of mind-to-mind transmission in the Chan tradition.

An important early source addressing the issue of how this transmission took place between Śākyamuni and Mahākāśyapa is the *Transmission of the Treasure Grove of Caoxi* (*Caoxi Baolin zhuan*), compiled in 801.[27] Caoxi refers to Huineng, victor in the battle for sixth patriarch in the

Platform Sūtra. The Treasure Grove (*baolin*) was the name of his monastery in Shaozhou (Guangdong). The *Transmission of the Treasure Grove* records Śākyamuni's words when transmitting the teaching to Mahākāśyapa as follows:

> The pure dharma eye, the wondrous mind of *nirvāṇa*, the true form of no form, the subtle and wondrous true dharma, I entrust to you. You must protect and maintain it. I decree that together with Ānanda as assistant, you perpetuate it, and not allow it to be cut off. The Buddha reiterated the explanation to Mahākāśyapa in a verse:

> The dharma is at root a dharma of no dharma,
> But that no dharma is yet the dharma.
> When I now transmit the dharma,
> What dharma could possibly be the dharma?[28]

According to Mahākāśyapa's biography in the same record, he was not present in the assembly when the Buddha entered *nirvāṇa*, but the Buddha made it known to his leading disciples that upon his return, Mahākāśyapa would clarify the treasury of the true dharma eye (*zheng fayan zang*), that is, the true teaching. Later, Mahākāśyapa verified that the treasury of the true dharma eye was none other than the collection of *sūtras* preached by the Buddha, recited at the assembly by Ānanda.

In this way, the *Transmission of the Treasure Grove* reflected an ambiguous understanding of the true nature of the Buddha's teaching transmitted to Mahākāśyapa. On the one hand, it contended that this teaching was "formless" and subtle, alluding to the mind-to-mind transmission that became the hallmark of Chan identity. On the other hand, it identified the teaching with the canonical tradition compiled through Ānanda at the council of the Buddhist assembly at Rājagṛha, as being verbal rather than formless.

There is no hint of the story of Mahākāśyapa responding with a smile when Śākyamuni holds up a flower to the assembly in early Chan records. In the *Transmission of the Treasure Grove* the whole episode is implausible given Mahākāśyapa's absence from the assembly where his role in clarifying the Buddha's teaching is announced. Likewise, the transmission between Śākyamuni and Mahākāśyapa is acknowledged in the *Transmission of the Lamp Record* as a transmission of "the pure dharma eye, the wondrous mind of *nirvāṇa*," but there is no mention of the episode.

The first mention in Chan records of this transmission involving the presentation of the flower before the assembly and Mahākāśyapa's smile in response is in the *Expanded Lamp Record*. This comes as no surprise in light of the role of this text in establishing Song Chan identity in terms of "a special transmission outside the teaching." In the *Expanded Lamp Record*, Śākyamuni presents the flower to the assembly as a test of the attendees' knowledge of the true nature of the dharma. This is the version of the story that made its way into the *Gateless Barrier*:

> At an assembly on Vulture's Peak, the World-Honored One held up a flower and showed it to the assembly. At that moment, everyone in the assembly was silent except Mahākāśyapa, who broke into a smile. The World-Honored One said, "I have the treasury of the true dharma eye, the wondrous mind of *nirvāṇa*, the true form of no-form, the subtle and wondrous gate to the dharma, the special transmission outside of scriptural teachings, not established on words and language. I now entrust it to Mahākāśyapa." (see p. 255)

The content of the treasury of the true dharma eye, the essence of Buddhist teaching that Śākyamuni was said to possess and entrust to Mahākāśyapa, was not yet explicitly connected to the expression "a special transmission outside the teaching," but the basis for identifying the two was clearly drawn. In the *Expanded Lamp Record*, the dharma transmitted from the Buddha to Mahākāśyapa is contrasted with the Buddha's preaching career, characterized in terms of the three vehicles. The implication is that the Chan dharma, transmitted between master (the Buddha) and disciple (Mahākāśyapa), is superior to the exoteric message preached in the *Lotus Sūtra*, the teaching of the three vehicles, and particularly the supreme dharma, the "one vehicle." Moreover, the *Expanded Lamp Record* was the first record to emphasize an interpretation of Chan as a tradition independent of Buddhist scriptural teaching by associating the phrase "a special transmission outside the teaching" with the teachings of prominent Chan masters active in the early Song dynasty. The inclusion of a story about how that independent tradition began forms a natural parallel to the kind of image that early Song Chan masters were projecting about the unique and superior nature of the dharma they were transmitting. What is remarkable is that both developments—the story of silent transmission between Śākyamuni and Mahākāśyapa as unequivocally associated with a superior Chan teaching and the identification of

Chan as "a special transmission outside the teaching"—were Song rather than Tang innovations.

The first version of the story to make explicit what was only implicitly drawn in the *Expanded Lamp Record* is the one recorded in the *Sūtra Where Brahman Asks Buddha to Resolve His Doubts* (*Dafan tianwang wenfo jueyi jing*). It is ostensibly part of the Buddhist canon, but there is no evidence that this "*sūtra*" existed prior to the Song dynasty. It is widely regarded as apocryphal, even more so for the scriptural support it conveniently provided for the story involving Śākyamuni and Mahākāśyapa. According to the version in the *Sūtra Where Brahman Asks Buddha to Resolve His Doubts*, when Śākyamuni sat before the assembly holding a lotus blossom that had been given him by Brahman, Mahākāśyapa, without uttering a word, broke into a smile. The Buddha proclaimed, "I have the treasury of the true dharma eye, the wondrous mind of *nirvāṇa*, the true form of no form, not established on words and letters, a special transmission outside the teaching," and went on to entrust it to Mahākāśyapa.[29] This established the origins of the Chan tradition in terms that directly linked the content of the Buddha's teaching, silently bequeathed to Mahākāśyapa, to the Chan identity. It did so, ironically, under the pretext of scriptural authorization, the very premise it was meant to defy.

Subsequently the story of the transmission of the dharma from Śākyamuni to Mahākāśyapa as told in the *Sūtra Where Brahman Asks Buddha to Resolve His Doubts* began to appear in Chan transmission records. The *Essential Collection of the Lamp Connections within the [Chan] Tradition* (*Liandeng huiyao*), compiled in 1189, records this rendition by explicitly connecting the transmission with "a special transmission outside the teaching." The story also appears in a Ming dynasty collection of Chan biographies, the *Special Transmission Outside the Teaching* (*Jiaowai biechuan*), preface dated 1633. This work organizes the lineages of the "five houses" around the motif of its title, thus suggesting that the entire tradition can be subsumed under this phrase.[30]

The full popularity of Chan that combined scriptural authorization with the interpretation of "a special transmission outside the teaching" was not realized through either the transmission record where it originated or the *sūtra* account that supported it, but instead through the uniquely Song literary form, the collections of *gong'an* case studies. The *Gateless Barrier*, compiled at the end of the Song dynasty in 1228, includes the story of the interaction between Śākyamuni and Mahākāśyapa as one of its case studies, following the version established in the apocryphal *Sūtra Where Brahman Asks Buddha to Resolve His Doubts*. Thus the interpretation of

Chan as "a special transmission outside the teaching" has reached countless numbers of Chan and Zen students, continuing down to the present day.

The *Gateless Barrier gong'ans* overwhelmingly feature Linji lineage-affiliated masters. The opening case, "Zhaozhou's Dog," features Zhaozhou Congshen (778–897), a disciple of Nanquan Puyuan (748–835), a successor of Mazu Daoyi (709–788). Zhaozhou also appears in six other *gong'ans*: case 7, "Zhaozhou's 'Wash the Bowl'"; case 11, "Zhaozhou Discerns the Hermits"; case 14, "Nanquan Kills a Cat"; case 19, "Ordinary Mind Is the Path"; case 31, "Zhaozhou Tests the Old Granny"; and case 37, "The Cypress in the Courtyard." Nanquan also features prominently in some of these: case 14, the famous "Nanquan Kills a Cat" *gong'an*, and case 19, as well as case 27, "Not the Mind, Not the Buddha, No Things," and case 34, "Wisdom Is Not the Way." Mazu figures prominently in case 30, "Mind Is Buddha," where Wumen Huikai comments about the impact of discerning the meaning of Mazu's pronouncement, "This mind is Buddha," when asked by his student Damei, "What is Buddha?"

> If you can directly grasp this meaning, then you will be wearing Buddha's robe, eating Buddha's food, speaking Buddha's words, and carrying out Buddha's practices. You will be Buddha. Even though this is the way it is, Damei has misled a lot of people, based on a wrong measurement of standard. One should know that just by saying the word "Buddha" you should wash your mouth for three days! If you are a genuine person, upon hearing someone say that mind is Buddha, you should cover up your ears and just walk away. (see pp. 271-272)

The point of Chan, as articulated here by Wumen Huikai, is that you are already Buddha. As articulated elsewhere in the *Gateless Barrier*, "ordinary mind is the path" (case 19). Put another way, there is no distinction between secular and sacred. The secular is already sacred; you do not have to do anything special to make it so. Just understand that it already is, just as it is. Upon realizing it, do not reify it as some kind of higher truth. That is the "wrong measurement standard." Saying the word "Buddha," as if Buddha was someone other than yourself, is a mark of delusion. Saying "mind is Buddha" as if it represented an abstract truth is equally debilitating. Wumen summarizes this point in his verse to this case:

> Stop seeking after it
> Under the clear blue sky in broad daylight.

Asking how it is [that mind is Buddha]
Is like holding on to stolen goods and claiming you're innocent! (see
    p. 272)

Throughout the *Gateless Barrier*, this point is made repeatedly. The aim of *gong'an* "study" is to bring one to this realization, not as an idea but as an existential experience. It is hardly surprising that the cast of characters in the *Gateless Barrier* are from lineages and masters who embraced the principle of "a special transmission outside the teaching" asserted in the "lamp records" (*denglu*).

In spite of the success the interpretation of Chan as "a special transmission outside the teaching" enjoyed, the history of Chan in the Song dynasty reveals a mixed legacy. Even with the dominance of the Linji lineage, this interpretation was not universally acknowledged. There was a reluctance among Chan masters to deny the Buddhist scriptural tradition and give voice to this interpretation of Chan. Many masters continued to exhibit the influence of "*sūtra* friendly" Chan, more or less continuing to to see Chan in terms of a basic harmony with the teachings of the scriptures, however much they otherwise fell under the sway of its rhetoric.

Even in the Song dynasty, when the Linji branch rose to dominance, the interpretation of Chan as "a special transmission outside the teaching" did not go unchallenged. Members of the Yunmen branch took the lead. The *Record of Chan Master Huai* (992–1064), the *Huai chanshi lu*, included in the aforementioned *Collection of Topics from the Garden of the Patriarchs*, Yunmen lineage records compiled in 1108, contests the interpretation of "a special transmission outside the teaching" promoted in Linji Chan circles. After citing the four slogans in connection with Bodhidharma, Chan master Huai remarks, "Many people mistake the meaning of 'do not establish words and letters.' They speak frequently of abandoning the scriptures and regard silent sitting as Chan. They are truly the dumb sheep of our school."[31]

In addition, there were limits to what Chan rhetorical claims to be "a special transmission outside the teaching" could, in practice, allow. The success of Chan in the Song dynasty led to official recognition and support. The fledgling movement of the Tang dynasty came to dominate Chinese Buddhism in the Song. The success of Chan institutions made them highly dependent on activities, rituals, ceremonies, and other forms of conventional Buddhist practice rhetorically denied in the interpretation of Chan as "a special transmission outside the teaching." In short, the social reality was predictably inconsistent with the radical rhetoric: the more successful Chan became institutionally, the more dependent it became on Buddhist scholastic teachings, and in turn, Song Chan institutions, by and large, inherited the rituals and conventions of Tang Buddhist monasteries.

CONCLUSION

Scholars have argued that the model for Buddha in Chan is not Śākyamuni but the illustrious Chan masters of the Tang dynasty as imagined through the eyes of their Song dynasty lineage descendants.[32] The *Gateless Barrier*, moreover, is constructed on the premise that achieving awakening is modeled on these Tang Chan masters, that buddhas "made in China" belong to the tradition of "a special transmission outside the teaching." The utterances and actions of these native Chinese Chan masters became the utterances and actions of buddhas, memorialized first through "lamp records" (*denglu*) and "discourse records" (*yulu*), and ultimately as episodes in *gong'an* collections like the *Gateless Barrier*. In this way, Chan created a new canon based on the repository of words and deeds left by the masters. Using *gong'an* as foci for meditation, the new buddhas provided case studies and a new methodology for the realization of awakening. In this way, the *Gateless Barrier* represents the crystallization of a new Buddhism made in China.

The acknowledgment of Chan as "a special transmission outside the teaching" was a decidedly Song innovation, however much it was inspired by earlier records. The myth of a silent transmission between Śākyamuni and Mahākāśyapa enshrined in case 6 of the *Gateless Barrier*, relating how Mahākāśyapa broke into a smile when the Buddha held up a flower to an assembly of the clergy on Vulture Peak, became the prototypical transmission myth in the Chan tradition. This case symbolizes the special transmission that animated the Song Chan imagination and substantiated Chan's unique identity. As such, it constituted a creative alternative to conventional ways the transmission of truth in Buddhism was conceived via textual means. Ironically, it did so by resort to scriptural authorization and textual codifications.

NOTES

This chapter is based on research completed in association with my previously published article, "Mahākāśyapa's Smile: Silent Transmission and the Kung-an (*kôan*) Tradition," in *The Kôan: Text and Context in Zen Buddhism* ed. Steven

Heine and Dale Wright (Oxford: Oxford University Press, 2000) and is an edited and altered version of it.

1. A position reflected in Heinrich Dumoulin, *Zen Buddhism: A History, Volume 1: India and China* (New York: MacMillan, 1988).

2. The *Zuting shiyuan* is a collection of records of masters associated with the Yunmen branch of Chan (X. 1261: 64). The four slogans are attributed to Bodhidharma in two places by Chan master Huai in fascicle 5.

3. Kamata Shigeo, ed., *Zengen shosenshū tojo, Zen no goroku,* vol. 9 (Tokyo: Chikuma shobō, 1971), 44 and note on 47.

4. Yanagida Seizan and Shiina Kōyū, *Shoki zenshū shisho no kenkyū* (Kyoto: Hozōkan, 1967), 475.

5. T. 1763: 37.490c. Isshu Miura and Ruth Fuller Sasaki, *Zen Dust: The History of the Koan and Koan Study in Rinzai (Lin-Chi) Zen* (New York: Harcourt, Brace & World, 1966), 228–230.

6. Iriya Yoshitaka, *Denshin hōyō, Enryu roku, Zen no goroku* (Tokyo: Chikuma shobō, 1969), vol. 8, 85.

7. The *Zutang ji* (K. *Chodong chip*) is noteworthy for promoting lineages descending from Mazu Daoyi, including those from Linji Yixuan. The phrase *jiaowai biechuan* appears in fascicle 6, in the biography of Shishuang Qingchu, 130b.

8. T. 1985: 47.506c.

9. Ruth F. Sasaki, trans., *The Recorded Sayings of Chan Master Lin-Chi Hui-chao of Chen Prefecture,* 24.

10. X. 1553: 78.496a–b.

11. X. 1553: 78.504c.

12. X. 1553: 78.443a.

13. The transmission in these biographies is usually invoked with a standard formula: "In the past, Śākyamuni transmitted the treasury of the true dharma eye to Mahākāśyapa. It continued to be transmitted from one to another until it came down to me. I now transmit it to you. Protect and maintain it so that it will flourish in the future. Do not let it be cut off. Receive my teaching, listen carefully to my verse . . . ," followed by the master's transmission verse.

14. X. 1553: 78.559c.

15. T. 2061: 50.789c.

16. T. 2126: 54.240a.

17. T. 2126: 54.240a.

18. T. 2061: 50.790a.

19. Peter N. Gregory, *Tsung-mi and the Sinification of Buddhism,* Kuroda Institute, Studies in East Asian Buddhism, 16 (Honolulu: University of Hawaii Press, 2002), 225–226.

20. T. 2016: 48.961a. These phrases were used in Chan circles (see *Jingde chuandeng lu,* fascicle 19; T. 2076: 51.356b). The expression "whatever one has contact with is Way" is attributed to the Hongzhou school by Zongmi.

21. T. 2016: 48.958b.

22. T. 2016: 48.958c.

23. T. 2016: 48.961b.

24. T. 2016: 48.958c.

25. Ishii Shūdō, *Sōdai zenshūshi no kenkyū: Chūgoku Sōtōshū to Dōgen Zen* (Gakujutsu sōsho Zen Bukkyō) (Tōkyō: Daitō Shuppansha, 1987), 22a.

26. X. 1553: 78.511c–512a.

27. Yanagida Seizan and Shiina Kōyū, eds., *Sōzō ichin: Hōrinden, Dentō gyokuei shū, Zengaku sōsho* no. 5 (Kyōto-shi: Chūbun Shuppansha, Kyōto-shi, 1983).

28. Yanagida and Shiina, *Sōzō ichin: Hōrinden*, 10a–c.

29. X. 26: 1.442a.

30. X. 1580: 84.440b–441a.

31. X. 1261: 64.379a. T. Griffith Foulk, "Myth, Ritual, and Monastic Practice in Sung Ch'an Buddhism," in *Religion and Society in T'ang and Sung China*, eds., Patricia Ebrey and Peter Gregory (Honolulu: University of Hawaii Press, 1993), 199 n. 17.

32. Kevin Buckelew, "Becoming Chinese Buddhas: Claims to Authority and the Making of Chan Buddhist Identity," *T'oung Pao* 105 (2019): 357–400.

[2]

DAHUI ZONG'GAO AND HIS IMPACT ON THE *GATELESS BARRIER*

Jimmy Yu

T HE *GATELESS Barrier* not only is different in character from earlier *gong'an* collections such as the *Blue Cliff Record* (C. *Biyan lu*)
but also serves a different purpose. Much of this difference has to
do with the shifts in society and religion from the Northern to the Southern Song dynasty. Chan master Dahui Zong'gao (1089–1163) stands out
during this transitional period. He strongly condemned literary engage-
ment with *gong'ans* and viewed it as an obstacle to awakening. Instead,
he advocated meditation on the critical phrase (C. *huatou*) as an anti-
dote to the over intellectualization of Chan practice. To appreciate the
Gateless Barrier and its significance in Chan Buddhism, it is absolutely
crucial to understand the sociohistorical context of this transitional
period.

Scholars have long recognized the vitality of the Chan tradition during
the Song dynasty (960–1279) and the extent to which Chan was integrated
into cultural life and the larger societal structure. Great political changes
occurred during this period, one of which was the invasion by the Jurchens from the north, who took over half of the Song empire in the twelfth
century, splitting the dynasty into the Northern Song (960–1127), preinva-
sion, and the Southern Song (1127–1279), post invasion. This tumultuous
transition affected Chan Buddhism on multiple social, cultural, and religious levels. There were also internal changes within the Chan community, as mentioned by Albert Welter in the previous chapter. This chapter
further explores the contingencies that led to a radical shift in the way
gong'an collections were compiled and used from the twelfth through the

thirteenth centuries. The *Gateless Barrier* embodies the shift away from *gong'an* study to *huatou* practice, or contemplation of the critical phrase. Dahui advocated *huatou* as a remedy in response to the external turmoil of dynastic transition and internal intellectualization of Chan.

I begin with the development of some salient historical and literary features of Chan in the Northern Song dynasty, particularly the "Chan of belles lettres" phenomenon epitomized by the *Blue Cliff Record*. With the turbulent dynastic fall of the Northern Song, the Chan practice approach changed in the Southern Song period as well. Historians have characterized this period as the inward turn among the literati in their dissatisfaction with the state and politics in general, in favor of their inner cultivation pursuits. Chan master Dahui's rise to prominence during the Southern Song, his radical departure from his teacher and contemporaries, and his exclusive focus on the *huatou* practice ultimately led to the publication of Chan master Wumen Huikai's (1183–1260) *Gateless Barrier*, which celebrated this new approach to Chan.

"CHAN OF BELLES LETTRES" IN THE NORTHERN SONG

In order to appreciate the emergence of *gong'an* collections writ large during the Northern Song dynasty and why the *Gateless Barrier* collection was different from its predecessors, it is important to contextualize the development of Chan during the tenth through the twelfth centuries from a historical and literary perspective.

The Chan tradition of the Northern Song flourished not only in the religious institutional sphere but also in the cultural sphere. Its vitality was inextricably linked to its relationship to the vibrant literati culture that followed the violent demise of the Chinese aristocracy in the final decades of the Tang dynasty (618–907), allowing Chan to become one of the most powerful schools of Buddhism. Even though the Northern Song court was far less hospitable to the monastic order than the previous Five Dynasties and Ten Kingdoms, strictly regulating especially the distribution of the monastic wealth, Buddhism as a whole, and Chan specifically, received considerable patronage from regional rulers, scholar-officials, and other literati elites. For example, during the Northern Song, for the first time, the grand and public Chan institutions were imperially and locally sponsored and recognized throughout the empire.[1]

In earlier centuries, the central government posts were filled mostly on a hereditary system of aristocracy. However, the Tang dynasty began the transition from rule by aristocracy to rule by meritocracy through civil service examinations. After a few centuries, during the Northern Song, the examinations had produced so many educated elites that the growth of this scholarly class ready for officialdom far outstripped the growth of state posts, leaving most degree holders without any practical opportunity to enter the professional civil service. However, the growth of rural market communities with their need for local leadership attracted scholars to their home localities. These local elites became increasingly powerful in their dense networks of familial, scholarly, personal, and religious connections.[2]

This class of literati exerted broad influence over much of the cultural production at the time—they were involved extensively in the production of local gazetteers, belletristic works, and Buddhist and Chan literary collections—and as they attained positions of power, high-profile Buddhist masters of the day also enjoyed eminence not only within clerical circles but also at court due to their relationships with other local literati elite. With the advent of woodblock printing during the Northern Song,[3] Chan teachings were circulated widely outside the monastery by the literati, influencing not only the religious life but also the literature and arts in the public sphere. In many cases, the literati were involved in the editing of Chan masters' discourse records, epistolary writings, and collectanea. The innovation and impact of woodblock printing cannot be underestimated; it led to a episteme shift, much like our current age of the internet.

During this time, Chan teachings began to be largely directed toward the laity, particularly the literati class, as much as, if not more than, toward Buddhist clerics. This phenomenon was not limited to Chan but can be seen in the ways the literati contributed to the overall vitality of Buddhism at large.[4] Confucian terms and ideas started appearing more frequently in Buddhist and Chan literature during this time. Arguably, even the flavor of Chan teachings began to change, addressing the concerns of lay life in areas of Confucian education and morality, literary theory and aesthetics, family and civil service obligations, politics and bureaucracy, and even foreign relations. What was important to the literati became topics for Chan masters to address.[5]

This does not mean that Chan simply became secularized; rather, its teachings actively engaged with lay concerns and encouraged the literati to go beyond the transience of the world in which they lived and the insubstantiality of their pursuits. In the bureaucracy, officials participated in intense factional conflicts and spent a great deal of energy engaging in political battles, intrigues, and attempts to win imperial favor. Political controversies could range from carefully reasoned policy discussions to personal slander and vilification. Many were dissatisfied with the state of affairs. All of these contingencies opened a vacuum in the hearts of the literati, and many were drawn to Buddhism in pursuit of spiritual release. Chan teachings offered them purpose and meaning beyond anything the secular world could provide.

Chan's close connection with this literati class and its impact on the cultural flourishing of the Northern Song led to the burgeoning of literary productivity. Despite the received image of Chan as a tradition "not established on words and letters," modern scholars have noted how Northern Song Chan traditions vigorously supported a systematic integration of traditional Buddhist doctrines and practices. As Albert Welter argues, during the Northern Song period, Chan was considered in harmony with the mainline Buddhist scriptural tradition; this only changed during the Southern Song period when Chan was espoused as a "special transmission outside the teaching." Thus, eloquent phrases such as "the union of Chan and the doctrine" (*Chan jiao heyi*) and "using the doctrine to awaken to the principle [of Chan]" (*jiejiao wuzong*) were common slogans of the Northern Song. There was a renaissance of scriptural study during this time that coincided with the innovation of woodblock printing, which fostered wide circulation of Chan texts.

Printing also led to a trend in Chan circles toward documenting (or inventing, in some cases) master-disciple Chan transmission records, also referred to as "lamp records" (*denglu*), allowing practitioners to align themselves with the special transmission of Buddha's awakening. In this milieu, under the aegis of the literati elite, the Chan tradition produced numerous chronicles, hagiographical compendia, epistolary collections, and hundreds of proto-*gong'an* texts called "old cases" (*guze*), carefully collated and drawn from the relatively new historical genre of "discourse records" (*yulu*). These cases ultimately led to *gong'an* collections.[6] The unprecedented accessibility of Chan texts among practitioners led to what Juhn Ahn, in chapter 7 of this volume, notes as a "reading craze" during the Northern Song.

This focus on reading, education, and literary erudition reflected the larger cultural milieu and the interests of the educated elite, and they greatly supported the Chan tradition in their literary productions. An emic term during this period, "Chan of belles lettres" (*wenzi Chan*), aptly captures this phenomenon of Chan's harmony with literary productivity as a new form of doctrinal development.[7]

THE *BLUE CLIFF RECORD* AS THE EPITOME
OF LETTERED CHAN

Perhaps the most prominent *gong'an* collection of the Northern Song period is the *Blue Cliff Record*, which consists of Chan master Yuanwu Keqin's (1063–1135) secondary comments on Chan master Xuedou Chongxian's (980–1052) 100 cases with his poetic verses. Yuanwu's comments were given fifteen years before the end of the Northern Song but were published at the beginning of the Southern Song dynasty in 1128. His articulate and complex interlinear commentaries, embellished with both prose and verses, must be understood as the epitome of "Chan of belles lettres."

Yuanwu was one of the most high-profile Chan masters of the time. He himself came from a long line of Confucian-trained elites. As he was already well versed in Confucian classics and learning before becoming a monk, his erudition greatly shaped his Chan teachings, particularly his *Blue Cliff Record*.[8] In the early phase of his monastic career, he sojourned to study under several Chan teachers of the day until eventually he met with Wuzu Fayan (1018–1104) on Mount Huangmei in present-day Hubei Province. Their first meeting led to a falling out between the two men because Yuanwu displayed his cleverness with words, which did not impress Wuzu at all. Instead, the teacher admonished him for his quick wit and verbal eloquence. When Yuanwu left, Wuzu predicted that he would soon fall gravely ill and would eventually return to him to study. Sure enough, Yuanwu became ill with typhoid at Jinshan. Recollecting what Wuzu had said to him, Yuanwu returned and studied diligently. Only half a month later, he experienced his initial awakening, which later played a significant role in his Chan teachings of *gong'ans*. Continuing his study with Wuzu, he soon developed a network of lay patrons, literati followers, and high-ranking officials, one of which was the very prominent Zhang Shangying (1043–1121). The two developed a close relationship. Zhang Shangying was a retired grand councilor and devout Buddhist with profound understanding of the Huayan Buddhist teaching.[9] He was also a lay disciple of Chan master Zhantang Wenzhun (1061–1115) of the Huanglong branch of Linji Chan. Impressed with Yuanwu's eloquence, Zhang Shangying arranged to have him serve as the abbot at Lingquan monastery in Lizhou, in which Yuanwu began his series of lectures on Chan master Xuedou Chongxian's 100 old cases, which became the basis of the *Blue Cliff Record*.

Yuanwu's *Blue Cliff Record* is essentially an intricate scripture-like commentary, albeit in vernacular form. At its core are Xuedou's 100 "root cases," on which Yuanwu provides elaborate comments, articulating how each case and Xuedou's verses are to be properly appreciated. After opening each case with an introductory prelude or set of "pointers," Yuanwu adds interlinear annotations—also known as "capping phrases"—to both Xuedou's root case and his verse. He then concludes with an overarching long commentary in prose. In other words, the *Blue Cliff Record* is multilayered, with comments upon comments. Yuanwu uses rhetorical devices, literary tropes, and allusions to convey the complexities of how each *gong'an* ought to be understood. Soon after the volume was printed, his fame spread widely throughout the empire, which eventually led to Emperor Huizong bestowing upon him a purple robe—the highest honor given to any clergy—and the honorific title "Fruition of Buddhahood" (*foguo*). He was also subsequently appointed as abbot of other large public Chan monasteries. When the Jurchens seized northern China in 1127, Yuanwu moved to the south and resided in Jinshan Monastery in Jiangsu Province. Some years later he relocated to his hometown in Sichuan Province and eventually retired there; he passed away in 1135.

There were other literary works tied to Yuanwu. In 1134, his *Yuanwu Foguo chanshi yulu* (*The Discourse Record of Yuanwu Foguo*), compiled by his disciple Huqiu Shaolong (1077–1136), circulated widely. Three years after his passing, in 1138, his *Foguo Keqin chanshi xinyao* (*Chan Master Foguo Keqin's Essentials of the Mind*), which consisted of 145 epistolary writings compiled by Yuanwu's disciple Hongfu Ziwen (d.u.), was published. Both works, especially the latter, reveal his close connection with members of the Song literati. More than one-third of his private instructions or letters were written to scholar-officials. In his discourse records, many of the sermons are listed as having been sponsored by literati-officials.

In the context of the "reading craze" of the time, his words were studied, revered, and memorized by many Chan adherents, both lay and monastic. His primary successor, Chan master Dahui, however, was disgusted by that fact that practitioners were merely mimicking Yuanwu's words without having any actual Chan insights. His criticism of Chan of *belles lettres* states: "Mental cultivation is the root; literary composition and learning are the branches. Contemporary scholars often discard the root to pursue the branch as they search out passages and pick phrases, vying with each other in the study of flowery words and clever remarks . . . which is pitiable!"[10] Dahui was quick to condemn pretentious, discursive approaches to Chan, which he believed, to his distress, were common in his day. He found true Chan practice replaced by merely rote intonation of deep-sounding Buddhist catchphrases and often warned his students against wasting their energy on literary pursuits. Instead, he encouraged them to "escape the dark caverns of vehicles and doctrines" and cease "groping about in the vacuousness" of texts that are at best "fingers pointing at the moon."[11]

A NEW SOUTHERN SONG EPISTEME

The broad shifts in society and religion that occurred in the late Northern and Southern Song period included changes in the elite's relationship to imperial and local institutions and a deep transformation in their understanding of their place in the world. With this change in the episteme, society by the end of the Southern Song was fundamentally different from what it had been in the North.

The consequences of the loss of the Northern Song region to the Jurchens were considerable. Even though the capital moved to the south, defense of a long northern frontier continued to drain the resources of the state into military expenditures. At the same time, the catastrophe had largely discredited the expansive state-building efforts of the literati-official reformers in the imperium. In the new climate of the Southern Song dynasty, the state attempted to address problems in the localities, to strengthen order, generate wealth, and redress the consequences of economic change. But through a complex of sociopolitical contingencies, its power diminished further.

Because of the focus on the local, the literati and the educated lost interest in large-scale state action or reform. This helped give rise to the school of Neo-Confucianism called the "Learning of the Way" (*Daoxue*), which retained the utopian view of a lost classical age and a belief in the potential for human perfectibility. Transformation depended on the individual's moral learning or the private actions of local communities. The inward turn in the sociopolitical identity of the educated elite focused on the question of how to rediscover within themselves the minds of the great sages of Confucian tradition. Many considered the embellished aesthetics of literary pursuits an indulgence. They were disheartened by the failure of the state, riven with corruption and factionalism. In their search for certainty, they sought the inherent sanctity of the true mind.

The immediacy of Chan awakening was appealing and was reflected in the writings of the Southern Song dynasty educated elite. Their pursuit of awakening appeared not only in their daily life but also in a new kind of literary sensibility.[12] This inward turn directly coincided with and provides a historical context to Dahui's teaching of *huatou* practice.

DAHUI'S RISE TO PROMINENCE

At the turn of the Southern Song dynasty, Dahui was arguably the most influential Chan master among the literati elite. He played a decisive role in shifting their attention away from the study of elaborate *gong'an* commentaries to the concrete contemplative practice of meditating on the "critical phrase" or *huatou*. This shift, and the renewed interest in embodying awakening for themselves, ultimately resulted in the birth of the *Gateless Barrier*, a new collection of *gong'ans* of a different kind—designed for meditative and contemplative practice. To appreciate this shift from *gong'an* to *huatou*, as reflected in the *Gateless Barrier*, it is necessary to discuss Dahui as a person, his connections with the literati, his approach to spiritual cultivation, and the mechanism of *huatou* practice.

Dahui was born in Anwei. He became a monk at the early age of sixteen and began his sojourn to various Chan monasteries to study with different Northern Song Chan teachers of his time.[13] In 1108, having studied with several already, he stayed with a Caodong master, Dongshan Daowei (d.u.), an eminent disciple of Chan master Furong Daokai (1043–1118). In 1109, Dahui met Chan master Zhantang Wenzhun (1061–1115) of the Huanglong branch of the Linji Chan and began his formal study in *gong'an*. His study was cut short when Wenzhun passed away. Dahui then established a very close relationship with Wenzhun's patron, the eminent layman and retired grand councilor Zhang Shangying, who introduced Dahui to the rich teachings of Huayan Buddhism and its connections to Chan.[14] It was not until 1124, when he was thirty-seven—at the advice of Zhang Shangying—that he began training under Chan master Yuanwu Keqin.

During a short period of eight months, Dahui practiced with Yuanwu, realized full awakening through working with a *huatou*, received the seal of approval from Yuanwu, and became his successor. By 1126, while he was still practicing under the tutelage of Yuanwu and had not yet held any official post as abbot, his fame had reached the imperial court, and he received a purple robe from Emperor Gaozong. This public recognition of an "ordinary monk" was unprecedented in the history of Chan. When the Northern Song dynasty fell in 1127, Dahui left for the south with Yuanwu, but they parted ways for a year. In 1128, he revisited Yuanwu for a year before parting again to go into seclusion from 1129 to 1133. China was still experiencing the tumultuous trauma of the dynastic relocation to the south. When Dahui reemerged on the scene, he traveled around the region and periodically stayed with prominent literati-officials who supported him.

Dahui's formal teaching career began in 1137, two years after Yuanwu's passing, when he took his first abbotship at Nengren monastery in Jingshan, the most prominent imperially sponsored monastery at the time. He attracted a large following—over two thousand Chan practitioners during the off-season and more during summer retreats—in addition to many lay supporters. After four years, however, due to Dahui's close association with officials such as Zhang Jiucheng (1092–1159), who was a scholar, imperial teacher, and leading high official in the Daoxue-led protest of the court's policy to negotiate peace with the Jurchen invaders, he fell from imperial grace and was forced to return to lay life and into exile in Hunan and then Canton provinces, the far southern regions of China.[15]

By 1140, it was already clear that Emperor Gaozong was ready to sign a treaty with the Jurchen who had occupied Northern China. The emperor's chief councilor, Qin Gui (1090–1155), was pushing for peace, and he suppressed the protests of the pro-war faction closely tied to the Daoxue movement and immediately began a wholesale purge of opponents at the court. Many were executed or exiled. Qin Gui perceived the close relationship and exchanges between Dahui and Zhang Jiucheng as an oblique way of stressing the importance of literati self-cultivation and awakening to achieve the political goals of the Daoxue, namely, the defeat of the pro-peace faction and the revitalization of the Song dynasty.[16] Therefore, Dahui was laicized (forced to give up his monkhood) and exiled between the years 1141 and 1155.

During his fourteen-year exile, Dahui kept in close contact with his literati students, monastic friends, and disciples through letters. The recipients were nearly all elite literati or officials, with only a few monastics. The literati-officials' ranks ranged from an illustrious grand councilor and vice ministers of various ministries at the imperium to low-ranking local magistrates and instructors in Confucian academies. Through his letters, Dahui's network grew steadily and his *huatou* teachings came into sharper focus among the educated elite.

In 1156, following Qin Gui's death in 1155, his exile was lifted. At the recommendation of the Caodong Chan master Hongzhi Zhengjue (1091–1157), he was immediately given the abbacy at Mount Ayuwang in present-day Zhejiang province. Dahui served for some time and then returned to serve as abbot at Jingshan, becoming one of the most illustrious Chan masters of his time, with thousands of students, scores of dharma successors, and many disciples among the educated literati and officials.[17]

DAHUI'S *HUATOU* CHAN

Dahui's prominence derived from his charismatic personality, the accessibility of his teachings, his social connections, and his supposed success in bringing many students, both lay and monastic, to awakening through his exclusive focus on the *huatou* practice. In a time when the literary *gong'an* collections were becoming an obstruction rather than an aid to spiritual insights, Dahui promoted the more effective and direct approach of meditating on critical phrases. The letters that he wrote during his exile years reveal the extent to which he focused on this method.

Gong'an collections were, by all standards, the literary endeavors of Northern Song dynasty Chan masters. Their internal structure was highly complex and convoluted, containing prose and verse comments, along with interlinear annotations called capping phrases. These compilations circulated only to the literate class, but in the aftermath of dynasty transition, in a state of moral ambiguity, *gong'an* collections had lost their relevance; they were becoming fossilized textual objects of intellectual speculation.

Dahui's vociferous critique of these cerebral trappings can be found repeatedly in his discourse records, as in the following excerpt from one of his letters:

> As of late, erroneous teachings flourish in the Chan forests. Those who blind the eyes of sentient beings are countless. If you don't bring forth the *gong'an* of the ancients to investigate, then it would be like a blind man giving up his cane—you wouldn't be able to take a single step. There are those who categorize the causes and conditions of ancient worthies' entrance to the path into different types: "these [*gong'an*] cases deal with attaining the eye of the way; those cases deal with the transcendence of sound and form; and those other cases deal with ending passions." They pursue each case, from beginning to end, case after case, in a sequential manner, considering and assessing them—even discuss them with others from a literary perspective. . . . Taking idle words and nagging admonitions [of ancient worthies] as topics of consideration, they transmit them and call them the "essential teachings" of the school. Yet in their heart it is still pitch black. Originally they wanted to eradicate attachment to self and

others, but their sense of self and others became great; originally they aimed to extinguish fundamental ignorance, but fundamental ignorance became enormous. They can hardly realize that this matter [of awakening] can only be personally actualized. The beginning is the end. They take a single word or phrase [of teaching] to have some kind of special understanding, subtle meaning, or esoteric teaching. That which can be transmitted or received is not the correct teaching. The correct teaching cannot be transmitted or inherited; it can only be actualized by you and me.[18]

In this passage he rebukes Chan teachers who discursively analyze the gong'an cases, dividing them into categories and groupings without truly investigating them as part of their meditation practice. In Dahui's eyes, these teachers reified the words of earlier masters as objects of attachment and blinded people, denying them the opportunity to awaken. The problem went both ways, though. Dahui also criticized students of Chan, particularly the literati elite who were fascinated with gong'an:

Most of the literati who study this path seek quick results. Before the master even opens his mouth [to speak], these people will have already formulated a [conceptual] understanding using their mind, consciousness, and perceptions. When [real obstructions] creep up on them, they lose all self-control like crabs in boiling water; they become busy with their hands and feet without having anything to hold on to. They don't know that it is actually their conceptual understanding that leads them to King Yama[19] to receive the [blows of the] iron rod and to [swallow] the blazing iron ball. The person who seeks quick results is no one else [other than you]. And so it is said, "Those who wish to acquire it will lose it" or "Those who try to be meticulous will end up being more negligent." The Tathāgata considers such people pitiable.[20]

The problem that Dahui perceived among the educated elite captivated by Chan was that they treated gong'an as objects of conceptual understanding, entangling themselves with words and ideas. But when vexations arose, they had no way of responding to them.

According to the Yuan dynasty postscript of the reprint of the Blue Cliff Record, Dahui felt that studying gong'an collections was useless for guiding practitioners to awakening. Instead it blocked them from giving rise to the sense of wonderment or existential questioning of birth and death. Thus, he was prompted to burn the printing woodblocks or xylographs of Blue Cliff Record before his exile. The postscript says:

Chan master Dahui found that when students came into his room [to present their realization], their replies [to his questions] were unusual. Suspecting [their insights], he questioned them further, and their cleverness fell apart of its own accord. When he brought up other [cases to question them], they would capitulate and confess, "I memorized [that answer] from the *Blue Cliff Record*; I really have not actually experienced awakening." Because he feared that future practitioners might not perceive the fundamental truth [of awakening] but instead merely develop eloquence with words, [Dahui] burned [the *Blue Cliff Record*] to save [practitioners from] this grave mistake. The intention that originally compiled this book and that which burned it were one. How could they be different?[21]

If we take this postscript at face value, it suggests that practitioners were memorizing his teacher Yuanwu's *Blue Cliff Record* comments without actually realizing the true significance of the words. It is indeed possible to acquire sufficient familiarity with Chan language to know how to respond to a *gong'an*, just as it is possible to theorize about the metaphors in the various Mahāyāna scriptures and develop a conceptual appreciation of the Buddhist teachings. Dahui's act was a forceful and radical departure from the kind of Chan taught by Yuanwu and Dahui's contemporaries.

Dahui criticized not only the intellectual study of *gong'an* collections but also the language of passivity with regard to seated meditation. In particular, he attacked the practice of what he coined as "silent illumination" or *mozhao*. Scholars typically associate this method with his contemporary, Chan master Hongzhi Zhengjue. Yet the practice instructions from Northern Song Chan masters (irrespective of their Chan lineage affiliations), particularly his own teacher, show that Yuanwu most prominently guided practitioners by using what I consider the "motif of passivity." Elsewhere I have demonstrated how he consistently emphasized words such as "the great rest" (*daxiu daxie*), "one thought for ten thousand years" (*yinian wannian*), and being like "cold ashes" (*hanhui*), a "withered tree" (*kumu*), or a "withered log" (*xiuzhu*) to put to rest the mind of discrimination through seated meditation.[22] There is evidence that Yuanwu's other disciples, Dahui's own dharma brothers, taught this form of meditation as well.[23] The motif of passivity was simply part of a shared repertoire of Northern Song Chan instructions for practitioners.

Responding to what he perceived to be an intellectualization of *gong'ans* and an overemphasis on sitting meditation in passivity, Dahui emphasized an active practice at the junctures of daily life:

During the six periods of day and night, if you can be diligent whether you're having tea or a meal, whether you're happy or angry, whether you find yourself in places of purity or filth, whether you're having a gathering with your spouse or children, entertaining guests or at work, dealing with personal affairs, or hosting a wedding banquet, all of these situations are foremost opportunities to engage in practice and bring [the *huatou*] to your awareness. Haven't you heard of the Military Commandant Li Wenhe,[24] who amid his prestige practiced Chan and realized great awakening? When Yang Wengong[25] was investigating Chan, he was residing in the Hanlin Academy. When Zhang Wujin[26] was investigating Chan, he was the officer in charge of imperial transportation. These three elder exemplars did not destroy the appearances of the world while engaging in the true form of reality. Since when must one leave one's wife, quit one's official duties or jobs, and go chew on vegetables and treat one's form with harshness, or avoid commotion to seek shelter in quietude? How can one realize the way by becoming like a withered wooden log or by entering the ghost cave to give rise to all sorts of deluded thinking?[27]

Dahui was vociferous about passivity, both in the realm of politics and in spiritual practice. In recounting his early years, he said that he never saw seated meditation as a means to awakening. While his peers focused on sitting, he just wanted to "stretch out his legs and sleep." It wasn't sitting meditation that led to his own awakening—it was his investigation of a *huatou* and the wonderment it generated that persisted in daily life.[28] Dahui made the same point in another sermon: "I studied Chan for seventeen years amid drinking my tea, eating my rice, when I was happy, when I was angry, when I was still and quiet, when I was disturbed; I never once let myself be interrupted."[29]

Dahui taught a nondiscursive practice of *huatou*, which can be rendered "observing the critical phrase" (*kanhua*). It was a direct way of engaging with a phrase, a word, and a brief turning point within a *gong'an* story without relying on literary accomplishments, poetic skills, or even familiariity with Buddhist theories. In fact, relying on knowledge of any kind was counterproductive, because the *huatou* typically presented a paradox that could not be resolved by logic.

The "phrase" or *hua* refers to the central question of the *gong'an*, expressed as the keyword of a turning point—the impenetrable essence of the story. *Tou* refers to the "source" of the key phrases. Thus, *huatou* literally means "source of spoken words." Meditating on the *huatou* or the critical words thus involves observing the source of all constructs, including *gong'an* stories. In fact, *huatou* points to the unfathomable, unconditioned, existential beingness, or the selfless state that is free from constructs. Facing this unknowable, ungraspable essence of *huatou*, the practitioner is to generate what has been translated as the "sense of wonderment," "uncertainty," or literally "doubt" (C. *yiqing*). According to Dahui, this wonderment serves as a catalyst for the sudden dropping away of self that is awakening.

As stated in the introduction of this volume, the significance of this wonderment cannot be overemphasized. It does not mean doubt or suspicion in the ordinary sense. It is a feeling (*qing*) that arises from the fundamental existential question of (*yi*): Who am I? or Where do I come from? This existential concern lies at the depth of one's being. Each *gong'an* essentially points to this uncertainty, which cannot be articulated or answered through constructs such as words or language. Wonderment interrupts the ordinary thought process and leaves the practitioner with no pat answers, only a gnawing sense of not knowing, enhanced by a deep and unescapable sense of humility, as Dahui describes:

> For those of you who are great adepts, determined to thoroughly resolve the causes and conditions of this great matter [of birth and death], you must first and foremost tear through your façade by intently straightening up your backbone and forsaking all human emotions. Take up the fundamental wonderment about your own existence, and stick it on your forehead, as if you owe tens and thousands of amounts of money to someone, and he's coming for you, but you—in humiliation—have absolutely nothing to give to him. Only then would you be apprehensive when feeling unconcerned, diligent when feeling lax, and develop insights with regard to this matter [of birth and death].[30]

In Chan, the "great matter" (*dashi*) refers to the conditioning of one's samsaric existence. For Dahui, one only needs to engage with a *huatou* and observe it with all of one's being to generate this great sense of wonderment (C. *dayi*). He declared, "With great wonderment comes great awakening" (C. *dawu*).[31]

With the shift from the Northern to the Southern dynasty, and his perceived degenerate tendency in Chan circles to attach to *gong'an* collections, Dahui's solution was the *huatou* method, which has inspired new generations of Chan masters and practitioners in subsequent periods.

DAHUI'S IMPACT ON THE *GATELESS BARRIER*

The *Gateless Barrier*, published in 1229, a century after the *Blue Cliff Record*, embodies the shift in practice from commentarial Chan to the Chan of paradoxes; from the extravagantly embellished, even bombastic, *gong'an* collections as literary products to the contemplative efficacy of the *huatou* practice; and from the Chan of belles lettres, marked by a self-conscious discursive quality, to the nondiscursive and nondiscriminatory experience of *huatou* wonderment. The forty-eight cases in the *Gateless Barrier* are terse, unpolished, and confrontational in nature. Its focus on generating wonderment by creating paradoxes can only be appreciated as the result of Dahui's influence and his elevation of the *huatou* method above all else.

Dahui's use of "A monk asked Zhaozhou, 'Does a dog have buddha nature or not?' Zhaozhou said, '*Wu!*'" or "No!" appears pervasively in all of his works, including his famous collection of letters to practitioners. This is also the first case that appears in the *Gateless Barrier*. Consider Dahui's letter to Lu Jiyi (d.u.):

> You must always fix at the tip of your nostrils the two affairs of not know-ing from where you were born and to where you will go after death. Whether you are drinking tea or eating your meals, amid quiet places or commotion, thought after thought it should be as if you owe someone ten thousand or hundreds of thousands of dollars without having any means of paying it back. Feeling anxious, stifled, with no way out, you are unable to live and unable to die. At this time, the paths to good and evil are sev-ered. Experiencing this is how to gain an entry and derive power. Only observe this *huatou*: "A monk asked Zhaozhou, 'Does a dog have buddha nature or not?' [Zhao]zhou replied, '*Wu!*'"
>
> When you observe this [*huatou*], there is no need for effortful spec-ulation; no need for explanations; no need to acquire any understand-ing; no need to open your mouth; no need to figure out some signifi-cance to the source from which you bring forth [the *huatou*]; no need to wallow in a state of empty quiescence; no need to wait for awaken-ing; no need to try to fathom the words of Chan masters; and further-more, there is no need to [dwell] in the shell of nondoing. Instead, sim-ply bring forth [this *huatou*] at all times, whether you are walking, standing, sitting, or lying down: "Does a dog have buddha nature or not? [Zhao]zhou replied, '*Wu!*'"

When you are familiar with your practice of bringing forth this "*Wu!*" then you will arrive at a place where words and thoughts do not reach. Your mind will be unsettled like a person biting on a raw metal or wooden rod— absolutely no taste whatsoever. Don't give up your determination, because it is precisely at this point in time that you will gain some "good news." Haven't you heard the words of the ancient worthies, "All the dharma spoken by the Buddha is for the purpose of delivering all [kinds of] minds. If there is no mind, of what use is all the dharma?"[32]

The purpose of these instructions is to drive the practitioner into an abyss, where all roads are cut off, with nowhere to advance or to retreat, unable to conceptualize or to rest in quietude. Indeed, the marvelous state of unsettling wonderment.

His instructions on how to meditate on this *huatou* consistently list several prerequisites: the urgent necessity of resolving birth and death; the exclusive focus on the *huatou*, allowing it to permeate one's daily activities; the irresolvable wonderment; comprehending the futility of discursive thinking or speculations; and not anticipating awakening. Central to these prerequisites is the great matter of birth and death, a Chan synecdoche for *saṃsāra*, the purpose of the whole Buddhist path, which Dahui integrated into the existential wonderment. When the irresolvable wonderment is strong, all discursive thinking is severed on its own accord.

In fact, the compiler of the *Gateless Barrier*, Chan master Wumen Huikai (1183–1260), experienced his great awakening working on this very *huatou*. Wumen was a disciple of Chan master Yuelin Shiguan (1143–1217). One day, as Wumen was doing walking meditation, absorbed in the *huatou*, a wave of drumming sounds from the kitchen suddenly shattered the great wonderment that had been pent up in him for six long years. After his insight, he wrote the following verse to present to Yuelin to affirm his realization:

A thundering clap breaks through the clear blue sky in broad daylight.
All beings on this great earth suddenly open their eyes.
Myriad forms and the multitudes bow down together
As they dance and celebrate on Mount Sumeru!

When Yuelin heard this verse, he shouted at Wumen, "What did you realize for you to come up with this rubbish? What is this 'multitudes,' spirits or fairies dancing around?!" When Wumen heard that, he shouted back: "Haaa!" Yuelin then roared like a lion back at Wumen, to which Wumen repeated his verse, shouting, "A thundering clap breaks through the clear blue sky in broad daylight; all beings on this great earth suddenly open their eyes. Myriad forms and the multitudes bow down together as they dance and celebrate on Mount Sumeru!" In that instant, hearing his own words, Wumen had another awakening. He completely broke through all traces of self-attachment.

Wumen favored his *huatou* by placing it at the beginning of the *Gateless Barrier*. He offered very concrete practice instructions on how to engage with it, as a template for how to work with the rest of the cases in his *Gateless Barrier*. His instructions echo those of Dahui:

To study Chan, you must pass through the barrier of our lineage masters. To realize wondrous awakening, you must exhaust the ways of the [deluded] mind. If you do not pass through the barrier of the lineage masters and do not exhaust the ways of the mind, then all that you do would amount to being a spirit haunting the forests and fields. But tell me, what is this barrier of the lineage masters? It is just this single word, *Wu*, which is also the gate of Chan—the *Gateless Barrier* of Chan. If you can pass through it, you will not only see Zhaozhou in person but also be able to walk together hand in hand with all the generations of lineage masters, to see through the same eyes as they do and hear through the same ears as they do. Wouldn't that be delightful? Do any of you want to pass through this barrier?

Arouse a mass of wonderment throughout your whole being, extending through your 360 bones and your 84,000 pores, as you come to grips with the word *Wu*. Bring it up and keep your attention on it day and night. Don't construe [this *Wu*] as void or nothingness, and don't understand it in terms of having or lacking. It is as if you had swallowed a red-hot iron ball that you cannot spit out—extinguishing all the erroneous knowledge and experiences. In time you will become ripe, and your practice will become pervasive and whole. Like a mute who has a dream, only you will know it for yourself.

Suddenly, [awakening] bursts forth, astonishing heaven and shaking the earth. It is like snatching General Guan Yu's sword into your own hands— slaying both buddhas and lineage masters as you meet them. On this shore of birth and death, you are free. You roam and play in *samādhi* in the midst of the six paths and four types of birth in all existence. Still, how will you take up [Zhaozhou's *Wu*]? With all of your life force to bring forth the word *Wu*. If you can do this without interruption, then, like a dharma lamp, it needs only a single spark to [suddenly] light up!

A dog, buddha nature—
The truth manifests in full.
As soon as there is having or lacking,
You will be harmed, and life will be lost. (see pp. 251-252)

These instructions have an entirely different structural and soteriological aim than the discursive literary comments found in the *Blue Cliff Record*—they encourage practitioners to take up the *huatou* and meditate on it without falling into the dualism of conceptuality.

In the *Gateless Barrier*, two-thirds of the cases contain paradoxes to be resolved. For those cases that do not, Wumen creates paradoxes in his comments. In other words, he teases them out and forces readers to confront them in order to generate wonderment. Often his comments point right to the source of the paradoxes, exacerbating the sense of not knowing and angst. The paradoxes are essentially *huatou*s for practitioners, and they are pervasive in the *Gateless Barrier* whether in the original text or in Wumen's comments. Sometimes the cases are so absurd that the stories themselves are paradoxes. The chart exhibits these features.

It is beyond the scope of this chapter to provide an in-depth analysis of how these paradoxes are featured in all forty-eight cases of the *Gateless Barrier*, so I encourage the reader to use the chart as a template to read the translation provided at the end of this volume, or consult *Passing through the Gateless Barrier*[33] or other commentaries. These paradoxes embedded in cases are scenarios of impossibility—the essential structure of any *huatou*. For Wumen, the paradoxes are, as he states in his introduction, "barriers of the lineage masters" that one must pass through.

Consider case 5:

Master Xiangyan said, "It is like a man being up in a tree hanging on to a branch by his teeth, with his hands and feet not touching the tree branches at all. Beneath the tree there is someone who asks about the meaning of [Bodhidharma's] coming from the west. If this man does not reply, he is evading the questioner's question. If he does reply, he perishes. At such a moment, how could he answer?" (see p. 254)

GATELESS BARRIER PARADOXES

Case	Paradox built into the case	Wumen gives concrete instructions	Paradox(es) provided by Wumen	Wumen exacerbates paradox(es)	Critical phrase or *huatou* (* = explicitly stated)
1. Zhaozhou's Dog	✓	✓		✓	*What is *Wu*?
2. Baizhang and the Wild Fox	✓		✓	✓	Not falling, not evading—which is it?
3. Juzhi Holds up a Finger			✓	✓	What is it, if not the finger?
4. Barbarian Has No Beard	✓	✓		✓	*Why does the Barbarian have no beard?
5. Xiangyan Is up a Tree	✓			✓	*How could he answer?
6. World-Honored One Holds up a Flower			✓	✓	*Transmission or no transmission?
7. Zhaozhou's "Wash the Bowl!"			✓	✓	Wash the bowl?
8. Xizhong Makes a Carriage			✓	✓	*What will the carriage be?
9. Great Penetrating and Supreme Wisdom			✓	✓	*Why did he not achieve the buddha path?
10. Destitute Qingshui	✓		✓	✓	*How did Qingshui drink the wine?
11. Zhaozhou Discerns the Hermit	✓	✓		✓	*Why is one affirmed and other denied? Who has it and who does not?
12. Ruiyan Calls His Master			✓	✓	*Who's the master?

Case	Paradox built into the case	Wumen gives concrete instructions	Paradox(es) provided by Wumen	Wumen exacerbates paradox(es)	Critical phrase or *huatou* (* = explicitly stated)
13. Deshan Carries His Bowl	✓		✓	✓	Why does Deshan have the last word?
14. Nanquan Kills a Cat	✓			✓	Why would sandals on the head save the cat?
15. Dongshan's Three Rounds of Blows	✓		✓	✓	*Did Dongshan deserve thirty blows?
16. The Sound of the Bell, the Seven-Piece Robe	✓		✓	✓	*Why put on the robe at the sound of the bell? How to hear with eyes and see with ears?
17. National Teacher's Three Calls	✓	✓	✓	✓	How did the attendant wrong the National Teacher?
18. Dongshan's Three Pounds of Flax	✓	✓	✓	✓	Why is Buddha three pounds of flax?
*19. Ordinary Mind Is the Path	✓		✓		Ordinary mind is the path?
*20. A Person of Great Power	✓	✓	✓		*Why can't a person of great strength lift his own feet?
*21. Yunmen's Dried Shitstick	✓		✓	✓	*The Buddha—a shitstick?

(continued)

Case	Paradox built into the case	Wumen gives concrete instructions	Paradox(es) provided by Wumen	Wumen exacerbates paradox(es)	Critical phrase or huatou (* = explicitly stated)
22. Mahākāśyapa's Temple Flagpole			✓	✓	*What did the Buddha transmit? Mahākāśyapa calls, Ānanda responds?
23. Not Thinking of Good or Bad		✓	✓		*What's my original face?
24. Apart from Words	✓		✓	✓	*Why does he not cut off the tongue of the former [poet]?
25. The Third Seat Preaches the Dharma			✓	✓	*Did Yang-shan preach or not?
26. Two Monks Rolled up Blinds			✓	✓	*One gained? One lost?
27. Not the Mind, Not the Buddha, Not Things			✓		What is it?
28. Long Have We Heard of Longtan			✓	✓	*Seeing him face-to-face or hearing of his name?
29. Not the Wind, Not the Flag			✓	✓	*Not wind, flag, or mind?
30. Mind Is Buddha			✓	✓	*Why isn't the mind Buddha?
31. Zhaozhou Tests the Old Granny	✓		✓	✓	*How did Zhaozhou see through the old granny?
32. An Outsider Questions the Buddha			✓	✓	*How far apart was the outer path and Ānanda?

Case	Paradox built into the case	Wumen gives concrete instructions	Paradox(es) provided by Wumen	Wumen exacerbates paradox(es)	Critical phrase or *huatou* (* = explicitly stated)
*33. Not Mind, Not Buddha	✓				*Not mind, not Buddha?
*34. Wisdom Is Not the Way	✓				*Wisdom is not the way?
35. When a Beautiful Woman's Spirit Departs	✓		✓	✓	*Which is the real person?
36. If You Meet a Person Who Has Reached the Path	✓		✓		*How to greet such a person with neither word nor silence?
37. The Cypress in the Courtyard	✓		✓		The cypress tree?
38. Water Buffalo Passing Through a Window Frame	✓		✓	✓	*Why can't the tail pass through?
39. Yunmen's Your Words Fail	✓		✓		*How did the monk's words fail?
40. Kicking Over the Water Jar	✓		✓		*What would you call it?
41. Bodhidharma Pacifies the Mind			✓		Mind already pacified?
42. The Girl Comes out of *Samādhi*	✓		✓	✓	*Why can't Mañjuśrī bring the girl out of *samādhi?*
43. Shoushan's Bamboo Stick	✓		✓	✓	*How would you call it?
44. Bajiao's Staff	✓			✓	Having, lacking, taking, leaving?
45. Who Is He?	✓			✓	*Who is he?

(continued)

GATELESS BARRIER PARADOXES (*continued*)

Case	Paradox built into the case	Wumen gives concrete instructions	Paradox(es) provided by Wumen	Wumen exacerbates paradox(es)	Critical phrase or *huatou* (* = explicitly stated)
46. A Step Beyond the Hundred-Foot Pole			✓	✓	*How to take a step beyond the hundred-foot pole?
47. Tuṣita's Three Barriers	✓			✓	*Where is this nature? How will you be liberated? Where will you go?
48. Qianfeng's One Path	✓		✓	✓	*Where does this one path begin?
Total	32	7	34	37	36* out of 48

The *huatou* in this case is explicitly stated as the last line of Xiangyan's story. Wumen's instruction pushes further this paradox: "Even if you have eloquence that flows like a river, it is totally useless here. Even if you can preach the whole great [Buddhist] canon of the teachings, that, too, is useless." In other words, all intellectual and discursive thinking, and indeed all words and language, must be cast aside in working on this *huatou*, "How could he answer?"

Here are case 21 and Wumen's comments: "When a monk asked Yunmen, 'What is buddha?' Yunmen said, 'A dried shitstick.'"

Wumen's Comment:

It can be said that Yunmen was too poor to prepare even a simple meal and too busy to write a composition. In response, he took a shitstick and propped open the gate [of our school]. The rise and fall of the buddha-dharma can be witnessed here.

Like a flash of lightning
Or sparks struck from flint,
In the blink of an eye,
It is already gone. (see p. 265)

This is a case where the absurdity of the whole story is the *huatou*; one could also say that the *huatou* is built into the story. Wumen's comment focuses on the critical word, "shitstick." He states that "the rise and fall of the buddhadharma can be witnessed here." Why is buddha a dried shitstick? What is a shitstick used to prop open the gate of our school or Chan? Either one of these can serve as the *huatou*.

Case 30 is also quite short and direct, presenting as a seemingly unproblematic statement:

When Damei asked, "What is buddha?" Mazu said, "This mind is buddha." (see p. 271)

In cases like this where the *gong'an* presents a straightforward statement, Wumen offers a paradox in his comment as a *huatou*. He states that "Even though this is the way it is, Damei has misled a lot of people, based on a wrong measurement of standard. One should know that just by saying the word 'buddha' you should wash your mouth for three days!" He goes on to say that real practitioners when hearing the words "mind is buddha" ought to just cover their ears and walk away. In saying that Damei was misleading people and denying that the mind is buddha, Wumen creates a paradox, leaving the reader to wonder: If mind is *not* buddha, then what? Why isn't mind buddha? Why would one need to wash one's mouth just by saying the word "buddha"?

Paradox or no paradox, the point of the *huatou* is not the words or phrases themselves but that they act as springboards to generate great wonderment, the sense of not knowing. For this reason, Wumen repeatedly states in the *Gateless Barrier* that "there is no gate to pass through." Still, he advises: "to realize wondrous awakening, you must exhaust the ways of the deluded mind." For Dahui and Wumen, the way to do so is to work through the *huatou* and give rise to great wonderment until both the wonderment and one's sense of self are shattered.

CONCLUSIONS

It could be said that it was during the Northern Song period that Chan became accepted as an important and integral component of mainstream culture, and that Chan Buddhists during this time cultivated both secular and sacred traditions, took Chan outside of its monastic walls into the world, and participated more readily in literati life. When the Song dynasty fell to the Jurchens and moved its capital to the South, everything changed. The traumatic transition led to a crisis among the educated elites interested in the Chan of belles lettres (*wenzi Chan*). Dahui's teachings on the *huatou* contributed to a shift from literary Chan to the practice of Chan.

There were considerable distinctions between the literati culture and Chan Buddhist teachings, and despite their greater mutual involvement, they did not entirely coalesce. Chan Buddhism in the Northern Song period and its general outlook were still very much aloof from the world, and its participation in secular culture was limited. Certain high-profile Chan masters such as Yuanwu were more literary in their religious orientations than their predecessors, and much of the Chan literature that we know of today was produced during the Northern Song period, but at least rhetorically, Chan maintained its suspicion of words and language. Likewise, the educated literati of the day, pious Buddhists though they may have been in certain areas and periods of their lives, nonetheless confined their Buddhism to matters of relatively private religious and intellectual concern, remaining wholeheartedly Confucian in their civil and political lives. Nor can we ignore those who were far less accommodating of Buddhism in the realm of politics and statecraft. Such ambivalence, perhaps better understood as a continuing tension in Buddhism in China, was never fully overcome or relaxed.

Yet, at the beginning of the Southern Song, living in the center of Chan's dialogue with secular literati culture, Dahui brought the secular and the sacred closer together. Eschewing the Chan of belles lettres and all indicators of passivity in spiritual practice, he advocated the *huatou* practice as a remedy for the literati when they took an inward turn, seeking solace and awakening for themselves. Dahui's impact on the whole of the Southern Song Chan tradition culminated in Wumen's publication of the *Gateless Barrier*, a new kind of *gong'an* collection focused on *huatou* practice instead of literary embellishment, with imaginative diction that is sparse, direct, and terse.

The question of Chan's relation to the post-Song period and its impact on Korea and Japan is addressed in chapters 7 and 8 of this volume. To this, our remarks about Dahui and the *Gateless Barrier* are only a prelude.

NOTES

1. Peter N. Gregory and Daniel A. Getz, Jr., eds., *Buddhism in the Sung* (Honolulu: University of Hawaii Press 1999), 5.
2. See Peter Bol, "The 'Localist Turn' and 'Local Identity' in Later Imperial China," *Late Imperial China* 24 (2003):1–51; and "Neo-Confucianism and Local Society,

Twelfth to Sixteenth Century: A Case Study," in *The Song-Yuan-Ming Transition in Chinese History*, ed. Paul Jakov Smith, Richard von Glahn, et al. (Cambridge, MA: Harvard University Asia Center; 2003), 241–283.

3. See Barend J. ter Haar and Maghiel van Crevel, eds, *Knowledge and Text Production in an Age of Print: China, 900–1400* (Leiden: Brill, 2011). For a masterful study of printing in China and its effect in the West, see Thomas Francis Carter, *The Invention of Printing in China and Its Spread Westward* (New York: The Ronald Press, 1955).

4. See the many chapters in Peter N. Gregory and Daniel A. Getz, Jr., eds., *Buddhism in the Sung* (Honolulu: University of Hawaii Press, 1999).

5. Much has been written on the characters of the Northern Song period from many perspectives; for examples, see Peter Bol, *Neo-Confucianism in History* (Cambridge, MA: Harvard University Asia Center distributed by Harvard University Press, 2008); Robert Hymes, *Statesmen and Gentlemen: The Elite of Fu-chou, Chiang-hsi, in Northern and Southern Sung* (Cambridge: Cambridge University Press, 1986); Robert M. Gimello, "Mārga and Culture: Learning, Letters, and Liberation in Northern Sung Ch'an," in *Paths to Liberation: The Mārga and Its Transformations in Buddhist Thought*, ed. Robert E. Buswell, Jr. and Robert M. Gimello (Honolulu: University of Hawaii Press, 1992), 371–437.

6. For an excellent survey on the nature and characteristics of *gong'an* collections and other various records, see T. Griffith Foulk, "The Form and Function of Koan Literature: A Historical Overview," in *The Kōan: Texts and Contexts in Zen Buddhism*, ed. Steven Heine and Dale S. Wright (Oxford: Oxford University Press, 2000), 15–45.

7. This phenomenon in the Northern Song can be traced back to tenth-century Wuyue Chan Buddhism, as articulated in the previous chapter by Albert Welter.

8. See Steven Heine, *Chan Rhetoric of Uncertainty in the Blue Cliff Record* (Oxford: Oxford University Press, 2016).

9. For an overview of Huayan Buddhism, see Francis H. Cook, *Hua-yen Buddhism: The Jewel Net of Indra* (Philadelphia: Pennsylvania State University Press, 1977); see also Miriam Levering, "Dahui Zonggao and Zhang Shangying: The Importance of a Scholar in the Education of a Song Chan Master," *Journal of Song-Yuan Studies* 30 (2000): 115–139.

10. From instructions to the otherwise unknown lay disciple Luo Zhixian 羅知縣 (d.u.) found in the *Dahui Pujue chanshi yulu* 20 (T. 1998A, 47: 898a6–8). See also the discussion in Miriam Levering, "Ch'an Enlightenment for Laymen: Ta-hui and the New Religious Culture of the Sung" (PhD diss., Harvard University, 1978), 82–102.

11. See *Dahui Pujue chanshi yulu* T. 1998A, 47:9 16c23–917b6.

12. See Michael A. Fuller, *Drifting among Rivers and Lakes: Southern Song Dynasty Poetry and the Problem of Literary History* (Cambridge, MA: Harvard University Press, 2013), 130–131.

13. For a general account of Dahui's life and teachings, see Levering, "Chan Enlightenment for Laymen," 18–38, and Chun-fang Yu, "Ta-hui Tsung-kao and Koan Chan," *Journal of Chinese Philosophy* 6 (1979): 211–235.

14. See Levering, "Dahui Zonggao and Zhang Shangying."

15. During his exile, Dahui continued to teach and write letters to his lay students. His letters were collected by several students and circulated as an independent epistolary record, "Letters of Chan Master Dahui Pujue" (*Dahui Pujue chanshi shu*), which has been translated into English; see Jeffrey L. Broughton and Elise Yoko

Watanabe, trans., *The Letters of Chan Master Dahui Pujue* (Oxford: Oxford University Press, 2017).

16. See Ari Borrell, "Ko-wu or Kung-an? Practice, Realization, and Teaching in the Thought of Chang Chiu-ch'eng," in *Buddhism in the Sung*, ed. Peter N. Gregory and Daniel A. Getz, Jr. (Honolulu: University of Hawaii Press, 1999), 62–108.

17. It was during this time that the new emperor, Xiaozong, bestowed on him the title "Dahui," meaning Great Wisdom. Prior to this he went by the name Zong'gao.

18. See *Dahui Pujue chanshi yulu* T. 1998A, 47: 892a13–b04.

19. King Yama in Buddhist mythology is the lord of the dead, who judges the dead in hell (S. *nāraka*).

20. See *Dahui Pujue chanshi yulu* T. 1998A, 47: 898c19–25.

21. See *Foguo Yuanwu chanshi Biyanlu* (The Blue Cliff Record of Chan Master Foguo Yuanwu), T. 2003, 48:224c21–25.

22. See Jimmy Yu, "The Polemics of Passivity and Yuanwu's Usage of It," *The Journal of Chinese Buddhist Studies* 36 (2023): 31–71.

23. See, for example, Morten Schlütter, *How Zen Became Zen: The Dispute over Enlightenment and the Formation of Chan Buddhism in Song-Dynasty China* (Honolulu: University of Hawaii Press, 2008), 124–125. Schlütter argues for an alternative view that Dahui was attacking the passive form of practice associated specifically with Hongzhi and generally with the whole Caodong tradition. My article cited in note 22 complicates this view.

24. This is Li Zunxu (988–1038), compiler of the *Tiansheng guangdeng lu* (Tiansheng Extensive Record of the Flame). See Albert Welter, *Yongming Yanshou's Conception of Chan in the Zongjing lu: A Special Transmission within the Scriptures* (Oxford: Oxford University Press, 2011), 210–211.

25. This is Yang Yi (974–1020), editor of the *Jingde chuandeng lu* (Transmission of the Lamp Record in the Jingde Era). See Welter, *Yongming Yanshou's Conception of Chan*, 210–211.

26. This is Zhang Shangyin (1044–1122).

27. See *Dahui Pujue chanshi yulu*, T. 1998A, 47: 899c23–a03.

28. This passage is from *Dahui Pujue chanshi pushuo* in *Dai Nihon kōtei daizōkyō* (Zokyo shoin, 1905), 1.31.5:418. The information given here is drawn from Miriam Levering, "Dahui Zonggao (1089–1163): The Image Created by His Stories about Himself and by His Teaching Style" in *Zen Masters*, ed. Steven Heine and Dale S. Wright (Oxford: Oxford University Press, 2010), 91–115, especially 99; and Ishii Shūdo "Daie goroku no kisoteki kenkyū (jo)," *Komazawa daigaku bukkyō gakubu kenkyū kiyō* 31 (1973): 283–292.

29. *Pushuo*, 421a.

30. See *Dahui Pujue chanshi yulu*, T. 1998A, 47: 899c6–11.

31. See *Dahui Pujue chanshi yulu*, T. 1998A, 47: 886a28–29.

32. See *Dahui Pujue chanshi yulu*, T. 1998A, 47: 901c21–902a08. The quote at the end of this passage appears to be a paraphrase of Huineng's conversation with a monk named Zhichang in the *Platform Sūtra*. However, there is no corresponding passage in the *Platform*. The earliest formulation of this quote in the form cited above appears in Zongmi's *Chanyuan zhu zhuji duxu*, T. 2015, 48: 411b09–10, which attributes it to the *Platform Sūtra*. The closest passage in the Dunhuang version of the *Platform* appears in *Nanzong dunjiao zuishangcheng mohe bore*

boluomi liuzu Huineng dashi yu Shouzhou Dafan si shifa tanjing, T. 2007, 48: 343a07–15.

33. See Guo Gu, *Passing through the Gateless Barrier: Kōan Practice for Real Life* (Boulder, CO: Shambhala, 2016).

[3]

THE *GATELESS BARRIER* AND
THE LOCUS OF TRUTH

Jin Y. Park

THE *GATELESS BARRIER*:
THE TEXT AND CONTEXT

The *Gateless Barrier*, or *Wumenguan* in Chinese, compiled by the Chinese Chan master Wumen Huikai (1183–1260), is one of the renowned collections of *gong'ans*, or "encounter dialogues," in the Chan Buddhist tradition. An encounter dialogue usually involves a conversation between a Chan master and disciples; it is often characterized by an apparent gap or disconnect between the question and the answer. The Chan masters featured in these *gong'an* stories from the *Gateless Barrier* mostly lived in China between the eighth and thirteenth centuries. Literally, *gong'an* refers to a legal precedent in law courts. The *Gateless Barrier* and other encounter dialogue collections preserve case stories in an orderly manner for easy referral by usually assigning a number to each case. The *Gateless Barrier* holds 48 cases. Another encounter dialogue collection titled the *Blue Cliff Record* (C. *Biyan lu*) contains 100 cases, some of which are also in the *Gateless Barrier*. In Korean Buddhist tradition, there exists a collection of *gong'ans* (K. *kongan*) compiled by Hyesim (1178–1234), the thirteenth-century Korean Sŏn master, titled *Collection of Prose and Verse Comments on Cases of the Sŏn School* (K. *Sŏnmun yŏmsong chip*), which contains over a thousand cases.

I interchangeably employ the expressions "cases," "stories," and "dialogues" to refer to *gong'an*. Stories always have context, and that distinguishes them from generalized rules or principles, intended to be applied in the same manner regardless of the specific context. For example, if a society has a principle that "One should not kill other living beings," it expects this to be applied in all situations. By contrast, when we consider "stories" or "cases," we can see context differences that may prevent any universal application of a rule or a principle. When a war occurs, on battlefields, taking the life of the designated "enemies" becomes a matter of justifiably defending one's own life and protecting the lives of others in society. Stories tell us when, how, and under what circumstances such a principle might be suspended or modified. Hence, the expression "*gong'an* stories" tell us that in understanding them, the context of *how* something happened is as important as, if not more important than, *what* happened.

The expression "encounter dialogue," an often-used English translation of *gong'an*, reflects the nature of *gong'an* stories. A story can be a narrative or a monologue, but a dialogue is a conversation, and the verbal exchange provides a high level of contextualization. With these opening points in mind, let's examine the first case story of the *Gateless Barrier*, known as "Zhaozhou's Dog":

A monk asked Zhaozhou, "Does a dog have buddha nature or not?" Zhaozhou said, "Wu!" (see p. 251)

Zhaozhou (778–897) was a Chinese Chan master who frequently appears in encounter dialogues. One of the most-cited *gong'an* stories, "Zhaozhou's Dog" is also known as "Wu" *huatou* or "Wu" ("No") *gong'an*. To understand the context of this dialogue, a basic grasp of the notion of "buddha nature," a key concept in Mahāyāna Buddhism, especially in Chan Buddhism, is needed. The foundational teaching of Buddhism holds that nothing in the world has its own self-subsisting nature, meaning that nothing has an independent and permanent essence to make it what it is. Instead, things exist through causes and conditions. The Buddha, the title we use to refer to the founder of Buddhism, is in fact not a proper name but an expression meaning "the awakened one." In other words, anybody who is awakened can be called "a buddha."

Awakening obviously is an experiential dimension, so all we can do is to theorize to understand it. One way of describing awakening could be to envision a state in which one sees through the reality of existence; from the Buddhist perspective, this means that one's existence is not based on a certain self-sufficient and unchanging essence or quality but rather is possible because of different contributing factors that come to be part of one's self through causes and conditions. Since there is no single denominator that identifies a person, a being, or a thing, Buddhism uses the expression "emptiness" to describe the interdependent conditions that makes up a person or a being. For example, Buddhism can say, "The cup is empty," which does not mean that it does not contain water, but that the cup does not have a singular essence that defines its identity. One might challenge this idea, claiming that a cup is a cup. That is true. A cup is not a chair and hence has its singular identity "on the surface." Buddhism does not deny that a cup exists or that one cup differs from another or from a table. But Buddhism brings our attention to a deeper level of existence to show that the independent identity at the surface level does not tell us everything about that cup. In fact, a cup is made up of noncup, from the Buddhist perspective.

To illustrate this point, try the following thought experiment: Count how many factors are required for a cup to be on your desk. A cup needs materials to be created, a designer to design it, a factory and factory workers to produce it, people who deliver the cup to the place where you must have bought it, and so on. If we think about a being from this perspective, their existence requires innumerable elements that we usually do not consider. This is exactly what Buddhism means by "emptiness." Hence, it is said, emptiness is fullness. A being is empty of one essence but full of everything.

Buddha nature can be understood as another name for the Buddhist understanding of how we exist: as a complex network of all the different factors that contribute. From the Buddhist perspective, this nature of existence does not change whether one is a buddha (an awakened being) or a sentient being (an unawakened being), a human being or a dog, or even an inanimate being like a rock or a laptop. This radical equality is one of the fascinating aspects of Buddhism, and buddha nature is a way of referring to the nonsubstantial nature of our existence.

This existential condition applies to all beings, both animate and inanimate, which means all beings have buddha nature. Therefore, a dog must have buddha nature as well. It would seem that the "correct" answer to the student's question, "Does the dog have buddha nature?" should be "Yes, it does." But instead, the renowned Chan master Zhaozhou said, "Wu!" which can be translated into "no" or "nothing."

If we just apply "the principle" of Buddhism that all beings have buddha nature, we might simply say that Zhaozhou's answer was wrong. But then, he is "the" well-known Chan master. Knowing his wisdom, the student must ponder why his teacher gave the answer "Wu," instead of "Yes, the dog has buddha nature."

Another issue to consider is that if the student knows Zhaozhou's answer apparently misses the mark, the student must know the answer to his own question. Why, then, ask Zhaozhou to begin with? If the student did not know the Buddhist teaching that all beings have buddha nature, he student would not know that his master's answer, "Wu," was inappropriate.

We can also ask, if the student found the answer unsatisfactory, why did he not ask Zhaozhou a follow-up question, as my students would do in my class? The student should have told Zhaozhou that Buddhist literature says all beings have buddha nature and asked him why he did not confirm the buddha nature of the dog and instead said "Wu."

In Chan Buddhist tradition, students usually do not ask a follow-up question that perhaps could resolve the problem quickly but instead agonize over the meaning of an answer such as "Wu" for days, months, and sometimes years. "How inefficient!" one might say in our time, but this lack of follow-up conveys as much about Chan training as it does about the topic of our inquiry, the locus of truth in the *Gateless Barrier*'s *gong'an* stories.

RIGHT ANSWER, WRONG ANSWER, AND QUESTIONING THE ANSWER

In examining the first *gong'an* story in the *Gateless Barrier*, we raised several questions instead of specifying what the right answer should be. According to the principle in Buddhist literature, the correct answer is "Yes, the dog has buddha nature," but then questions emerge about why the renowned Chan master didn't say that, and because he didn't, whether this textbook answer is really the right one. It might not be an issue of which is correct, but rather, the *gong'an* making us consider what it means to make an inquiry and search for a right answer or truth.

We tend to identify truth with "correctness" and "right" and many other positive values. Obviously, there is an "inconvenient truth," an expression that has become popular recently, and that would make people uncomfortable. Still the assumption is that learning the truth, even if it makes one uncomfortable, is a right and correct thing to do. But how do we encounter truth? Is it an expression, a fact, a situation, or a condition? "Truth," in English is related to the adjective "true" in its etymology. The French expression, *la verité*, is also related to the word for true, *vrai*, which in turn is related to being faithful. What are we faithful or true to when we want truth?

Traditionally the faithfulness related to truth is understood as the correspondence between the proposition and the reality it refers to. For example, if one says, "This is an apple" and points at an apple, it is true, because the statement or proposition corresponds to what it refers to. When we deal with the truth of a simple statement and a simple referent, this is relatively easy, but when we search for truth, the context is not always as simple as in this case.

In the first case story in the *Gateless Barrier* about the buddha nature of a dog, the situation is not clear either. The proposition or claim is "A dog has buddha nature," because all things have buddha nature according to Mahāyāna Buddhist teaching. This proposition needs to correspond to what it refers to, which is the buddha nature of the dog. How do we identify the buddha nature of the dog, when Buddhism says that having buddha nature means that a dog does not have one essence that defines it? The proposition is impossible to prove in our familiar way of matching a statement with its reference.

Here we find a hint of why Zhaozhou responded to his student's question with such an ambiguous answer, "Wu," instead of a straightforward yes or no. Wumen, the compiler of the *gong'ans* in the *Gateless Barrier*, adds the following verse as his response to the story:

A dog, buddha nature—
The truth manifests in full.
As soon as there is "having" [yes] or "lacking" [no],
You will be harmed, and life will be lost. (see p. 252)

The *gong'an* dialogue and Wumen's verse demand that we look for a different possibility beyond a right or wrong answer. What is this third way? We can question the question and also question possible answers. Let's explore this idea in another case in the *Gateless Barrier*.

In case 7, entitled "Zhaozhou's 'Wash the Bowl!'," Zhaozhou answers a question from a student:

A monk said to Zhaozhou, "I have just entered this monastery. I beg for your instructions, teacher."
    Zhaozhou replied, "Have you eaten porridge yet?"
    The monk said, "Yes, I have eaten."
    Zhaozhou said, "Then go wash your bowl!"
    The monk had an insight. (see p. 256)

Unlike the first *gong'an*, "Zhaozhou's Dog," "Zhaozhou's 'Wash the Bowl!'" does not require any knowledge of Buddhism. But on first reading, it might sound peculiar. Between the heaviness of the student's request, which must have carried great import for him, and the Chan master Zhaozhou's mundane answer there does not seem to be a balance, and that gives the reader pause. Even more perplexing is that the student attains insight at the end of this conversation, instead of being dumbfounded.

There are some similarities the two stories share. In both, the student is looking for truth, either through the confirmation of the buddha nature of a dog or through instruction about Buddhist practice. "Wu!" and "Wash the bowl!" are far from providing anything we might consider truth. And the *gong'an* "'Wash the Bowl'" adds another component of unconventional ways of searching for truth: the daily routine gets into the picture.

Think again about this dialogue's context. The monk reported to the master that he had just joined the monastery. That means that the monk had given up his life outside, his only goal was to attain awakening, and he was seeking a way to do so by asking for instructions from the renowned Chan master. This must be a life-and-death question for the monk, in terms of seriousness. And the answer he received was that he needed to do the dishes after a meal.

Here we find another important aspect of the Chan Buddhist approach to the locus of truth. We tend to think of truth as something outside our daily routine, or at least something rather extraordinary, different from our mundane existence. But if we think about life, we realize that life is a continuation of routine activities, like eating meals and doing dishes afterward, taking a shower, having a cup of coffee, going to work, coming back home. There are milestone events, such as birthdays, commencements, marriage, and so on, but most of the time we repeat what we did the day before, and even milestone events are not the revelation of truth itself but are a continuation of what we've done before. Where then do we find truth? Where is its locus?

At least in this *gong'an*, Chan master Zhaozhou is telling us—or telling his student who expects a life-changing instruction that will let him attain awakening—that if there are teachings, if there is a way to encounter truth, it should happen in the midst of our daily activities.

Truth is always related to meaning. If something has a meaning, it should be true, and the human desire to know truth is directly related to human beings' desire to have meaning in their lives. As with truth, we tend to think that meaning is something out there that we can reap, like picking an apple during the harvest season. But is the meaning of life ready-made like a ripe apple or something we constantly have to produce? Even apples are not simple items but are products of the collaborative work of farmers, sunshine, rain, soil, and many other elements for a substantial period of time.

Owen Flanagan, a philosopher of mind, observes in his book *The Really Hard Problem*, "How to make sense of living meaningfully is the hardest question."[1] How we find meaning in our lives is a fundamental question, but we do not always ask it. Rather, we think we are leading a meaningful life without asking where that meaning resides, or how it comes to be meaning in our lives. To quote Flanagan again, "Meaning, if there is such a thing, is a matter of whether and how things add up in the greater scheme of things."[2] What is it that holds things together to make meaning of life?

If one is a believer, one might say the meaning is given by God or a transcendental being. But the situation would not be so simple; even if a transcendental being or designer of the universe has assigned a meaning to humans, it does not follow that humans have access to that meaning or to the intention of this being. Hence, even a believer still needs to find the meaning of existence to match the intention of the superior being they believe in.

"Zhaozhou's 'Wash the Bowl!'" teaches us that there is no specific locus of truth, no specific time or activities that bring us truth, but that rather the locus could and should be everywhere and at every moment in one's life.

The idea that meaning can be anywhere at any moment offers a way to think about the power dynamics in our lives. The twentieth-century French philosopher Maurice Merleau-Ponty said, "Philosophy's center is everywhere and its circumference nowhere."[3] Philosophy in this case is directly related to the search for truth in the Western tradition. Like Zhaozhou, Merleau-Ponty asserted that there is no specific philosophical tradition, such as German philosophy or Greek philosophy, that contains more truth than others, or a specific event that reveals more truth than other events. He observed, "Philosophy is everywhere, even in the 'facts,' and it nowhere has a private realm which shelters it from life's contagion."[4] Like Zhaozhou, who advised his student to do the dishes after the meal, Merleau-Ponty said that there is no pure realm in which one can reap truth outside of the mundaneness or "contagion" of daily existence.

Truth is always related to power. Those who know truth can have power by virtue of possessing meanings and values that are precious to our existence. But the reverse is also the case. That is, people tend to equate power with truth. What is claimed by those who have power too often passes as truth, simply because of their ability to control people and information. This is becoming more and more the case, as social media and simultaneous sharing of information become the norm around the world.

Truth and power coupled together occupy the center of the life space in our time, which means that those who do not have truth or power linger at the periphery of existence. Such a hierarchical understanding of truth is ubiquitous, and Zhaozhou's advice to his student debunks that hierarchy by showing that washing the dishes can and should reveal truth. This means that anybody has the capacity to discover truth and has power to control their life and produce meaning for their existence.

Scholars often like to compare *gong'an* stories with discussions in Daoism, a major East Asian thought tradition. The *dao* literally means way or path in Chinese, and it is a key concept. Zhuangzi (who died around 286 BCE) was one of the main thinkers of that tradition. In the *Book of Zhuangzi*, he recounts a conversation with a person named Dongguo. Like Zhaozhou's student who wanted advice to attain awakening, master Dongguo wanted to know how to find the *dao* or the "Way" so that he could find truth. In answer to the question, "This thing called Dao, where does it exist?" Zhuangzi responded, "There's no place it doesn't exist." Master Dongguo demanded that Zhuangzi pin down the specifics of the locus of the *dao*, and Zhuangzi said it exists even in an ant or in a tile. Zhuangzi's dialogue partner could not believe this and said, "How can it be so low?" Zhuangzi responded, "It is in the piss and shit."[5]

The centrality and the power that one might believe to accompany truth dissipates in the cases discussed—"Zhaozhou's 'Wash the Bowl!,'" Merleau-Ponty's idea that philosophy's center is everywhere, and Zhuangzi's confirmation that the *dao* is even in the piss and shit. One might wonder at this point: If truth is so ubiquitous, does this mean that the power of truth can be shared by everybody? If so, realizing the ubiquity of truth can be a way of actualizing our idea of equality for all. But what's the value of truth if everybody can have it and it is so mundane? What is truth for? With these questions in mind, let us consider another *gong'an* from the *Gateless Barrier* that is different from the previous two in its approach to truth.

KILL THE CAT, KILL THE TRUTH

Some *gong'an* have a jaw-dropping effect upon first encounter. One such story is case 14 of the *Gateless Barrier*, "Nanquan Kills a Cat." Since this case story is directly related to our investigation of the locus of truth, I briefly restate a point made previously.[6]

The title of the *gong'an* itself is puzzling if we know that the first precept of Buddhism for both monastics and lay practitioners is "do not kill." Nonkilling or nonviolence is a flagship principle of Buddhism, and this title says that a renowned Chan master kills a living being. Here is the entire story:

> Master Nanquan saw that the monks from the eastern and western quarters were arguing over a cat, so he held it up and said, "If any of you can say something about it, you save the cat. If you cannot say anything, it will be killed." No one in the assembly could reply, so Nanquan killed the cat.
>
> That evening Zhaozhou returned from a trip outside the monastery. Nanquan recounted the story to him. Zhaozhou then took off his sandals, put them on top of his head, and walked out. Nanquan said, "If you had been there, the cat would have been saved." (see p. 260)

The case does not say what the monks were quarreling about, but some scholars have interpreted that they were arguing about the ownership of the cat, though this isn't clear from the text. Even though we cannot verify the cause of the argument, the details have little bearing on our investigation of the locus of truth. One thing is clear: the life of a cat, a living being, was at stake in a Buddhist monastery, and the monks held the key to saving it. Nanquan demanded that the monks "say something" and the cat would be saved. Nobody was able to say anything, and the cat was killed. Nanquan did not state what the monks should say. What if a monk had come forward and just said, "Please do not kill it" or "I'm sorry," or anything, just to save the cat? But the monks were unable to do so. What does that indicate?

One way of answering this question is to consider what we might call the "burden of truth," which is closely related to the connections between truth and power, center and periphery. We tend to think that truth is something precious and therefore should not be contaminated by "just saying." But what could the truth have been in this situation? Wouldn't the only truth have been to save the living being that is facing death? Who owned the cat, or what was right or wrong, could have been decided after the cat was saved.

Nanquan's instruction was exact: "Say something." But the imaginary nature of truth was so heavy that it pressed the monks down and paralyzed them. In a situation where an urgent action was needed to keep their oath of not killing living beings, they were unable to act and kept silent, even when that would violate the first precept of not killing. In the *gong'an*, Nanquan was the one who did the killing, but monks were just as guilty for the death of the cat.

People's first question upon reading this story could well be focused on the reply that Nanquan demanded from the monks. What was it— expression, idea, or something else—that Nanquan expected? The "what-ness" of truth as the primary and sometimes the only way of recognizing it often precedes and overrules a more important issue in a situation like the killing of the cat. Whatever Nanquan or the monks were looking for, the clear truth was a death of a living being, which the monks failed to recognize, causing a tragic result.

One way of thinking about the *gong'an* case "Nanquan Kills the Cat," using today's terms, could be as a case of conflict resolution. When a conflict arises and a complaint or grievance is filed, people usually approach it by trying to find out who is right and who is wrong: they try to decide what the truth is in the situation. Finding out the whatness of truth is also anchored in a mindset that is accustomed to competition, because who is right and who is wrong are directly related to who is the winner and who is the loser. The truth, the rightness, the winner—all these add up to create the heaviness of truth, which hampers people from making a decision to resolve conflicts.

In early Buddhist scripture, there is a story about a poisoned arrow. The Buddha asks his followers, if someone was shot by a poisoned arrow, what the most appropriate response would be. If people ask who shot the arrow and why, then while they try to figure out the "truth" of the situation, the victim will die. The first thing to do is to remove the arrow and treat the patient. That is the truth at that moment. Like in the story just discussed, the Buddha is telling us that the importance of truth is not in its what-ness but in its relation to us.

The twentieth-century German philosopher Martin Heidegger once proposed that truth should be understood as *aletheia* instead of *veritas*. *Veritas* means truth in Latin and indicates a correspondence between the idea and the reality. In the previous section, we asked: When we say something is true, how is that truthfulness confirmed? For truth to be understood as a correspondence between the idea we have and the reality it refers to, two conditions must be met: we must know exactly what our ideas are, and we must have all the information about the external reference. But confirming truth in this manner is like completing a jigsaw puzzle. Only when we could put together all the fragmentary pieces of information could the picture be completed and the truth be confirmed. But events in life are not like a jigsaw puzzle. We almost never have all the pieces we need to complete a picture. And even if we complete the picture, what is the goal of doing so?

Heidegger pointed out the problems with this approach and proposed that we think about truth in terms of *aletheia*, a Greek word for truth that means disclosure, unconcealedness, and revealing.[7] We can use Heidegger's method to understand the locus of truth in *gong'an* stories. Thinking of truth as disclosure or revealing does not mean that the truth will miraculously show itself. Rather, it suggests that in each case the truth needs to be detected in relation to the situation and the truth seeker.

More often than not, the weight of truth's whatness is related to our understanding of justice. Justice means fairness, as in the image of Themis, the Greek goddess of justice, who is holding a two-tray scale symbolizing balance of or fairness to two sides. The fairness of a justice system is also often understood in terms of punishment commensurate with the crime committed. However, there is also the practice of restorative justice, which gives priority to reconciliation between the victim and perpetrator, the victim and what happened, through which trauma is overcome and normalcy is restored. Restorative justice cannot take place if the parties involved remain in the mode of winning and losing and whatness of truth. One might ask whether this approach sacrifices truth in order to recover normalcy. When we ask such a question, we are already in the mode of thinking that takes truth as a fixed entity we can pick up, single out without context. This attitude can also partly explain why we might not feel comfortable in reorienting our understanding of truth.

Most of us might agree that the value of maintaining justice should be considered a universal truth. However, justice as universal truth is an idea, not reality. When an idea appears in reality, it appears in the context of our lives, which are contingent upon networks of social, political, cultural, and personal dimensions. Truth might be universal, but when we encounter it, if we ever do, the encounter happens in a context that is charged with varying conditions of existence. If truth can appear in its universal form, we should not even have to make efforts to find it out, since we should be able to recognize it. This is not the case in our lives.

In the second part of "Nanquan Kills the Cat," Naquan tells Zhaozhou what happened during the latter's absence. Zhaozhou places his shoes on his head, and Nanquan acknowledges that if Zhaozhou had been at the scene, he could have saved the cat. As horrifying as the story is, Zhaozhou's reaction and Naquan's acknowledgment of his response as a valid way of saving the cat seem absurd. But in the context of our interpretation of the story and the locus of truth, one's relation to truth, the second section of the *gong'an* aligns. Any response, even such an absurd one as placing shoes on one's head, could have saved the cat. The truth of truth might not lie in its whatness but in how we perform, cultivate, and connect with the truth in the context at hand.

IN SEARCH OF TRUTH

A pattern has emerged in our investigation of the locus of truth in the *gong'an* stories from the *Gateless Barrier*. These encounter dialogues tell us that truth is not something fixed; nor is it out there for us to pick up. This is so because truth is not a principle or even a rule, with which people often confuse it. Nor does truth occur only at extraordinary moments. Instead, in our daily activities we can encounter and discern its nature.

Several other stories in the *Gateless Barrier* offer occasions to further elaborate on the nature and the locus of truth proposed by the Chan tradition. In case 18, a monk asks Chan master Dongshan, "What is buddha?" and Dongshan responds, "Three pounds of flax." In case 21, the same question is posed to Chan master Yunmen, who responds, "A dried shitstick." In case 30, the question is asked of Chan master Mazu, and his response is "The mind is buddha." And again in case 33, the same question is asked of Mazu, who this time responds, "Not mind, not buddha."

Keep in mind that the question was about "what" buddha is rather than "who." These cases show that stating the "what" does not get us close to the truth of buddha, or to what buddha should mean to practitioners of Buddhism. If the whatness of buddha were what the practitioner needed to learn, Mazu wouldn't give two opposite answers to the same question. And what would be the point of answers like three pounds of flax or a dried shitstick if in order to get to know truth, one should focus on its whatness? All these responses seem to have the purpose of facilitating a certain state of mind and a certain relationship between truth and the truth seeker instead of offering information in the way a questioner usually expects.

In all the *gong'an* cases discussed so far—"Zhaozhou's Dog" (case 1), "Zhaozhou's 'Wash the Bowl!'" (case 7), and "Nanquan Kills a Cat" (case 14)—the students are looking for a fixed answer, in terms of the truth as defined by a "what," and the Chan masters give responses that are off track rather than straightforward right or wrong answers.

The twentieth-century French philosopher Jacques Derrida once claimed that we need to change our mode of questioning to get a better understanding of reality.[8] The question "what is" asks about the essence of the thing mentioned and demands a definitive declaration of its value. That value is presented as a property of the being or thing, independent of others. The whatness of beings preemptively excludes beings' indebtedness to others in the construction of the what, the value of the being. Derrida challenged this and claimed that we understand a being, a thing, or a concept through difference and trace. For example, we understand a chair as a chair because a chair is not a desk or a cup or the sky. Take the letter *b* as another example. We recognize *b* not because it has its own *b*-ness but because it is not *p* or *t* or *s*. The difference between *b* and other letters gives the identity of *b*: there is no exclusive whatness of *b*.

Why would it be a problem, then, from the Buddhist perspective, to define the identity of something by using a definitive expression, its whatness? To declare "what" is to declare an essence of the being, and this essence assumes a being is an independent entity. What we call individualism today is directly related to this mode of thinking, and at least since the beginning of the modern period, individual identity has been celebrated with ideas such as autonomy, independence, and freedom. All these traits of a free individual sound positive. What our claim of an independent and autonomous identity of ourselves as "human beings" fails to account for is that these qualifications always accompany various power dynamics. The truth might be that all humans are autonomous, independent, free beings. The reality, however, is that "all humans" does not include everybody and only refers to specific groups of people.

The problem of the individualist claim about our existence and the power dynamic as its corollary appears in different forms. A hierarchical and competitive relationship has been a common factor of human existence, whether in eighth-century China or twenty-first-century America. Does Buddhism say that a hierarchical and competitive relationship is always bad? The Buddha might respond that the question misses the point of his teachings. From the Buddhist perspective, the issue is not so much whether something is good or bad, or right or wrong, as whether an action is likely to cause suffering.

The Buddha was clear from the beginning that the goal of his teaching was to eliminate suffering, and it is not difficult to imagine how a hierarchical and competitive relationship could cause pain to the self and others. In order to exercise power in a hierarchical structure and defeat others in competition, the invasion of others' physical and mental space is inevitable. One becomes either an invader or a victim of invasion, which not only is not conducive to positive coexistence but also causes suffering for both oneself and others.

If we use the expressions of our time, understanding a being in terms of the essence of that being easily leads to a world in which self-centeredness hampers one's capacity to understand beings. We could say that one function of *gong'an* practice is to expose the practitioner to situations that help them realize the limitations of their habitual views and facilitate new ways of seeing things so that they can create environments in which people can make changes.

How does that change occur? Case 46 of the *Gateless Barrier*, "A Step Beyond the Hundred-Foot Pole," is related to this issue:

> Venerable Shishuang asked, "How do you take a step beyond the hundred-foot pole?" Another ancient worthy said, "Although the person sitting on top of the hundred-foot pole has found an entry [into the practice], it is still not real. At the top of the hundred-foot pole, you must step forward and expose the full body of reality throughout the worlds in the ten directions." (see p. 281)

As one reads this *gong'an*, one might picture a person standing on a hundred-foot pole. Just the idea of being in such a high place and atop a pole is dizzying. But this *gong'an* says that if you are on the hundred-foot pole, you should go one step farther. What would happen? A fall?

Different interpretations of this story are possible. One way to understand it is to read it as a simile of awakening. The very fact that a person is able to stand on a hundred-foot pole means that they have already achieved a certain level in practice. We might even say that they have attained awakening. But this case story tells us that the expression "to attain awakening" is misleading, because when one is in that state, one should also be able to push to move forward at the end of the hundred-foot pole.

My students often ask me what happens after awakening. I say that they need to modify the question, since there cannot be an "after" to awakening. It would be like standing at the base of the hundred-foot pole and holding on to it. For what purpose? Life is movement. It doesn't stay still. And awakening must be the same. Awakening should not be a static state that one can maintain but be constantly taking place, and this *gong'an* says that the constant activation of awakening is not easy but requires extreme rigor, like taking a step forward from the end of a hundred-foot pole.

At this point, we can circle back to consider the *gong'an* cases discussed earlier. Awakening sounds easy, like washing dishes, according to case 7, but it requires radical courage to break our habits of mind, as in the case of killing of a cat or stepping forward from a hundred-foot pole. For transformation of the mind to take place, conventional questions and answers will not help, because they will keep us repeating the same habits of mind. The point is not getting an answer to whether a dog has buddha nature or not. It is more about why the practitioner wants to know whether a dog has buddha nature and confirming this information or knowledge, because buddha nature affirms the possibility of their own awakening. But confirming a theory or idea is not the same as actualizing it. By offering an answer that is off track, such as "Wu!" or "dried shitstick," Chan masters in *gong'an* traditions push their students to struggle with their own existential reality and to embody the teaching that all beings are equipped with buddha nature.

Pojo Chinul, the thirteenth-century Korean Sŏn master who endorsed the efficacy of the *gong'an*-related meditation known as *hwadu* (C. *huatou*), repeatedly said that Chan or Sŏn Buddhism does not offer new theories. All the great theorizations already had been made by other Buddhist schools. Rather, Chan or Sŏn Buddhism provides a way for practitioners to actually get to the path to awakening. The *gong'an*, according to Chinul, is like a catalyst. It facilitates a moment for practitioners to find their own way, but it is not a teaching. This method of the Chan *gong'an* tradition should help us rethink our relationship to truth.

THE LOCUS OF TRUTH AND OUR TIME

In *Thick and Thin: Moral Argument at Home and Abroad*, Michael Walzer, a scholar of moral and political philosophy, proposes "thin" ethics as a paradigm for a globalized society. "Thin" refers to the minimal elements that can function as shared moral concerns among people in different parts of the world. Walzer says that moral minimalism "has no imperialistic tendencies; it doesn't aspire to global rule" and is "reasonable enough and universal enough."[9] He claims that this should be "everyone's morality because it is no one's in particular; subjective interest and cultural expression have been avoided or cut."[10] As an example, he mentions his experience of seeing a picture of people marching with signs, such as "Truth" and "Justice," in Prague during what came to be known as the Velvet Revolution. Even though he did not know the Czech language, Walzer said, such expressions were sufficient for him to feel solidarity with the marchers.

That protest happened in 1989. In recent years, polarization in both distribution of wealth and value claims has been causing significant problems in American society. Traditionally, Americans had ideas and ideals that we believed most of us valued dearly and would protect even at a high cost, including justice, fairness, equity, human dignity, and democracy. The situation has changed. In various places in the United States, people still protest with signs about truth, justice, human rights, and human dignity. But these expressions seem to have very different meanings to different groups. Where and how do we find truth?

To answer this question, let's return to the first *gong'an* story, "Zhaozhou's Dog." We asked why Zhaozhou's student did not pose a follow-up question to the teacher about the meaning of his answer. We might think the student should have pointed out that Buddhist texts teach that all beings have buddha nature and asked why Zhaozhou did not confirm this and instead said "Wu!"

Gong'ans are allegedly spontaneous conversations, but there must be some strategy embedded in them. The lack of a follow-up question by the student and the lack of clear elaboration by Zhaozhou on the meaning of his answer are themselves the teaching. That is, truth is not something one can confirm just by saying it. The idea does not mean much unless truth itself is embodied in a person's life. The student knew that all beings have buddha nature and wanted his teacher to confirm his knowledge. Zhaozhou's response was in fact his teaching: unless that confirmation is embodied in the student's life, it would not be meaningful.

People have been eager to find out what the truth is, or should be, as if we would be able to recognize it or possess and own it. The attitude of understanding truth through ownership has blinded us to the fact that truth is not something one can possess and has been distorting our relationship to truth.

One of the many teachings of the *gong'an* stories today might be that we need to adjust our relationship to truth. Before we ask what it is, we can ask what it means to us. When truth is understood in terms of ownership, it has value because ownership leads to the power to exercise authority over others. Truth in this case has meaning because of its utility.

When truth is understood in terms of being enacted in one's life, it also leads to power, but not the kind that exercises authority over others. Rather, it is the power to guide people's efforts to improve themselves so as to live with others sustainably.

In this polarized world, one can make claims for justice and truth, but as slogans they no longer help in directing our society for the benefit of many people or guiding us toward a better life. Instead, the precious values in our life and society, such as justice, truth, fairness, and equity, need to be rethought in consideration of the diverse environments we live in. What Walzer tries to bring to attention with moral minimalism or thin ethics is not just justice or truth itself but our efforts to understand others and move toward a better life with differences of opinions still within the boundaries. In this context, I have proposed that Buddhist ethics is an ethics of tension.[11]

Unlike our tendency to think about ethics as based on rules or obligations, Buddhist teachings seem to pay more attention to people's efforts to improve themselves and thus avoid causing suffering to themselves and others. In making such efforts, one inevitably encounters different views, perspectives, and truth claims. A tension inevitably arises in the struggle to make the best moral or ethical decision. This has been considered an element that needs to be removed for an ethical agent to make a decision, but Buddhist ethics demands the practitioner face the nature of the tension by considering the different positions involved in the argument or situation. As one reviews different possibilities and positions, one should refine one's own position on the issues at hand. Still, accepting a viewpoint that is far different from one's own is not easy. I would say that this struggle and the tension in one's ethical space is itself moral training.

From the Buddhist perspective, nothing has a permanent independent essence. If that worldview is applied to ethical decision making, one realizes that a position taken by any individual or group is a product of causes and conditions. The response that Buddhism encourages is not assigning an unchanging value judgment of right or wrong but understanding the causal links that led to a certain action or decision. This process of figuring out the causal nature of one's actions and decisions should expand one's capacity to comprehend others and oneself. "Baizhang and the Wild Fox," case 2 of the *Gateless Barrier*, teaches this lesson.

In this *gong'an*, Chan master Baizhang (720–814) notices that each time he delivers a dharma talk, an old man he doesn't know attends. One day, the old man stays behind to explain who he is. He says that a long time ago, a student had asked him, "Does a person of great practice still fall into cause and effect or not?" (see p. 252). The old man answered that such a person does not fall into cause and effect, and as a result was condemned to five hundred rebirths as a fox. The old man was now asking the same question of Baizhang, who responded that such a person "does not evade cause and effect." The story concludes, "At these words, the old man is greatly awakened."

Causality is the foundational worldview of Buddhism. The same causal event can produce enormously different effects depending on the conditions in which it takes place. For instance, imagine adding a spoonful of salt to a cup of tea. The tea will become noticeably saltier. Now imagine adding the same amount of salt to the Pacific Ocean. The ocean becomes saltier, but human beings can't tell the difference. The same action can produce a significantly different result depending on the conditions. The Buddhist idea of karma is based on such a causal theory that evaluates actions through causes and conditions.

Depending on the nature of one's action, its results can be positive or negative, and they will then become the seed of one's next action. We might want to think that once a person attains awakening, they are free of any evaluation of their actions as either positive or negative, since the awakened person should always do the right thing. This *gong'an* tells us that is not the case. Causality means that the contexts of actions define their results. Depending on the context, the same action might cause harm or benefit. Medicine can cure an illness when used in the proper dosage, but it can harm or kill people in overdoses. The action that is beneficial requires knowing not just that one needs a certain medicine for a certain disease, but what dosage and when, depending on one's condition, one's understanding of the context.

The ethical dimension of action lies less in choosing premade positive actions and rejecting premade negative ones than in being alert to the mechanisms through which actions occur and in which we live our lives. Unlike a moral theory that assumes unchanging moral obligation, Buddhist ethics demands its practitioners consider the complexity of existence and thus refines their capacity to understand situations in a more nuanced way. Often life places us in circumstances where competing values and priorities require us to make the best decision with limited information. If ethics consists of human efforts to live together and aims for the flourishing of all beings, one of the most valuable qualities for its practice is not "what" but "how." Instead of identifying whether a certain action is good regardless of context, one needs to learn to decipher various elements that lead to certain actions and their consequences. Buddhism teaches that awareness of how things happen refines one's capacity to understand others, which leads to exercising compassion and embracing others' suffering as if it were one's own, and to efforts to eliminate the suffering.

Such ethical efforts also coincide with a path toward truth. That is so because truth is not a fixed, premade entity but a process. That should especially be the case in Buddhism, whose worldview is based on the idea of multilayered causality. Hence awakening does not have an endpoint as far as life continues, and neither does truth. Identifying the locus of truth then is not based on "what" truth should be, but on how one expands one's ethical capacity through self-cultivation so as to see causes and conditions of events that take place.

NOTES

1. Owen Flanagan, *The Really Hard Problem: Meaning in a Material World* (Cambridge, MA: MIT Press, 2007), xi.
2. Flanagan, *The Really Hard Problem*, xi.
3. Maurice Merleau-Ponty, "Everywhere and Nowhere," in *Signs*, trans. Richard C. McCleary (Evanston, IL: Northwestern University Press, 1964), 128.
4. Merleau-Ponty, "Everywhere and Nowhere," 130.
5. Burton Watson, trans., *The Complete Works of Zhuangzi*, Section 22 (New York, Columbia University Press, 2013), 183.
6. See, Jin Y. Park, *Buddhism and Postmodernity: Zen, Huayan, and the Possibility of Buddhist Postmodern Ethics* (Lanham, MD: Lexington Books, 2008), chapter 5, "Thinking and Violence: Zen Hermeneutics," 101–143; "Zen Hermeneutics vis Heideggerian and Derridean Detours," *Universitas: Monthly Review of Philosophy and Culture* 30, no. 3 (2003): 79–96.
7. See Martin Heidegger, "The End of Philosophy and the Task of Thinking," in *On Time and Being*, trans. Joan Stambaugh (1964; reprint, New York: Harper & Row Publishers), 1972. Also see Park, "Zen Hermeneutics vis Heideggerian and Derridean Detours."
8. Jacques Derrida, *De la grammatologie* (Paris: Les Éditions de Minuit, 1967), 31; *Of Grammatology*, trans. Gayatri Chakravorty Spivak (Baltimore, MD: Johns Hopkins University Press, 1997), 18.
9. Michael Walzer, *Thick and Thin: Moral Argument at Home and Abroad* (Notre Dame, IN: University of Notre Dame Press, 1994), 64.
10. Walzer, *Thick and Thin*, 7.
11. Park, *Buddhism and Postmodernity*, chapter 10, "The Ethics of Tension," 205–22. Also see Jin Y. Park, "Zen Buddhism and the Space of Ethics," in *A Mirror is for Reflection: Understanding Buddhist Ethics*, ed. Jake H. Davis (New York: Oxford University Press, 2017), 73–91.

{ 4 }

PARADOX IN THE *GATELESS BARRIER*

Robert H. Sharf

Mountains Are Just Mountains

The Chan master Qingyuan Weixin of Jizhou ascended the high seat and said: "Thirty years ago, before this old monk had begun to practice Chan, I saw mountains as mountains and rivers as rivers. Then later on I came face to face with a teacher and made some headway, and I saw that mountains are not mountains and rivers are not rivers. But now, having reached a place of rest, I once again see that mountains are just mountains and rivers are just rivers. To all of you I ask, as for these three ways of understanding, are they the same or are they different? Should there be a monastic or layperson among you who can find a way out of this, I will acknowledge your having come face to face with this old monk."[1]

Virtually nothing is known about Qingyuan Weixin (ca. thirteenth century) other than his putative authorship of this *gong'an*, which first appears in a Chan anthology dated to 1204.[2] But the anecdote is justly celebrated in both classical and modern sources, as it bears upon a problem that lies at the very heart of Buddhist path theory: liberation is impossible, and yet it is achieved.

We will use Qingyuan Weixin's case, and the paradox to which it points, as our gateway into the nature and widespread usage of paradox in the *Gateless Barrier*. Even the title of this work suggests paradox: it refers to a passageway through which there is no opening. This could mean either that it is impossible to enter or that there is nothing stopping one from entering.[3]

At first glance, the "mountains are mountains" case seems to be straightforward and the paradox only superficial. Virtually all modern commentators interpret it as follows: before one sets out on the Buddhist path, one unreflectively accepts the common-sense attitude toward objects, such as mountains and rivers, as existing "out there" in the natural world. This is what philosophers call the "natural attitude"—a viewpoint that unquestioningly accepts the existence of the world given to us by our senses. As one engages in Buddhist practice, one comes to realize that the world we perceive is a cognitive construct. Everything we know—everything that can be known—emerges as the result of causally determined, interdependent processes, and hence nothing can be said to exist in and of itself. In the language of Buddhist scholasticism, everything is causally conditioned and thus lacks an "intrinsic nature" (S. *svabhāva*). There is, in the end, no substantially existent mountain out there in the mind-independent world, and this is what it means to say that all things, including mountains, are "empty" (S. *śūnyatā*). (In Buddhist thought, to claim that something is empty does not mean that it doesn't exist. Rather, it means that its existence is entirely dependent on other things, and those other things are in turn dependent on other things, and so on. Nothing exists *in itself*.) At this stage, "mountains are not mountains and rivers are not rivers." But later still, as one matures in one's practice, one realizes that emptiness is also empty. In other words, to say that mountains are empty is to affirm that all there ever was, or ever will be, are conventionally existing mountains. The term "conventional" ceases to mean anything, as it makes no sense to talk about a world that lies beyond appearances. Hence, there is no intelligible distinction to be drawn between the phenomenal mountains that show up for us, and real ones. In the end, mountains are just mountains.

So when Qingyuan Weixin asks whether these three ways of understanding are the same or different, the answer seems straightforward: they are the same in some respects and different in others. The mountains never change—they have always been empty—but the mind does. The mind evolves in its understanding, from an initial naïve perception of things as having independent existence, to the realization of the emptiness of all phenomena, and finally to the understanding that emptiness too is empty. Objectively, the world remains the same, but subjectively, the Chan adept has come to appreciate its ephemeral and insubstantial nature, and this brings freedom from clinging and desire.

It is then possible to escape the apparent paradox in Qingyuan Weixin's case using the Buddhist doctrine of two truths. From the perspective of *conventional truth*, there is a difference between the way the mountains are viewed at the beginning and end of the path, but from the perspective of *ultimate truth* there is not. The mountains remain the same (ultimate truth, the domain of ontology), but our apprehension of and/or relationship to them is transformed (conventional truth, the domain of epistemology). If one follows this line of argument, the paradox disappears.[4]

Or does it? The problem is that, were it that simple, Qingyuan Weixin's challenge would be vapid. Sidestepping the contradiction by distinguishing between "perspectives"—ultimate versus conventional, ontological versus epistemological—does not work, as the *gong'an* genre is, among other things, questioning the coherence of precisely these distinctions. The relationship between ultimate and conventional is itself enmeshed in paradox, and thus the two truths cannot help to defuse the paradox at the heart of this case: there is no difference between the mountains before and after awakening; thus there is no path, no awakening, and no Chan; it is the understanding that there is no awakening and no Chan that constitutes Chan awakening; this awakening changes nothing and everything.

THE INDIAN BACKGROUND

The seeds of the "mountains are mountains" conundrum go back to the beginnings of Buddhist thought. Buddhism teaches that all conditioned existence (*saṃsāra*) is impermanent, that there is no eternal soul or self or godhead, and that the only genuine escape from suffering is the peace of *nirvāṇa*, which is the cessation of the five aggregates (*skandhas*) that constitute the person. (The introduction to this volume explains the five aggregates.) Early Buddhist scriptures sometimes depict final *nirvāṇa* as tantamount to death, as death is now understood by secular materialists: there is no future rebirth, and hence sentient existence simply ceases. This led rival teachers to accuse the Buddhists of propagating nihilism. The Buddhists responded that their goal is not nihilistic; rather, whether there is something that survives final *nirvāṇa* is "undetermined" (S. *avyākṛta*, also translated as "unexpounded," "inscrutable").[5]

Various rationales for this answer can be found in Buddhist sources. However, whether one considers *nirvāṇa* an absence pure and simple; imagines that something, however subtle and unimaginable, survives *nirvāṇa*; or holds that the question is simply wrongheaded, all Buddhists agree that *nirvāṇa* is "unconditioned" (S. *asaṃskṛta*), meaning that it cannot be the result of, or affected by, any cause. (If *nirvāṇa* came about through causes, then it would be impermanent and would not be an escape from *saṃsāra*.) Some early Buddhist schools (Theravāda, Saṃmitīya, Vātsīputriyā) consider *nirvāṇa* to be the only unconditioned dharma, while other traditions, notably Sarvāstivāda, expand the list, sometimes by adding different types of "extinction" (S. *nirodha*) or including metaphysical or logical absences such as "space" (S. *ākāśa*).[6] A Newtonian notion of space is a useful analogy for thinking through the logic of the unconditioned: space exists, yet nothing touches or affects it.

The problem, then, is that activity (S. *karma*) of any kind, including Buddhist practice, cannot logically bring about *nirvāṇa*. Anything one does, including trying not to do anything, can only be a cause for a subsequent effect, but *nirvāṇa* cannot be the effect of any cause. No activity can bring about the final cessation of all activity.

There are various ways the early Buddhist commentators tried to respond, directly or indirectly, to this problem, none particularly satisfying. The most common response was to simply caution against fretting about it. *Nirvāṇa*, being unconditioned, lies beyond our (conditioned) comprehension, so we should just have faith that the Buddha's teachings will lead one there. This strategy has scriptural support in a famous parable from the *Cula-Malunkyovada-sutta*, in which a man is shot by a poisoned arrow and a surgeon is called to extract it. What if, before allowing the surgeon to remove the arrow, the man were to insist on first knowing the identity of the person who shot the arrow (his caste, name, clan, village, complexion, etc.), the nature of the bow and arrow that were used (the materials and design of the bow, the species of bird from which the arrow feathers came, etc.), and so on? Surely this benighted fellow would die from the poison before the surgeon could get on with his work.[7] The Buddha's teachings are simply a means to an end—a raft to cross the river of *saṃsāra*. Or, in an image popular in East Asia, the Buddha's teachings are likened to a finger pointing to the moon; understanding entails looking not at the finger but at the moon to which it points. It is counterproductive to ponder inconsistencies and contradictions in the teachings, since they are, in the end, mere expedient devices (S. *upāya*) leading the way to a goal that transcends conceptual understanding.

One indication that Buddhist exegetes themselves found this solution inadequate is that they continued to wrestle with it, reworking their doctrinal formulations and interpretative strategies. The Mahāyāna doctrine of emptiness (S. *śūnyatā*), for example, holds that every phenomenon is devoid of "intrinsic nature," rendering the distinction between conditioned things and unconditioned things moot. If the nature of *everything* is empty, then there is ultimately no distinction between conditioned *saṃsāra* and unconditioned *nirvāṇa*, and hence there is nothing to attain. This claim is made repeatedly and forcefully in the early *Perfection of Wisdom* (S. *Prajñāpāramitā*) genre of literature, as well as in early Madhyamaka texts such as the *Verses on the Middle Way* (S. *Mūlamadhyamaka-kārikā*) by Nāgārjuna (ca. 150 CE). The *Vimalakīrti-nirdeśa-sūtra* uses the language of nonduality, insisting that there is no difference between ignorance and awakening, impurity and purity. The matrix of buddhahood (S. *tathāgatagarbha*) teachings declare that since buddhahood—the unconditioned—cannot be attained, it must already be present within all beings; ergo *nirvāṇa* is not so much achieved as it is disclosed. While there are significant differences in the way these doctrines are fleshed out, they all address the seemingly insuperable gap between the mundane and supramundane (conditioned and unconditioned, *saṃsāra* and *nirvāṇa*) by maintaining that there is ultimately no gap to be bridged.

However, these important strands of Mahāyāna thought solved one problem only to generate others. If everything is empty, if buddhahood already abides within us, what stands in the way of our recognizing this? If there is ultimately nothing to achieve, why practice in the first place? And finally, if *everything* is contingent and empty, doesn't this apply to the teachings of the Buddha as well?

These questions lie behind the doctrine of the two truths as it appears in chapter 24 of Nāgārjuna's *Verses on the Middle Way*. In the first twenty-three chapters, Nāgārjuna is intent on showing that nothing has any intrinsic or substantial nature. Chapter 24 opens with the interlocutor raising the question: if it is indeed the case that nothing exists in and of itself—that everything is empty—then can't the same be said of the Buddhist teachings? Aren't they also empty, and thus ultimately false? In other words, in the interlocutor's mind, the Buddha's teachings—the four noble truths, the stages of liberation, the three jewels (Buddha, dharma, and *saṃgha*)—should be subject to the same critique that Nāgārjuna applies to everything else.

Nāgārjuna begins his response by insisting that the interlocutor makes a mistake in thinking that emptiness is the equivalent of nonexistence. According to Nāgārjuna, to claim that something is empty is not tantamount to claiming that it is unreal or false. He then goes on to introduce his understanding of the two truths, namely, the truth of worldly convention and an ultimate truth. He explains that both are necessary: "Without a foundation in the conventional truth, the significance of the ultimate cannot be taught. Without understanding the significance of the ultimate, liberation is not achieved."[8]

In other words, the conventional way of using language—the language associated with the "natural attitude" that unreflectively accepts things as they appear—is required to convey the Buddha's liberative insight into ultimate truth, which is the truth of emptiness. Nāgārjuna then explains that emptiness is nothing more and nothing less than the central Buddhist doctrine of dependent origination—the teaching that *everything* arises through causes and conditions. As there is nothing that is not dependently originated, there is nothing that exists in and of itself, and this is what it means to say that things are empty. In sum, for Nāgārjuna, to assert emptiness is not to claim that things are false or nonexistent but to claim that all things exist in dependence on other things.

The problem is that this response is satisfying only to the extent that one exempts the doctrine of dependent origination from the logical thrust of Nāgārjuna's critique. To put this another way, how does the claim that all things are dependently originated fit within the rubric of the two truths? Is dependent origination itself conventionally true or ultimately true?

This is not a trivial issue. The two-truths doctrine holds that the teachings of the Buddha—the four noble truths, three jewels, etc.—are conventionally *true* because they lead to the ultimate truth of emptiness. This is what distinguishes them from the conventional *falsehoods* taught by non-Buddhists. But the ultimate truth to which conventional truth points turns out to be that anything one says about the world must pertain to the domain of the conventional. We are now up against a limits-of-thought paradox: the doctrine of two truths cannot be asserted ultimately, because the ultimate does not allow for conceptual distinctions. (Properly speaking, the ultimate cannot be a "truth claim" or a "perspective" or a "view" at all, as that would entail being one among many.)

It would then seem that the two-truths doctrine itself belongs to the realm of the conventional. Indeed, the whole point of Nāgārjuna's *reductio ad absurdum* arguments is to demonstrate that *nothing* can be asserted ultimately, including the claim that nothing can be asserted ultimately. This leaves conventional truth as the only truth left standing, in which case the conventional truth that there is no ultimate truth is as true as it gets. This is tantamount to the final realization that "mountains are just mountains." But now we cannot use the two truths as a conceptual tool to eliminate the contradiction in Qingyuan Weixin's *gong'an*, since they are themselves contradictory. Rather than resolving the paradox, applying the two truths to this *gong'an* merely relocates it.

So Nāgārjuna uses the doctrine of two truths to situate the Buddha's teachings within his understanding of emptiness and dependent origination. He draws a distinction between conventional and ultimate—between finger and moon—and then claims that the Buddha's teachings are conventionally *true* by virtue of the fact that they point to the ultimate. But if ultimate truth is the truth that all truth is dependent, we are left with no stable point of reference—no nonconventional foundation—on the basis of which to distinguish between the conventional truth of the Buddha's teaching and the teachings of his rivals. The claim that the truth of any statement is context dependent and hence only relatively true must apply to the statement that all statements are context dependent and only relatively true. The two truths turn out to be paradoxical, so using them to escape from the paradox in Qingyuan Weixin's case simply kicks the can down the road.

It is unclear whether Nāgārjuna himself endorsed the use of paradox in his writings—indeed, this is a topic of debate among modern scholars.[9] What is clear, however, is that later Buddhist commentators in India and Tibet did everything they could to avoid it, lest they be accused of countenancing contradiction and thus incoherence. But China was a different story: Chinese Buddhist commentators, steeped in the paradoxes found in early Daoist texts such as the *Zhuangzi* and *Laozi*, not only recognized the limits-of-thought paradox in the two-truth formulation but also ran with it.

THE *GATELESS BARRIER*

Chan writers were not the only Buddhist monks in China who recognized and responded to the logical conundrum created by the two truths. Medieval writers associated with the Tiantai school, for example, read chapter 24 of the *Verses on the Middle Way* as talking about not two truths but three, adding a "middle truth" that, somewhat paradoxically, is both identical to and different from conventional and ultimate truth.[10] Some would see this as a philosophical advance, as it allowed Tiantai exegetes to distinguish conventional wisdom (the middle truth) from mere conventional falsehood and thus provided a foundation for ethical thought and action. The Chan tradition, however, steadfastly refused to move in this direction. From their point of view, proliferating truths simply exacerbate the muddle. In what may have been a thinly veiled attack on the nascent Tiantai tradition, one of the founders of Southern Chan, Heze Shenhui (670–762), said, "There is only the middle way, and it too is not in the middle, since the meaning of 'middle way' is predicated on the basis of the extremes. It is the same with three fingers—it is only by virtue of the two fingers on either side that we can posit a finger in the middle. If there are no sides, there is also no middle finger."[11]

Shenhui is claiming that the conventional and the ultimate are themselves codependent—that the label "conventional" is meaningful only in relation to the label "ultimate," and vice versa. Being relational and hence empty, the two truths cannot be construed as independent positions or perspectives between which one might locate a middle. Whether Shenhui's polemics fail to do justice to the conceptual sophistication of the Tiantai position need not concern us here. My point is simply that the Chan tradition refuses to mitigate or resolve the contradiction at the heart of the two-truth doctrine (is the doctrine itself conventional or ultimate?). Rather, they embrace it. And this means rejecting any attempt at mediation—any attempt to circumscribe a third position that resolves or transcends the paradox.

One possible mediating stance might be silence, in which one refrains from speech altogether so as to avoid positing any view, perspective, or truth. Some *gong'ans* do in fact depict Chan masters, like the Greek philosopher Cratylus or the Buddhist sage Vimalakīrti, resorting to nonverbal gestures. In response to students' challenges to say something "real" or "true" (i.e., something not conventional or relative), Huangbo Xiyuan (d. 850) was famous for hitting the interlocutor, Linji Yixuan (d. 866), for letting out a shout, and Jinhua Juzhi (ca. 810–880) for simply raising one finger. Yet should their disciples mistake these actions as pointing toward some inexpressible truth—as fingers pointing to the moon—they are immediately chastised. Take, for example, case 3 of the *Gateless Barrier*:

Whenever he was questioned, Venerable Juzhi would hold up a finger.

One time, one of the boys in the congregation was asked by an outsider, a visitor to the monastery, "What is the essential teaching of Juzhi, your master?" The boy also held up a finger.

When Juzhi heard about this, he took a knife and cut off the boy's finger. As the boy ran out howling in pain, Juzhi called him back. When the boy looked back, Juzhi held up a finger. The boy suddenly understood. (see p. 253)

The boy's transgression, of course, was mistaking the finger for the moon, which is why the master cuts it off. But an absent finger (the refusal to signify, the posture of silence) is just as contextually dependent as the shout, the strike, the wordless finger, or any other attempt at resolving the dilemma. This is why the case ends with the master once again raising his finger. There is no escape.

This same point is driven home in case 6, in which Śākyamuni Buddha, instead of preaching a sermon, silently holds up a flower. The elder Mahākāśyapa alone smiles, indicating his understanding, and the Buddha responds by acknowledging his transmission to the elder. But instead of celebrating the Buddha's skillful teaching, Wumen, the author of the *Gateless Barrier*, in his commentary castigates the Buddha as a swindler who offers his audience dog's meat and calls it mutton. "If the whole assembly had smiled, how would the Buddha have passed on the treasury of the true dharma eye?" Wumen asks. Silence is no less conventional, no more direct, than any other signifier, a point driven home in Hakuin Ekaku's (1686–1768) famous *kōan*, "What is the sound of one hand clapping?"

The attempt to circumscribe a third medial position (or "nonposition") that tames or resolves the paradox, that signifies by refusing to signify that which can't be signified, whether through a mute gesture or knowing silence, is rejected as futile and misguided. Rather than trying to insulate the tradition from the force of its own deconstructive logic, Chan holds back nothing. Wumen calls the Buddha a swindler; the sixth patriarch Huineng is depicted tearing up the sacred scriptures;[12] Yunmen likens buddha to a "dry shitstick" (case 21); and Linji famously declares, "If you meet the Buddha, kill the Buddha." There is no special pleading here—no special dispensation for expedient teachings.

It would seem then that transmission of the dharma is impossible—that speech and silence both fail. And yet in saying this, I have transmitted the truth of the matter. This paradox, at the heart of so many Chan cases, is drolly illustrated in *Gateless Barrier* case 5, "Xiangyan's Man Is Up in a Tree."

Master Xiangyan said, "It is like a man being up in a tree hanging on to a branch by his teeth, and his hands and feet not touching the tree branches at all. Beneath the tree there is someone who asks about the meaning of [Bodhidharma's] coming from the west. If this man does not reply, he is evading the questioner's question. If he does reply, he perishes. At such a moment, how could he answer?"

Wumen's Comment:

Even if you have eloquence that flows like a river, it is totally useless here. Even if you can preach the whole great [Buddhist] canon of the teachings, that, too, is useless. If you can give an appropriate answer, you bring back to life what before was a dead end and you put to death what before was your life's path. If you cannot answer, you must wait until Maitreya comes and ask him. (see pp. 254-255)

To appreciate this case, the reader has to know what any literate Chan monk would know: that the Indian patriarch Bodhidharma traveled to China in order to transmit the dharma. But the moment the man in the tree opens his mouth to respond in this or any other fashion, he falls to his death. The man under the tree is asking for the moon—the true dharma that Bodhidharma brought to China—but to respond in any fashion at all is to offer a mere finger. Xiangyan is saying that transmission of the dharma—the moon—is impossible, since all we have are empty fingers. But this very truth *is* the moon, and hence the case succeeds in transmitting the dharma. This is why Bodhidharma came from the west.

Bodhidharma's transmission of the dharma to his sole Chinese successor, Huike (487–593), is the subject of case 41 of the *Gateless Barrier*.[13] This famous (but no doubt apocryphal) anecdote begins with Huike waiting patiently outside Bodhidharma's cave hoping to catch the master's attention, while the falling snow piles up around him. Finally, in an act of desperation, Huike cuts off his arm, presents it to Bodhidharma, and says,

"Your disciple's mind is not at peace. Please, Teacher, pacify my mind!"
Bodhidharma said: "Bring me your mind, and I'll pacify it for you."
The second ancestor replied: "When I search for my mind, it cannot be found."
At that point Bodhidharma said: "I've already pacified it!" (see p. 278)

In this paradigmatic Chan encounter dialogue, Bodhidharma pacifies Huike's mind by showing him that there is no mind to pacify. Huike gets it and becomes the second Chan ancestral master in China.

The temptation at this point might be to resort, once again, to a distinction between conventional and ultimate, or between epistemology and ontology. There must, in the final analysis, be *some* difference, however "conventional," between those who understand that there is ultimately nothing to attain and those who have not yet come to this understanding. There must be *some* difference between Huike before the transmission and Huike after the transmission, even if, from the ultimate or ontological perspective, the point of the story is that there is no mind in need of awakening and thus no awakening to be gained. What could be more central to Buddhism in general and Chan in particular than the notion that

Buddhist practice leads to, or discloses, wisdom—the buddha mind—and that this wisdom is transformative?

Yet the moment one asserts these venerable Buddhist truths, claiming that there must be *something* gained through practice (whether ultimately or conventionally), Wumen will respond that nothing is attained (either ultimately or conventionally). Case 11, for example, takes aim at the premise that there are some grounds on which to distinguish the awakened from the unawakened.

> Zhaozhou went to a hermit's place and asked, "Have you got it? Have you got it?" The hermit held up his fist. Zhaozhou said, "Shallow water is not a place to dock a ship." And he left.
>
> Zhaozhou went to another hermit's place and asked, "Have you got it? Have you got it?" The hermit also held up his fist. Zhaozhou said, "Able to give and take; capable to kill and save." He paid his respect.

Wumen's Comment:

> "Both raised their fists. Why is one affirmed and the other denied? Tell me: Where is the fault? If you can utter a turning word here, then you can see that Zhaozhou's tongue has no bone in it. He can hold up and put down with great freedom. While this is so, these two hermits have also exposed Zhaozhou; they saw right through him. If you say that one hermit was better than the other, you do not have the eye to investigate and learn. If you say that there is no better or worse, you also do not have the eye to investigate and learn. (see p. 258)

This case is a clever trap into which you fall if you believe there is something *behind* Zhaozhou's approval of one hermit and his disapproval of the other. Wumen declares that the choice is arbitrary; he says Zhaozhou's "tongue has no bone in it," and that he raises one and disparages the other "with great freedom" (*da zizai*)—a term that references the unconstrained and unconditioned activities of a buddha. Zhaozhou is thus free from any investment in or attachment to attainment or nonattainment. But to claim that there is no difference between them is to establish a medial position, and this is precisely what Zhaozhou does *not* do. Rather he mischievously denigrates one hermit and acknowledges the other, thereby enacting his freedom from positions in the very act of "testing" the hermits.[14] This is not to say that Zhaozhou has something the hermits lack—i.e., "freedom." Note how Wumen flips things around, stating that the two hermits exposed Zhaozhou's ruse and were actually the ones doing the testing. Who now has it and who does not?

The same point is made in an almost identical manner in case 26 in the *Gateless Barrier*, "Two Monks Rolled Up Blinds."

A monk came forth and requested a teaching before the midday meal, and the great master Fayan of Qingliang [Temple] gestured with his finger at the blinds. At that, two monks went up to roll them up. Fayan responded, "One succeeds, the other fails."

Wumen's Comment:

Tell me, who has succeeded and who has failed? If you can obtain the eye [of awakening], you will perceive how Fayan himself failed! That being said, don't try to fathom this in terms of success and failure. (see p. 268)

Like Zhaozhou, Fayan acknowledges the attainment of one anonymous monk and denies that of another, without any apparent criteria to guide him. Should you be tempted to try to deduce what lies *behind* Fayan's pronouncement—what is concealed beneath or beyond the surface—you are immediately lost. There is only surface, only the conventional, only fingers. And to drive the point home, in his commentary Wumen once again reverses the hierarchy between master and disciple, between the awakened and the unawakened, by suggesting that it is actually Great Fayan who is at fault.

Many of Wumen's cases are rather cryptic, leaving it to the reader to tease out the paradox at the core of the anecdote. But case 2 of the *Gateless Barrier*, Baizhang Huaihai's (720–814) "Baizhang and the Wild Fox," foregrounds the paradox for all to see. This case is particularly salient for our discussion, as it deals directly with the problem of liberation—whether final escape from karmic conditioning and rebirth is possible at all.

Every time Baizhang taught, there was an old man who followed the congregation to listen to dharma talks. When the congregation dispersed, so would the old man. Unexpectedly, one day this elderly man stayed behind, so Baizhang approached him: "Who is it that stands before me?"

The old man said, "I'm actually not human. In the time of the ancient Buddha Kāśyapa, when I was dwelling here on this very mountain, a student asked me, 'Does a person of great practice still fall into cause and effect or not?' I replied that he does not fall into cause and effect. As a consequence, I have been condemned to be a fox for five hundred rebirths. I now ask you, Master, for a turning phrase so as to release me from being a wild fox."

Then he asked, "Does a person of great practice still fall into cause and effect or not?"

Baizhang said, "He does not evade cause and effect."

At these words, the old man was greatly awakened. He bowed in reverence and said, "I have now shed this fox's body behind the other side of the mountain. Please, Master, give me a funeral service due to a dead monk." . . .

After their meal, Baizhang led the congregation to a cliff on the other side of the mountain, where he used his cane and dragged out the body of a dead fox from a crevice in the rocks. They then formally cremated the body as they would for a monk.

That night, Baizhang ascended to the dharma hall and related the full story of what had happened. Huangbo then asked, "One wrong reply and this old man was condemned to be a fox for five hundred rebirths. If his reply had been correct, then what?"

Baizhang said, "Come here and I'll tell you." Huangbo then went up and gave Baizhang a good slap in the face. Baizhang clapped his hands and laughed and said, "I knew the [Western] barbarian's beard was red but didn't know that red was the beard of the barbarian!" (see p. 253)

Buddhist doctrine holds that Buddhist practice leads to *nirvāṇa*—to freedom from causation and escape from the karmically determined cycle of life and death. Hence the orthodox response to the initial question would seem to be that the person of great accomplishment—an awakened sage—is indeed free of causation. Yet precisely because he gave this doctrinally sanctioned answer, the old man found himself bound to the cycle of life and death. The challenge, then, is to answer in a manner that does not reify causation or liberation—that does not confuse the conventional with the ultimate—and at the same time does not posit a medial or transcendent position (that is, a perspective that neither affirms nor denies causation and liberation). Baizhang asserts the inverse of the old man's response, saying that even an awakened person cannot escape causation. (Zhaozhou uses precisely the same strategy in case 1 of *Gateless Barrier*, in which he categorically denies that dogs have buddha nature.)[15] Baizhang's claim that there is no escape from karma is tantamount to declaring that there is no final *nirvāṇa*, no buddhahood, no end to life and death, no freedom. And this answer—the assertion that there is no freedom—is what frees the old man. The paradoxical structure could not be more explicit: if you claim liberation is possible, it is not. If you claim it is not possible, it is.

At the end of the story, after Baizhang relates this improbable tale to his assembly, his leading disciple, Huangbo, confronts the master with a counterchallenge: what would have happened had the old abbot given the answer that liberated him in the first place—the doctrinally "incorrect" answer that there is no escape from karma? After all, it would seem that the answer that freed the fox—that no liberation is possible—is only effective insofar as it is the antithesis of the answer previously given, that liberation is in fact possible.

Huangbo is raising the specter of radical contingency—that there is, in the end, no determinate truth of the matter, so ultimately both answers are equally true and equally false.[16] In response to this challenge, the master invites Huangbo to approach the dais. Those versed in Chan literature know what to expect next: the master will strike the student, as a means of bringing closure to the exchange if not to the conceptual loop. But in yet another reversal, Huangbo manages to get his slap in first. Baizhang, delighted, offers Huangbo the ultimate compliment, using a pun to associate him with both the wily fox of the story and Bodhidharma, two inveterate tricksters.[17] The way out of the loop is to understand that there is no way out. The task of the Chan master is simply to drill this home.

CLOSURE (AND NOT)

Wumen understands that there is no ultimate position, perspective, or point of view, since ultimate truth can only be the truth that all truth is context dependent. Again and again, following impeccable Mahāyāna scriptural precedents, he asserts the identity of *nirvāṇa* and *saṃsāra*, wisdom and ignorance, freedom and entrapment. He does not do this from the perspective or standpoint of the ultimate, since there is no ultimate "perspective" to be had. This is precisely Wumen's point: his cases are traps, intended to catch the unwary student who imagines some transcendent ground beyond the vagaries of contingency and conception—a final escape from life and death. There is no stepping outside oneself, no view from nowhere, no escape from causality. This is the truth of emptiness, *the realization of which frees one from causality*. Rather than running away from this dialetheia, Wumen runs toward it.

Wumen refuses to hold anything sacred. He does not distinguish between the truths of Chan and the mundane truths of everyday life. No special dispensation is made for Chan skillful means. Chan is nothing special. And this, of course, is what makes it special.

Wumen thus endorses, and indeed revels in, a number of related contradictions. Liberation is impossible to achieve and yet it is achieved. Transmitting the dharma is impossible and yet it happens. *Nirvāṇa* and *saṃsāra*—ultimate and conventional—are identical and yet different. The truth cannot be spoken, and yet it is spoken. Indeed, it is difficult to find a single case in Wumen's revered collection that isn't constructed around a paradox held to be both true and pressing.

To return to where we began, Qingyuan Weixin asks if the three views of the mountains—those at the beginning, middle, and end of one's practice—are the same or different. It should now be clear that Qingyuan Weixin, like Wumen, does not want to avoid the dialetheia but rather to rub your nose in it. To assert that they are different *in any respect*—to maintain that there is anything to attain, either conventionally or ultimately—is to fall from the path. But at the same time there must be a difference; if awakening were not an achievement, there would be no path from which to fall. There is nothing to be attained, and when you see this, you have attained something, both conventionally and ultimately. Everything is left precisely as it was before, and everything has changed, both conventionally and ultimately.

If what one attains is the understanding that there is nothing to attain, if Chan is nothing special, why practice Chan in the first place? This is the subject of *Gateless Barrier* case 16: "Yunmen said, 'The world is so vast and wide! Why put on the seven-piece robe at the sound of the bell?'" (see p. 262). In other words, of all the possible things one might do with one's life, why choose the ritually regimented life of a monk? Yunmen provides no rationale because in the end there is no rationale to give. There is no nonempty moon by which to determine that one finger is better than another.

Yunmen puts on his robe because the bell has sounded.

NOTES

This chapter is adapted from the chapter "Chan Cases" in Yasuo Deguchi, Jay L. Garfield, Graham Priest, and Robert H. Sharf, *What Can't Be Said: Contradiction and Paradox in East Asian Thought* (Oxford and New York: Oxford University Press, 2021).

1. The earliest source for this anecdote appears to be the *Jiatai pudenglu*, compiled in 1204 by Leian Zhengshou (1146–1208; X. 1559: 79.327a24–b4). It is reproduced,

with minor changes, in a number of later Chan collections, including the *Wudeng huiyuan, Xu chuandeng lu,* and *Wudeng quanshu.* The *gong'an* is popular in Western accounts of Zen, owing largely to D. T. Suzuki's discussion in his influential *Essays in Zen Buddhism,* First Series (London and New York: Rider, 1926), 24. It was subsequently picked up in popular culture, featured in the 1967 hit song by Donovan Leitch, "There Is a Mountain" and later in songs by The Allman Brothers Band and the Grateful Dead.

2. Qingyuan Weixin's spiritual genealogy is recorded in the *Jiatai pudenglu zongmulu* (X.1558: 79.274b13). For an account of how *gong'an* were used in the curricula of Song Dynasty Chan monasteries, see Robert H. Sharf, "How to Think with Chan *Gong'ans,"* in *Thinking with Cases: Specialized Knowledge in Chinese Cultural History,* ed. Charlotte Furth, Judith Zeitlin, and Hsiung Ping-chen (Honolulu: University of Hawai'i Press, 2007), 205–243. The analyses of some of the cases raised in this chapter borrows directly from that essay.

3. The title of the *Gateless Barrier,* like so many of the *gong'an* contained therein, contains a pun: in addition to the "gateless barrier," it could be read as "the gateless passageway," or "the passageway that is the word 'no' (or 'nonbeing')," a reading that is suggested in Wumen's commentary to the first case, Zhaozhou's "No." Or it could be read as referencing the author himself: "Wumen's Pass."

4. For an alternative resolution of this paradox, based on an analysis of the syntax of the "signature formula," see Paul Harrison, "*Vajracchedikā Prajñāpāramitā:* A New English Translation of the Sanskrit Text Based on Two Manuscripts from Greater Gandhāra," in *Manuscripts in the Schøyen Collection,* ed. Jens Braarvig, Paul Harrison, Jens-Uwe Hartmann, Kazunobu Matsuda, and Lore Sander, vol. 3 (Oslo: Hermes Publishing, 2006), 136–140, and "Resetting the Diamond: Reflections on Kumārajīva's Chinese Translation of the *Vajracchedikā ('Diamond Sūtra'),"* *Journal of Historical and Philological Studies of China's Western Regions* 3 (Beijing Science Press, 2010): 241–245.

5. See, for example, the *Sariputta-kotthita-sutta* (SN 44.6; iv.388), and *Anuradha-sutta* (SN 22.86; iii.1160). On the relationship between *nirvāṇa* and insentience, see Robert H. Sharf, "Is *Nirvāṇa* the Same as Insentience? Chinese Struggles with an Indian Buddhist Ideal," in *India in the Chinese Imagination: Myth, Religion, and Thought,* ed. John Kieschnick and Meir Shahar (Philadelphia: University of Pennsylvania Press, 2014), 141–170.

6. Andre Bareau, "The List of the Asamskrta-dharma According to Asanga," in *Researches in Indian and Buddhist Philosophy: Essays in Honour of Professor Alex Wayman,* ed. Alex Wayman and Rāma Karaṇa Śarmā (Delhi: Motilal Banarsidass, 1983), 269–308.

7. *Majjhima-nikāya* 63, i. 426.

8. *Verses on the Middle Way* 24.8, 10; trans. Jay Garfield, *The Fundamental Wisdom of the Middle Way: Nāgārjuna's Mūlamadhyamakakārikā* (Oxford and New York: Oxford University Press, 1995), 68.

9. See, for example, Jay L. Garfield and Graham Priest, "Nāgārjuna and the Limits of Thought," *Philosophy East and West* 53, no. 1 (2003): 1–21; Yasuo Deguchi, Jay L. Garfield, and Graham Priest, "The Way of the Dialetheist: Contradictions in Buddhism," *Philosophy East and West* 58, no. 3 (2008): 395–402; Tom J. F. Tillemans, "How do Mādhyamikas Think? Notes on Jay Garfield, Graham Priest, and Paraconsistency," in *Pointing at the Moon: Buddhism, Logic, Analytic Philosophy,* ed.

Mario D'Amato, Jay L. Garfield, and Tom J. F. Tillemans (Oxford and New York: Oxford University Press, 2009), and "'How Do Mādhyamikas Think?' Revisited," *Philosophy East and West* 63, no. 3 (2013): 417–425; Mark Siderits, "Does a Table Have Buddha-Nature?" *Philosophy East and West* 63, no. 3 (2013): 373–386; Yasuo Deguchi, Jay L. Garfield, and Graham Priest, "Does a Table Have Buddha-Nature?: A Moment of Yes and No. Answer! But Not in Words or Signs! A Response to Mark Siderits," *Philosophy East and West* 63, no. 3 (2013): 387–398, and "How We Think Mādhyamikas Think: A Response To Tom Tillemans," *Philosophy East and West* 63, no. 3 (2013): 426–435.

10. On the Tiantai doctrine of three truths see Paul L. Swanson, *Foundations of T'ien T'ai Philosophy: The Flowering of the Two Truths Theory in Chinese Buddhism* (Berkeley, CA: Asian Humanities Press, 1989), and Brook Ziporyn, *Evil And/or/as the Good: Omnicentrism, Intersubjectivity, and Value Paradox in Tiantai Buddhist Thought* (Cambridge, MA: Harvard University Press, 2000).

11. *Nanyang heshang dunjiao jietuo chanmen zhiliaoxing tanyu,* Pelliot 2045; Hu Shih, *Shenhui heshang yiji—fu Hu xiansheng zuihou de yanjiu* (Taibei: Hu Shi jinian guan, 1968), 248; Tōdai goroku kenkyū han, ed., *Jinne no goroku: dango* (Kyoto: Zen bunka kenkyūjo [Hanazono University]), 2006, 117.

12. The attribution of this painting (now in a private Japanese collection) to the celebrated painter Liang Kai (ca. 1140–1210) is controversial, but the theme is clear enough.

13. This exchange, which marks the beginning of the transmission of the dharma in China, served as the prototype for all meetings between master and disciple in Chan monastic training; an image of Bodhidharma was placed outside the master's chamber when the senior disciples came for a formal interview known as "entering the chambers" (*rushi*; T. Griffith Foulk and Robert H. Sharf, "On the Ritual Use of Ch'an Portraiture in Medieval China," *Cahiers d'Extrême-Asie* 7 (1993): 194.

14. On the notion of "enacting" or "performing" buddhahood, see Robert Sharf, "Ritual," in *Critical Terms for the Study of Buddhism*, ed. Donald S. Lopez, Jr. (Chicago: University of Chicago Press, 2005), 245–269.

15. For an extended analysis of "Zhaozhou's dog," see Sharf, "How to Think with Chan *Gong'ans.*"

16. Such a position is sanctioned, arguably, in the *Mahāparinirvāṇa-sūtra*, which claims that the Buddha teaches non-self to those who hold to the existence of a self. For those who cling to non-self, he teaches the existence of a self (*Dabanniepan jing*, T. 374: 12.407b29–c19, *et passim*).

17. In medieval times, as in modern Mandarin, the Chinese characters for "barbarian" and "fox" were homophones. (In modern Mandarin both are pronounced *hú*.)

TESTING, CONTESTING, BESTING

AMBIGUITY IN *GONG'AN* DIALOGUES

Steven Heine

AMBIGUITY IN CASE 31

This chapter examines how the fundamental role played by the rhetorical elements of ambiguity, uncertainty, and ambivalence impacts our understanding of the meaning of the Chan experience of awakening, as expressed in the "encounter dialogue" (*jiyuan wenda*) that forms the basis of *gong'an* case 31 ("Zhaozhou Exposes the Old Granny"; see pp. 272-273) in the *Gateless Barrier*. The term "encounter dialogue" refers to a witty, competitive exchange of words and sometimes gestures between two people seeking to test and contest with each other in dharma combat. This usually brief account is then interpreted through the incisive prose and poetic commentary of Wumen, the compiler of the collection.

Case 31 involves a brief and intriguing yet perplexing exchange between master Zhaozhou, an exalted figure in the Chan tradition who leads a large assembly of monks at a local temple and is cited in the *Gateless Barrier* more times than any other teacher, and an old woman or "granny" (C. *pozi*), who is unaffiliated with and somewhat defiant of the monastic institution. Despite her lack of credentials, the woman has been able to consistently outwit numerous novice monks who walk by as she stands on the side of a road that leads toward the renowned Buddhist pilgrimage site of Mount Wutai (C. *Wutai shan*). News of this ongoing disturbance to his acolytes exasperates Zhaozhou and causes him to leave his temple compound in order to confront the granny directly.

It is altogether unclear, however, which of the competitors, the master or the granny, bests their adversary to prevail as the winner of this contest. During their repartee Zhaozhou at first seems to be one-upped by the old woman, who mocks him just as she had been doing with the lesser-ranked monks; by the end of the encounter, however, he proclaims himself the victor. Therefore, a basic sense of uncertainty pervades the dynamic yet enigmatic give-and-take. Furthermore, Wumen's commentarial remarks, which serve as a kind of "scorecard" regarding the outcome of the dispute, indicate that "Examining them, both had transgressed" (see p. 272). Because the result remains inconclusive in the story as well as in the commentary on the case, I suggest that by studying this encounter carefully in light of other "public records" or gong'an narratives involving Zhaozhou and/or comparable grannies, we find that ambiguity is a foundational conceptual factor that helps determine the significance of many, though by no means all, of the entries in the Gateless Barrier.

To explain how equivocality contributes to interpreting this and related cases, the following questions are considered: What is the symbolism of the confrontation taking place on the path to a prominent shrine that lies far afield from, and in some ways seems antithetical to, the customary circumstances in a Chan temple compound? Which person, if either, has upheld their status in the intense face-to-face meeting? How are readers to evaluate the apparently contradictory conclusion to the narrative that is reinforced by Wumen's poetic remark, "The questions were the same, and so were the answers" (see p. 272)? Moreover, to what extent does examining the complicated situation and ironic comments concerning case 31 help clarify the significance of ambiguity in the overall discourse of gong'an narratives?

CASE 31, PART 1: ADDITIONAL ASPECTS OF AMBIGUITY

There are several crucial aspects of ambivalence, or of intricate and unsettled discursive connections and institutional disconnections, that occur when Zhaozhou purposefully but warily goes to meet his adversary. She is not a typical disciple lurking in the halls of the monastery, nor a rival teacher visiting there, but an unusual and bewildering outsider known to repeatedly deceive and upset members of his congregation. Promising to test, investigate, or check out (C. *kanguo*) this granny, suddenly in the midst of their impromptu chat, the eminent teacher Zhaozhou becomes the one who is caught off balance and vulnerable. His sense of ecclesial authority and existential authenticity as a well-established clerical leader is deeply challenged and threatened by the savviness of the seemingly disrespectful though ingenious and self-confident granny. He must try to overcome the profound difficulties presented during their exchange to recover his good standing, yet the degree of his success remains in question.

According to the case record, the granny is found waiting to greet itinerant monks traveling on their way to visit Mount Wutai, a sacred place in Buddhist lore considered the earthly abode of the bodhisattva Mañjuśrī (C. Wenshu). This group of five peaks (the literal meaning of *wutai*) is located in remote Shanxi province but also relatively near, or about 225 miles from, Zhaozhou's monastery in northeastern China. Mount Wutai was considered highly ambivalent in terms of its function in Chan discourse. It housed dozens of temples often featuring remarkable accounts of visions of the deity appearing as multicolored clouds or as a king riding on a lion's back in the skies above to inspire seekers; sometimes, however, the deity was said to manifest as a meager or unruly beggar traipsing the hills to test the will power and compassion of lone pilgrims.

This fantastic pilgrimage site attracted Chan travelers from all over the country, even though Zhaozhou and several other prominent teachers were on the record as refuting the mountain's spiritual efficacy and discouraging their students from journeying there. These teachers feared that the esoteric practices associated with the mountain sanctuary would distract trainees from a strict adherence to formless meditation or unobstructed quiet sitting, and ultimately that seeking insight through external means would leave them feeling disillusioned and unfulfilled in their quest to attain awakening.[1] Or perhaps, conversely, the Chan leaders were fearful of competition from an alternative and increasingly popular form of Buddhist symbolism that impressed many practitioners.

In traditional biographical materials, Zhaozhou is represented as having wished to visit Mount Wutai during his early days of training before he became a temple abbot. However, he met with criticism from a colleague, leaving it uncertain whether he ever made the journey or not. According to the Chan warning about the illusory quality of the mountain that was expressed to Zhaozhou in a poem,

> What green mountain anywhere is not a place to learn the Way?
> Why hike with your staff all the way to Qingliang (Wutai)?
> Even if the golden lion (Mañjuśrī) is revealed in the clouds,
> When looked at with the true dharma eye, this is not auspicious.[2]

Zhaozhou's own recorded sayings do not contain the kind of blunt refutation that was proffered by other leading teachers, who asserted that the bodhisattva is not present on Mount Wutai or otherwise declared the deficiency of imaginative images seen in the mountains because "[Meditation] is better than worshipping at Wutai and is better than seeking the Western Paradise."[3]

By the time case 31 takes place, Zhaozhou had ascended to serving as head of a major monastery in an area not far from Beijing, which is unusual because the Chan school thrived mainly in the southern parts of Jiangxi and Hunan provinces, located below the Yangzi River that flows across central China. Some wayfarers coming all the way from southern districts likely stopped at Zhaozhou's temple to spend time learning from him. That type of transiency, allowing novice monks to study with different teachers, was generally encouraged by Chan monastic leaders.

Following up on complaints from some visitors, who in principle should not have been venturing to Wutai since it was considered off limits, Zhaozhou proceeds to meet the granny, an apparently wise yet mysterious and provocative stranger—i.e., "a person of wit and resourcefulness who is usually marginal and ambivalent in social status and who crosses social boundaries."[4] The old woman may denote the function of various non-Buddhist teachings based on Daoist or shamanistic wizardry, or spiritual approaches that, like Mount Wutai's visionary form of religiosity, were perceived as a threat to the sanctity of Chan's cloistral training procedures and perhaps intimidated Zhaozhou.

The granny's inscrutable manner of speaking had already confounded various clerics hoping to reach the mountain destination; similarly, when the esteemed master goes to test the mystifying interlocutor on their behalf, she appears to overcome and quickly dispense with him in the same way. At the very least, their dialogue is said to be identical in terms of Zhaozhou making a simple query and the granny giving a puzzling reply. But at the end of the narrative, in a talk delivered at his monastery on the day following the encounter, Zhaozhou declares to the assembly, "I've thoroughly exposed [or seen through] (C. *kanpo*) the granny of Wutai for you all" (see p. 272). The compounds *kanguo* for "testing" and *kanpo* for "exposing" share the first character *kan*, which means "to perceive."

Is Zhaozhou offering an idle claim made to save face or a reluctant and ironic admission of defeat? Are Wumen's dubious comments on the encounter dialogue meant to teach readers that they should abandon the expectation of clear-cut answers and embrace ambiguity as an inevitable part of the path to an awakening to nondual truth that lies beyond the divisions of right versus wrong, or apparent winners and losers? As Wumen remarks by borrowing from art of war discourse, "The old granny only knew how to sit within her headquarters tent and launch her stratagem to catch the thieves. She did not know that old man Zhaozhou was good at creeping into her tent and menacing her fortress." That is, she is unprepared for such an illustrious adversary, versed in methods used for fending off putdowns or comebacks. "But tell me," Wumen adds provocatively, "what is it that is exposed by Zhaozhou in the old granny?" (see p. 272). Thus, neither of the exchange partners fares well in Wumen's estimation, as both exhibit flaws, partiality, or limitations revealed by his commentary.

My analysis of case 31 therefore considers the pattern whereby a verbal/nonverbal interchange creates a fundamental degree of uncertainty about the consequences of a dialogue in that the participants reach a puzzling crossroad or standstill without a clear-cut or unambiguous result. To clarify my approach: it is said in the prose commentary on the *Blue Cliff Record* (*Biyan lu*) *gong'an* collection, published in 1128, that because unraveling the mysteries of a case or deciphering the uncertainties of an encounter dialogue is quite complicated, an interpreter must take a round-about or circuitous path.[5] Rather than trying to be straightforward or direct, an analysis of a *gong'an* should explore the full background and multiple ramifications of the core story.

In that vein, I will reflect on a variety of related topics before circling back toward the end of the chapter to a more detailed view of case 31. These include considering the character of Zhaozhou as depicted in various *gong'an* cases and taking into account additional dialogues that feature the role of ambiguous nonclerical women trying to outsmart clerical male counterparts.

For example, I will discuss the significance of case 11 ("Zhaozhou Discerns the Hermits"; see pp. 258-259) in the *Gateless Barrier*, in which Zhaozhou has an unconventional and inconclusive encounter with a couple of recluses meditating in huts outside the temple grounds, who react in identical ways to his challenge but receive opposite evaluations from the teacher. This dialogue is very similar to case 31 because both refer to the process of "testing" adversaries and "exposing" their true status. I will also consider case 28 ("Long Have We Heard of Longtan"; see pp. 258-259), which according to Wumen's prose comments refers to another roadside contest, this time between a clever granny selling refreshments and the master Deshan, whom she apparently exposes for being stubborn and arrogant. Cases 11 and 28 help illuminate our understanding of what

Zhaozhou means when he claims to have bested the granny in case 31, and why Wumen calls the master's attitude into question without drawing a firm conclusion.

Furthermore, I will compare the pithy hermeneutic approach of the *Gateless Barrier*'s remarks with the more elaborate commentarial style concerning the same story that appears, with a few minor textual variations, as case 10 of the *Record of Serenity* (*Congrong lu*), a *gong'an* collection with comments on 100 cases by the master Wansong Xingxiu (1166–1246) that was first published in 1224. The two collections were both composed during the 1220s, but the respective commentators were located at temples in faraway regions. Wumen, a member of the Linji branch of Chan, led a temple in Hangzhou, the capital of the Southern Song dynasty, and Wansong, a leader of the Caodong school, compiled the *Record of Serenity* while he dwelled at a retreat known as the Serenity Hermitage in Beijing. Then part of the Jurchen empire, Beijing was being affected by the early stages of Mongol expansion. Thus, the two commentators were unaware of each other's interpretative style, so it is especially interesting to be able to link their writings today.

HOW AMBIGUITY IS EMBEDDED IN VARIOUS ENCOUNTER DIALOGUES

I will first reflect on the structure of encounter dialogues, a particular kind of oral exchange featured in numerous Chan writings, in which masters and students interact in certain clearly discernible, albeit spontaneous and unpredictable, ways in order to trigger spiritual insight. This awakening usually occurs on the part of the junior partner or learner who is roused by virtue of a mentor's expression of wisdom through a probing inquiry, paradoxical instruction, or cryptic declaration.[6]

These dialogues initially appeared in various textual sources first published at the beginning of the early eleventh century, including the voluminous transmission of the lamp and recorded sayings genres. Stories of exchanges were culled from those materials to form the core literary unit that is crucial in the teachings of *gong'an* included in the *Gateless Barrier* and other major Song dynasty compilations with commentaries. The additional parts of the literary structure of cases include prose and poetic comments on the dialogues and an introductory statement or ironic capping remarks on key passages of the core exchange and verse. Introductions and capping phrases are not contained in the streamlined interpretative approach featured in the *Gateless Barrier*.

According to the primary pattern of encounter dialogues, during a contest of wills epitomized by pithy banter and nonverbal reactions, such as striking a rival or feigning a posture of defeat, two exchange partners test each other.[7] This contest determines whether their mettle can withstand the scrutiny instigated in a highly competitive, if not necessarily antagonistic, interpersonal context. One party emerges from the exchange as the vanquisher while the other gets their comeuppance. Yet, through the process of engaging in the encounter, the apparent loser undergoes a spontaneous transformation from stubborn ignorance to genuine self-awareness.

Nearly half of the forty-eight cases in the *Gateless Barrier* lead toward or specifically culminate in a triumphal assertion by or about how a disciple, who is often but not always anonymous, attains an experience of awakening. For instance, in case 7 ("Zhaozhou's 'Wash the Bowl!'"; see p. 256) an unnamed monk has "an insight" when instructed by Zhaozhou, serving as his teacher, to wash his dishes after eating breakfast. Zhaozhou's point is that the novice should focus all his attention on the next mundane daily task at hand, rather than holding on to grand expectations by anticipating in an overly eagerly way a quick path to awakening. Also, in case 19 ("Ordinary Mind Is the Way"; see pp. 263-264) Zhaozhou, at the time still a disciple, is "greatly awakened" upon hearing the words of his teacher, Nanquan, about the meaning of nonduality, which is "neither known nor unknown," and is "free from doubt" and "vast like open space." This view of going beyond divisions or polarities seems to have greatly influenced Zhaozhou's encounter with the granny.

An interesting variation occurs when the master is bested at the hands of a tables-turning underling but happily acknowledges this circumstance. For a Chan teacher, overseeing the development of a worthy follower, even or especially when the student demonstrates their own capacity through criticizing the mentor, proves in the final analysis the merits of the teacher's ability. In case 13 ("Deshan Carries His Bowl"; see pp. 259-260), the head of the temple, Deshan, is disparaged at first by his follower Yantou for a minor breach of hermetic protocol when he inexplicably enters the lunchroom before the proper time. However, after the master provides an outstanding dharma talk for the assembly the next day, the disciple proclaims, "This old man has the last word. From now on, no one in the world will be able to cope with him," and Deshan accepts the praise. Also in case 40 ("Kicking Over the Water Jar"; see pp. 277-278), Guishan ridicules a challenge from his teacher Baizhang, when he is pitted against a monk ranked higher in the temple pecking order, by kicking over a water pitcher and abruptly walking away from the scene. For this absurd action he is praised by Baizhang instead of being criticized. Moreover, Baizhang invites Guishan "to open a new monastery at Mount Dagui."

Although these cases appear to be rather clear-cut and decisive while featuring the positive outcome of a participant, whether junior or senior, learning a lesson from the encounter, there is another discernable gong'an pattern whereby the dialogue ends abruptly after posing a challenge that leaves matters deliberately inconclusive. Such a standstill implies the disciple or rival is not yet capable of grasping the essential point and must continue training before a realization can be gained. For instance, case 5 ("Xiangyan's Man Is Up in a Tree"; see pp. 254-255) raises the specter of a dire conundrum when someone hangs by their teeth from the branch of a tree and is asked an unanswerable question. Xiangyan demands, "At such a moment, how could they answer?" Indeed, there seems be no way out of this enigma. Also, case 8 ("Xizhong Makes a Carriage"; see pp. 256-257) speaks hypothetically of deconstructing the various parts of a carriage and inquires, "What will the carriage then be?" Again, this leaves the reader with uncertainty. In case 38 ("A Water Buffalo Passing Through a Window Frame"; see p. 276), Wuzu says that all the large parts of a buffalo can be pushed through a window and asks, "Why can't the tail pass through?" The reader is thus confronted with an illogical situation. Lastly, case 45 ("Who Is It?"; see p. 281) posits that even buddhas and bodhisattvas are slaves of an unnamed master, asking the unfathomable, "Who is he?"

Furthermore, even though the results of many dialogues seem clear enough, one of the general goals of gong'an commentaries in the Gateless Barrier and other collections is to call into question the outcome. Regarding case 13, for example, Wumen remarks, "As for the last word, neither Yantou nor Deshan could ever dream of it" (see p. 260). Moreover, despite an emphasis on contesting a topic or theme, with one exchange partner eventually defeating the other, the message suggested in numerous commentaries is that readers should not get preoccupied with keeping track in a way that pigeonholes the simple categories of winner and loser.

Instead of expecting a fixed outcome concerning the dialogue in case 26 ("Two Monks Rolled Up Blinds"; see pp. 268-269), in which the master Fayan says enigmatically of novices raising a set of bamboo blinds in identical fashion, "One gains, the other loses," Wumen instead suggests, "Don't try to fathom this in terms of gain or loss!"[8] In case 48 ("Qianfeng's One Path"; see pp. 282–283), although the masters Qianfeng and Yunmen seem to offer productive if obscure responses to a disciple's query about the pathway to nirvana, *nirvāṇa*, which they express from opposite peda-gogical angles, Wumen cautions, "But, when observing them with the correct eye [of wisdom], neither of the two great elders knows where the path begins." These examples of Wumen's commentaries illustrate that accepting a basic level of ambiguity is frequently the key to understand-ing the significance of an encounter dialogue.

THE CHARACTER OF ZHAOZHOU IN RELATION TO AMBIGUITY

Since the ambiguity featured in case 31 reflects an approach fostered by Zhaozhou, it is important to discuss briefly the historical and philo-sophical significance of his method. Are there qualities regarding Zhoazhou's pedagogical outlook that are particularly conducive to an emphasis on open-endedness rather than decisiveness? Or is the uncer-tainty reflected in Zhaozhou's contests typical of other dialogues in the *Gateless Barrier*?

As mentioned, Zhaozhou is featured as the main or, in two instances, the secondary figure in seven cases (1, 7, 11, 14, 19, 31, 37) in the collection, which makes him the most frequently cited of any master. The teacher with the second highest number of citations is Yunmen, founder of one of the five main branches of Chan often mentioned in *gong'an* compilations, who appears in five cases (15, 16, 21, 39, 48). Zhaozhou's mentor, Nanquan, has the next highest number, four cases (14, 19, 27, 34; the first two over-lap with Zhaozhou's dialogues that occurred when he was still a student).[9] In the *Record of Serenity*, Zhaozhou is the key figure in six cases, with five identical to cases in the *Gateless Barrier*.[10]

Zhaozhou's teaching style is considered by most commentators on *gong'an* to epitomize the tradition of Chan adepts awakening their disci-ples through cryptic banter. Yet the unfolding of his career is anomalous in several ways, especially compared to the exploits of some illustrious col-leagues of the Tang dynasty as depicted in Song-dynasty writings.[11] First, Zhaozhou's ascendancy to the role of a temple abbot was long delayed because he remained under the tutelage of Nanquan, a disciple of the emi-nent teacher Mazu. When Nanquan died, Zhaozhou was already sixty years old. Even then, he did not inherit or open his own temple right away, but instead began a period of itinerancy that lasted a couple of decades, during which he continued to train with various leading masters all over China.

As noted by Guo Gu, "Zhaozhou was so cautious in his practice, not taking anything for granted, that after decades of practicing under his teacher, who passed away when Zhaozhou was close to sixty, he continued to practice for twenty more years, refining his understanding by studying with other teachers."[12] It is likely that during this itinerant career phase Zhaozhou thought about visiting Mount Wutai. Then, around the age of eighty, the master finally settled in a northern temple, not far from the monastery of Linji, founder of the main Chan school named after him. Zhaozhou supposedly then led his own monastery for nearly forty years until his death. This is where he taught a multitude of disciples and received many visitors seeking instruction, although his legacy does not include initiating an independent lineage that survived him.[13]

A key difference between Zhaozhou and several other Chan leaders of the period involves his distinctive pedagogical flair. He stands in contrast to noteworthy contemporaries, especially Linji and Deshan, who were both known for an assertive method that included frequent bouts of shouting or slapping deficient trainees, or of striking them repeatedly with a staff as a corporal punishment designed to resemble the kind of chastisement typically meted out by the Chinese legal system. Instead, Zhaozhou relied on his great patience and deep sense of wit and irony combined with innate wisdom.

According to a comment in the *Blue Cliff Record*, "Zhaozhou's adamantine eye is completely devoid of dust," which praises how the master's teaching surpasses both the delusions characteristic of unenlightened people and the distractions of everyday sensations. Furthermore, "Through words he shows his full capacity by giving an answer as part of an approach known as 'linking activity with circumstances': when encountering a monk, Zhaozhou transforms the follower by fully illumining (*zhaopo*) their innermost heart."[14] In addition, the *Blue Cliff Record* claims, "When people carry their misguided views of Chan while visiting Zhaozhou, they learn to never resort to that deficient outlook. Instead, he sets them free all at once by eliminating deception without leaving a trace of disquiet." This thought-provoking teaching method is referred to paradoxically as "Being already awakened is the same as not yet being awakened."[15] In other words, Zhaozhou is credited with an impeccable understanding of how to help followers overcome their spiritual insufficiencies. But what happens when his own impenetrability faces an ambivalent exchange partner, specifically one who resists playing a conventional institutional role and instead tries to undermine all expectations?

CASE 11: ZHAOZHOU DISCERNS THE HERMITS

The single main dialogue in Zhaozhou's ample repertoire that resembles the degree of ambiguity evident in case 31 is case 11. In this story Zhaozhou hears that two recluses, or nonclerical practitioners residing in separate huts (or caves, in some versions) somewhere in the vicinity of his temple, have attained a significant level of spiritual awareness. Their status is perhaps equal to or greater than that of the master himself, thus posing a grave threat to his sense of identity as a figure of authority. Zhaozhou decides to go outside the temple compound, which is by no means a regular occurrence for a Chan abbot, to visit the respective hermitages and test the recluses' abilities.

As in case 31, the master enters uncharted territory to face unusual exchange partners, so he summons the utmost resourcefulness in his responses. Who are these mysterious figures? Should they be considered representative of alternative kinds of contemplative practice, such as from a different Buddhist school or a Daoist or shamanistic cult that challenges Chan hegemony in the region? Might they embody a polished form of sitting meditation cut off from all attachments, or do they represent a defective method because they are not ordained with Buddhist precepts? It is clear the hermits are avoiding monastic commitments, and thus, their degree of accomplishment probably cannot be verified. Zhaozhou's mission, ideally, is to bring them into the fold by leading them to an ordination ceremony. However, this does not occur.

Zhaozhou asks both hermits the same question: "Have you got it? Have you got it?" In effect, this means, "Show me now your original face or true self!"—that is, express your loftiest degree of insight. Both recluses give a nonverbal response by holding up a fist, perhaps defiantly to proclaim their independence from the master's ecclesial rank or as a symbol of self-reliance. However, despite their identical actions, the hermits receive opposite evaluations. Zhaozhou walks away from the first one after saying, "Shallow water is not a place to dock a ship," but he bows deeply while telling the second recluse, "Able to give and take; capable to kill and save." It seems that the first hermit has lost the contest with Zhaozhou, who breezily dismisses him, yet the second hermit has equaled or even bested the master, which he acknowledges. However, it is also possible to reverse that interpretation and read the initial response as disingenuous praise for a nonclerical practitioner and the the second as mocking. Perhaps neither recluse expresses truth, or maybe both do.

On an institutional level, ambiguity is heightened in that the reader wonders if the hermits, especially the second one who seems to emerge as a victor, can be considered fully legitimate practitioners and participants in the Chan transmission process although they have not accepted the basic Buddhist behavioral rules that reflect monastic ranking based on seniority. According to the *Chan Monastic Rules for Purity* (*Chanyuan qingqui*) compiled in 1103, which summarizes the main guidelines for practices carried out by the entire religious community, an emphasis on strict adherence to codes of conduct, at the risk of suffering excommunication, was to be enforced for monks at all temples.[16]

On a philosophical level, these interactions evoke ambiguity by demonstrating the neither/nor reasoning of nonduality that is beyond logic, as expressed in case 19 when Nanquan tells Zhaozhou, "The way is not something known or not known. Knowing is false perception. Not knowing is just being oblivious . . . How is it possible to impose affirmation and denial?" (see p. 264). In other words, ultimate truth defies bifurcation or any kind of categorization, so pointing to this level of transcendence is the rationale for Zhaozhou's mystifying remarks.

Wumen's comments reinforce the ambiguity in the encounters between the hermits and Zhaozhou, in addition to the reader's possible reactions to the dialogue. In his case 11 verse Wumen lavishly praises Zhaozhou's abilities:

An eye like shooting star,
A response swift as lightning.
A knife that kills,
A sword that brings life. (see p. 259)

Yet Wumen's prose remarks also complicate the situation while still flattering the master and challenging the reader to speak up. "Both raised their fists. Why is one affirmed and the other denied? Tell me: Where is the fault? If you can utter a turning word here, then you can see that Zhaozhou's tongue has no bone in it" (see p. 258).

Moreover, Wumen points out that, although the results of the contests seem clear enough, there is additional ambiguity in that "although Zhaozhou can hold up and put down freely, these two hermits have exposed (*kanpo*) Zhaozhou." Wumen's comments also highlight the sense of being caught in a double bind that is experienced by interpreters trying to appropriate Zhaozhou's dialogue: "If you say that one hermit was better than the other," Wumen maintains, "you do not have the eye to investigate and learn. If you say that there is no better or worse, you also do not have the eye to investigate and learn" (see p. 258).

The use of the term "exposed" in cases 31 and 11 highlights how encounter dialogues foster intense competition and a dramatic focus on one-upmanship based on repartee that encompasses verbal chitchat mixed with moments of silence or symbolic movements to produce productive interactions and mutually reinforcing collaborations. Yet the delicate balance between contesting with someone and claiming to have bested them is problematized when Wumen says, "But tell me, what is it that is exposed by Zhaozhou in the old granny?" (see p. 272). Thus, the repercussions of both dialogues are left unclear and deliberately ambiguous, since there is no well-defined message about who is the victor or whether one of the parties has gained an authentic awakening.

TWO EXAMPLES OF AMBIGUOUS CHAN WOMEN

The issues of gender and non- or anticlericalism as embodied by the ambivalent figure of the granny affect the significance of ambiguity in encounter dialogues. Here, I briefly discuss two examples of dharma battles between a man who is considered the true teacher, including an instance involving Zhaozhou, and a woman who challenges his authority and seems to best the cleric.

The first example of an exchange involving an inscrutable woman, in this instance a granny who stands by the road selling rice cakes, is mentioned in Wumen's prose comments on case 28 in the *Gateless Barrier* (see p. 270). At the time of the encounter, which took place shortly before he had a true experience of Chan awakening, the master-to-be Deshan considers himself an expert on the *Diamond Sūtra* (C. *Jingang jing*) and carries voluminous notes in his backpack. He travels south to the region of China where the prevalent approach to Chan is based on undergoing sudden awakening, rather than gradually studying scriptures. Before he crosses the border from his native place, it is said that his mind burns with resentment and his mouth utters only bitterness toward the southern school; he intends to stamp out the notion that meditation requires "special transmission outside the teaching."

During the journey Deshan stops to ask an old woman to sell him light "refreshments," a word that literally means "to point to the mind" (C. *dianxin*; pronounced *dimsum* in Cantonese). Using an ingenious wordplay as a putdown of the deluded monk, she responds, "I hear it is said in the *Diamond Sūtra*, 'The past mind cannot be found, the present mind cannot be found, and the future mind cannot be found.' Which mind (*xin*) do you wish to refresh (*dian*)?" (see p. 270). On hearing this question Deshan is struck silent but, recognizing his deficiency, he travels based on the granny's recommendation to learn from the master Longtan, and their ensuing dialogue soon leads to his awakening.

Although the besting of Deshan during his contest with the granny selling refreshments seems clear and conclusive, this result has been questioned by some interpreters. For example, in the chapter of his major work, the *Treasury of the True Dharma Eye* (J. *Shōbōgenzō*), titled "The Ungraspable Mind" (J. "Shin fukatoku"), Dōgen, the founder of the Sōtō (C. Caodong) sect in Japan, raises the issues of inconclusiveness and ambiguity by probing the relative positions of the exchange partners. Dōgen finds that both the granny and Deshan are deficient and in need of improvement. "If we think carefully about the encounter," he writes, "it is clear that, at the time, Deshan was still a latecomer to studying Chan and not yet an ancient buddha." Furthermore, "it is difficult to determine whether the granny was really enlightened because she does not explain the mind that can be grasped."[17] Therefore, for Dōgen, Deshan should have continued the dialogue to test the old woman, while she should have gone beyond quickly upsetting the monk to demonstrate more fully her own degree of prowess. Furthermore, "When Deshan failed to respond, why did she not say to him, 'Since you are incapable of speaking, ask me a question and I will give you an answer'?"[18]

The second example emphasizing the role of ambiguity regarding a woman also discussed by Dōgen involves an encounter between Zhaozhou and a granny. The woman donates funds to his temple and requests that the master "turn" (C. *zhuan*, J. *ten*) the *Great Treasury of Sūtras* (C. *Dazang jing*, J. *Daizōkyō*), which refers to the Buddhist canon. The verb "turn" used here is a multifaceted term that can mean to read or recite the scriptures but also the physical act of rotating the revolving sūtra repository that was held by many temples. As a surrogate for reciting the entire collection for those unable to complete this act, a common practice in Chinese Buddhism was to simply view the collection of scrolls stored in a special building, and in some cases priests and worshipers would circumambulate the sūtra hall. Such practices were conducted within the Chan ritual cycle even though the southern school advocated going beyond words and letters, and it recommended in a couple of flagrant stories—one involving Deshan in the aftermath of his awakening by Longtan—burning or ripping up scriptures to symbolize an interior breakthrough experience.

In this dialogue, Zhaozhou "gets down from his meditation seat, walks around it one time, and says to the old woman's assistant, 'I have completed the turning of the *Great Treasury of Sūtras*.'" While this clever yet quirky maneuver seems to have bested the granny, sometime later she says, "A little while ago, I asked to have the entire treasury turned; why did the teacher only turn half the treasury?"[19] Zhaozhou taunts the donor, but she gets the last laugh by calling him out and leaving an impression that he is the one with shortcomings.

According to the interpretation in the fascicle on "Reciting the Sūtras" (J. "Kankin"), where he cites a dozen dialogues with a similar theme of apparent disregard for the importance of sūtra recitation (although in other passages he supports this traditional practice), Dōgen suggests that the woman makes a misleading distinction between the entire sūtra treasury and half of it. He then says paradoxically that the master accomplishes the following: "Zhaozhou going around (J. *meguru*) the meditation seat, the meditation seat going around Zhaozhou, Zhaozhou going around Zhaozhou, and the meditation seat going around the meditation seat." "However," Dōgen points out, "the complete turning of the canon is not only circumambulating the meditation seat, nor is it only the meditation seat doing the circumambulating."[20]

Thus, once again, a puzzling Chan interpretation calls into question the apparent victory of the granny vis-à-vis the mainstream male cleric. Dōgen questions the aptitude of both the granny selling refreshments and Deshan, whom she seems to confound. And despite the appearance that Zhaozhou and the granny requesting the turning of the sutras reach an impasse that exposes the Chan teacher, the commentator praises the master and at least mildly criticizes the old woman.

CASE 31, PART 2: IMPLICATIONS OF ZHAOZHOU EXPOSING THE GRANNY

How do the various instances of uncertainty embedded in stories like case 11 involving Zhaozhou and two hermits, as well as those featuring ambivalent women interacting with men who try to exert their authority, shed light on the significance of ambiguity concerning the roles of the master and the granny in the encounter dialogue of case 31? Furthermore, is the sense of indecisiveness reflected in Wumen's commentary on the dialogue unique, or is this rhetorical element found in other interpretations of the narrative?

I will first consider in more detail exactly what triggers the main encounter between two figures who stand so far apart in terms of their rank, or lack of any, in Chan institutional hierarchy. According to the case record, a monk traveling from Zhaozhou's temple, presumably one of numerous clerics who have endured the granny's humiliation, asks the old woman about the way to Mount Wutai, and she just says, "Straight ahead," which is no doubt a misleading and impractical directive. Once the novice foolishly takes a few steps forward, she remarks sarcastically, "Yet another fine monk goes off like that!"[21] It's as if she had deliberately duped him because she sensed that he was clueless and would follow without knowing better any meaningless instruction she would offer.

Perhaps the message intended by the granny's sarcasm is that ambitious seekers must learn not to take anything at face value. Or perhaps, in her own way, the granny is trying to prevent itinerants from ever reaching the exotic Mount Wutai, known for visionary experiences that distract from concentrating on meditation. Given the warnings against going there issued by leading teachers, including Zhaozhou, the granny's scornful attitude resulting in the devastating putdown of a series of anonymous monks evokes the wariness that all Chan practitioners must have felt about visiting Mount Wutai's sacred but forbidden peaks.

Zhaozhou assures the monk who complains to him about the granny, "Wait until I go and check out this old granny for you," which is quite like his reaction to hearing about the hermits, whose reclusive presence poses a threat to monastic regulations. But he does not reprimand the monk for journeying to Mount Wutai, which may indicate an underlying connection linking the master and the granny. In any event, a mischievous outsider causes enough anxiety to stir a reaction in Zhaozhou. He must venture from the comfort zone of his quarters to demonstrate his mettle and reassure his assembly of followers, for they have been shaken to the core by a nonclerical figure and thus are questioning their own status and that of their teacher. This high degree of symbolic value represents how much is at stake in setting up the encounter.

The next day Zhaozhou decides to settle differences by asking the granny the same question posed by the novice, and she gives the identical answer. However, instead of stepping ahead toward the mountain like the previous monk, he returns to the monastery. Once there, among a crowd of disciples who have not seen for themselves the results of the encounter, Zhaozhou claims to have thoroughly exposed his adversary. But according to Wumen's skeptical prose comments, neither the master nor the granny is justified in claiming victory because Zhaozhou "did not have the outward marks of a great man." Wumen's poetic comment further highlights that with more questions than answers, only riddles, rather than solutions, remain: "Sand is mixed in the rice; thorns are hidden in the mud."

What does the *Record of Serenity* commentary say about the outcome of the dialogue? Does it reduce or enhance the ambiguity found in the *Gateless Barrier*'s interpretation? The main difference between the intricate commentarial style of the *Record of Serenity* and the more simplified approach of the *Gateless Barrier* is that the latter text reflects only Wumen's explanations, whereas the *Record of Serenity* contains diverse interpretative voices. In *Serenity*, Wansong provides introductory comments and capping phrase remarks on each line of the case, and in the section of prose commentary he often cites the words of previous Chan interpreters; those additional discursive elements are not found in Wumen's much shorter though compelling and persuasive text. Some of the interpretative expressions Wansong evokes convey standpoints that are at odds with or contradictory to others, thus adding additional layers of ambivalence.

The *Record of Serenity*'s discursive structure thus intensifies the degree of ambiguity concerning the encounter between the master and the granny. Wansong's capping phrases for the concluding section of the dialogue question Zhaozhou's prowess by suggesting that, although his questioning of the granny "sets a trap to fell a tiger," the master's claim of victory is premature because "I (Wansong) am much more devious than he is."[22] Then the last two lines of the *Record of Serenity*'s verse (written by Chan master Hongzhi in the twelfth century) further problematize the outcome by suggesting,

Zhaozhou exposes the old woman's understanding of Chan,
But what he later tells people isn't worth a dime.[23]

Also, in a section of prose commentary, Wansong points out that the master Langya once said of this case, "Even the great Zhaozhou couldn't help but walk straight into the woman's lair and lose his life. Yet, most people misunderstand this."[24]

Wansong cites several additional commentators whose remarks similarly highlight ambiguity. For example, the master Xuanjue says of the limitations of the old woman's approach, "The granny is not only exposed by Zhaozhou, but she is also exposed by me," and Wansong comments, "I say, not only has she gotten Xuanjue involved but me, too." Moreover, Wansong suggests that Zhaozhou's status is equally uncertain: "Although the old woman exposes the monks, she cannot avoid being exposed by Zhaozhou, and although Zhaozhou exposes the old woman, he cannot avoid being tested by Langya. In the practice of meditation this is called the rule of gold and manure: if you don't understand another person, then their status is like gold; but once they're exposed, it's like manure."

Wansong concludes, "Just leave behind emotional calculations concerning gain and loss, or victory and defeat, and you'll naturally always deceive the granny and look down on Zhaozhou."[25] Therefore, the message of the case as presented in the *Record of Serenity* is that readers should not idolize the master or iconize (or demonize) the granny, but instead investigate truth for themselves and come to their own conclusion. Wansong finally suggests that this case can be referred to as "Zhaozhou's Barrier" (using the same character, *guan*, as in the title of Wumen's text), since it is unavoidably difficult to pass through.

In a later commentary, a seventeenth-century nun named Baochi augments the notion of uncertainty that stems from examining the dharma battle between Zhaozhou and the old woman with the following verse comment:

> Although each appears to have sealed their border,
> In the end, neither one is able to get themselves out.
> Let's sit leisurely on top of the mountain peak
> And watch as the one falls and the other rises.[26]

The poem provides an important perspective regarding ambiguity by referring in the first couplet to both figures being stuck inside an imaginary boundary as victims of their own self-deceptions, from which there is no escape. Then in the second couplet Baochi indicates that the standpoint of the reader/observer is like that of a third party surveying diverse interpretations of the outcome of the encounter dialogue from a lofty standpoint, while gaining peace of mind by embracing an ambiguity that views the possibilities for, yet does not remain fixated on, the matter of gain and loss. This remark resonates with the commentaries by Wumen and Wansong that refuse to declare—or to deny—a winner of the contest by finding both merit and deficiency in the actions of Zhaozhou and the granny.

CONCLUSION: AMBIGUATION AND DISAMBIGUATION

Earlier in this chapter I showed that a key pattern characterizing encounter dialogues included in the *Gateless Barrier* and other major *gong'an* collections is that the intricate exchange, as a testing process involving two competitors, results in a positive and conclusive result. Often the deluded or misguided junior interlocutor is led through interactions with a skillful yet enigmatic teacher to spontaneously gain insight as an experience of awakening. By virtue of being bested in the dialogue, the trainee unexpectedly is enabled to transform obstinate ignorance into flexible wisdom and thorny attachments into sublime detachment. Zhaozhou participates in three such dialogues when he is instructed as Nanquan's disciple in cases 14 and 19, and functions as the teacher of an anonymous monk in case 7.

However, the narrative pattern evident in case 31 and other dialogues undermines the paradigm of certainty because the implication is that the conclusion is altogether ambiguous. The scorecard provided by ironic commentaries further casts doubt and problematizes the indecisive quality of the situation concerning the master and the granny. Seen from a perch on a proverbial lofty peak, as Baochi's verse indicates, the overall paradigm of the encounter dialogue appears to shift because many exchanges have a strong element of vagueness or are purposefully inconclusive, including some that appear triumphally decisive on an initial reading.

Therefore, rather than understanding equivocality as an exceptional or unusual element in *gong'an* discourse, I suggest that readers should consider the notion of ambiguity as a foundational component. The apparent sense of clarity in numerous cases transpires not so much because the approach is straightforward, but due to a process of disambiguation or an unraveling of mysteries stemming from underlying uncertainty. This is why it is often said in Chan lore, borrowing an expression from the ethics of commerce, "To gain an advantage" (*de pianyi*) is "to lose the advantage" (*luo pianyi*). This is because in the context of the repartee, trying to declare a firm conclusion can be seen as self-serving and therefore self-defeating. Ambiguity is thus the means to enabling disambiguation, which leads to a new level of insightful and fair-minded awareness that triggers awakening beyond typical polarities.

NOTES

1. See Steven Heine, "Visions, Divisions, Revisions: The Encounter between Iconoclasm and Supernaturalism in Kōan Cases about Mount Wu-t'ai," in *The Kōan: Texts and Contexts in Zen Buddhism*, ed. Steven Heine and Dale S. Wright (New York: Oxford University Press, 2000), 137–167; and T. H. Barrett, "How Important Is Mount Wutai? Sacred Space in a Zen Mirror," in *The Transnational Cult of*

Wutai: Historical and Cultural Perspectives, ed. Susan Andrews, Jinhua Chen, and Guang Kuan (Leiden: Brill, 2021), 238–252.

2. In the *Transmission of the Lamp Record in the Jingde Era* (*Jingde chuandeng lu*), T. 2076: 51.277a.

3. See Barrett, "How Important Is Mount Wutai?," 249.

4. According to Guo Gu, "This word *granny*, or *po*, refers to an old woman but also suggests a person of wit and resourcefulness who is usually marginal and ambivalent in social status and who crosses social boundaries. In premodern popular fictions, a granny is depicted as a witch or a sorceress. There are many of these old grannies in Chan or Zen stories." In *Passing Through the Gateless Barrier: Kōan Practice for Real Life* (Boulder, CO: Shambhala, 2016), 268.

5. This is perhaps the most famous collection of *gong'an* published in 1128 by Yuanwu, a leader of the Linji faction who taught at a temple in Hunan province a century before Wumen.

6. For a discussion of the literary structure of *gong'an* collections see Steven Heine, *The Rhetoric of Uncertainty in the Blue Cliff Record: Sharpening a Sword at the Dragon Gate* (New York: Oxford University Press, 2016).

7. John R. McRae, "The Antecedents of Encounter Dialogue in Chinese Ch'an Buddhism," in *The Kōan: Text and Contexts in Zen Buddhism*, ed. Steven Heine and Dale S. Wright (Oxford: Oxford University Press, 2000), 47–48. McRae points out the encounter dialogues do not include questions that seek to elicit explanations about Buddhist doctrine or the spiritual path in general, or answers meant to provide information. See also John R. McRae, "Encounter Dialogue and the Transformation of the Spiritual Path in Chinese Ch'an," in *Paths to Liberation: The Mārga and Its Transformations in Buddhist Thought*, ed. Robert E. Buswell Jr. and Robert M. Gimello (Honolulu: University of Hawaii Press, 1992), 339–370; Miriam Levering, "The Dragon Girl and the Abbess of Mo-shan: Gender and Status in the Ch'an Buddhist Tradition," *Journal of the International Association of Buddhist Studies* 5, no. 1 (1982): 9–35; and Ben Van Overmeire, "Reading Chan Encounter Dialogue during the Song Dynasty: The *Record of Linji*, the *Lotus Sutra*, and the Sinification of Buddhism," *Buddhist-Christian Studies* 37 (2017): 209–221.

8. See a comment on case 23 of the *Blue Cliff Record* says, "Where there is no gain and no loss, / No affirmation and no negation, / There the Golden Peak stands fully revealed." T. 2003: 48.164c.

9. The ranking of masters is reversed in the *Blue Cliff Record*, where Zhaozhou is featured in twelve cases, the second highest number, but Yunmen is the most oft-cited teacher in eighteen cases. This is mainly because Xuedou, the original compiler in 1038 of the cases and verses included in the *Blue Cliff Record* with prose comments provided nearly a century later by Yuanwu, was a member of the Yunmen school lineage and in part saw his collection as a way of reviving the fortunes of the school.

10. These include, in addition to case 10 corresponding to case 31, case 9 of Wansong's text corresponding to case 14 of Wumen's version on "Nanquan Kills a Cat," case 18 to case 1 on "Zhaozhou's Dog," case 39 to case 7 on "Zhaozhou's 'Wash the Bowl!,'" and case 47 to case 37 on the "The Cypress in the Courtyard." Zhaozhou is also the focus of case 63 in The *Record of Serenity* and is mentioned in cases 57 and 69.

11. See Steven Heine, *Like Cats and Dogs: Contesting the Mu Kōan* (New York: Oxford University Press, 2014), 132–142.

12. Guo Gu, *Passing Through the Gateless Barrier*, 395–396.

13. In the recorded sayings of both masters, the two meet for a dharma battle, with Linji portrayed as the winner in his text whereas Zhaozhou bests his rival according to his record.

14. T. 2003: 48.150a; Thomas Cleary and J. C. Cleary, trans., *The Blue Cliff Record* (Boston: Shambhala, 2005), 64.

15. T. 2003: 48.182b; Cleary and Cleary, *The Blue Cliff Record*, 273.

16. See Yifa, trans., *The Origins of Buddhist Monastic Codes in China: An Annotated Translation and Study of the Chanyuan qinggui* (Honolulu: University of Hawai'i Press, 2002).

17. Kawamura Kōdō, et al., eds., *Collected Works of Zen Master Dōgen* (*Dōgen Zenji zenshū*), 7 vols. (Tokyo: Shunjūsha, 1989–1993), I: 84; Kazuaki Tanahashi, trans., *The Treasury of the True Dharma Eye* (Boulder, CO: Shambhala, 2010), 193.

18. *Dōgen Zenji zenshū* I: 84, Tanahashi, *The Treasury of the True Dharma Eye*, 194.

19. *Dōgen Zenji zenshū* I: 233; Tanahashi, *The Treasury of the True Dharma Eye*, 220. In another dialogue, Zhaozhou meets a woman carrying a basket of bamboo shoots that, she tells him, she is taking to Zhaozhou. When he asks her what she would do if she were to unexpectedly run into the master, she abruptly gives him a slap; see Beata Grant, trans., *Zen Echoes: Classic Kōans with Verse Commentaries by Three Female Chan Masters* (Boston: Wisdom, 2017), 33 n. 43.

20. *Dōgen Zenji zenshū* I: 234; Tanahashi, *The Treasury of the True Dharma Eye*, 220.

21. See appendix 1, xxx; T. 2005: 48.297a.

22. T. 2004: 48.233b; Cleary, *Book of Serenity*, 43.

23. T. 2004: 48.233b; Cleary, *Book of Serenity*, 43.

24. T. 2004: 48.233b; Cleary, *Book of Serenity*, 43.

25. T. 2004: 48.233c; Cleary, *Book of Serenity*, 44.

26. Grant, *Zen Echoes*, 94 (modified).

[6]

A GATE OF THEIR OWN?

WOMEN IN WUMEN'S WORLD

Natasha Heller

T HE *GATELESS Barrier* opens with a question ostensibly about a dog; this is followed by a case centered (as we learn) on a fox. The cases feature any number of objects—water bottles, poles, shitsticks, staves, flags—as props for Chan challenges. Most of the people who appear are male, and they too can serve as props, their actions something for more advanced students of Chan to talk about. Men often are interlocutors and teachers, engaged in challenging each other as they seek a true way of looking at the world. There are not very many women. Only four cases mention them: a woman who has been split in two, a girl in meditation, and two old women. This raises several questions: Why do these kinds of women appear in these cases? What does this tell us about the status of women in Chan? And what does this tell us about the *Gateless Barrier* as a Chan text?

Wumen Huikai (1183–1260) explains in his introduction to the text that the *Gateless Barrier* was compiled from teachings he gave over a summer retreat with male monastics. Wumen did not intend the cases that he worked through with students to become a formal collection. As I will discuss below, such collections and cases and commentaries are part of the maintenance of Chan lineages, which were almost exclusively male. Given the social and literary context of the *Gateless Barrier*, it is perhaps not surprising that women play a limited role and the work is intended for a male audience. As we will see, the *Gateless Barrier* does not represent the status of women in Chan; in Wumen's own time women were awakened and acknowledged as such. Yet this text, whether intentionally or unintentionally, was created in a way that repeats tropes about women's roles and places them outside of the Chan establishment.

When women appear in the *Gateless Barrier*, they are on the margins of the monastic tradition or outside it entirely. Two of the four female persons mentioned in this text are figures from literature, further distanced from the historical figures whose dialogues and encounters make up a large portion of the cases. The *Gateless Barrier* is a constructed text, not a reflection of reality—that is, the dialogues themselves have been manipulated for literary and ideological effects, and the selection process shapes how the cases fit together. Because this is a work of literature and not history, we can read it as arguing (if obliquely) for how women fit into Chan lineages of transmission. Among these four cases, only one figure is from within the Buddhist tradition—a young girl in a brief extract from a sūtra—and she does not herself speak. In the other three cases, the women have things to say but are outsiders to Chan institutions. As a closer analysis of these cases will show, women are given a voice only when that voice cannot speak directly to the tradition.

LITERARY WOMEN

Let's start by considering the cases that mention women, girls, or grannies in the *Gateless Barrier*, beginning with those farthest from Wumen and the Chan tradition of his time. Cases 35 and 42 concern literary women—that is, women who appear in literature rather than as part of the lived experience of these monks. Case 35 seems cryptic to modern readers, a mere sentence long: "Wuzu [Fayan, d. 1104] asked a monk, 'Lady Qian's spirit has divided; which is the real person?'" (see p. 274). The four characters translated as "Lady Qian's spirit has divided" (*qiannü lihun*) are an alternate title for a popular Tang dynasty story and would have been well known to readers of the time. It appears in the *Extensive Records of the Taiping Era (Taiping guangji)*, a collection of stories and anecdotes completed in 978. This massive collection was not published at the time of compilation, so it is not the source of Wuzu Fayan's knowledge of the story.[1] The story is attributed to Chen Xuanyou (d.u., active eighth century) and concerns the younger daughter of the high-ranking official Zhang Yi (d.u., active late seventh century). The daughter became attached to one of her cousins, a young man by the name of Wang Zhou. Zhang Yi held Wang in high esteem, and often said that he should marry his daughter Qian when both were of the appropriate age. Qian and Wang thought of each other often and with affection, but their families did not know of their feelings. When Qian was of the age to be married, a promising young official sought her hand, and Zhang Yi assented. Qian was depressed by this turn of events, and Wang Zhou, both angry and sad, felt he had no choice but to leave the area. He left by boat that same evening and had not gotten very far when he heard someone walking quickly on the riverbank. When the person reached the boat, it was none other than Qian, who could not bear to be parted from him. The reunited lovers continued on their journey to a distant province, where they settled and had two children. After five years, Qian confessed that she missed her parents and felt guilty about what they had done by running off. They decided to return home, again by boat, and when they arrived Wang Zhou went on ahead. He apologized to Zhang Yi, explaining what had happened. Zhang Yi replied that Qian had been lying ill in bed for years; Wang Zhou retorted that she was on the boat. A messenger was dispatched to the boat, and upon his return he confirmed Wang Zhou's report. At this point the Qian who had been ill in her bed arose and went out to greet the Qian who had arrived by boat. When the two Qians met they merged into one body. Although the story had a happy ending, the family thought this was "not right" (*bu zheng*) and did not talk about these strange events with outsiders.

Wuzu raises the case because it addresses one of Chan's fundamental critiques of unenlightened thinking—the belief that there is a "real" (*zhende*) self that can be located. This case also exemplifies the problem with dualistic thinking, the belief that there is a decision to be made about whether boat Qian or sickroom Qian has ontological priority. Wumen's prose and verse commentary place this anecdote in two contexts. The first, in the prose commentary, is that of reincarnation: "If you can awaken to the real person here, then you realize that both leaving and entering the shell of worldly existence is like sojourning in a traveler's inn" (see p. 274).[2] Wumen then notes that the elements that make up our physical bodies will suddenly break apart. Our bodies are temporary lodging places, and in an extended time frame, not a permanent home. The story of Qian can in this way be read as a reflection on the instability of our physical form.

Wumen's verses emphasize nonduality and the fundamental ground all things share:

> Clouds and moon are the same,
> Streams and mountains are different.
> Myriad blessings, countless fortunes!
> Are they one and two? (see p. 275)[3]

Not only are boat Qian and sickroom Qian both different and the same, but this also could be said for any other two objects or phenomena. In later citations, "Qian's soul left her body" is a way of raising these issues.

This is the only case in the *Gateless Barrier* that points directly to non-Buddhist literature, and so serves as a reminder that monks were immersed in a broader culture that included narratives such as this and the practice of composing poetry—and they participated in the gender norms of that literary culture. This story comes from a body of tales of unusual encounters that circulated in elite circles at that time. Sarah M. Allen has identified prominent themes, including: "demon exposure, unexpected passage to another realm . . . unions with nonhuman women (most often goddesses, ghosts, and were-beasts), and unexpected encounters with women or men who prove not to be what they seem." By the late eighth century—when Chen Xuanyou would have been writing down his tale—there were "basic models" for telling stories about these themes. In one of these, "a traveling man who meets a woman who seems too easily available will eventually discover that she is not what she seemed."[4] These tales reflect male anxiety that women dissemble and that they are not reliable. There is an undercurrent of this concern reflected in Wang Zhou's experience: although he knows Qian already, he is pursued by her while traveling and does indeed find out that she is not exactly who he took her to be.

Qian is effaced both in the story itself and in its use in *gong'an* collections. Of course, Qian is a character, and a variation on a stock character at that. In the story she does not have agency, as a whole person at the beginning, to determine her marriage. She gains control over her fate only by splitting herself in two, although it is not clear that the split happened through her own volition. Yet Qian continues to be subordinate to her father and husband: when the couple returns home, the husband does all the speaking, and we never hear her perspective. The *Gateless Barrier* reduces her even more, and "Qian" becomes simply a name intended to evoke the story.

THE GIRL IN *SAMĀDHI*

Case 42 also focuses on a female character known only through textual sources. It is one of a handful of cases in the *Gateless Barrier* that center on exchanges between the Buddha and his disciples, or between senior disciples (as in case 12); Buddha's role in these dialogues is that of enlightened master. Case 42 is comparatively long, comprising a series of exchanges rather than a pithy back-and-forth. It begins with Mañjuśrī, the bodhisattva of wisdom, approaching the Buddha with a question. No emotion is attributed to Mañjuśrī, but the question itself suggests some irritation on the bodhisattva's part: he wants to know why a girl—who happens to be deep in meditation—is permitted to sit next to the Buddha when he is not. Her place near the Buddha is unexpected because it seems to go against norms in which seating arrangements reflect monastic hierarchy. The Buddha tells him to rouse the girl from her meditation and ask her. The girl is said to have *ruding*, or "entered into meditative concentration." *Ding* is often translated as *samādhi*, which is a high level of concentration. We know from this description that the girl is accomplished in meditation; no background or other details are given.[5] Mañjuśrī does various things—circumambulation, snapping of fingers, transporting the girl to one of the heavens, displaying his other spiritual powers—but she remains in deep concentration. The Buddha tells the bodhisattva that even if he were multiplied one hundred thousand times, he would be unable to bring the girl out of *samādhi*. There is, however, a bodhisattva who *could* rouse her, and not only does he live in a land far, far below, he is named "Ignorance" (*wangming*).[6] At this, Bodhisattva Ignorance appears from the earth; the Buddha charges him with rousing the girl, whereupon the bodhisattva snaps his fingers once—something that Mañjuśrī had also tried—and immediately she emerges from *samādhi*.

The girl does not do nothing, because being in *samādhi* is a kind of activity, but we do not see her move or speak. The exchange ends when she comes out of her concentrated state. Whether she has something to say about the actions of the bodhisattvas Mañjuśrī and Ignorance is beside the point, because this exchange is about Mañjuśrī. He is the student receiving Chan instruction from the Buddha, as Wumen's comment notes.

This story, even though comparatively lengthy for the *Gateless Barrier*, is considerably shortened from its source in the *Scripture of the Collected Essentials of All Buddhas* (*Zhufo yaoji jing*), translated by Dharmarakṣa (d. 316). It is useful to consider this longer version to see the choices Wumen makes when he pares it down. One of the key differences in this lengthier text is that the Buddha and the girl are named. The Buddha is not Śakyamuni Buddha, as readers might have concluded from the case as Wumen provides it, but Devarāja Tathāgata (Ch. Tianwang rulai), who is none other than Devadatta, Śakyamuni's miscreant cousin and enemy, once he has finally straightened out his lives and become a buddha. The girl—who may be older here, as she is referred to as a *nüren* or "woman"—is named "Departing from Thought" (*liyi*), appropriate given that she is in deep concentration.

In the *Scripture of the Collected Essentials of All Buddhas*, the lengths to which Mañjuśrī goes to bring the girl out of *samādhi* demonstrate the limits of his powers while also adding humor. In part because each of Mañjuśrī's attempts is detailed, the narrative takes several pages to unwind, rather than the paragraph given in the *Gateless Barrier*. He snaps his fingers, and she is not roused from *samādhi*. He makes his body incredibly large so that when he snaps his fingers it makes a thunderous sound, and this again does not bring her out of meditation. He makes the musical instruments of all the different kinds of beings in countless worlds play music, but this has no effect.[7] Entering into meditative concentration, Mañjuśrī makes Mount Sumeru and all the other mountains of the world crash into each other, creating an unbelievably loud din that penetrates all the worlds—but this too does not rouse the girl from her *samādhi*.[8] He picks her up in his right hand and takes her through all the many buddha lands of each direction, and none of the activities therein causes her to emerge from her concentration.[9]

After all these efforts, Devarāja Buddha tells Mañjuśrī that the depth of the girl's concentration—so profound that she cannot hear any of the various sounds he caused—is like the limitlessness of the awesome virtue of the wisdom of the path.[10] Mañjuśrī then asks who *would* be able to make the girl emerge from concentration. The bodhisattva whom Devarāja suggests has a different name than the one Wumen uses: Remover of Hindrances Bodhisattva (Ch. Qizhuyingai pusa, Skt. Sarvanīvaranaviṣkambhin). Given the condensed nature of the narrative, the name in the *Gateless Barrier* works better to deflate Mañjuśrī's overconfidence in his own achievements. One of the themes in Chan is the decoupling of knowledge from enlightenment; being erudite does not equate to having insight. Although Mañjuśrī is closely associated with wisdom, we see him here exercising various supernatural powers. These make a related point: sometimes vast attainments are obstructions, which is also the paradox Wumen emphasizes.

However, there is another important difference in these bodhisattvas: in the scriptural version, Remover of Hindrances Bodhisattva does *not* rouse the girl from meditation. It is Devarāja Buddha who ultimately does so. This brings us to the final major difference with Wumen's recounting of this episode: in the sūtra version, Liyi has an extended conversation with Mañjuśrī when she finally emerges from her concentration. One section goes as follows:

Mañjuśrī asked the girl, "Why didn't you transform your female form?"

The girl replied, "Stop! Do not harbor delusions. You have insight—is there 'male" and "female' among those who penetrate all dharmas?"

Mañjuśrī replied, "There is not."

The girl said, "Considering form, is there male and female?"

"There is not."

"As for sensation, thought, volition, and consciousness, is there male and female?

"There is not."

"Do earth, water, fire, and wind have male and female?"

"They do not."

"Does space, vast without limit and unoccupied, have male and female?"

"It does not."

She again asked Mañjuśrī, "From beginning to end of the words that have been preached, is there a place where there is male and female?"

He replied, "There is not."

The girl declared, "Why did you just now say, 'Why didn't you transform your female form?' If I perceived male and female from the female position I occupy, would I then give up the female appearance and take a male form? I do not obtain the female form or manifest the male, so what reason would there be to discard the female form and take a male form? Consider that all dharmas are without unification and without dispersal, without basis or point of origin, empty and void without unification or dispersal. All dharmas are empty, so what reason would there be to transform a female appearance into a male form? Why is that? This is the first teaching of the tathāgatas!"[11]

In this version, not only are Mañjuśrī's powers not all he thought they were, but he also harbors some rigidly dualistic ideas about gender—and which is better. The girl exposes the accomplished bodhisattva's limitations.

SCRIPTURAL SOURCES

We can place this episode from the *Scripture of the Collected Essentials of All Buddhas*, and, by extension, case 42 of the *Gateless Barrier*, in the context of a series of narratives about girls and their achievements within Buddhism. The most well-known of these narratives is that of the dragon king's daughter in the *Lotus Sūtra*. In chapter 12, "Devadatta," a bodhisattva by the name of Accumulated Wisdom asks Mañjuśrī if there is anyone who could rapidly attain buddhahood based on assiduous practice of the scripture. Mañjuśrī says that indeed there is—the eight-year-old daughter of the dragon king, whose achievements and virtues he praises. Accumulated Wisdom Bodhisattva expresses his doubts, whereupon the dragon king's daughter appears. The Buddha's disciple Śāriputra then questions her, listing the obstructions that all women have. The dragon king's daughter does not respond to his disparagement but asserts that she can become a buddha in an instant. She then transforms into a male form, fulfills all the bodhisattva practices, ascends a bejeweled lotus throne, and achieves unsurpassed perfect enlightenment, attested in physical form by the thirty-two major and eighty minor marks of buddhas.[12]

This passage has attracted much comment from modern scholars because of its ambiguity. On the one hand, that the dragon king's young daughter achieves buddhahood suggests that it is open to anyone. On the other, that she must transform into a male form first is usually read as misogynistic. Access to buddhahood is universal but entails a process that includes both specific bodhisattva practices and passage through a male body. Jan Nattier notes that the dragon king daughter's story is "not at all unique" but rather is among a body of texts in which female bodhisattvas undergo transformation. The passage itself has an interesting history, not appearing in Kumārajīva's translation but interpolated decades later.[13] From that point on, it was a core episode in both the Chinese and Japanese traditions.

There is also a group of texts that feature little girls, and many can be read as more egalitarian than that of the dragon king's daughter. Stephanie Balkwill has identified roughly twenty scriptures in which a young girl is a central figure. These girls use their female forms, and their ability to transform them, as an argument for the inherent emptiness of all physical manifestations.[14] Balkwill traces a rise in texts that feature women or girls taking on male forms before achieving buddhahood and concludes that in the medieval period "just as women's access to modes of intellectual production decreased with the rise of dominant forms of institutionalized Buddhism, so too did texts that feature female protagonists."[15] Buddhist institutions, it seems, had an interest in protecting the patriarchy.

Although *sūtras* featuring young girls were largely ignored by later Chinese Buddhists, the episode with the dragon king's daughter was often taken up by Chan teachers. In the Chan biographical collection *Transmission of the Lamp Record in the Jingde Era* (*Jingde chuandeng lu*), dating from 1004, for example, a nun cites the dragon king's daughter when her qualifications to teach are challenged by a monk.[16] Dahui Zong'gao (1089–1163)—whose female disciples will be discussed at greater length below—also used this episode in several of his sermons as a means to emphasize the importance of awakening in a single moment, not the form of the person achieving awakening.[17] It is clear that for Buddhist authors young women provide an interesting example to think with,[18] and that at different points in the history of Buddhism in China there have been positive assessments of women's potential for achieving the highest stages of spiritual attainment. The dragon king's daughter and others are models for later Buddhists, including in the Chan tradition.

But not all Chan masters took up the examples provided by Dahui and the *Transmission of the Lamp Record in the Jingde Era*. In the *Scripture of the Collected Essentials of All Buddhas*, Wumen reduces the role of the girl to a prop. He says as much in his prose comment:

> Old man Śakyamuni staged this comedy; the inferior would not be able to appreciate it. What is more, Mañjuśrī is the teacher of seven buddhas, so why couldn't he bring the girl out of *samādhi*? Ignorance [Sarvanivāraṇaviṣkambhin] was only a bodhisattva of the first *bhūmi*. Why then could he bring her out? If you can perceive this intimately, then this frantic consciousness of karma is precisely the great *samādhi* of the dragon kings. (see p. 279)[19]

Let's briefly unpack this comment. First, Wumen's focus is squarely on the success or failure of Mañjuśrī and Ignorance, and he says that this set piece was staged to this end. Mañjuśrī is a bodhisattva of great attainment and thus he (and perhaps the audience of the scripture) assumes that the task set for him by Śakyamuni will be one he can readily dispatch. In contrast, the bodhisattva with the name Ignorance is at a much lower stage but succeeds where his superior cannot. Wumen's last sentence points to the ultimate identity between our normal muddled mental state and profound meditation; this is another way of equating *saṃsāra* and *nirvāṇa* and critiquing the false dualisms that govern most people's worldviews. Thus the reason for Ignorance's success would seem to lie in his lack of attachments—either to the notion of the achievement or to the distinction between deluded and awakened states. Wumen is concerned with what these two bodhisattvas learned through the scene Śakyamuni created. Although the girl is doing something—meditating—her capacity to speak for herself has been excised and with it her critique of the deluded dualistic thinking that distinguishes male and female. Indeed, the critique of distinctions has been taken over by Wumen himself. An insider (albeit fictional) based on her attainments, the girl is made an outsider through

Wumen's silencing. However, the power dynamics of raising Chan cases means that the person offering a commentary assumes the greatest authority, and this is true whether the cases involve men or women.

WORDS WITH OLD WOMEN

Indeed, the women who speak in the *Gateless Barrier* are only those outside the monastery walls. The first appears in case 31:

> A monk asked an old granny, "Which way is the road to Mount Tai?" The old granny said, "Straight ahead." When the monk started walking [in that direction] three or five steps, the old granny said, "Yet another fine monk goes off like that!" Later the monk brought this up to Zhaozhou, who said, "Wait till I go and check out this old granny for you." The next day Zhaozhou went to the old granny and asked the exact same question. Her answer was the same as before. When Zhaozhou returned, he gathered his congregation and said, "I've seen through the old granny of Mount Tai for you all." (see p. 272)[20]

The case itself presents Zhaozhou as having the upper hand. In his prose comment Wumen criticizes the old woman for only knowing how to "strategize within her tent" (*zuochou weiwo*) but also remarks that they both "had errors" (*youguo*), asserting his authority over Zhaozhou and the granny. This woman plays more of a role than those in the first two cases discussed. She is given a voice and treated as a legitimate participant in a Chan dialogue with the right to critique the monk's understanding.

Much rests on the assumptions that go along with Chan dialogues. When she says, "Yet another fine monk goes off like that!," we read it as sarcastic or dismissive because of expectations associated with the genre, and because *how* she says this is not detailed in the anecdote. We could also imagine her saying it while sighing in admiration, truly impressed at the piety of a monk on pilgrimage. In such a reading, it is not at all surprising that she would give the same response to a second monk—and that she would serve unwittingly as a player in a Chan drama.

That we do *not* take this brief narrative in the second way is also due to the other grannies in Chan texts. One appears in the commentary to case 28, in which Wumen recounts the famous meeting between Deshan and an old woman selling refreshments:

Before Deshan passed through the barrier, his heart had been burning with zeal and his tongue was very sharp. He traveled south, with the intent to wipe out "the special transmission outside of the scripture" teaching [i.e., Chan teaching].

When he reached Lizhou, he told an old woman selling refreshments by the road that he wanted to buy some dessert to eat. The old woman asked him, "What are those writings that you have in your cart, virtuous one?" Deshan said, "That's my commentary and annotation on the Diamond Sūtra." The old woman said, "Ahh . . . doesn't it say in the Diamond Sūtra that the past mind cannot be found; the present mind cannot be found; and the future mind cannot be found? Which mind do you wish to refresh, virtuous one?"

When Deshan heard this question, his mouth remained shut, unable to answer. Yet he was still unwilling to die under the old woman's words. He asked her, "Are there any Chan teachers around here?" The old woman said, "Yes. About five miles from here lives Chan master Longtan." (see p. 270)[21]

This granny knows even more than the one in our first example—she has memorized at least one passage from a key Buddhist scripture, can cite it at an apt moment, and is also aware of the local Buddhist teachers. Equally important, she knows how to employ her knowledge in such a way as to startle Deshan out of his habits of thinking; in this she is a true Chan adept.

These are the only two grannies in the *Gateless Barrier*, but variations on these meetings appear elsewhere in the Chan corpus. One other example is from the *Transmission of the Lamp Record in the Jingde Era*:

Once there were three monks traveling, intending to visit Master Jingshan. They met a granny, just at the time of the rice harvest. One of the monks asked her, "Where is the road to Jingshan?" The granny said, "It's straight ahead." The monk said, "Does the depth of the water ahead allow us to pass or not?" The granny replied, "You won't get your feet wet." The monk asked again, "Why is the rice on the upper bank so fine, and the rice on the lower bank so scraggly?" The woman responded, "The rice on the lower bank keeps being eaten by crabs." The monk said, "Too fragrant!" The granny said, "There's no scent." The monk again asked the granny, "Where do you live?" She replied, "Right here." The three monks thereupon went into her shop, and the granny put the kettle on to boil and placed three cups on a tray, saying, "Any monk who has supernatural powers, drink up!" The three monks did not respond, and they also did not dare drain their cups. The granny said, "Look at this old crone showing off her supernatural powers!" And with that, she picked up her cup and drained it.[22]

Both the granny selling snacks to Deshan and this one, on the road to Jing-shan, are given larger speaking roles than the granny in case 31. Both confidently assert their knowledge, but longer dialogues make the extent of their abilities more apparent. The granny Deshan meets and has a lon-ger exchange with knows enough about Buddhism to call forth an apt quote from scripture. This granny goes even further, challenging the monks over supernatural powers and tweaking them by drinking up when they are too abashed (or confused) to do so. (Remember that the bodily transformation of the dragon king's daughter was understood as a super-natural power.) In short, the more women speak or are represented as speaking, the more they are shown as able to hold their own with Chan monks. As I will argue below, there are dimensions of Chan doctrine that suggest this is exactly as it should be—that there is no inherent reason a Chan monk should have a better understanding of ultimate reality than an old peddler by the roadside.

On the roadside, in a teahouse, selling snacks—where old women are encountered tells us about their social status. All these are interstitial spaces, between places like monasteries and homes. That the women are alone and operating small businesses suggests that they are not attached to homes and families and are on the lower end of the socioeconomic spec-trum of the time. In other words, they are on the edges of the social fabric of medieval China. Being old further marginalizes them, and in some ways they are the mirror opposites of the very young girls discussed above, at the other end of the age spectrum.

Old age has its own set of associations. It can be associated with wis-dom, as in the aged depictions of Confucius and Laozi, along with the more general idea that those who have lived longer know more. Grannies, wise to the ways of the world, might possess knowledge that younger men do not. Yet old age can also connote a retreat or distance from the world, as men retire from office and its associated sociality and women see their childrearing and homemaking responsibilities diminish. Such changing commitments also marked a diminishment of power.[23] For women, fertil-ity (and by extension sexual availability) was central to their gender role, so passing beyond reproductive age in some ways made them less female. Along with their social marginalization, Chan grannies occupy an ambig-uous position that grants them some authority but leaves them nonthreatening.[24] Indeed, they could even serve as a model for the behavior of Chan teachers in certain contexts. Chan masters are often likened to grandmothers or said to have "grandmotherly kindness" as a way of acknowledging their concern with their students' progress and their patient instruction.[25]

As clever as these old grannies are—and as much as they seem capable of speaking of and in the Buddhist tradition—they remain outsiders. They can point the way or point out teachers, but that is the extent of their input. As the text presents it, the real learning takes place when a Chan master instructs his disciples, which most often happens within the monastery walls.

NONDUALITY AND EGALITARIANISM

Should we expect women's marginalization? That is, if being a woman meant that one could not be a full participant in other dimensions of society at the time the *Gateless Barrier* was written, would it not follow that women would be sidelined in Chan texts? I think not, given both Chan's distinctive and strong position on nondualism and the historical record of prominent Chan women.

Being a woman is not the only way one might be marginalized in society. One might be economically disadvantaged, like the old women selling roadside snacks, or limited to service or menial positions. One might live outside what was considered the most civilized part of the Song dynasty and therefore speak a dialect or have customs that marked them as regionally different. One might be illiterate or undereducated. Many of these qualities were attached to Huineng (638–713), perhaps Chan's most famous outsider. He would later be considered the sixth patriarch of the Chan tradition, but as the *Platform Sūtra* recounts, he was very different from other monks in training. When he arrives at the temple where Hongren (601–674) is teaching, the elder Chan master calls him to introduce himself. Huineng tells him that he is a commoner from Lingnan, which immediately prompts a challenge from Hongren: "If you're from Lingnan, then you're a barbarian. How can you become a buddha?" Huineng points out that such distinctions should not matter, according to Buddhist doctrine: "Although people from the south and people from the north differ, there is no north and south in Buddha nature. Although my barbarian's body and your body are not the same, what difference is there in our Buddha nature?"[26] The term Hongren uses carried the implication that Huineng was from a place of hunters and meat eaters, so took part in practices firmly forbidden to monks, and may have even suggested cannibalism.[27] Huineng denies that his place of origin disqualifies him from pursuing awakening within the Chan tradition, which holds that buddha nature is universal.

The *Platform Sūtra* was written to establish or strengthen Huineng's place within the Chan patriarchy, so it is no surprise that the narrative confirms that his background is not an impediment. He is initially sent to do menial labor within the monastery and learns from recitation rather than reading. In the poetry contest that is a central moment in the text, he composes his verse orally and then asks someone to write it out for him. Although he is within the monastery, Huineng is akin to the old grannies in the stories above, outside the elite and literate center of the tradition. His achievement—being recognized as his master Hongren's true heir—confirms the universality of buddha nature and suggests a Chan egalitarianism.

Another early Chan text suggests that this egalitarianism could be extended to gender as well. The *Record of the Dharma Treasure in Successive Generations* (*Lidai fabao ji*) is the first text to mention the nun Zongchi as a disciple of Bodhidharma and the one who attained his "flesh."[28] It also contains an anecdote in which the Chan master Wuzhu (714–774) meets a woman who will later become his disciple. She introduces herself by acknowledging that she is hindered by her status as a woman yet wishes to study with Wuzhu so as to "cut off the source of birth and death." He responds by pointing out that "male" and "female" do not exist in the no-thought that he teaches: "No-thought is thus no 'male,' no-thought is thus no 'female.' No-thought is thus no-obstruction, no-thought is thus no-hindrance. No-thought is thus no-birth, no-thought is thus no-death. At the time of true no-thought, no-thought itself is not. This is none other than cutting off the source of birth and death."[29] In other words, the goal that the woman seeks ("cutting off the source of birth and death") is inseparable from transcending the categories of gender. Following this exchange, the woman takes tonsure, is given a dharma name, and becomes a leading nun. In the scriptural examples above, discussions of the emptiness of sex and gender come from the mouths of young girls; here a male Chan master uses a similar logic to instruct female students.

One might argue that the gap between a doctrine of universal potential and the realities of a patriarchal society was always going to be wide. Yet later historical examples also complicate the picture and suggest how women show up in Chan history. In premodern China there have always been fewer records of nuns than of monks, an accurate reflection of the lower number of female monastics. This reflects not a lack of interest in Buddhism on the part of women but that "leaving home" was more vexed for them. Through the centuries these nuns preserved the only fully ordained order for women. Laywomen were also Buddhist practitioners and donors. Women in Chan echo these larger trends, with both nuns and female lay disciples seeking out teachers for instruction and pursuing awakening. Those in the circle of Dahui Zong'gao are good examples of how women might pursue Chan in the Song dynasty.

HISTORICAL EXAMPLES OF CHAN WOMEN

Wumen Huikai's life spanned the end of the twelfth century and the first half of the thirteenth. Dahui lived a century earlier. The recipient of imperial patronage and the teacher of a large number of students, Dahui was a well-recognized Chan master. Among those students was the nun Wuzhuo Miaozong (1095–1170). Although she is the best known of Dahui's female disciples, she was far from alone: Dahui's writings attest to fourteen nuns and twenty-seven laywomen who could be counted as his students.[30] Miaozong entered Dahui's circle long before she became a nun. Drawing on the biography by Tanxiu in his *Precious Mirror of Gods and Humans* (*Rentian baojian*, 1230), Beata Grant writes that Miaozong received a robust education in literature and classics as a young girl, as befitted her family's elite status. Tanxiu records that she had early experiences of awakening but, following social expectations, married a man of similar background. After her marriage, she continued and intensified her interest in Chan, visiting eminent monks for instruction. She developed a particularly close relationship with Dahui. It was not until after her husband died, however, that Miaozong was ordained as a nun. Already quite well known for her penetrating understanding, she was appointed abbess of a nunnery, although her advanced age meant that she was in this role for only a few years.[31]

We see in her biography evidence that being married, or a woman, was not an obstacle to spiritual attainment or being treated as a worthy student by an eminent monk. However, Dahui may have been unusual in his capacious welcome to female disciples: several episodes from Miaozong's Chan career show how she had to grapple with gendered assumptions. The first of these resonates with the conversation the girl in *samādhi* has with Mañjuśrī and more distantly with the dragon king's daughter in the *Lotus Sūtra*; it turns on whether being a woman or a man matters for spiritual attainment. Tanhui records the following: "Then she went to pay her respects to Chan master Yanyuan. Yuan said, 'How could a beauty of the women's quarters participate in the matters of great gentleman?' Miaozong replied, 'Is the teaching of the Buddha divided into male and female ranks?'"[32] Having refuted the assumption that there should be binaries dividing the Buddhist teachings, Miaozong goes on to exchange Chan thrust-and-parries with Yanyuan. As Tanhui records it, the exchange ends with Yanyuan telling Miaozong that she is a "true disciple of the Buddha" (*zhen shizi er*).[33] Note, though, that the term Yanyuan uses is *er*, which can mean "child" but usually implies "son." Miaozong's achievements make her seem male in Yanyuan's eyes; he might at this point in their exchange also have recognized her as a "great gentleman" (*da zhangfu*), a term used for virtuous men and also as an epithet for bodhisattvas. In both its pre-Buddhist and Buddhist usages, *zhangfu* or *da zhangfu* is masculine, emphasizing qualities of courage and directness. In a Chan context, a *da zhangfu* is someone with great capacity, who perceives the truth immediately and does not hesitate to act. Women also took on this label when they were understood to be living up to its ideals. Because not all men were worthy of being called *da zhangfu*, it was possible that a woman could be seen as more manly (in the Chan sense of the word) than a man. That said, the term remains within a discourse that privileges the male and masculinity. Although applying it to women is not as radical as insisting that they must change bodily forms, it follows a similar logic: Buddhist achievement is marked as male, and women must take on its gendered qualities.[34]

Miaozong drew on her gender and used her body to instruct monks, at least according to a story recorded in *Encomia of the Correct Teachings of the Five Houses* (*Wujia zhengzong zan*), compiled in the mid-thirteenth century by Xisou Shaotan (d.u.). Here Miaozong is referred to as Wuzhuo:

When Wuzhuo was not yet ordained, [Da]hui sometimes lodged her in the abbot's quarters. The teacher [i.e., Wanan Daoyan] often rebuked him. Dahui said, "Although she is a married woman, she truly has some strengths." The teacher would not assent to this. Hui then ordered him to visit her, and the teacher had no choice but to do so. When he announced his arrival, Wuzhuo said, "Chief seat, is this visit about the Buddhist teachings or about mundane affairs?" The chief seat said, "It's a visit about the Buddhist teachings." Wuzhuo told him to dismiss his attendants and invited him to enter. When the teacher reached the curtains, he saw that she had nothing on and was lying back on the bed. The teacher pointed and said, "What kind of place is *this*?" Wuzhuo replied, "Buddhas of the past, present, and future, the six generations of patriarchs, and all the monks in the world all emerge from within it." The teacher said, "Can an old monk enter or not?" Wuzhuo said, "This place does not let asses pass, but horses can pass." The teacher was speechless. Wuzhuo said, "My visit with the chief seat is over," then rolled over and cast a look at him. The teacher was embarrassed and left.[35]

Miaozong here not only shows that she is not embarrassed or fettered by her female form but also points out that women are the source of the buddhas and patriarchs—and then slyly insults the visiting monk. This story postdates her life by several decades, so we might question its veracity. Interestingly, it echoes a much less explicit anecdote mentioned in the *Blue Cliff Record*. Following a case centered on the Tang dynasty monk Juzhi, the commentary provides some background on the monk and how he came to pursue Chan in a serious way:

> The monk Juzhi was a man of Jinhua in Wuzhou. When he first lived in a hermitage, there was a nun by the name of Shiji who arrived at his hut and went in straightaway without even taking off her bamboo rain hat. Grasping her staff, she circled the meditation seat three times and said, "If you can speak then I'll take off my rain hat." She asked like this three times. Juzhi had no response. The nun then left. Juzhi said, "It's getting late; you should stay the night." The nun said, "If you can speak, I'll stay." Juzhi again had no response, and so the nun left. Juzhi sighed. "Although I have the physical form of a man, I do not have a man's spirit."[36]

Juzhi, in his concluding comment, uses *zhangfu*, although not the "great gentleman" of above; he has realized his own limitations. Thrown by the nun's boundary-crossing behavior, Juzhi cannot respond. He is bound by his sense of his gendered role in a way that the nun is not.

Both Wanan Daoyuan's visit to Wuzhuo and the nun's visit to Juzhi were included in texts that would eventually become part of the Buddhist canon. They were not marginal or extra-Buddhist literature. By showing monks as being wrong about gender, these anecdotes teach the reader as well. The reader is in the position of Wanan Daoyan and may be a little shocked or embarrassed by Miaozong, but the story challenges our views, bringing us (perhaps) a little closer to Dahui's stance.

There were other prominent female disciples of Dahui. The nun Miaodao likewise came from an elite background but never married. Ordained at twenty, she studied with several teachers before meeting Dahui; she hoped to make swifter progress with him. Dahui's sermons for Miaodao are the earliest examples of instruction in investigating *huatou* in his written works. This practice did indeed result in her awakening, and she went on to be a teacher in her own right, with several of her sermons and dialogues preserved in Chan lineage texts.[37] A laywoman, Madame Qinguo, studied with Dahui, and like his other disciples, engaged in the investigation of *huatou*; her biography too merited inclusion in lineage texts.[38] These were not the only women prominent in Chan circles during the Song dynasty, and their numbers in official records grew over the course of the dynasty.[39] The *Transmission of the Lamp Record in the Jingde Era* includes one nun. The *Compendium of Linked Lamps* (*Liandeng huiyao*) of 1189 contains the records of Dahui's two disciples and of one other woman. The *Comprehensive Lamp Record of the Jiatai Era* (Jiatai pudeng lu), of 1204, includes sixteen women as part of the Chan lineage it describes.

The types of female Chan practitioners Wumen might have himself encountered are for the most part very different from the women who appear in the *Gateless Barrier*. There women are on the margins, silent for the most part, and have no opportunity to speak to the Chan tradition. Why are they *especially* marginalized? We do not and cannot know—it is hard enough to analyze the presence of themes in texts from several hundred years ago, let alone try to discern the reasons for their absence. We might take Wumen at his word that, as he asserts in the introduction, the *Gateless Barrier* was composed over a summer working through cases with monks. If this is true, we might not want to read too much into the paucity of women or their marginalization. Yet another factor may have influenced Wumen's choices: Chan as a lineage, and *gong'an* collections as lineage texts.

THE *GATELESS BARRIER* AND CHAN LINEAGES

As we saw above, Huineng is an example of the principle that there should be no dualistic discrimination in Chan, but the *Platform Sūtra* is above all a text that establishes a lineage—and a patriarchal one at that. The Chan tradition claimed that authority came not from mastery of scriptural knowledge or meditation but from personal realization. A student's insight was cultivated through close association withand verified by a teacher. As Wendi Adamek writes in connection to the *Platform Sūtra*, for Chan to be distinct from the broader practices of Buddhism, it had to "create a sense of privileged transmission that could not be reproduced through monastic rules and rituals, images, and texts."[40] Chan's authority rested on its lineage, and lineages depend on articulating who does and does *not* belong—who is outside the path of transmission. In this the Chan tradition followed models of male transmission in the secular world. In family lineages, expressed through both genealogical charts and ritual performances, primogeniture dictates that the firstborn son has the most significant role. Women, necessary for the continuation of the family, are not part of their natal lineages and have only peripheral roles in the lineages of their husband; their reproductive contributions are denied by their marginalization. Dynastic succession reiterates male family lineages on the level of the state, and attempts by women to intervene in the transmission of power were viewed as highly problematic.[41] In short, Chan's lineage claims echoed and were supported by other social forms.

The *Gateless Barrier* is less obviously a text concerned with establishing lineage than the *Platform Sūtra*, yet it is well within this tradition. Its anecdotes are drawn from biographies and lamp-transmission texts compiled from individual biographies; the latter genre makes explicit the idea of transmission through the analogy of a flame passed from (male) person to (male) person. Collections of Chan cases reflect an awakened master instructing students: what might seem to be inscrutable encounters are given meaning through the assumption that one person operates from a position of greater insight.[42] The story in case 6 in the *Gateless Barrier* might be considered the origin of this paradigm: the Buddha holds up a flower, and his disciple Mahākāśyapa smiles, whereupon the Buddha acknowledges the wordless transmission of the dharma.[43] All cases are variations on this form, with an enlightened teacher acting in the hope that a student will recognize what is being taught, a transmission by which the student will be able to take authority in the future. Ben Van Overmeire has argued that the format of encounter dialogues—which make up a large percentage of cases in *gong'an* collections—prompts readers "to imagine themselves in the presence of their lineage ancestors." Wumen says as much in his commentary to case 1 in the *Gateless Barrier*, promising that those who penetrate this and other cases will "walk together hand in hand with all the generations of lineage masters," seeing and hearing as they do.[44] The cases are the means by which later Chan students place themselves within the lineage.

In the cases that include women or girls in the *Gateless Barrier*, we can see the effects that flow from the fact that the original audience was male. In case 28, the exchange with the old woman discussed in the commentary is the setup and background for the main case. Primed by the old woman's remarks, Deshan is ready to receive teachings from Longtan. Their exchange, resulting in Deshan burning his notes on the *Diamond Sūtra*, serves as the model for teacher-student interaction. Likewise, case

31 starts with a granny but ends with Zhaozhou telling the assembly that he has "fully investigated" or "seen through" her; Zhaozhou, not the granny, is the authority. In case 35, a reader is not in conversation with Qian but with Wuzu, who raises her example. Case 42 places the reader in the position of Mañjuśrī in dialogue with Devarāja Buddha, eliminating the girl as an interlocutor and making her into a prop. In these four cases, female figures who might have spoken from a position of awakened authority are sidelined in favor of male-male interactions. As a text that reaffirms and extends lineage, the *Gateless Barrier* does not offer women a role.

Lineages are not just about transmission, but about *controlled* transmission: to the firstborn son, to the next rightful ruler in a dynasty's line. Wumen's title uses the metaphor of gates and barriers to emphasize that not all can pass. Whether it was intended or not, the text leaves the impression that those who succeed not only must understand the cases he offers but also must be men. Women are never shown to occupy positions of authority, and Wumen uses his source material in a way that constrains female voices. Chan masters handled the matter of women in various ways, ranging from the broad acceptance exemplified by Dahui to silence or exclusion.[45]

*Gong'an*s and the anecdotes from which they derive ask readers to imaginatively inhabit one part of a dialogue or, through the commentaries, to take a position of critique. By consigning women to secondary or silent roles, the *Gateless Barrier* appears to restrict the ideal of Chan transmission to men only and thereby forecloses the possibility of truly overcoming the gender binary, one of the most salient dualisms late medieval Chinese Buddhists encountered. By removing gender dualism as a topic of inquiry Wumen narrows the gate, both for women and for men. However, the *Gateless Barrier* does not necessarily reflect how women participated in Chan, or how male Chan masters saw their participation. Although never more than a small number, women like Miaozong showed that their gender need not be an impediment to realization and indeed could be used to catalyze awakening in those who cling to false dualisms.

NOTES

1. Li Fang, et al., comps., *Taiping guangji*, vol. 8 (Beijing: Zhonghua shuju, 1961), 2831–32. See discussion of the story as an exemplary romance of the Tang dynasty in Daniel Hsieh, *Love and Women in Early Chinese Fiction* (Hong Kong: The Chinese University Press, 2008), 158–161. Hsieh discusses its likely origin in "folk tale and urban legend." This story continued to be popular after the Song dynasty and was

the basis of the Yuan dynasty play; it was also included in the Ming dynasty story collection *New Tales for Trimming the Lamp* (*Jiandeng xinhua*), published in 1378 by Qu You (1341–1427).

2. T. 48, 2005: 297b18–9.

3. T. 48, 2005: 297b23–4.

4. Sarah M. Allen, *Shifting Stories: History, Gossip, and Lore in Narratives from Tang Dynasty China* (Cambridge, MA: Harvard University Press, 2014), 119–120.

5. As we will see below, the scripture from which this case is taken provided more information.

6. Sarvanivāraṇaviṣkambhin in the translation in the appendix, xxx.

7. T. 17, 810: 765c28–766a9.

8. T. 17, 810: 766a28–b6.

9. T. 17, 810: 766b13–18.

10. T. 17, 810: 766c12.

11. T. 17, 810: 768b14–21.

12. T. 9, 262: 35b–c.

13. Jan Nattier, "Gender and Hierarchy in the *Lotus Sūtra*," in *Readings of the* Lotus Sūtra, ed. Stephen F. Teiser and Jacqueline I. Stone (New York: Columbia University Press, 2009), 97.

14. Stephanie Balkwill, "Disappearing and Disappeared Daughters in Medieval Chinese Buddhism: *Sūtras* on Sex Transformation and an Intervention into Their Transmission History," *History of Religions* 60, no. 4 (June 2021): 259–263.

15. Balkwill, "Disappearing and Disappeared Daughters," 286.

16. Miriam L. Levering, "The Dragon Girl and the Abbess of Mo-shan: Gender and Status in the Chan Buddhist Tradition," *Journal of the International Association of Buddhist Studies* 5, no. 1 (1982): 25.

17. Levering, "The Dragon Girl and the Abbess of Mo-shan," 27.

18. The expression "good to think with" (*bonnes à penser*) was first used by the anthropologist Claude Lévi-Strauss in 1962 but popularized—especially as it relates to women and religion—through the work of Peter Brown. See, for example, his *The Body and Society: Men, Women, and Sexual Renunciation in Early Christianity* (New York: Columbia University Press, 1990), 154. See also Marjorie Garber, "Good to Think With," *Profession* (2008): 11–20.

19. T. 2005: 48:298b7–10.

20. "Investigate" translates *kanguo*. Zhaozhou says that he has *kanpo*—also translated as "to see through"—the old woman. I have used "fully investigated" to preserve the link between the two expressions.

21. T. 2005: 48:296c02–c10.

22. T. 2076: 51:435c28–436a8.

23. For a thoroughgoing investigation of what old age represented in the context of Japanese Buddhism, see Edward R. Drott, *Buddhism and the Transformation of Old Age in Medieval Japan* (Honolulu: University of Hawaiʻi Press, 2016).

24. By the Ming dynasty, however, "no one thought a granny was harmless." Victoria Cass, *Dangerous Women: Warriors, Grannies, and Geishas of the Ming* (Lanham, MD and Oxford: Rowman & Littlefield, 1999), 47. See her discussion of the different roles grannies played in late imperial China, 47–64.

25. This comparison became more popular during the Song dynasty. Ding-hwa E. Hsieh, "Images of Women in Ch'an Buddhist Literature of the Sung Period," in

Buddhism in the Sung, ed. Peter N. Gregory and Daniel A. Getz, Jr. (Honolulu: University of Hawai'i Press, 1999), 172; see also her longer discussion of this term, 171–176. Most grannies were nameless, or fictional figures; Hsieh highlights Granny Yü, a snack seller who studied under an eleventh-century Chan master, confidently participating in dialogues with him.

26. Philip B. Yampolsky, trans., *The Platform Sutra of the Sixth Patriarch: The Text of the Tun-huang Manuscript* (Columbia University Press, 2012), 127–128. I have changed the Wade-Giles transliteration in the original to *pinyin*.

27. John Jorgensen, "The Figure of Huineng," in *Readings of the Platform Sutra*, ed. Morten Schlütter and Stephen F. Teiser (New York: Columbia University Press, 2012), 27.

28. Wendi Adamek, *The Mystique of Transmission: On an Early Chan History and Its Contexts* (New York: Columbia University Press, 2007), 312.

29. Adamek, *Mystique of Transmission*, 380. See also Wendi L. Adamek, "Revisiting Questions about Female Disciples in the *Lidai fabao ji* (Record of the Dharma-Treasure through the Generations)," *Pacific World*, Third Series 18 (2016): 57–65.

30. Beata Grant, *Zen Echoes: Classic Kōans with Verse Commentaries by Three Female Zen Masters* (Boston: Wisdom, 2017), 6.

31. Grant, *Zen Echoes*, 7–15.

32. Z. 87, 1612: 21b7. Grant, *Zen Echoes*, 8.

33. Z. 87, 1612: 21b14–5.

34. Miriam Levering, "Lin-Chi (Rinzai) Ch'an and Gender: The Rhetoric of Equality and the Rhetoric of Heroism," in *Buddhism, Sexuality, and Gender*, ed. José Ignacio Cabézon (Albany: State University of New York Press, 1992), 141–146.

35. Z. 78, 1554: 598b23–c6. This passage is partially translated and paraphrased in Grant, *Zen Echoes*, 13, which I have consulted and adapted.

36. T. 48, 2003: 159a27–b03. See also the translation in Thomas Cleary and J. C. Cleary, trans., *The Blue Cliff Record* (Boston and London: Shambala, 2005), 124.

37. Miriam Levering, "Miao-tao and Her Teacher Ta-hui," in *Buddhism in the Sung*, ed. Peter N. Gregory and Daniel A. Getz, Jr. (Honolulu: University of Hawai'i Press, 1999); Dahui's *huatou* instruction is discussed on 201. On *huatou* as it relates to the *Gateless Barrier*, see Jimmy Yu's chapter in this volume.

38. Ding-hwa E. Hsieh, "Images of Women in Ch'an Buddhist Literature of the Sung Period," in *Buddhism in the Sung*, ed. Peter N. Gregory and Daniel A. Getz, Jr. (Honolulu: University of Hawai'i Press, 1999), 158–159. See Dahui's letter to her in Jeffrey L. Broughton with Elise Yoko Watanabe, trans., *The Letters of Master Dahui Pujue* (Oxford and New York: Oxford University Press, 2017), 157–159.

39. Levering, "Miao-tao and Her Teacher," 189.

40. Wendi L. Adamek, "Transmitting Notions of Transmission," in *Readings of the Platform Sūtra*, ed. Morten Schütter and Stephen F. Teiser (New York: Columbia University Press, 2012), 116.

41. John Jorgensen writes that "Shenhui's emphasis on the unbroken lineage of one male patriarch per generation also resonated with the reassessment of Empress Wu's reign." Wuzhao (Empress Wu, although many scholars now refer to her as Emperor Wu) was the most famous example of a woman claiming dynastic succession. Jorgensen elaborates on how Shenhui's *Platform Sūtra* offered a vision of Buddhism that rejected the forms of the religion most prized by Wuzhao. John Jorgensen, "The Figure of Huineng," in *Readings of the* Platform Sūtra, ed. Morten

Schütter and Stephen F. Teiser (New York: Columbia University Press, 2012), 40–41.

42. Mario Poceski shows that commentaries on the case of Nanquan killing a cat rely on the "operative assumption" that Nanquan is a "genuine Chan master" and "enlightened person." Mario Poceski, "Killing Cats and Other Imaginary Happenings: Milieus and Features of Chan Exegesis," in *Communities of Memory and Interpretation: Reimagining and Reinventing the Past in East Asian Buddhism*, ed. Mario Poceski (Freiberg: Projekt Verlag, 2017), 123.

43. Wumen's commentary on this case points out that the Buddha's gesture and the flower are themselves forms of what is supposed to be inconceivable and ineffable. See the discussion in T. Griffith Foulk, "The Spread of Chan (Zen) Buddhism," in *The Spread of Buddhism*, ed Ann Heirman and Stephan Peter Bumbacher (Leiden: Brill, 2007), 448–449.

44. Ben Van Overmeire, "Reading Chan Encounter Dialogue during the Song Dynasty: *The Record of Linji*, the *Lotus Sutra*, and the Sinification of Buddhism," *Buddhist-Christian Studies* 37 (2017): 211, 218. Wumen's comment appears at T. 48, 2005: 292c29–293a1.

45. The debate on the role of women and gender determinism continued for centuries. For late imperial examples, see Beata Grant, "Da Zhangfu: The Gendered Rhetoric of Heroism and Equality in Seventeenth-Century Chan Buddhist Discourse Records," *Nan Nü* 10 (2009): 177–211.

{ 7 }

PUBLIC CASES IN KOREAN SŎN BUDDHISM

Juhn Y. Ahn

I N 1485, a new legal-administrative code—known as the *Great Code of State Administration* (K. Kyŏngguk taejŏn)—was promulgated within the Korean Chosŏn dynasty (1392–1910).[1] The new code was not created ex nihilo. It replaced an earlier code, the *Six Codes of Administration* (K. Kyŏngje yukchŏn), which had been established in 1397. Although still less than a few decades old, the earlier legal framework of the *Six Codes* was found to be full of lacunae and shortcomings. Initially, these problems were addressed hurriedly with supplemental codes. However, this temporary solution ultimately proved ineffective. As the expansion of the *Six Codes* progressed in this unsystematic and need-driven manner, the number of inconsistencies and contradictions naturally grew. Continuous revisions therefore became necessary and were quickly made, but the intrinsic limitations of relying on addenda or supplemental codes had become all too evident. Rather than continue the practice of adding and revising supplemental codes, the Chosŏn court worked to create a new code that would be more comprehensive and coherent. This turned out to be an arduous process that also took several decades to complete.

One reason the Chosŏn court found it so difficult to complete the new code was its broad scope. Not finalized until 1485, the *Great Code of State Administration* covered everything from officials' salaries and appointment letters to taxation, inheritance, loans, weights and measures, and Buddhism. Another reason was that many of the statutes contained therein were about ongoing, controversial issues. This was certainly true of the statutes concerning Buddhism. They had been codified to bring some sense of closure to the ongoing efforts to reform the Buddhist establishment, which began not long after the founding of the dynasty in 1392. This chapter will cover how the new legal code also addressed the matters related to Buddhism, specifically, how the development of Sŏn (C. Chan; J. Zen) in Korea was contingent on these political changes.

At the heart of the reform effort was the issue of state support.[2] As part of a larger plan to maintain a balanced budget and prevent taxable resources from escaping state control, the new dynasty first designated eleven official Buddhist schools, with their 242 monasteries, worthy of state support. Then, in 1406, land and bondservants were confiscated from all other (presumably) state-supported Buddhist monasteries, some of which had fallen into disrepair during the Red Turban incursions of 1359, 1360, and 1361. Part of this confiscated wealth was likely redistributed to the 242 monasteries as their permanent endowments, to ensure that they would all be able to operate and support their permanent assemblies without further financial assistance. Not surprisingly, the monasteries located in the old capital of the previous Koryŏ dynasty (918–1392) and the new Chosŏn capital were granted the largest endowments. Two monasteries from each capital were selected to receive enough land and bondservants to support a hundred permanent resident monks. All other state-recognized monasteries in these and other urban centers received half that amount. The Chosŏn court also granted smaller endowments to monasteries in the countryside, but they seem to have struggled to attract talented abbots as well as wealthy patrons. Perhaps for this reason, the number of state-recognized Buddhist schools was reduced from eleven to seven by 1407, the very next year. These were further consolidated into two schools—the Sŏn (C. Chan; J. Zen) school, which specialized in Buddhist theories of *dhyāna* or meditative absorption, and the Kyo (C. Jiao; J. Kyo) school, which specialized in the study of Buddhist scriptures and scriptural commentaries—in 1424. As part of this downsizing and consolidation process, the Sŏn and Kyo schools were each effectively limited to eighteen monasteries. The total number of state-recognized monasteries was thus reduced from 242 to 36.

It was during this process of reforming the state's support of the Buddhist establishment that the court attempted to codify statutes concerning Buddhism. These specified, among other things, the conditions for acquiring official ordination certificates and the qualifications necessary to join the Buddhist monastic order as a Sŏn or Kyo monk. According to the new code, examinations for aspiring monks had to be administered every three years. The Sŏn and Kyo schools were each allowed to select thirty new ordinands from the candidates who passed the exams. Kyo candidates had to be tested on their knowledge of the *Avataṃsaka* and *Daśabhūmika Sūtras*. Sŏn candidates were tested on their knowledge of the *Transmission of the Lamp* (K. *Chŏndŭng*)—presumably referring to the *Transmission of the Lamp Record in the Jingde Era* (C. *Jingde chuandeng lu*; hereafter *Transmission of the Lamp Record*)—in addition to the *Collection of Prose and Verse Comments on Cases of the Sŏn School* (K. *Sŏnmun yŏmsong chip*; hereafter *Prose and Verse Comments*), completed in 1226 and attributed to Sŏn master Chin'gak Hyesim (1178–1234).[3]

The use of these two collections to test Sŏn candidates was hitherto unprecedented in Korea. There is little evidence to suggest that Korean monks regularly studied the *Transmission of the Lamp Record* before this period. The label "Sŏn" was basically an administrative shorthand for two different Buddhist traditions that specialized in either the tradition of Ch'ŏnt'ae (C. Tiantai; J. Tendai), founded by Zhiyi (538–597), or the tradition of the Chinese Chan patriarchs, represented by the Korean Chogye Sŏn school.[4] Before the fifteenth century, these two traditions had separate and distinct examinations for entering the state-controlled ecclesiastical bureaucracy. The Chogye Sŏn lineages, known collectively as the Nine Mountains, even had their respective preliminary examinations administered by the lineages themselves. However, these earlier methods of evaluating candidates were ignored and replaced with a much simpler examination system in the *Great Code of State Administration*. In this new system, all monks belonging to the Sŏn school were tested on their knowledge of just the two collections mentioned above. Neither collection had anything to do with the Tiantai or Ch'ŏnt'ae tradition, which was nominally part of the Sŏn school.

Why did the Chosŏn court ignore earlier conventions and limit the new Sŏn examination to the *Transmission of the Lamp Record* and *Prose and Verse Comments*? Why were these two specific collections chosen, and what does that tell us about Sŏn Buddhism and more specifically, Sŏn learning during this period? To answer these questions requires a closer look at Hyesim's *Prose and Verse Comments*.[5] This massive collection of 1,125 *kongans* (C. *gong'an*; J. *kōans*) was compiled to promote a unique style of Buddhist learning that began to acquire its more characteristic forms—verse commentaries, capping phrases, commentarial remarks, and so on—in China during the Northern Song dynasty (960–1127).[6] The new fifteenth-century clerical examination in Korea tested a Sŏn monk's proficiency in precisely this style. The significance of Hyesim's collection and the style of learning it promoted is evident on a closer look at the broader context of *gong'an* learning in the thirteenth century, to which both Wumen Huikai's *Gateless Barrier* and Chin'gak Hyesim's *Prose and Verse Comments* belong.

GONG'AN LEARNING

Kongan or *gong'an* typically refers to texts selected and edited by Chan masters for careful study, analysis, and observation. They are more commonly known in their Japanese pronunciation today as *kōan*s. We do not know the precise origins of the genre, but the crisis precipitated by the collapse of the great Chinese Tang dynasty (618–907) seems to have served as an important catalyst for the collection, collation, and preservation of the textual material that later became *gong'an*. Rather than take this historical rupture as an irreparable moment of despair (i.e., the fall of a dynasty), the Chan community seems to have used it as an opportunity to reinvent itself. Indeed, sometime between the An Lushan rebellion of 755 and the Huang Chao rebellion of the late ninth century, literate members of the community began the process of transforming the inchoate past into sacred memory and legacy.[7] Biographies, anecdotes, and sermons of Chan masters were carefully edited into collections known as "discourse records" (C. *yulu*) and published in large numbers during the tenth and eleventh centuries. Eventually, the publication of discourse records was so common that it became de rigueur for eminent masters to be honored with a collection of their own.

The advent of the printing press in China during this time and the rising popularity of this new genre inevitably affected Chan learning. Most notably, as the number of discourse records grew, extensive reading became possible and more feasible.[8] Rather than engage in the intensive perusal of one book or text, for example, students of Chan could now more easily read broadly, moving rapidly from one discourse records collection to the next. The growing popularity of this new reading practice led to the invention of a new related Chan genre. The warm support that Buddhism received from the rulers and the ruling elite of southern kingdoms such as the Southern Tang (937–975) and Wuyue (907–960) was a critical factor behind this development, as it made the completion of ambitious Buddhist publication projects possible. In the safe environs of the south, Chan monks and their literati followers collected discourse records and edited them together into comprehensive "transmission of the lamp" records. The *Patriarchs Hall Collection* (C. Zutang ji, published in 952) and the *Transmission of the Lamp Record* (published in 1004) are the earliest known examples.

We must not underestimate the significance of these developments in Chan learning. Extensive reading enabled students to appreciate the teachings of masters in novel ways.[9] Students were now able to more easily compare a wide variety of Chan teachings and use what they deemed to be more effective or superior. Differences in teaching style naturally acquired newfound importance. Nevertheless, the wide variety of teachings now at their disposal simultaneously made it difficult to gain depth of understanding and a sense of mastery over this massive literature. In this context Chan masters began to collate what they deemed to be highly instructive examples into case collections. Old Chan stories were thus turned into "public cases" or *gong'an*. More important, some masters such as Fenyang Shanzhao (947–1024) and Xuedou Chongxian (980–1052) also began to offer their own judgments or verdicts on these cases in the form of verse commentaries. These commentaries and literary productions challenged readers to once again practice a form of intensive, close reading.

Chan learning was thus thrust into a deep dilemma. *Gong'an* collections with verse commentaries provided students with a convenient way to access the wide variety of teachings or styles of teaching that the old Chan masters had developed but also encouraged students to focus on developing not only breadth of knowledge but also depth of understanding. One could argue that the perfection of both styles of reading, extensive and intensive, is what Fenyang and Xuedou intended. Nevertheless, the two styles were not necessarily regarded as compatible or commensurable. The question of which to privilege continued to trouble the Chan and, later, Sŏn communities in China and Korea. This is precisely why the *Prose and Verse Comments* was compiled.

CHAN VERSUS DAO

During the Northern Song, the Chan community witnessed the spread of its own modest version of what the Germans call a *Lesewut* or "reading craze." The emic term at the time was the "Chan of belles lettres" (C. *wenzi chan*).[10] For instance, a disciple of the eminent Chan master Yunmen Wenyan (864–949) named Dongshan Qingbing (d.u.) "collected discourse records from all over the country."[11] Chan master Fenyang Shanzhao similarly visited no fewer than seventy-one masters and learned "all of their wondrous styles of teaching."[12] Fenyang even wrote a poem titled "Song of Extensive Wisdom" (C. Guangzhige) to celebrate this kind of erudition and to help others appreciate the diversity of Chan teaching styles that they could encounter through extensive reading and learning.

Lest Chan students hastily conclude after acquiring a saying or two that they had thus completely figured out the *dao* (which could be understood in many ways as "truth," "point," "intent," or "the Way" in this context), Fenyang's disciple Dayu Shouzhi (d.u.), while praising the "Song of Extensive Wisdom," urged them to "seek extensively for wisdom and travel far and wide for factional styles."[13] In his reading of Fenyang's poem, Chan master Juefan Huihong (1071–1128) reached the very same conclusion: "Having witnessed later generations resting content with what little they have attained by consulting [only a Chan saying or two], how could [Fenyang] not warn against this by [encouraging us] to consult far and wide?"[14]

Evidence of this reading craze as a significant cultural phenomenon can be found as early as the ninth century. After he failed to answer his teacher Weishan Lingyou's (771–853) question about Chan, Xiangyan Zhixian (d. 898), the subject of case 5 of the *Gateless Barrier*, is said to have burned the discourse records he had gathered from all over the country out of frustration and disappointment.[15] To be sure, the explicit aim of this episode from Xiangyan's official biography is to point out the shortcomings, not the benefits, of the Chan reading craze. It is trying to suggest that a good teacher like Weishan is far more valuable than a large pile of Chan books. Still, the very fact that the author felt it necessary to make this point indicates that there was a real tension between the advocates of intensive and extensive reading in the tenth-century Chan community.

This tension was created and exacerbated, of course, by the Chan reading craze, which enabled members of the community such as Fenyang and Dayu to see the benefit of reading widely and extensively. Although a Chan student could potentially attain awakening by intensively reading and studying one or two sayings or *gong'an*, there was, as noted above, a growing consensus that this awakening had to be verified by consulting more teachers and their divergent styles. Diversity was something to celebrate, not fear. This view had broader implications. Those who advocated extensive reading and its systemetization as the "Chan of belles lettres" were effectively dismantling the unique bond that existed between Chan master and disciple, which Xiangyan's story was clearly seeking to restore. If the advocates of extensive reading were right, then it was no longer good enough to acquire expertise in only what one had learned from one's master, such as their take on the famous "three barriers" teaching.[16] A dutiful and diligent Chan student had to test for himself this factional understanding of the "three barriers" against others to see if his master's understanding was right or wrong, superior or inferior. Needless to say, the more a single understanding was tested, the better.

However, extensive reading presented its own set of problems. Chief among these was the tendency to develop a shallow, literalistic, and superficial understanding of Chan sayings. This was neatly pointed out by Chan master Yungai Shouzhi (d.u.), who deemed it necessary to mock those who made poor use of the Chan reading craze:

A while ago I went again to Mount Huangbo. When I arrived at the reservoir, I saw a monk coming from the mountain, so I asked him, "Brother, how have you been recently making sense of the words of the three barriers?" The monk replied, "There are some very marvelous words that can allow you to see their intent. [In response to] 'Why does my hand look like the Buddha's hand?' some say, 'Play the lute under the moon' and others say, 'Holding an empty begging bowl on a long road.'[17] [In response to] 'Why does my leg look like an ass's leg?' some say, 'A white egret stands on snow and yet they are not the same color'[18] and others say, 'Stepping on fallen flowers in an empty mountain.'[19] [In response to] 'Wherein lie the conditions of your birth?' some say, 'I am so and so from such and such a place.' At that time, I made fun of him, saying, 'Along the way if someone asks you about the meaning of the Buddha's hand, an ass's leg, and conditions of your birth, will you answer him with 'Holding an empty begging bowl on a long road' or with 'A white egret stands on snow and yet they are not the same color'? If you use both, then you will bring great confusion to buddhadharma. But if you pick just one reply, then the test of your aptitude in Chan will prove to be underwhelming."[20]

Here, Yungai does not hide his contempt for the monk who just visited Huanglong Huinan, Yungai's teacher, famous for his use of the "three barriers" to instruct students. What troubled Yungai was the unnamed monk's seemingly clueless attachment to the "marvelous words" used in Chan exchanges, which sources from this period simply called *chan*.[21] Instead of trying to comprehend the intent or meaning of the words, the monk merely learned to parrot them. The larger purpose of Yungai's story is to point out the limitations of extensive reading—and relatedly, to promote, as an alternative, a style of intensive Chan learning that took depth of comprehension as its ultimate goal.

Concerns about the need for better comprehension in Chan learning were voiced often by the dharma heirs of Huanglong Huinan. There was, however, no easy or straightforward way to address these concerns. Huanglong's dharma heir Zhaojue Changcong (1025–1091) tried to do so by distinguishing *chan* from *dao*—that is, Chan "sayings" from their "intent."

He made this bold claim during an important ritual. When Zhaojue became abbot of Donglin si on Mount Lu and thus Huanglong's dharma heir in 1080, he did what any new Chan abbot was expected to do.[22] He displayed the broad range of rhetorical skills that he had at his disposal and answered questions from the assembly with references to classical poetry, well-known *chan* catchphrases, and new lyrical expressions of his own making. At the end of his first public sermon as the new abbot, Zhaojue made his stance on the proper use of *chan* clear. He explained that the practice of asking about the Patriarch's (i.e., Bodhidharma's) intention in coming from the West and answering with the repetition of a *chan* catchphrase such as "the essence of the Southern school" was nothing but an expedient. This catchphrase was not the ultimate truth. Beyond *chan*, Zhaojue claimed, there was *dao*. Zhaojue thus declared that "the singular path of going beyond [i.e., attaining awakening] was not transmitted by the thousand sages—the sight of students toiling away [in the study of *chan*] is like that of a monkey trying in vain to grasp its shadow."[23]

According to Zhaojue, looking for *dao* in *chan* was pointless, because the sages—that is, the Chan masters—had never transmitted a separate method for attaining *dao*. The *dao* therefore had to be pursued directly. Zhaojue, of course, made this bold claim to distinguish himself from other masters and abbots whom he treated as specialists of *chan* and not *dao*. He was explaining why he, the new abbot, deserved the respect of everyone in the assembly. The desire to set himself apart did not stop there. Zhaojue is said to have even claimed that his own dharma brothers Huitang Zuxin (1025–1100) and Zhenjing Kewen—fellow dharma heirs of Huanglong—had acquired their master's *chan* and not his *dao*. This bold statement did not sit well with a Chan master named Dahui Zong'gao (1089–1163), who issued the following rebuttal:

Zhaojue takes being ordinary, doing nothing, and not establishing conceptual views and understandings as the *dao*. He thus forsakes the pursuit of sublime awakening. He considers the teaching of a true sudden awakening and seeing into one's own nature taught by the buddhas and patriarchs like Deshan, Linji, Caodong, and Yunmen as mere contrivances. . . . By taking the ancients' discussion of the mysterious and their explanations of the sublime as *chan* [and not *dao*], he has slandered the past sages and has rendered the next generation deaf.[24]

Although Dahui voices his strong disagreement with Zhaojue here, the two actually advance remarkably similar claims. Neither thought there was a separate method for attaining *dao*. For Zhaojue, *dao* had to be pursued through *dao*. For Dahui, *chan* was itself nothing other than *dao*. Zhaojue's mistake, if we are to believe Dahui, was to see *chan* and *dao* as two different things.

To bolster his criticism of Zhaojue, Dahui cited Huitang and Zhenjing, the two dharma brothers that Zhaojue belittled. Dahui felt justified because he believed that Huanglong, contrary to Zhaojue's claim, actually acknowledged only those two real dharma heirs.[25] Huitang, Dahui says, used to tell learned men, "You should go to Mount Lu [i.e., Donglin si] and sit in the primordial state of doing nothing." Zhenjing similarly referred to Zhaojue's students at Donglin si as "dead ashes" who only knew how to sit quietly and not do anything.

"Dead ashes" is an expression that Dahui used frequently throughout his illustrious career, to ridicule not only the students of Zhaojue but also any teacher who taught this way, including the Linji and Caodong Chan traditions.[26] Dahui was convinced that Zhenjing had good reason to mock the students of Zhaojue as "dead ashes." According to Zhenjing, they "stubbornly insisted that 'the ordinary mind is *dao*' and considered this the ultimate rule." They also made the mistake of using the same *chan* catchphrases as in Yungai's story to answer questions about the "three barriers." Put simply, they either parroted Chan sayings (*chan*) without comprehension (*dao*) or did nothing, thinking ordinary mind (i.e., the mind in its current state) was *dao*. Zhenjing sums up their grave mistakes accordingly: "they take the hundred artifices [i.e., *chan* catchphrases] as the only essential thing and the single road of being ordinary as the legitimate [path]." What Zhaojue and his students pursued, in other words, was not *dao*, but a *dao*-less *chan* and a *dao*-less ordinary mind. This, in Dahui's opinion, was a grave mistake.

EARLY *GONG'AN* LEARNING IN KOREA

Dahui's opinion of *chan* and *dao* (and hence extensive reading) is important for understanding the compilation of the *Prose and Verse Comments* in the thirteenth century. The volume was meant to preserve and promote a unique style of *gong'an* learning that Dahui considered to be a good way of addressing these concerns about *chan* and *dao*. What was this style, how did Dahui himself explain it, and why did he deem it necessary to do so? The lessons that Dahui learned from the discourse records of Huitang and Zhenjing proved to be extremely useful throughout his illustrious career. Teachers of the rival Caodong tradition such as Hongzhi Zhengjue

(1091–1157) taught a popular style of Chan—known more commonly as silent illumination (C. *mozhao*)—that was remarkably similar to the teachings of Zhaojue. Using words taken straight out of Zhenjing's discourse records, Dahui was able to claim, for instance, that certain masters taught practitioners to rest and relax like "dead ashes, withered trees, strips of white silk, and incense burners in old shrines."[27] But the rest and relaxation thus attained was nothing more than a mind afflicted by what Dahui calls the malady of meditation and therefore "not a matter that concerns those who learn *dao*."[28]

This malady of meditation was the product of not a particular factional teaching or style but larger problems related to the spread of extensive reading and extensive reading fatigue. There is evidence of this in Dahui's own diagnosis of the problem. According to Dahui, Chan students were exhausted by the demands of the reading craze and therefore tended to gravitate toward teachers like Zhaojue and Hongzhi who instead taught them to just rest and relax. Dahui's remedy was a unique form of "intensive reading":

> Just once put down the mind of deluded ideas and perverse notions, the mind of thinking and discrimination, the mind that loves life and hates death, the mind of opinion and understanding, the mind that enjoys calm and dislikes bustle. Then where you have put down [such minds], observe this critical phrase: "A monk asked Zhaozhou, 'Does a dog have buddha nature?' Zhaozhou answered, 'Wu!' (or No!)" This one word, "no," is a weapon that will crush a multitude of perverse perceptions. Do not try to understand it through "have" or "not have"; do not try to understand it with reason. Do not rely on the mind to think it through or figure it out; do not be fixated on raising the eyebrows and blinking the eyes. Do not try to make your way on the path of words; do not just float in idleness. Do not simply assent to its source; do not cite proof from writings.[29]

This form of reading came to be known as "critical phrase *chan*" (C. *kanhua chan*), popularly known as *hwadu* (C. *huatou*; J. *wato*). There is no reason to think that Dahui invented the practice, but his advocacy did play a critical role in its spread throughout East Asia. In fact, when members of the Sŏn community in thirteenth-century Korea tried to promote it, they cited the discourse records of Dahui as the authoritative grounds for doing so.

Even so, the promotion of meditation on the critical phrase and the publication of the most systematic presentation of this form of *gong'an* learning in Korea—i.e., Hyesim's *Prose and Verse Comments*—did not happen in a vacuum. There is evidence to suggest that prior to Chinul and Hyesim, there were already traces of *gong'an* learning, and possibly the critical phrase method, in Korea. The Sŏn community must have already had *some* understanding of how to study the sayings of old Chan masters. Exactly how is unknown. That being said, in the fall of 1076, a Sŏn master named Tamjin (d.u.) traveled to Song China as part of an official Koryŏ embassy.[30] Not long after his arrival, Tamjin took up temporary residence at the Upper Tianzhu monastery in Hangzhou. His stay did not last long. At the request of Emperor Shenzong, Tamjin relocated to the Song capital early the next year. There, he was placed in the care of Chan master Daozhen (1014–1093), the influential abbot of the grand public Jingyin Chan Monastery.[31] This proved to be a great opportunity for the Korean monk. Tamjin gained firsthand knowledge of the rituals regularly performed at public Chan monasteries such as the ritual of ascending the hall (C. *shangtang*).[32] During this ritual, Chan masters like Daozhen brought old *chan* stories up for comment and discussion. Tamjin also got the chance to learn more about these stories and how to interpret them in the informal sermons (C. *xiaocan*) delivered by the abbot. Furthermore, he was given plenty of time to soak in everything he heard and saw and spent three long years studying under Daozhen. Tamjin managed to receive dharma transmission from Daozhen before his return to Koryŏ.

Although there is no mention of him acquiring Chan discourse records during his pilgrimage in China, it seems reasonable to assume that Tamjin had a few when he returned to Koryŏ, at least a copy of Daozhen's sermons. We know that he managed to get a copy of the "pure rules" (C. *qinggui*)—i.e., monastic rules—used by public monasteries. There were also more opportunities for him to acquire new books in China. In 1085, Tamjin was able to accompany the famous Korean monk Ŭich'ŏn (1055–1101) on another pilgrimage. Like Ŭich'ŏn, who is known to have returned with a thousand scrolls of Buddhist texts, Tamjin probably returned with a large collection. His ability to acquire Buddhist texts was impressive enough for Koryŏ's King Yejong (r. 1105–1122) to entrust him with the task of purchasing a copy of the Khitan canon, which Tamjin did a few decades after his pilgrimage to Song China with Ŭich'ŏn.

The funerary epitaph for Tamjin's student T'anyŏn (1070–1159) recounts how T'anyŏn sent a copy of some of his verses and "sayings" prepared for the ritual of ascending the hall to the Chinese Chan master Wushi Jiechen (1080–1148), the abbot of Guangli si on Mount Ayuwang, to ask for his seal of approval.[33] This seems to imply that Sŏn masters, especially those who studied under Tamjin, already knew how to practice *chan* and *gong'an* learning in the twelfth century. If so, there must have been growing interest in how to better engage in this practice in Korea. In the writings of Sŏn master Pojo Chinul (1158–1210) and the *Prose and Verse Comments* attributed to his student Hyesim, we find evidence of not only *gong'an* learning but also, more specifically, observing the critical phrase *chan*.

CHINUL, HYESIM, AND SUSŎN MONASTERY

Initially, Chinul showed no interest in *chan, gong'an* learning, or observing the critical phrase.[34] He was far more interested in pursuing a career in the state-controlled ecclesiastical bureaucracy. To that end, in 1182 he traveled to the capital to take the clerical examination for Sŏn monks, which seems to have involved engaging in a doctrinal debate. Chinul passed, but exam success did not result in official titles or desirable monastic appointments as he expected. Disappointed, he left the capital and sought refuge in a rustic monastery in the southeast. Chinul's funerary epitaph claims that he had his first moment of awakening during this period, after reading a passage from the *Platform Sutra*. Chinul was so excited after he discovered the passage that he paced around the Buddha Hall, reciting and contemplating it until he figured out its intent. Three years later, Chinul found himself at another rustic monastery where he developed a deeper appreciation for the *Avataṃsaka Sutra*.

Chinul experienced a third and final awakening in 1197. By then, he had established himself as the leader of a sizable monastic community he helped create nine years earlier. The community quickly grew and was eventually large enough to warrant relocation to a monastery with a larger endowment of land and probably slaves. Plans were made after a monastery that met the community's needs was found, but Chinul seems to have wanted to resolve some lingering doubts first. He therefore decided to retreat at a hermitage on top of Mount Chiri. During this three-year retreat, Chinul read the discourse records of Dahui and had his final awakening. This seems to have been a very important transformative experience. To celebrate the completion of the restoration of his new monastery (later renamed Susŏn sa) in 1205, Chinul chose to deliver lectures on Dahui's discourse records for 120 days.

There is no extant record of these lectures, but we may be able to glean what he said from a treatise, *Resolving Doubts About Observing the Phrase* (K. Kanhwa kyŏrŭi ron), discovered and published posthumously by Chinul's chief disciple, Hyesim, in 1215.[35] It is unclear how much, if any, of the treatise was actually written by Chinul, but issues raised and addressed conform neatly with those that appear in his biography. Written in question-and-answer format, the treatise offers a meticulously argued defense of Dahui's understanding of the *chan* method of observing the critical phrase. Chinul's interlocutor, who is portrayed as an expert on the *Avataṃsaka Sutra*, raises doubt about Dahui's notion of seeking awakening without relying on conceptual understanding and the written word. Is the *gong'an* and its critical phrase, for instance, not written words full of conceptual understanding? In response, Chinul reminds his interlocutor that students of Sŏn "investigate the live word," which cannot be done by relying on established knowledge (i.e., doctrinal teachings) and conceptual understanding. He also carefully distinguishes this method from the teachings of radical subitism (or sudden awakening), which present the ordinary mind as *dao*. As Chinul explains, there is a difference between investigating the "idea" and investigating the "word" (i.e., *chan*). The shortcut approach advocated by Dahui, he claims, does the latter.

Chinul's interest in the *chan* method of observing the critical phrase continued to define the intellectual and spiritual endeavors of the community of monks and scholars at Susŏn Monastery and later, its growing number of branch monasteries, which thrived with the support of Ch'oe U (1166–1249) and his family. Susŏn Monastery and its abbots were able to wield great influence and power. This, in turn, enabled the *chan* method of observing the critical phrase to dig deep roots in Korea. Ch'oe U was the son of Ch'oe Ch'unghŏn (1149–1219), a general who seized control of the military-led Koryŏ government through a bloody coup in 1196. The age of military rule in Koryŏ had begun less than three decades earlier in 1170, also as a consequence of a coup.[36] As the heir of the Ch'oe House, Ch'oe U was one of the most powerful figures in Koryŏ at this time.

Ch'oe U seems to have developed a deep interest in Susŏn Monastery when he was tasked with lending his calligraphic skills to the writing of the monastery's restoration record in 1207. This opportunity seems to have led to Ch'oe becoming an enthusiastic patron of Chinul's successor, Hyesim, who regularly offered him guidance on the practice of observing the critical phrase through pastoral letters.[37] The trust between them grew so strong that Ch'oe even had his two sons become monks and serve Hyesim as their master. Ch'oe's patronage predictably led to Susŏn Monastery's material prosperity. He and his supporters at court furnished Susŏn Monastery and its branch monasteries with handsome endowments of land and movable wealth. One of these branches was Ch'oe U's grand

memorial monastery, Sŏnwŏn Monastery on Kanghwa Island, built to perform yearly memorial rites for Ch'oe and his family.

Susŏn Monastery benefited immensely from Ch'oe's patronage, but this
also meant that it had to bear a greater responsibility. Rapid expansion of
the network of monasteries under Susŏn's control naturally created a need
for standardization and quality control. Fortunately, Chinul had already
prepared a rudimentary set of monastic rules, *Admonitions to Beginning
Students* (K. Kye ch'osim hagin mun), for the newly restored monastery
in 1205.[38] These rules were most likely observed by monasteries belonging to its growing network. However, this network did not yet have a reliable tool for practicing the critical phrase method.

GONG'AN LEARNING IN THE
THIRTEENTH CENTURY

It is for this purpose that Hyesim compiled his massive compendium of
gong'an commentaries, *Prose and Verse Comments*, which is part of the
literary genre of "classified books" (C. *leishu*). As Hyesim states in his preface, students strongly requested that such a resource be made available to
them.[39] To ensure that the new compendium would meet their expectations, Hyesim consulted as many discourse records as he could and gathered old cases (i.e., *gong'an*), verse comments, commentarial remarks, comments from sermons delivered during ascending the hall rituals,
comments from something called "universal sermons" (K. *posŏl*), as well
as comments from informal sermons delivered by abbots to his disciples.
All of this material was then arranged in chronological order like the
Transmission of the Lamp Record. Old cases featuring the Buddha and
related commentaries were placed at the beginning. These were followed
by old cases about his successor Kāśyapa and the other Indian patriarchs,
which in turn were followed by old cases about Bodhidharma and the Chinese Chan patriarchs.

Despite his best efforts, Hyesim admits in his preface that he was unable
to consult recorded sayings for everyone. His *Prose and Verse Comments*
nevertheless turned out to be one of the largest and most comprehensive
gong'an commentary collections ever to be published, exactly as it was
intended to be. Its intended function becomes much easier to see when
compared with other *gong'an* commentary collections from Song China.

The first and perhaps most important *gong'an* commentary collection
to present the old cases of Chan patriarchs in chronological order is the

Essence of Succession in the Chan School (C. *Zongmen tongyao ji*) published in 1093.[40] This early ollection featured more than 500 patriarchs and 11,000 *gong'an*. Each *gong'an* consisted of an old case accompanied by commentarial remarks. Each case had at least one remark, but it was more common for several remarks to accompany a single case. A similar layout was used in another important *gong'an* commentary collection, the *Anthology of the String of Pearls Verse Commentaries on Old Cases of the Chan Lineage* (C. *Chanzong songgu lianzhu ji*), published in 1175. This work also arranged *gong'an* in chronological order but focused on verse commentaries, not commentarial remarks. In this anthology too, a single case could have as few as one and as many as a dozen or more appended verse commentaries. Hyesim's *Prose and Verse Comments* is arranged in the same manner, but it appends both commentarial remarks and verses to each case.

The way these three collections organized old cases and their commentaries tells us something important about their intended function and purpose. All three clearly tried to be comprehensive. Each and every generation of Chan's extended lineage was represented. But none of them included cases for which commentarial remarks or verses could not be found. These collections, then, were not intended to be used as resources for looking up old cases but instead for looking up commentarial remarks and verses. For looking up old cases, one could always rely on the *Patriarchs Hall Collection* or *Transmission of the Lamp Record*. This is exactly why Hyesim explains in his preface that *Prose and Verse Comments* should be used together with the *Transmission of the Lamp*.

The production of a *gong'an* commentary collection like *Prose and Verse Comments* in thirteenth-century Korea should, again, be understood as a response to the specific needs of a growing network of influential monasteries. Had Susŏn Monastery not developed its network with Ch'oe House support, Hyesim might have produced a very different kind of collection—perhaps a commentary that looked a lot more like the *Gateless Barrier*. The *Gateless Barrier* was based on teaching material that Wumen prepared for a winter retreat at Longxiang Monastery in 1228 and therefore includes only forty-eight *gong'an*, which are not presented in any obvious order. Each *gong'an*, moreover, has only one prose and one verse commentary. The commentaries were all written by Wumen himself. As the record of what Wumen taught during a winter retreat, the *Gateless Barrier* could not but bear these characteristics. In effect, it presents a list of one Chan master's favorite *gong'an* and explanations, in prose and verse form, why he likes them so much. The *Gateless*

Barrier grants us privileged access to Wumen's take on *chan*. Hyesim's *Prose and Verse Comments* offers something very different. There is no trace of Hyesim whatsoever. There is no privileged access to anything or to anyone. All we have (or are supposed to have) is *chan* in its entirety.

CONCLUSION

Although they are both *gong'an* commentary collections from the early thirteenth century, Hyesim's *Prose and Verse Comments* and Wumen's *Gateless Barrier* have been shown to be different in many ways. In essence, whereas the *Gateless Barrier* focuses on one Chan master's comprehension and appreciation of *chan, Prose and Verse Comments* makes such a focus virtually impossible. Context is important to understanding this difference. Wumen's work was based on material prepared for a winter retreat at his monastery Longxiang si, a public monastery that was granted an imperial plaque in 1130. As the abbot of a public monastery, Wumen had no personal ties to the institution. He also could not expect his dharma heirs to succeed him. In fact, to have dharma heirs, he needed to impress and win over the talented Chan monks in his assembly, for it was up to them to decide whether or not they should declare Wumen their master when they later deliver their first public sermons as abbots. When Wumen prepared the material that became the *Gateless Barrier*, he did so for himself and to commemorate an event that took place in 1228; he did not do it for the monastery. The event was an integral part of the Chan cult of awakened abbot. Participants in the winter retreat were given privileged access to an enlightened being, Wumen, and his insights on *chan*.

The circumstances under which *Prose and Verse Comments* came into being were quite different. Hyesim was also the abbot of a grand Buddhist monastery, but it and its many branch monasteries belonged to Hyesim and his dharma heirs. Susŏn was not a public monastery. When Hyesim published his compendium, he did so for this network of monasteries and monks. The compendium was not meant to bear testimony to Hyesim's own greatness (though it certainly did) but instead to demonstrate to the monks who belonged to the network that their practice of observing the critical phrase was consistent and congruent with the *chan* practice of the various lineages of Chan. It was meant to serve as a tool for practicing extensive, not intensive learning.

Although the two *gong'an* commentary collections aspired to advance the practice of observing the critical phrase, they assumed different styles of learning. Hyesim's compendium adhered more closely to the style of learning that emerged during the Chan reading craze, which Chan master Fenyang Shanzhao regarded as an effective remedy for the problems inherent to learning *chan* from one master. *Prose and Verse Comments* assumed extensive learning. Wumen's collection, in contrast, adhered more closely to the style of learning—the unique style of intensive reading—advocated by Dahui. This, as Wumen makes clear in the prose commentary to the first *gong'an* of his collection, is best encapsulated by Zhaozhou's "Wu" or "No."

Despite these differences, both Hyesim and Wumen remained faithful to Dahui's vision of *chan*. As noted earlier, Dahui refused to separate *chan* from *dao* and *dao* from *chan*. In his preface to *Prose and Verse Comments*, Hyesim used this vision of *chan* to explain why it was necessary and also possible for him to publish the compendium:

> Those who obtain the origin or the source, even though they speak of it in different ways, have always hit the mark, and those who have not obtained this, even though they have eliminated words and have kept to that, have always been deluded. For this reason, the venerable elders from all over are not alienated from letters and not sparing of compassion, sometimes (using) examination, topics picked up for comment, substitute answers, separate answers, and verses or songs to display the profound tenets and to leave them to later people.[41]

Chan provided models, not ideas. Both Hyesim and Wumen therefore sought to make sure that old *chan* models like Zhaozhou's "Wu" continued to work properly. Both knew that, when these models worked ("hit the mark"), there was no longer any need to think that comprehension or awakening (i.e., *dao*) lies elsewhere. Only someone attached to ideas such as "ordinary mind is *dao*" and desperate to eliminate words would mistakenly think so.

Why did the early Chosŏn court make this specific type of observing the critical phrase the law of the land for Sŏn monks? The answer, not surprisingly, lies in Hyesim and his *Prose and Verse Comments*. Hyesim succeeded not only in building a network of monasteries under the control of Susŏn Monastery but also in developing a *gong'an* commentary compendium that could be employed as a universal tool for all monks within this network. This success, however, did not necessarily guarantee that the lineage established by his teacher Chinul would remain the primary beneficiary of everything that he accomplished. Indeed, in 1371, King Kongmin (r. 1351–1374) appointed his royal preceptor, Naong Hyegŭn

(1320–1376), abbot of Susŏn Monastery. Naong had no prior relation to the monastery, but Sŏn masters who received dharma transmission from him continued to serve as its abbots. After Naong, his disciples Muhak Chach'o (1327–1405) and Hwanam Honsu (1320–1392) served as abbots. Hwanam, who served for less than a year, was succeeded by his disciple Hyeam Sangch'ong (d.u.) in 1376.

On May 29, 1398, the same Hyeam submitted a letter to the new king, Yi Sŏnggye (1335–1408).[42] Yi had just founded the new Chosŏn dynasty in 1392. As the chief monastic officer of the late queen's memorial monastery Hŭngch'ŏn sa, Hyeam could wield much influence at court. He decided to put this political clout to good use. As the court continued to debate the fate of state-recognized monasteries, Hyeam wanted to make sure that the attempted reform was done properly. He recommended the division of the *saṃgha* into Sŏn and Kyo. Sŏn monks, he claimed, should specialize in Hyesim's *Prose and Verse Comments* and *Transmission of the Lamp*. Kyo monks should continue to focus on the words of the Buddha (i.e., *sūtras*) and authoritative Buddhist commentaries. Hyeam also urged the king to have all prominent monasteries outside the capital follow the model of Susŏn and place themselves under the authority of a single head monastery and be subject to regular inspection and monitoring. This, according to Hyeam, would prevent any lapse or decline in monastic discipline and the *saṃgha*'s ability to meet its ritual obligations to the state. Not unexpectedly, Hyeam also urged the king to have all Korean monasteries study, practice, and permanently observe the monastic rules outlined by Chinul. He was referring, of course, to Chinul's *Admonitions to Beginning Students*. Hyeam's proposal was adopted. In 1485, it became law. Dahui's observing the critical phrase thus became synonymous with Sŏn Buddhist practice in Korea.

NOTES

1. For the code, see *Kyŏngguk taejŏn*, Reprint (Keijō: Chōsen Sōtokufu, Chūsūin, 1934). The code was first promulgated in 1471 but revised, enlarged, and republished in 1474 and again in 1485.

2. For a brief discussion of this reform effort, see Juhn Y. Ahn, *Buddhas and Ancestors: Religion and Wealth in Fourteenth-Century Korea* (Seattle: University of Washington Press, 2018), 46–48.

3. *Kyŏngguk taejŏn*, 296.

4. Another tradition known as Ch'ongnamjong, which seems to have been created by combining two earlier traditions known as Ch'ongjijong and Namsanjong, was also classified as Sŏn. We know close to nothing about these traditions.

5. For *Hyesim's Prose and Verse Comments*, see Dongguk taehaekkyo Ha'guk Pulgyo chŏnsŏ p'yŏnch'an wiwŏnhoe, ed., *Han'guk Pulgyo chŏnsŏ* (hereafter HPC) 5.1a–923a. For a partial English translation of this work, see Juhn Y. Ahn, trans., *Gongan Collections I*, Collected Works of Korean Buddhism, Vol. 7–1 (Seoul: Jogye Order of Korean Buddhism, 2012).

6. The recension of the *Prose and Verse Comments* that was preserved as part of the supplemental blocks of the Koryŏ Buddhist canon contains a total of 1,462 old cases. This is the recension currently extant. The other 337 cases were added later, but we do not know by whom or exactly when.

7. For more on the impact of the An Lushan and Huang Chao rebellions, see Nicholas Tackett, *The Destruction of the Medieval Chinese Aristocracy* (Cambridge, MA: Harvard University Asia Center, 2014). For their impact on Buddhism, see Stanley Weinstein, *Buddhism Under the T'ang* (New York: Cambridge University Press, 1987).

8. For a brief but useful explanation of the distinction between "intensive" and "extensive" reading, see Robert Darnton, "History of Reading," in *New Perspectives on Historical Writing*, ed. Peter Burke (University Park: Pennsylvania State University Press, 1991), 148. Although I refer to intensive and extensive reading here, I am not trying to imply that China experienced something like the "reading revolution" of eighteenth-century Europe.

9. For a more extensive discussion, see Juhn Y. Ahn, "Who Has the Last Word in Chan? Secrecy, Transmission, and Reading During the Northern Song Dynasty," *Journal of Chinese Religions* 37 (2009).

10. See Robert M. Gimello, "Mārga and Culture: Learning, Letters, and Liberation in Northern Sung Ch'an," in *Paths to Liberation: The Mārga and Its Transformations in Buddhist Thought*, ed. Robert E. Buswell, Jr., and Robert M. Gimello (Honolulu: University of Hawai'i Press, 1992), 371–437.

11. *Jingde Record* (T. 2076: 51.390a29–b1).

12. *Chanlin sengbaozhuan* (XZJ 137.455b1–2); *Linjian lu* (XZJ 148.631b5), and *Jingde Record* (T. 2076: 51.305a16–27).

13. *Chanlin sengbaozhuan* (XZJ 137.508b4–5).

14. *Linjian lu* (XZJ 148.635b1–2).

15. *Song gaoseng zhuan* (T. 2061: 50.785b1–2).

16. See Ahn, "Who Has the Last Word in Chan?"

17. This expression was most likely borrowed from a sermon by Huanglong Huinan's (1002–1069) dharma heir, Zhenjing Kewen (1025–1102), delivered at Puli chanyuan on Mount Dong; see the sermon in the *Guzunsu yulu* (XZJ 118.711b11–13) and the *Xu guzunsu yuyao* (XZJ 118.929b3–5).

18. The *Chanlin sengbao zhuan* (XZJ 137.539b12) attributes this reply to Huanglong Huinan's dharma heir, Rongqing Qingxuan (1027–1082). See also the *Rentian yanmu* (T. 2006: 48.310b13–14) and Rongqing's entry in the *Xu chuandeng lu* (T. 2077: 51.568c27).

19. This expression was most likely borrowed from the sermon by Zhenjing noted above (see n. 14).

20. *Linjian lu* (XZJ 148.588a9–16).

21. The character *chan* was used by the Chinese Buddhist traditions to denote a number of different things, for instance, the tradition or school of monks who claimed to have received mind-to-mind transmission and thus traced their lineages back

to Bodhidharma. When the character is used in this sense, I capitalize the romanized term ("Chan"). The same character was also used as part of a transliteration of the Sanskrit word *dhyāna*. During and after the Song dynasty, it was used as a convenient name for the unique style of locution and thought found in Chan *gong'an*. When the character is used in this sense, I italicize and lowercase ("*chan*").

22. In the Song, only those who were appointed abbots of public monasteries were considered dharma heirs. It was customary for the new abbot to declare his dharma master in his first public sermon. See Morten Schlütter, *How Zen Became Zen: The Dispute over Enlightenment and the Formation of Chan Buddhism in Song-Dynasty China* (Honolulu: University of Hawai'i Press, 2008), 65–69.

23. *Jianzhong Jingguo xudeng lu* (XZJ 136.184a4–5).

24. *Zongmen wuku* (T. 1998B: 47.948a).

25. *Zongmen wuku* (T. 1998B: 47.951c18–22).

26. *Yunan Zhenjing heshang xingzhuang* (XZJ 120.213ap11–12). Elsewhere, Jimmy Yu has complicated the scholarly portrayal of Caodong practice as a form of passivity, using language such as "dead ashes, withered trees, strips of white silk, and incense burners in old shrines." He shows that of all the high-profile Song masters at the time, it was Yuanwu Keqin, Dahui's own teacher, who consistently used this kind of language in a positive way to describe the process of meditative practice; see Jimmy Yu, "The Polemics of Passivity and Yuanwu's Usage of It," *Journal of Chinese Buddhist Studies* 36 (2023): 31–71.

27. *Dahui Pujue chanshi yulu* (T. 1998A: 47.885c4–5 & 25–28). For Zhenjiing's use of these expressions to attack silent illumination, see *Baofeng Yunan Zhenjing chanshi zhu Jinling Baoning yulu* (XZJ 118.745a8–13).

28. *Dahui Pujue chanshi yulu* (T. 1998A: 47.918b24).

29. *Dahui Pujue chanshi yulu* (T. 1998A: 47.921c5–13).

30. For more on Tamjin, see Juhn Y. Ahn, "Pure Rules and Public Monasteries in Korea," in *Approaches to Chan/Sŏn/Zen Studies: Chinese Chan Buddhism and Its Spread Throughout East Asia*, ed. Albert Welter, Steven Heine, and Jin Y. Park (Albany: State University of New York Press, 2022), 220–224.

31. Chŏng Sua, "Hyejo kuksa Tamjin kwa 'Chŏnginsu': Puk-Song Sŏnp'ung ŭi suyong kwa Koryŏ chunggi Sŏnjong ŭi puhŭng ŭl chungsimŭro," in *Hanguk sahak nonch'ong: Yi Ki-baek sŏngsaeng kohŭi kinyŏm*, vol. 1, ed. Yi Ki-baek sŏngsaeng kohŭi kinyŏmhoe (Seoul: Ilchogak, 1994), 618–619.

32. For more on this ritual, see Mario Poceski, "Chan Rituals of the Abbots' Ascending the Dharma Hall to Preach," in *Zen Ritual: Studies of Zen Theory in Practice* (New York: Oxford University Press, 2007), 83–112.

33. See Juhn Y. Ahn, "Have a Korean Lineage and Transmit a Chinese One Too: Lineage Practices in Seon Buddhism," *Journal of Chan Buddhism* 1 (2019): 201.

34. For Chinul's biographical sketch provided below, see Robert E. Buswell, Jr., trans., *The Collected Works of Chinul* (Honolulu: University of Hawai'i Press, 1983), 17–30.

35. For a superb English translation of this text, see Buswell, *The Collected Works of Chinul*, 238–261.

36. For a study of the age of military rule in Koryŏ Korea, see Edward J. Shultz, *Generals and Scholars: Military Rule in Medieval Korea* (Honolulu: University of Hawai'i Press, 2000).

37. For these letters, see John Jorgensen, trans., *Seon Dialogues*, Collected Works of Korean Buddhism, Vol. 8 (Seoul: Jogye Order of Korean Buddhism, 2012), 175–187.

38. Buswell, *The Collected Works of Chinul*, 135–139.

39. HPC 5.1a; see also Ahn, *Gongan Collections I*, 30. See Jimmy Yu's discussion of leishu in the introduction, pp. 19-20.

40. For more on the *Essence of Succession in the Chan School*, see Ishii Shudo, "Kung-an Ch'an and the Tsung-men t'ung-yao chi," trans. Albert Welter, in *The Kōan: Texts and Contexts in Zen Buddhism*, ed. Steven Heine and Dale S. Wright (New York: Oxford University Press, 2000). Yanagida Seizan pointed out the similarity between Hyesim's text and the *Essence of Succession in the Chan School*; see Yanagida, "Zenseki kaidai," in *Zenke goroku*, vol. 2, ed. Nishitani Keiji and Yanagida Seizan (Tokyo: Chikuma shobō, 1974), 509.

41. Ahn, *Gongan Collections I*, 28–29.

42. For the following account of Hyeam, see Ahn, "Pure Rules and Public Monasteries in Korea," 215–217.

[8]

FROM SECRECY TO OPENNESS

THE *GATELESS BARRIER* IN PREMODERN JAPANESE ZEN

Marta Sanvido

T HIS CHAPTER illustrates the arrival and dissemination of the *Gateless Barrier* in relation to the evolution of Japanese Zen from the thirteenth to the eighteenth century. During this time, Zen groups underwent significant changes that reflected how Buddhist communities adapted and responded to different historical and social circumstances. Initially, the transmission of the *Gateless Barrier* occurred in the context of the medieval culture of secrecy, which was characterized by distinct *kōan* interpretative styles representative of each Zen faction. Through the late sixteenth century, the *Gateless Barrier* was read outside Zen groups, as attested by the allusion to *kōan* displayed in Japanese comic theater (*kyōgen*) plays. When secrecy became obsolete around the end of the seventeenth century, religious texts such as the *Gateless Barrier* started circulating widely, reaching even laywomen. Accordingly, the *Gateless Barrier* followed the evolution of medieval and early modern Japanese Buddhism from a strong culture of secrecy to the large dissemination of Buddhist notions among the lay population, especially women. By casting light on the overarching evolution of the *Gateless Barrier*, the present chapter investigates the social, cultural, and religious function of *kōan* against the backdrop of the history of Buddhism in Japan. In addition, this chapter highlights the different usages of *kōan* according to readership and historical moment, revealing how the understanding of *kōan* may be seen as a projection of larger tendencies and concerns within the transmission of Zen and Buddhist teachings.

The transmission of Zen in Japan is traditionally dated back to the monk Myōan Eisai (alt., Yōsai, 1141–1215), who introduced Chinese Song dynasty Chan in the archipelago and established the Rinzai school. A few years after Eisai, another pivotal figure joined the stage of the Japanese religious landscape, Dōgen (1200–1253), the founder of Sōtō Zen. Rinzai and Sōtō are usually considered emblematic examples of the new Buddhism movements (*Shin bukkyō*, also known as Kamakura Buddhism) characterized by alternative paths toward salvation.[1] Nevertheless, these new movements originated within preexisting Buddhist schools such as the Tendai group,[2] wherein both Eisai and Dōgen began their monastic career. Therefore, Zen's practice and teachings presented from the very beginning an interesting combination of local components and traces of continental Zen, visible in the transmission and adaptation of *kōans* imported from China.

By the mid-fourteenth century, Japanese Zen had gained considerable favor among the ruling elite. Less than one century later, hundreds of Rinzai and Sōtō monasteries had been established throughout the country, confirming the exponential growth of Zen communities.[3] Scholars have distinguished between Sōtō and Rinzai monasteries known as Rinka (beneath the grove) vis-à-vis Sōrin (the grove), represented by the Gozan (the Five Mountains) Zen temples, based on the location and institutional status of Zen temples in medieval Japan. While Rinka includes Zen temples not pertaining to the Gozan ranking system and mainly located in rural areas, the categorization of Sōrin only applies to the Gozan monasteries, and their affiliates situated in the capital or centers of power.[4] In spite of this taxonomy, the boundaries between the groups were oftentimes more blurred. It was not unusual to move from one lineage to another to follow one's inclinations or aspirations to study with famous masters. Accordingly, medieval Zen monks were encouraged to spend time in Gozan monasteries to achieve a good level of literacy and then transferred to other factions belonging to Rinzai and Sōtō groups. In other words, monastic education was not dissimilar from present-day universities.

Starting in the fourteenth century, *kōan* became the common ground of interaction between these lineages. The arising of different hermeneutical styles, the readaptation of motifs used by competing groups, and the inclusion of local knowledge were only a few of the many strategies formulated by Zen communities to develop their own *kōan* training style. This became particularly important for Sōtō and Rinzai temples, which used secret *kōan* knowledge to attract new practitioners and patrons. In the case of Gozan Zen, however, considerable efforts were directed to the study of Chinese poetry, as well as Chinese classic texts from the

Confucian and divinatory traditions. The widespread interest in *kōan* displayed by Rinka monks generated harsh criticism among the well-educated Gozan clergy. Gozan teachers such as the famous master Musō Soseki (1275–1351) critically noted that Japanese Zen monks of the Rinka system would collect sayings of Zen masters only to provide the right responses to *kōan* interviews. Rather than mechanically repeating words ascribed to the masters of the past, Musō was instead convinced that Zen monks should focus on how to read and interpret Chinese classics and Zen texts.[5] These intense debates over *kōan* corroborate the centrality of this practice during the early stages of Zen development, uncovering the historical dynamics surrounding the arrival of the *Gateless Barrier* in the archipelago.

THE TRANSMISSION OF THE GATELESS BARRIER IN JAPAN

The *Gateless Barrier* arrived in Japan through the Zen monk Muhon Kakushin (1207–1298). After spending time studying with several Zen masters in Japan, Kakushin embarked for China in 1249. Although he initially intended to practice under Wuzhun Shifan (1177–1249)—who, by the time he arrived, was no longer alive—Kakushin decided to stay with Wumen Huikai (1183–1260), the compiler and commentator of the *Gateless Barrier*. It was Wumen who donated Kakushin the *Gateless Barrier* along with other Chan texts to bring back to Japan.[6] The centrality of the *Gateless Barrier* in Kakushin's experience is stated in his biographic record reported in the first history of Buddhism in Japan, the *Genkō-Era Biographies of Eminent Monks* (*Genkō Shakusho*). Here, the author, the Zen monk Kokan Shiren (1278–1347), highlights a specific teaching in the monastic training received by Kakushin, the *kōan* of Zhaozhou's dog, which opens the *Gateless Barrier*.[7]

Following his predecessors, Kakushin's approach to Zen teachings resembles Eisai's, presenting a combination of Zen with esoteric Buddhism as well as Pure Land practices. Nevertheless, his doctrinal view hinges clearly on Zen and lacks any systematic attempt to theorize the combination of Zen with other teachings.[8] This is particularly evident in his *Dharma Words* (J. *Hōtō kakushi hōgo*), a collection of his sayings on different topics ranging from Buddhist cardinal concepts to *kōan* and meditation. On the practice of *kōan*, Kakushin comments, "Whatever doubts we have that cannot be known in our own minds are made clear by these *kōans*. If, while sitting in meditation, we do not seize a *kōan*, we are like a blind man who has lost his staff and cannot proceed a single step. It is also said that a person should practice *kōan* meditation three times during the day and three times during the night. It is like living with an enemy who has entered one's house. Do not relax your hold on your mind."[9] Here, *kōan* is seen as a practice through which the practitioner focuses their mind, integrally part of their daily monastic life. Most interestingly, *kōan* practice is paired with sitting meditation. Kakushin reiterates the centrality of sitting meditation because through meditation, one can "destroy within a single moment of thought countless crimes and come to know intimately one's own nature."[10] This confirms how *kōan* and meditation coexisted within medieval Zen training.

Upon its transmission in Japan, the *Gateless Barrier* drew attention for its connection with Kakushin, who at the time was a prominent exponent of Zen. The first attested printed edition of this work was made in 1291 by the Gozan monks who, in medieval Japan, would use wood-block printing to make copies of Chan texts and Chinese classics. However, the *Gateless Barrier* was reprinted only once after the first edition, in 1405, suggesting that it took a while for Zen monks to include consistently this collection of *kōans* in their curriculum. Although there is not sufficient historical evidence to explain this century of relative silence, the presence of other famous *kōan* collections such as the *Blue Cliff Record* (J. *Hekigan roku*) might have delayed the dissemination of the *Gateless Barrier* among Zen communities, which preferred commenting on more widely known works.[11]

SECRECY AND *KŌAN*: THE COMMENTARIAL CULTURE OF *KŌAN* IN MEDIEVAL JAPAN

Starting in the eleventh century, Japanese society witnessed the progressive growth of secrecy among Buddhist monks as well as within other fields of knowledge. The "culture of secrecy" in Japanese society cut across any distinctions of religious affiliation, localization, and social status, especially in Buddhist circles.[12] One of the sociocultural aspects that favored this dissemination was the Buddhist schools' organization into lineages and small groups (*ryū* or *ha*, lit., streams or cliques).[13] In the modern Japanese language, *shū* (school) is commonly used to indicate Buddhist schools, such as Sōtō-shū or Rinzai-shū. However, the term was far less common in the premodern period.[14] During the medieval period, Rinka lineages existed as relatively independent groups that developed different techniques to read and transmit *kōans* by adopting secrecy. Starting in the seventeenth century, each lineage had to develop a standard curriculum to train their acolytes. Slowly but steadily emerged the idea of a "school" composed of individuals committed to the same view regarding, for instance, their founder's teaching, or the doctrinal hallmarks of the group. For instance, Sōtō Zen monks rediscovered their founder, Dōgen, whose insights had been rather marginal during the late medieval period. Consequently, the centrality of *kōan* was progressively replaced by the study of Dōgen's writings, such as the *Treasury of the True Dharma Eye* (J. *Shōbōgenzō*).[15]

In this context, secrecy contributed to enhancing the doctrinal and soteriological peculiarities of each group, allowing the emergence of unique traits that in some cases are traceable in the extant secret texts. Nevertheless, we should not mistake secrecy for lack of sociality. On the contrary, premodern secrecy, especially in Zen, hinged on the creation of ties with other religious groups, as well as the mobility of monks and laypeople who would travel to different centers (and peripheries) home to other communities to learn teachings and rituals.

Both the Rinzai and Sōtō lineages fully embraced the Japanese culture of secrecy. Despite different hermeneutical methodologies, they had a common ground of secret exchange: commenting on *kōans*. *Kōan* collections and Buddhist scriptures were at the center of commentarial networks, which reveal that these sources were handed down from a master to his disciples, displaying the education and religious curriculum at the core of Zen communities, with a considerable variety of secret sources:[16]

- commentaries on lectures about *kōans*, in which a master presented to the assembly his interpretation of famous *kōan* collections or sayings by masters of the past (J. *gorokushō* or *kikigakishō*);
- manuals containing the teacher's correct answers to *kōans*. Usually the master would ask a question about a *kōan* or a theme and provide the correct answer when the student failed to respond to his examination (J. *daigo*);
- secret *kōan* commentaries exchanged between the master and his disciples (J. *monsan* or *missan*);[17]
- secret paper strips reporting the interpretation of a *kōan* as well as several ritual instructions (J. *kirigami*).[18]

Although *kōan* is only one of the many topics covered, it is undoubtedly one of the most common. Indeed, scholars have labeled premodern

Zen as "*kōan* Zen" due to the prominence given to *kōan* in the monastic education.[19]

Secret manuals such as *monsan* or *missan* often contain standardized ways to respond to questions about a *kōan*. The correct interpretation of a *kōan* was often measured by the ability to provide the apt answer, known as a capping phrase (J. *jakugo* or *agyo*). This would entail verbatim quotation from Chan classic literature, demanding that the student report the words of famous masters of the past. Although many secret texts hinged on the Chan repertoire, leaving little space for improvisation or creativity, *kōan* practice required a vast understanding and acquisition of the Chan/Zen textual corpus. Accordingly, Japanese Zen monks produced a genre of handbooks known as Zen phrase books (J. *kushū*), manuals containing collections of capping phrases, to facilitate the memorization of these formulae.[20] Indeed, students were required to practice a limited number of *kōans* and learn a set of capping phrases, thus reducing significantly the number of notions and texts to be studied and memorized during the monastic training.[21] Regardless of their affiliation, students would meet several times with their master to practice the question-and-answer format (J. *mondō*). These interviews produced secret *kōan* commentaries recorded by the student and treasured as a proof of the lineage's cultural capital they inherited.[22] In other words, secret *kōan* manuals recorded the gatherings that took place between the master and a limited number of acolytes elected as his dharma heirs. These manuals vary in length, yet the format is quite standard. Each paragraph opens with a title identifying the *kōan*, followed by questions and answers. The questions might be about certain terms used in the *kōan*, whereas the answers provide analogous capping phrases supplementing the terminology in the *kōan* along with a gloss explaining the capping phrase.[23]

For instance, the famous Rinzai Zen master and founder of the Rinzai temple Daitokuji in Kyoto, Daitō Kokushi (alt., Shūhō Myōchō, 1283–1338), compiled the *One Hundred Twenty Cases* (J. *Hyakunijussoku*) containing his capping phrases for *kōans* from both the *Blue Cliff Record* and the *Gateless Barrier*. In the *One Hundred Twenty Cases*, Daitō comments on case 1 of the *Gateless Barrier*: A monk asked Zhaozhou, "Does a dog have buddha nature or not?" Zhaozhou said, "*Wu!*" (see p. 251). Daitō's gloss of this episode reads as follows:

A monk asked Zhaozhou,
"Does a dog have buddha-nature or not?"
His tongue is already long.

Zhaozhou said, "Wu."
To buy iron and receive gold.
Completely fills emptiness.
To throw a holeless iron hammer head right at him.[24]

The lines in italics are Daitō's capping phrases. The connection between these expressions and the *kōan* is not evident at first glance. The initial question is commented on with "his tongue is already long," which refers to the dualistic manner in which the question is formulated. The answer to this poorly worded question is brilliant. The Zen master replies "*Wu*" (J. *Mu*), which means "no" or "nothing." In other words, the response is "to buy iron and receive gold," which indicates a very profound answer given to a silly question. The next phrase, "completely fills emptiness," complements the answer "Mu." From the enlightened perspective, void and form are not distinct, yet they are one and the same; thus emptiness is form and form is emptiness. The section concludes with, "to throw a holeless iron hammer head right at him." This is an oxymoronic metaphor. A holeless hammer lacks the place to stick the handle, thus it cannot be wielded and used normally. Likewise, "*Mu*" cannot be grasped by discriminatory thinking, requiring us to go beyond the dualistic thinking implied by the initial question.[25]

This example is particularly illuminating for several reasons. First it showcases the methods of *kōan* interpretation at the foundation of many secret texts. Daitō's capping phrases hinge on intertextual references that establish implicit ties with the masters of the past and their teachings. Second, it highlights the multiple layers of meaning composing a *kōan*. These layers are evoked by the capping phrases, yet they are never totally explicit. It was part of monastic training to penetrate each of these expressions in relation to the examined *kōan*, and if possible, to follow the master's footsteps in the method for reading it.

Although Daitō's *One Hundred Twenty Cases* reflects a widely accepted adoption of capping phrases to read *kōans* in both Rinzai and Sōtō communities, other hermeneutical strategies emerged during the late medieval period, revealing that *kōan* interpretation changed over time. An emblematic example of this sort is the Genjū stream, a Rinzai-Gozan Zen faction established during the fourteenth century. Genjū's approach to *kōan* introduced several innovations in the repertoire of capping phrases. Their commentarial style certainly echoes many of the characteristics of Daitō's *One Hundred Twenty Cases*, such as commenting on each expression of the *kōan* by quoting the capping phrases borrowed from the Chan corpus; however, Genjū monks expanded their symbolic and literary references to interpret *kōans* by borrowing from outside the Chan/Zen textual corpus. The incorporation of embryological theories that employ gestational metaphors to explain the spiritual progression of practitioners toward buddhahood is an example. These theories, which originated from esoteric Buddhist schools, gained prominence during the medieval era and were embraced by various religious groups.[26] In simple terms, buddhahood was likened to the state of a fetus inside the womb, representing a condition of predualism and unity. The gloss to case 5 of the *Gateless Barrier* exemplifies some of these innovative characteristics:

> Master Xiangyan said, "It is like a man being up in a tree hanging on to a branch by his teeth, with his hands and feet not touching the tree branches at all. Beneath the tree there is someone who asks about the meaning of [Bodhidharma] coming from the West. If this man does not reply, he is evading the questioner's question. If he does reply, he perishes. At such a moment, how could he answer?" (see p. 254)

Case 5 presents the impossible scenario in which a man hanging on to a tree branch has to answer the question about the meaning of the first Chan ancestor, Bodhidharma, coming from the West, which symbolizes the innermost sense of Zen transmission. However, when replying, he will die immediately by opening his mouth, as his teeth are clenched on the branch. If he stays quiet and waits, he is not facing the question, ignoring the deepest meaning of Zen. The metaphor of the man up in a tree, unable to speak, and forced to choose between life and death thus conveys the attachment to words and discriminating thoughts. In the story, the man is encouraged to let go of any dualistic ways of thinking between knowing and not knowing, good and bad, right and wrong.

Genjū's secret *kōan* manuals give the following interpretation of case 5:

> **Main case:** The Chan Master Xiangyan . . . , addressing the community, said: "How about the man up a tree?"
> **Xuedou replied:** "Up the tree, easy to say; below the tree, hard to say."
> **The master asked:** "The tree, what is it?"
> **Explanation:** "The tree is the mother's body."
> **Commentary:** "A rootless tree on a rock."
> "What does 'up a tree' mean?"
> **Explanation:** "*He hangs to the branch* with his teeth means that he sucks the root of milk in the womb. *His hands cannot grasp the branch*

means that his hands are placed against his chest. *His feet cannot touch the trunk* means that his legs are folded when he faces his mother."

Commentary: "During nine years facing the wall,[27] his mouth is like that of a dumb person. During these nine years facing the wall, not a breath of wind has passed, yet the five petals have opened, flowers have scattered, and outside spring has come."

Explanation: The nine years spent facing the wall are the nine months within the womb, with the placenta. The fact that Bodhidharma, while facing the wall, wears his red robe over his head symbolizes the placenta.[28]

The focal point of the commentary revolves around the interpretation of Bodhidharma using gestational elements. In the *Gateless Barrier*, the monk asks the man the meaning of Bodhidharma coming from the West. Genjū's commentary builds upon the traditional depiction of Bodhidharma meditating for nine years and draws a parallel between these nine years and the nine months of gestation in the womb. To reinforce this connection, the commentary introduces the imagery of Bodhidharma's robe as a metaphorical placenta. Just as the placenta provides protection to the fetus, the monastic robe serves a similar protective function. By making this association, the commentary equates the monk wearing the monastic robe with the fetus inside the mother's belly. Consequently, during the monk's journey, the robe symbolizes protection, and the monastery becomes the nurturing womb where the attainment of buddhahood is revealed.[29]

Additionally, the embryological symbolism serves to elucidate the dilemma presented in case 5 of the *Gateless Barrier*: whether or not the man should respond to the question regarding the meaning of Bodhidharma's coming from the West. The answer is literally embodied in the figure of the Bodhidharma-embryo. Bodhidharma, during his nine-year meditation inside the cave-womb, remained silent, not uttering a single word. However, as a result the five schools of Chan flourished ("the five petals have opened"), and his teachings proliferated in all directions. In essence, Genjū's interpretation urges practitioners not to fixate on whether to respond. Instead, they are encouraged to direct their minds toward the state of predualism that transcends the dichotomies expressed through language. Thus, in line with these associations, the fifth case symbolizes the journey that commences with the initial steps into monastic life and culminates in the realization of buddhahood. When the practitioner grasps and embraces this predualistic reality—resembling the state of unity inside the womb—they will be able to go beyond the impasse of answering or not answering the question.

In Sōtō Zen, *kōan* interpretations were also transmitted as single documents reporting the explanation about one single *kōan*, oftentimes linking the specific *kōan* to a ritual. Although it is not clear why certain *kōan* were given particular attention and handed down separately, some cases from the *Gateless Barrier* circulated as secret paper strips (J. *kirigami*). Sōtō Zen secret paper strips about case 5 dated around the beginning of the seventeenth century resemble the interpretation found in the Genjū line. The similarities between the two groups should not be surprising. Not only had several Genjū monks been trained by Sōtō Zen masters, but the two factions were also notoriously closed during the early days of Genjū development, around the fifteenth century. This geographic and intellectual proximity is evident from the hermeneutical affinities found in *kōan* exegesis. In both groups, case 5 came to designate the experience of the practitioner inside the monastery, from the bestowal of the robe to the awakening. However, the symbolism adopted to express this process derived from other Buddhist traditions such as esoteric Buddhism. The combination of Zen and esoteric Buddhism in the interpretation of case 5 sheds light on many typical aspects of medieval Zen. In addition to being characterized by secrecy, medieval Zen, as well as *kōan* exegesis, combined the Chan textual corpus developed in China with religious tendencies originating within Japanese Buddhism. Accordingly, Zen incorporated teachings from other groups, showing the porosity of the factional boundaries as well as the mobility of ideas.

In sum, secret manuals produced during the medieval years showcase different styles for reading and integrating *kōans* within monastic life. Although commenting on *kōans* was initially a way to show one's knowledge of Chan tropes and texts, during the late medieval period, *kōan* hermeneutics disclosed the regional growth of Zen groups and their interactions with other Buddhist teachings that emerged in loco. As a result, the methods of reading and understanding *kōans* came to reflect social networks and the ability of Zen monks to adapt and reshape doctrines outside Zen.

THE *GATELESS BARRIER* BEYOND ZEN: *KŌAN* AND SATIRE IN *KYŌGEN* THEATER

During the medieval period, the *Gateless Barrier* predominantly circulated among the Rinka monks, as attested by the several secret commentaries produced during this time. Nevertheless, this collection of *kōan* seems to have had extended influence beyond Zen circles. Buddhist ideas played a crucial role in several fields of knowledge, including theater and literature. One example is in *kyōgen* (lit., mad words), a form of Japanese theater characterized by parodic tones performed during the interludes of Noh plays. Oftentimes, *kyōgen* pieces satirically portray Buddhist monks or religious rituals, offering an alternative viewpoint on how the Buddhist clergy was perceived.

The *kyōgen* play *The Monk's Staff* (J. *Shujō*) showcases how the *Gateless Barrier* was readapted to different contexts outside the cloister walls. This work narrates the story of an unnamed monk who travels to Kyoto to collect a lacquered walking staff he ordered from an artisan. When the monk meets the artisan, the two begin a *mondō*—that is, a typical interaction between master and disciple used in Zen and based on a series of questions and answers on a *kōan*—regarding the meaning of the staff.[30]

Although Zen has been considered traditionally reluctant to rely on materiality,[31] modest objects that were part of the monastic life synecdochically assume profound significance, being featured in Chan/Zen writings and *kōans*. Likewise, the walking staff held great significance in the daily lives of Zen monks, acquiring a multitude of meanings. It symbolized the journey toward enlightenment, represented the authority of the clergy, and ultimately signified the attainment of awakening. Revealingly, the founder of Sōtō Zen in Japan, the Zen monk Dōgen, defines the staff as follows: "The traveling staff is a *sūtra* offering free expression to the dharma in every conceivable way by spontaneously breaking up 'emptiness' and 'existence.'"[32] In this excerpt, the staff is akin to a *sūtra* capable of preaching and breaking up the meaning of emptiness and existence. In other words, it was not merely a walking aid; rather, this kind of object embodied several layers of symbolic meaning that evoked Zen masters' teachings in Zen texts.

In the play *The Monk's Staff*, the *mondō* between the artisan and the Buddhist monk is fueled by the discontent of the priest. In fact, the staff looks poorly crafted and still white—the natural color of the wood used—since it has not been properly lacquered. Baffled by the monk's discontent, the artisan asks to have one word with him and inquires why the staff seems unfinished. The monk replies, "Without lacquer, it remains unpainted." He then strikes the artisan's nose. Although this gesture might have been perceived as humiliating, the craftsman honestly recognizes that he has been negligent in his work,[33] impressing the monk with his humble behavior. The artisan promptly responds with another question,

"What will the monk do when the staff is broken?" The monk replies, "When one thought ends, another thought arises."[34]

This short dialogue includes numerous allusions to Zen/Chan literature, which must have struck a chord with the contemporary audience. First, the act of striking the nose derives from a famous Chan expression, "to strike the nose" (C. *zhuzhao bikong*). This formula indicates either the literal act performed by the master to awaken the disciple to their inherent buddha nature or a metaphor illustrating how the master uses language to disrupt his disciple's habitual patterns of deluded thinking.[35] Second, the dialogue between the two resembles case 44 in the *Gateless Barrier*: "Venerable Bajiao taught the assembly, 'If you have a staff, I will give you a staff. If you have no staff, I will take your staff away'" (see p. 280).

Case 44 reports the words of the Korean-born master Bajiao Huiqing (tenth century), known for having trained several disciples. The staff here represents the ultimate attainment and the role played by the master within the process of realization. Is awakening the conclusion of the learning path? Is awakening even the final goal? Is it something that can be possessed as if it were an object? While the students might expect the master to give them answers and teach them the way to awakening, the master instead gives the student what they already have or takes from them what they do not possess. Therefore, not only is the path to realization endless, but also there is no straightforward means or secret formula the master gives students in order to reach it.

In a commentary to the *Gateless Barrier* printed at the beginning of the seventeenth century (the *Mumonkan shō*), the staff in the case of Bajiao's staff expresses the dharma body and breaks through the endless illusions. Besides, this commentary adds, every human being is endowed with the staff—that is, buddhahood—yet they continue mistakenly searching for it outside themselves.[36] "Bajiao's staff" hinges on the classic Chan trope of having and lacking, which poses a frustrating dilemma to the Zen student. Likewise, in the *kyōgen* play *The Monk's Staff*, the monk draws on this same dichotomy and, when asked why the staff is unfinished, replies that without the lacquer, it remains unpainted. Yet the artisan's nose tip was stained with lacquer grease, so where is this lacquer? The monk's reply is reinforced by the gesture of rubbing the grease off the artisan's nose. This scene clearly echoes Bajiao's phrase in the *Gateless Barrier* and the dichotomy of having and not having. The artisan firmly believed that he lacked the lacquer to paint the staff, but the trace of color left on his nose indicated otherwise. As Bajiao expressed, "If you claim to have no staff, I will take away your staff." In this context, the artisan represents the deluded individual who believes that awakening can be possessed or even lost, while the monk, through the act of striking the nose, demonstrates that awakening transcends such dualistic thinking. The *mondō* between the two continues with the second question. The craftsman's question, "What will the monk do when the staff is broken?" implies a second, "What should I do when awakening falls apart?" The monk's answer introduces the concept of "one thought" (*ichinen*), which refers to the single unobstructed thought. In other words, when a person is truly focused and becomes one with realization, they should never be distracted by the deluded concern about losing awakening, since there is nothing to possess, and awakening is the natural state of beings rather than a condition to achieve.

In this short story, the staff creates the occasion that makes possible the encounter between the master and the craftsman. Yet this object is also the means that encourages the artisan to leave everything and become a monk. After the *mondō*, the man decides to follow the monk around the country to practice and preach the Buddhist teachings. Confident that the man has received his family's blessing, the monk agrees to take him along, shaves his head, and dresses him in a robe. When the artisan's wife discovers that her husband is about to leave his family, she becomes outraged that he has become a monk without her permission and angrily pulls him away. The man, in an attempt to escape, lies and claims that the monk forcibly shaved his head, and the wife wrestles the monk to the ground.

The Monk's Staff cleverly employs the enigmatic language of Chan and *kōans* to create a parody of the Buddhist clergy and its obscure teachings. The play revolves around an artisan who becomes captivated by the monk's inexplicable words and mesmerizing gestures, leading him to abandon his lay life and join the clergy. However, the comedic twist comes when his wife, depicted as a faithless and furious woman, takes matters into her own hands and restores order in the household by beating the monk. The intriguing exchange between the monk and the artisan, filled with allusions to complex Buddhist concepts and *kōans*, clashes amusingly with the practical and worldly minded nature of the wife, who finds herself in a comical battle with a Buddhist monk to keep her husband. This contrast generates a humorous effect, caricaturing the literary trope often found in the biographies of eminent monks, depicting renowned Buddhist figures leaving their families to embrace the priesthood. Although such actions are usually regarded as acts of devotion, in *kyōgen*, they are presented as grotesque and funny, evoking hilarity in the audience.

What is noteworthy about *The Monk's Staff* is the usage made of *kōan* language and its allusion to the *Gateless Barrier*. This implicit caricaturization of *kōan* highlights the widespread perception that Chan/Zen teachings were often seen as arcane and esoteric. However, it also suggests that the playwright and presumably the audience were familiar with *kōan* collections and the Zen practice of dialogic interaction known as *mondō*. Thus, in *The Monk's Staff*, the *Gateless Barrier* is reimagined to serve the parodical purpose characteristic of *kyōgen*. In other words, the inclusion of Zen texts in this context implies that *kōans* were not limited to the confines of the monastic setting. These collections had a broader reach and were known well beyond the boundaries of the Buddhist world.

KŌAN FOR EVERYONE: THE *GATELESS BARRIER* AND WOMEN IN EARLY MODERN JAPAN

The dissemination of Buddhist concepts and scriptures changed dramatically during the Edo period, significantly impacting the transmission of *kōan* collections such as the *Gateless Barrier*. This change was influenced by two major factors. The advancement of printing techniques made Buddhist ideas more accessible to a wider audience, and the reformation of Buddhist schools mandated by the Tokugawa *bakufu* brought about major alterations in the monastic learning curriculum, resulting in the progressive abandonment of secret manuals.[37] These transformations opened up access to Buddhist texts and concepts for individuals who had previously been marginalized by the tradition, including women.[38]

Little is known about the extent to which women had access to doctrinal texts and knowledge of *kōan* interpretation prior to the Edo period. There are scattered references suggesting that monks at the Rinzai temple Daitokuji imparted *kōan* teachings to nuns, but the secret *kōan* manuals produced during the medieval period were predominantly reserved for male monastics. As a result, tracing the study of *kōan* among women before the seventeenth century is a challenging task, further complicated by the scarcity of sources. Nevertheless, beginning with the seventeenth century, the large dissemination of printed books of every genre, including religious scriptures and texts, reached individuals who had hitherto been denied access. One of the most intriguing examples is Tachibana no Someko (1667–1705). Tachibana was not only interested in *kōan* but also compiled her own commentary on the *Gateless Barrier*. Tachibana's interpretation highlights the spread of *kōans* among lay individuals and is one

of the few instances of the voices of women in the interpretation of Chan/
Zen teachings from pre-nineteenth century Japan.

Tachibana was the consort of a local warrior, Yanagisawa Yoshiyasu
(1658–1714). She grew up reciting the name of the Bodhisattva Amida (the
nenbutsu recitation) and learning the teachings of the Pure Land tradition. However, at an early age, after losing three of her four children,
Tachibana sought spiritual refuge in Zen practice and began to attend sermons at a nearby temple, the Ryūkōji, with master Ungan (d.u.). Her
interest in Zen was probably encouraged by her husband. Yoshiasu, in his
twenties, spent a period practicing Zen at the same temple, where he met
several Zen masters. Tachibana elaborated her Buddhist faith and view in
her miscellany, the *Wastepaper Record* (J. *Koshiroku*, early eighteenth century), where she explores her Buddhist journey from childhood to the
seal of awakening acknowledged by her master Ungan. According to this
memoir, throughout her life, Tachibana had access to a variety of Buddhist
approaches. After marrying, she became closer with the Shingon Ritsu
master Jōgon (1639–1702), yet Tachibana did not agree with his teachings—
especially the idea that women could not achieve buddhahood—and
eventually abandoned the idea of studying Shingon Buddhism. It was her
husband who, after the loss of their children and symptoms of her
depression, encouraged Tachibana to practice Zen. During the first meeting with Ungan, she was introduced to *kōan* when the master asked her,
"Shaka and Maitreya are their servants. Who is this person [they serve]?"[39]
From that moment, Tachibana practiced diligently with Ungan, becoming knowledgeable about the *kōan* corpus. After one year, she was sufficiently prepared to provide her answer for this *kōan*: "The matter of birth
and death is great; Impermanence is swift."[40] She followed this with a comment about the practice of *kōan*, which, according to Tachibana, became
part of her everyday life; even during sleep, her mind was completely
devoted to the meditation on *kōan*.[41]

The *Wastepaper Record* provides an insightful depiction of women's
lives during the eighteenth century, revealing how Buddhism was ingrained
as part of their lived experience. For instance, Tachibana recalls one of her
first memories about how Buddhism shaped her understanding of death
and the afterlife. Around the age of eight, she heard for the first time the
story of Emperor Daigo (885–930), who was cast into hell for condemning
the famous poet Sugawara no Michizane (845–903).[42] Appalled that even
rulers could be reborn in hell, Tachibana comments on this episode wondering what kind of suffering would come to people like her, lower in rank

compared to the emperor, who committed innumerable sins throughout their lives.[43] One year later, at the age of nine, Tachibana lost of her mother. She was fearful of death and preoccupied with future rebirths in a conversation with her father, asking, "Could human beings ever escape the sufferings of hell by pursuing good actions?" He told his daughter that the only thing she could do was to recite the name of the Buddha Amida in her heart.[44]

Tachibana's experience is especially valuable for grasping the complex relationship among practice, monasticism, and women. Although as an already married woman she could not become a nun, in the *Wastepaper Record*, she reveals the support she gave both her husband and Ungan. Tachibana's story offers a glimpse into the lived experience of women and their relationship with Buddhism. While the majority of texts speak for the experience of male monastics, the writings left by Tachibana reveal how, in favorable circumstances, women could also find their space and personal growth within the Buddhist universe. In addition to the *Wastepaper Record*, a commentary on the *Gateless Barrier* entitled the *Bird's False Cry* (J. *Tori no sorane*) casts light on her approach to *kōan* practice.[45] The style used in this work differs from the aforementioned secret *kōan* manuals exchanged during the medieval period among Zen monks. Tachibana mixes religious and Japanese literary sources, relying on this uncommon combination to express her viewpoint on the *Gateless Barrier*, as well as on the female condition and salvation. The result is an eclectic juxtaposition of Japanese poetry (*waka*), quotations from Buddhist scriptures, and reflections on her personal experience.

Among her comments on forty-eight cases, Tachibana adds several reflections regarding female salvation. Case 9 is particularly detailed on these themes even though in the *Gateless Barrier* this *kōan* is not obviously linked to female buddhahood:

> A monk asked Master Rang of Xingyang, "The Buddha of Great Penetrating and Supreme Wisdom sat at the site of enlightenment for ten *kalpas*, but buddhadharma did not appear to him. How was it that he did not achieve the Buddha Way?" Master Rang replied, "This question is most appropriate." The monk said, "Since he sat at the site of enlightenment for ten eons, or *kalpas*, why did he not achieve the buddha path?" Rang said, "Because he did not." (see p. 257)

Tachibana uses the metaphor of a rough gem to express her understanding of awakening, drawing on the common symbolism of buddhahood as a gem.[46] In the first half of the commentary, she quotes a famous anecdote from the *Han Feizi*, the episode of Mr. He's jade. This story narrates that Mr. He found a piece of uncut jade in the mountains and decided to present it to King Li. The sovereign, however, ordered Mr. He's left foot cut off to punish the man for having fooled him. Mr. He did not desist and presented the same stone to King Li's successor, King Wu. Like his predecessor, King Wu was convinced that the gem was a worthless stone, and he ordered Mr. He's right foot cut off. To show his honesty, the man crawled to the foot of the mountain and wept over the stone for three days and nights until he cried blood tears. Hence the king sent someone to question the man. When asked why he wept over a mere stone, Mr. He replied, "I do not grieve because my feet have been cut off. I grieve because a precious jewel is dubbed a mere stone, and a man of integrity is called a deceiver."[47] The king then ordered that the stone be polished and soon discovered that it was in fact a precious jade.

Tachibana continues her disquisition by recalling another famous episode involving a gem, the parable of the Dragon Princess in the *Lotus Sūtra*.[48] The Dragon Princess is a creature of eight years old who, due to her gender and her species, cannot achieve buddhahood. In fact, as a woman she is obstructed by the five hindrances and three subordinates,[49] thus, theoretically, she cannot climb the ladder of Buddhist spiritual hierarchy and will always remain subordinate to men (i.e., her father, husband, and son). Nevertheless, against all odds, the Dragon Princess obtains the highest spiritual refinement and achieves buddhahood in the quickest time possible. The Buddha, upon witnessing her marvelous realization, acknowledges her enlightenment by accepting the precious pearl that the princess offers him. This episode is the most famous tale about female salvation in the history of Buddhism and has received much attention, especially in China and Japan. Its interpretation changed over time, swinging between exemplifying women's ability to attain buddhahood and reinforcing the patriarchal idea that women required male intervention to be saved.[50] The gem donated by the Dragon Princess symbolizes female awakening, suggesting that if a female dragon became a buddha, women in their very bodies should be allowed to do the same. Tachibana adds:

> Women are obstructed by the five hindrances, and in today's society and the monastic path, there are many obstacles such as the three subordinations; from [the years] of the childhood hair [you should listen to your parents],[51] then your eyebrows grow thick [when you become a wife], until your mouth deforms [and you depend upon your children], you realize that

not even your body belongs to your mind. Depicted like a vase, similar to a water lily [growing] in the distant mountains, resembling a plum blossom, on the inside, women's bodies hide solely defilement. Women spread clever words, fill [their mouths] with [delighted] laughs, and fool the dumb hearts: attractive appearance, mellifluous voice, deeply vindictive. [. . .]

Nevertheless, how is it even possible that a female creature who is not even a human being reached instantaneously the Southern Pure Land and helped innumerable people [to achieve awakening]? Given this quick way to disclose buddhahood, why then could the Buddha of Great Penetrating and Supreme Wisdom [. . .] after two, three, up to ten *kalpas* not manifest in front of him the buddhadharma? Was then [the Buddha of Great Penetrating and Supreme Wisdom] inferior to the light irradiated by the Dragon Princess's gem?[52]

This commentary displays two main characteristics of Tachibana's approach to *kōan*. First she focuses on one aspect of the *kōan* to connect it with themes from Buddhist scriptures. Tachibana highlights that the Buddha of Great Penetrating and Supreme Wisdom sat in meditation for more than ten *kalpas* and did not achieve awakening. She compares and contrasts the eternal time of practice carried out by the Buddha of Great Penetrating and Supreme Wisdom with the rapidity of the Dragon Princess, who, in the *Lotus Sūtra*, becomes a buddha in the blink of an eye. Second, Tachibana's view of practice is never detached from her personal experience. Here she equates women's enlightenment to an uncut gem considered worthless. The parable of the Dragon Princess reveals that whoever is capable of overcoming a gendered viewpoint on salvation will see the immense value of that gem. In addition, Tachibana reports some of the many preconceptions attached to women in early modern society— that they are deceitful, lustful, impure, etc.[53] In her gloss to case 9, she concludes that, given the bodhisattva's vow to be reborn in the triple world to save sentient beings, anyone should be able to achieve buddhahood in this life. In a similar vein, she reiterates the nonduality of awakening at the beginning of the *Bird's False Cry* where she writes that any living being has the potential to realize their buddha nature.

The story of Tachibana epitomizes many of the transformations that affected Japanese Buddhism during the seventeenth century, including the efforts to make Buddhist teachings accessible to the laity. One of the most renowned figures depicting these tendencies is the Rinzai monk Hakuin Ekaku (1686–1769). Although Tachibana's and Hakuin's paths supposedly never crossed, Hakuin's approach to *kōan* reveals his attempts to attract women to Zen practice.[54] In one of his letters, Hakuin praises one of the first Zen abbesses, Mugai Nyodai (1223–1298),[55] for her achievements within the Zen community.[56] When visiting Kyoto in 1751, Hakuin gave lectures in several temples and nunneries. In particular, his hall sermon on the *Blue Cliff Record* was attended by the fourth daughter of the Emperor Nakamikado (1702–1737), Princess Rishū (1725–1764), who served as abbess of the Hōkyōji in Kyoto.[57] Accordingly, Hakuin established close ties with aristocratic female devotees, also teaching *kōan* to the female audience. Indeed, Hakuin conceived *kōan* as the ideal practice for overcoming the trivial dualism of social dichotomies and hierarchies such as male/female, rich/poor, educated/ignorant.[58] In sum, Tachibana's experience reflects a broader trend during the Edo period: the increased dissemination of Buddhist scriptures and concepts among the general population.

CONCLUSIONS

The history of the *Gateless Barrier* in Japan reflects the evolution of the Zen schools and a process of the localization of teachings transmitted from the continent. This process initially occurred during the medieval age of secrecy, in which *kōan* commentaries became instrumental to showcase the acquisition of Chan classic tropes. Nevertheless, connoisseurship of Chan texts was progressively paired with teachings developed within the Japanese Buddhist lineages, as in the case of esoteric Buddhism. The commentarial manuals on the *Gateless Barrier* epitomize this evolution, revealing how the codified hermeneutics of *kōan* was adapted to the needs of each group. In other words, the understanding along with the role of *kōan* evolved in accordance with the historical changes in Zen schools. In addition, the *Gateless Barrier* gained popularity among the laypeople, for example, the resonance of episodes from the *Gateless Barrier* in the parodies of the *kyōgen* theater. While in the secret Zen encounters between master and disciples, *kōans* were the method to demonstrate one's ability to connect oneself with the past tradition, in *kyōgen* theater, the abstruse language is parodistic, generating hilarity in the audience, and becomes the cause of marital discord. During the seventeenth century, access to Zen texts was facilitated by the improvement of printing techniques, allowing even women to find their way within *kōan* practice. Not only did Tachibana no Someko discover in the *Gateless Barrier* her path to recover from the loss of her children, but she also turned this collection of *kōan* into the conceptual blueprint to express her social critique of misogynistic Buddhist theories regarding the salvation of women.

This chapter has introduced only a few of the many examples of how Zen texts adapted to various contexts and resonated with different audiences throughout the centuries. From doctrinal disquisitions to the everyday life of laypeople, the *Gateless Barrier* thrived within the plethora of meanings generated by its readers, hence disclosing the multifaceted character of Zen teachings.

NOTES

1. For an overview and critical analysis about the notion of Kamakura Buddhism, see William E. Deal and Brian Douglas Ruppert, *A Cultural History of Japanese Buddhism* (Chichester: Wiley Blackwell, 2015), 135–171.
2. The "Old" Buddhism, developed between the sixth and the eleventh century, included the Six Schools of Nara, the Tendai School (established by Saichō), and the Shingon School (founded by Kūkai, 774–835).
3. Martin Collcutt, "Zen and the Gozan," in *The Cambridge History of Japan Vol. 3*, ed. Kozo Yamamura (Cambridge: Cambridge University Press, 1990), 583–652. doi:10.1017/CHOL9780521223546.015.
4. William M. Bodiford, *Sōtō Zen in Medieval Japan* (Honolulu: University of Hawai'i Press, 1993), 256 n. 55. Nevertheless, this distinction is not accurate since Rinka temples were also located in the capital, Kyoto.
5. Bodiford, *Sōtō Zen*, 146.
6. Philip B. Yampolsky, "Hattō Kokushi's *Dharma Talks*," *Cahiers d'Extrême-Asie* 7, no. 1 (1993): 249–265.
7. In *Dazangjing Bubian* vols. 1–36 (hereafter *B*), ed. Lan Jifu (Taipei: Huayu chubanshe, 1985), CBeta Edition, *B*32, no. 173, 202c24–25.
8. Yampolsky, "Hattō Kokushi's *Dharma Talks*."
9. Translated in Yampolsky, "Hattō Kokushi's *Dharma Talks*," 263.
10. Translated in Yampolsky, "Hattō Kokushi's *Dharma Talks*," 265 (slightly modified).
11. Didier Davin, *"Mumonkan" no Shusse Sugoroku: Kikashita Zen no Seiten* (Tokyo: Heibonsha, 2020), 34–39.
12. Bernhard Scheid and Mark Teeuwen, "Introduction," in *The Culture of Secrecy in Japanese Religion*, ed. Bernhard Scheid and Mark Teeuwen (London: Taylor and Francis, 2015).
13. Scheid and Teeuwen, "Introduction." In addition, historical and religious developments such as the privatization of lands and the centrality of the bond between master and disciples were among the factors that accelerated the privatization of Buddhism, literature, and the arts. See Jacqueline I. Stone, *Original Enlightenment and the Transformation of Medieval Japanese Buddhism* (Honolulu: University of Hawai'i Press, 1999), 151.
14. On the terminology of "school," see Jason Ānanda Josephson, *The Invention of Religion in Japan* (Chicago: University of Chicago Press, 2012), 1–21. On the factional organization of medieval Japanese Zen, see Steven Heine, "Boundary-Crossing Zen in Fourteenth Century Japan: A Case Study of the Wanshi Stream (Wanshi-Ha)," *Des mots aux actes*, forthcoming

15. On the sectarian organization of Edo-period Buddhism, see Stone, *Original Enlightenment*, 66–77; David E. Riggs, "The Rekindling of a Tradition: Menzan Zuihō and the Reform of Japanese Sōtō Zen in the Tokugawa Era" (Ph.D. diss., University of California, Los Angeles, 2002).

16. These commentaries are known as *shōmono*, a general term used to indicate any kind of commentaries from Buddhist and non-Buddhist traditions. The categorization reported here is particularly common for Sōtō Zen *shōmono*. On this topic, see Stephan Kigensan Licha, *Esoteric Zen: Zen and the Tantric Teachings in Premodern Japan* (Leiden: Brill, 2023).

17. *Monsan* is the term used in Sōtō Zen, while *missan* in more common in Rinzai Zen. This terminology distinction is a mere formality since secret *kōan* commentaries produced by the two groups present striking similarities.

18. Ishikawa Rikizan, "Transmission of Kirigami (Secret Initiation Documents): A Sōtō Practice in Medieval Japan," in *The Kōan Texts and Contexts in Zen Buddhism*, ed. Steven Heine and Dale S. Wright (New York: Oxford University Press, 2000), 233–243.

19. Andō Yoshinori, "Chūsei Zenshū no kōan Zen nitsuite," *Komazawa Joshi Daigaku Kenkyū Kiyō* 7 (2000): 12–24.

20. On this topic, see Victor Sogen Hori, *Zen Sand: The Book of Capping Phrases for Kōan Practice* (Honolulu: University of Hawaii Press, 2003).

21. Bodiford, *Sōtō Zen*, 144–145.

22. For a historical overview of secret *kōan* manuals, see, Peter Haskel, *Bankei and His World* (Ph.D. diss., Columbia University, 1988), 55–107.

23. Bodiford, *Sōtō Zen*, 151–152.

24. Translated in Kenneth Kraft, *Eloquent Zen: Daitō and Early Japanese Zen* (Honolulu: University of Hawai'i Press, 1992), 136.

25. Kraft, *Eloquent Zen*, 135–137.

26. For an investigation of embryology across Asia and in different traditions, see Anna Andreeva and Dominic Steavu, eds., *Transforming the Void: Embryological Discourse and Reproductive Imagery in East Asian Religions* (Leiden: Brill, 2016).

27. According to Bodhidharma's hagiography, he spent nine years sitting in meditation facing a wall.

28. Translated in Bernard Faure, "From Bodhidharma to Daruma: The Hidden Life of a Zen Patriarch," *Japan Review* 23, no. 23 (2011): 45–71. For a more recent translation of this passage, see Licha, *Esoteric Zen*, 262–263.

29. For an in-depth analysis of this commentary and its intricate symbology in Sōtō and Genjū Zen, see Marta Sanvido, "On the Verge of Damnation and Buddhahood: Motherhood, Female Corporeality, and Koan Exegesis," *Japanese Journal of Religious Studies* 50, no. 1 (2023): 1–47. A recent and thoroughly investigation on Genjū Zen can be found in Licha, *Esoteric Zen*, 245–281.

30. For a complete analysis of the staff in Zen/Chan literature, see Steven Heine, "Thy rod and thy staff they discomfort me: Zen staffs as implements of instruction," in *Zen and Material Culture*, ed. Steven Heine and Pamela D. Winfield (New York: Oxford University Press, 2017), 1–36.

31. This idea has been revised by the excellent contributions in Heine and Winfield, *Zen and Material Culture*.

32. In "Self-Fulfilling *Samādhi*" (*Jishō zanmai*), partially translated in Heine, "Thy rod and thy staff they discomfort me," 12.

33. The script reports a wordplay based on the term *hananuri*, which can be understood as the technique of decorating with lacquer, as well as the paint grease on the nose (from *hana* meaning nose, and *nuri* meaning paint).

34. This translation is based on the Tenri Central Library's version quoted in Ōtani Setsuko, "Kyōgen *Shujō* to *Mumonkan* dai yonjūyon soku 'Bashō Shujō,'" *Seijō Kokubungaku Ronshū*, 41: 5–25. This play is also translated in A. L. Sadler and Paul S. Atkins, *Japanese Plays: Classic Noh, Kyogen and Kabuki Works* (Tokyo: Tuttle, 2010), 114–118. However, this version differs from the one adopted here.

35. T. Griffith Foulk, William M. Bodiford, Carl Bielefeldt, and John R. McRae, *Record of the Transmission of Illumination: Volume 2. A Glossary of Terms, Sayings, and Names Pertaining to Keizan's Denkōroku* (Honolulu: University of Hawaii Press, 2021), 217.

36. Yanagida Seizan and Shiina Kōyū, eds., *Zengaku tenseki sōkan*, vol. 9 (Kyoto: Rinsen Shoten), 175.

37. William M. Bodiford, "When Secrecy Ends: the Tokugawa Reformation of Tendai Buddhism and Its Implications," in *The Culture of Secrecy in Japanese Religion*, ed. Bernhard Scheid and Mark Teeuwen (New York: Routledge), 309–330.

38. For an excellent investigation of women's involvement in Japanese Buddhism, see Lori R. Meeks, *Hokkeji and the Reemergence of Female Monastic Orders in Premodern Japan* (Honolulu: University of Hawai'i Press, 2010).

39. This *kōan* is reported in several texts, including the *Essential Recorded Sayings of the Ancient Worthies* (*Guzunsu Yuyao*), and the *Gateless Barrier* case 45.

40. These are two of the four verses reported on the sounding board. The full poem reads, "The matter of birth and death is great; Impermanence is swift; You should be mindful of this; Do not waste your time."

41. Quoted in Sueki Fumihiko, "Tachibana no Someko no Zen rikai," in *Ejima Yasunori Hakushi Tsuitō Ronshū: Kū to Jitsuzai*, ed. Ejima Yasunori Hakushi Tsuitō Ronshū Kankōkai (Tokyo: Shunjūsha, 2001), 593–606.

42. This episode is illustrated in the *Foundation of the Kitano Temple and the Life of Sugawara no Michizane* (*Kitano Tenjin engi*). On this topic, see Conán Dean Carey, "In Hell the One Without Sin Is Lord," *Sino-Platonic Papers* 109 (2000): 1–60.

43. Quoted in Sueki, "Tachibana no Someko no Zen rinkai," 597.

44. Sueki, "Tachibana no Someko no Zen rinkai."

45. The authorship of the *Bird's False Cry* is still under debate. Although the author was most certainly a woman, there is no consensus that it was Tachibana.

46. One such famous example is the hagiography of the Chan monk Yushanzhu, who experienced awakening upon falling from his donkey when crossing a bridge. In the verses composed following the event, awakening is described as a gem covered in dust, which can finally shine and irradiate all the things around it. Reported in the *Compendium of the Five Lamps* (*Wudeng huiyuan*), in *Manji shinsan Dainihon zokuzōkyō* (abbreviated *X*), vols. 1–90 (Tokyo: Kokusho Kankokai, 1975–1989), CBeta edition, *X*80, no. 1565, 137c5–11. Tachibana quotes this anecdote in her commentary, see Shimauchi Keiji, *Shin'yaku "Tori no sorane": Genroku no josei shisōka, Iizuka Someko, Zen ni idomu* (Tokyo: Kasama Shoin, 2013), 387–389.

47. Translated in Burton Watson, "Han Feizi (d. 233 B.C.): Two Passages," in *Classical Chinese Literature Vol. 1*, ed. John Minford and Joseph S. M. Lau (New York: Columbia University Press, 2000), 224–225.

48. For an English translation of this episode, see Burton Watson, *The Lotus Sutra* (New York: Columbia University Press, 1993), 182–190.

49. The five hindrances refer to the five obstructions that prevent women from attaining buddhahood in their body and the impossibility of becoming a Brahmā, a Shakra, a devil king, a wheel-turning king, or a buddha. The five hindrances are usually paired with the three forms of obedience, as a woman must be subordinate to her father, husband, and son.

50. On this topic in the context of Japanese Buddhism, see Meeks, *Hokkeji and the Reemergence of Female Monastic Orders in Premodern Japan*, 253–284; Abé Ryūichi, "Revisiting the Dragon Princess: Her role in medieval engi stories and their implications in reading the *Lotus Sutra*," *Japanese Journal of Religious Studies* 42, no. 1 (2015): 27–70; Heather Blair, "Mothers of the Buddhas: 'The Sutra on Transforming Women into Buddhas' (*Bussetsu Tennyo Jōbutsu Kyō*)," *Monumenta Nipponica* 71, no. 2 (2016): 263–293. For a discussion on this topic within Mahāyāna Buddhism, see Jan Nattier, "Gender and Hierarchy in the Lotus Sūtra," in *Readings of the Lotus Sūtra*, ed. Stephen F. Teiser, and Jacqueline Ilyse Stone (New York: Columbia University Press, 2009), 83–106.

51. Refers here to the hair kept at shoulder length during childhood.

52. Shimauchi, *Shin'yaku "Tori no sorane,"* 388.

53. This aspect is also explored in the explanation of case 35. Shimauchi, *Shin'yaku "Tori no sorane,"* 424–425.

54. On Hakuin, see Juhn Y. Ahn, "Hakuin," in *The Dao Companion to Japanese Buddhist Philosophy*, ed. Gereon Kopf (Dordrecht: Springer, 2019), 511–535, doi.org/10 .1007/978-90-481-2924-9_22; Michel Mohr, "Emerging from nonduality: Kōan practice in the Rinzai tradition since Hakuin," in *The Kōan Texts and Contexts in Zen Buddhism*, ed. Heine and Wright, 244–279.

55. On this figure, see Patricia Fister, "Commemorating life and death: The memorial culture surrounding the Rinzai Zen nun Mugai Nyodai," in *Women, Rites, and Ritual Objects in Premodern Japan*, ed. Karen M. Gerhart (Leiden: Brill, 2018), 269–303.

56. Reported in the *Wild Thistles* (*Oniazami*, 1751), in *Hakuin Zenji hōgo zenshū*, ed. Yoshizawa Katsuhiro (Kyoto: Zen Bunka Kenkyūjo, 1999), 38–39; also quoted in Takeshita Ruggeri Anna, "Jendā ni taisuru Edo jidai no Rinzai shū: Hakuin Zenji wo chūshin ni," *Kenkyūjo hō* 研究所報 31 (2021): 12–25.

57. Reported in the *Wild Thistles*, in Yoshizawa, *Hakuin Zenji hōgo zenshū*, 79; also quoted in Takeshita Ruggeri, "Jendā ni taisuru Edo jidai no Rinzai shū."

58. However, Hakuin did not train many female students. Takeshita Ruggeri, "Jendā ni taisuru Edo jidai no Rinzai shū."

{ 9 }

KŌAN KUFŪ

EMBODYING THE *KŌAN* IN RINZAI ZEN PRACTICE

Meido Moore

T HE MEDITATIVE practice for which Japanese Rinzai Zen Buddhism is perhaps best known, making use of *kōans* (C. *gong'ans*), has straightforward purposes in common with all Zen practices: to dissolve the student's obstructions, to cause the student to arrive at the awakening called *kenshō* ("seeing [one's] nature") that is counted as the entrance gate of Zen, and subsequently to lead the student—taking awakening itself as the basis of practice—to revisit, polish, and deepen it along the path of liberation. Inheriting the vitally energetic teachings of late Song Chinese masters, Rinzai Zen teachers in Japan from the late twelfth century onward refined *kōan* practice to a high degree. This process reached its culmination with the great master Hakuin Ekaku (1686–1769) and his heirs, who organized the essential framework of the *kōan* curricula passed down to the present day in Rinzai Zen lineages. Within all of these curricula, the *Gateless Barrier* (C. *Wumen guan*; J. *Mumonkan*) figures prominently as a practice text.

This chapter will focus on the actual method that Rinzai Zen preserves for practicing with *kōans* from the *Gateless Barrier* and other sources. Called *kōan kufū*, it is a distinctively embodied way of engaging with *kōan* texts within the teacher-student encounter that goes beyond intellectual examination in order to experientially penetrate their meaning.

Even with the transplanting of Rinzai Zen lineages throughout the world since the end of the Second World War, Rinzai *kōan* practice remains little understood outside the tradition. Yet Mumon Eikai's (C. Wumen

Huikai's) commentary to the first *kōan* in his *Gateless Barrier*, the famous case in which Jōshū Jūshin (C. Zhaozhou Congshen) answers *"Mu!"* (C. *Wu*) to the question of a dog's possession of buddha nature, holds keys to grasping its meaning. We will thus examine Mumon's words informed by traditional oral instructions as they clarify the meaning for Rinzai Zen practitioners. Zen practice is made vital only through such oral instructions (J. *kuden*) received from one's master. In fact, much of what is considered indispensable in Zen practice is still transmitted primarily in this manner, from mouth to ear—something also little understood by many.

I am not a scholar, and so can only speak of these things from a practitioner's standpoint, and as someone who has been tasked in some small way with ensuring the transmission of Rinzai Zen teachings. I practice and carry a branch of one Japanese Rinzai Zen lineage: that transmitted to the West by the great twentieth-century master Ōmori Sōgen Roshi (1904–1994). Though this is a prominent and mainstream Rinzai Zen line, different lines can preserve unique teaching material depending upon the interests and predilections of past lineage holders. The transmission of Rinzai Zen lineages, in fact, is not an organizational matter but a wholly personal one between teachers and students. Thus, within the many lineage branches, as within individual monasteries, there arise over time unique cultures or atmospheres that we call the *kafū*, "house wind," of each.

Still, what I will discuss here is broadly applicable to the whole of traditional Japanese Rinzai Zen, and communicates something of the overall flavor of Rinzai *kōan* practice. I hope you will come to understand how texts like the *Gateless Barrier* still serve as supports for truly profound spiritual inquiry, and perhaps grasp something of how Rinzai Zen students are guided to harness their whole beings as they grapple with each *kōan*, entering into the situations and ultimately the minds of the great masters that feature therein.

Before turning to the *Gateless Barrier*, it is useful to examine two things. First is the essentially embodied or yogic nature of Rinzai Zen practice. Understanding this will allow us to clarify what is signified by the word *kufū*, and what implications this has for *kōan* practice in the Rinzai tradition. Second is the formal teacher-student encounter: not only the crux of Rinzai Zen *kōan* practice but actually the most important of all Rinzai practices. It is within the face-to-face meeting with one's master that the heart of *kōan* practice is realized and the *kōans* of the *Gateless Barrier* are brought to life.

KUFŪ: A YOGIC APPROACH

Rinzai Zen practice, marked by *kufū*, is fundamentally a *yogic* approach to spiritual inquiry. The Sanskrit word *yoga* is of course familiar today, referring popularly to systems of physical culture having Indian cultural origin. But here we use the word more broadly, with its original meaning of "union" or "joining." What we may call the systems of yogic spirituality, with roots stretching back at least to the *śramanic*[1] religious movements of ancient India, are marked not primarily by intellectualization, but rather by a harnessing and unification of the aspirant's entire being—body, breath, and mind—within a wholly psycho-physical project of spiritual exploration.

For millennia, practitioners of yogic disciplines have observed that specific ways of cultivating the body (for example, in the postures of meditation), regulating the breath (and with that the subtle energetics—the vital currents or "winds" perceived within the body), and directing the mind's attention or functioning can together transform the quality of one's experience in remarkably powerful ways. Buddhism, of course, has rested upon such an approach from its earliest days, taking the kind of meditative practice done by the Buddha as a foundation of its path and the insights at which he arrived through meditation as its core teachings. Penetrating the "three mysteries" (J. *sanmitsu*) of body, speech (including breath), and mind can be said to form the basis of all Buddhist praxis.

Observing Zen, we may certainly recognize seated meditation (J. *zazen*) in the familiar posture of the Buddha as the best-known practice. But even something like silent meditation has its inner yogic function; it is not simply an exercise of contemplation or mental rumination. Describing this more precisely according to the Rinzai Zen understanding: when in meditation the vital currents (J. *ki*) of the body are made to gather with the breath at the navel center (J. *tanden*)[2] by means of the methods transmitted through oral instruction, then meditative absorption (S. *samādhi*) quickly manifests and may be more easily sustained.

Samādhi is an important word, used frequently within yogic traditions. This meditative absorption can be of various kinds and depths and is not by itself the liberative wisdom to which Buddhism points. But crucially, for our understanding, we can say that the meditative absorption cultivated in Zen practice serves to dissolve obstructions and create conditions for genuine insight to arise. Within this absorption, realized as a relaxed, unified, and nonabiding or nonfixating state of body-mind, our habitual manner of viewing all phenomena from the standpoint of a reified "I" or "me"—that is, the habit of dualistic seeing that is at the root of human delusion—becomes less rigidly binding. In profound meditative absorption, this deeply ingrained fixation upon a self seems to drop utterly away for a time.

In such ways, *samādhi* aids us to begin seeing through our delusion. Later, after one arrives at a genuine awakening, such meditative absorption becomes crucial for fully integrating that wisdom. This, in fact, reveals the heart of the Rinzai Zen path: the cultivation of seamless meditative absorption, unified with the upwelling of wisdom first recognized with awakening, in a manner that causes that wisdom—riding the vital winds, so to speak—to penetrate the very fiber of one's body, even to the bones.

Nothing less than bodily realization of this kind constitutes liberation in Rinzai Zen. But it is made possible only through a kind of practice that encompasses, engages, and harnesses the body as well as the mind. As expressed by the twentieth-century Rinzai Zen master Ōmori Sōgen Roshi (1904–1994): "[The purpose of] Zen is to transcend life and death [that is, all dualism], to truly realize that the entire universe is the true human body, through the discipline of body-mind in oneness."[3] Dōgen Kigen Zenji (1200–1253),[4] the great founder of Sōtō Zen in Japan, expressed it thus in *Shōbōgenzō*: "The phrase, 'learning the Way through the body,' means that we learn the Way by means of the body, that we learn the Way by means of our living flesh."[5] From my own teachers I frequently received this similar oral instruction that is perhaps most pithy: "Zen is accomplished through the body."

Many anecdotes from Zen history reveal an abiding concern with such embodied, wholly yogic practice, including cultivation of the breath and focus upon the navel center. Perhaps the most amusing is this one from *Shōnan kattō roku*, a fascinating text preserving something of the flavor of practice that medieval Chinese Chan masters and monks who had arrived in Japan transmitted to their Japanese disciples. The main character, Giō,[6] was a Chinese monk from Sichuan Province:

At the outbreak of war in the first year of Kōan (1278)[7] Tokimune visited Bukkō[8] and gave the *katzu*! shout of dashing straight forward.[9] Priest Giō said: "The general has got something great below his navel, so the shout too is great."...

One of the regent's ministers, Masanori, when he came to know what Giō had said, asked him indignantly:

"When did Your Reverence see the size of what our lord has below his navel?"

The priest said: "Before the general was born, I saw it."

The courtier did not understand.

The priest said: "If you do not understand the greatness of what is below the general's navel, then see through to before you yourself were born, the greatness of the thing below the navel. How would that thing become greater or less by the honor or contempt of high or low?"

The courtier was still more bewildered.

The priest gave a *katzu*! shout and said: "Such is the voice of it, of that thing."[10]

The *katsu* (or *katzu*) shout, an explosive vocalization used in Zen practice that can strike the hearer with remarkable effect, only has such power when issuing from the body of someone who has cultivated breathing focused on the "thing below the navel": the navel center, or *tanden*. From this anecdote and others that survive, we can clearly see the intense physicality of the training these masters and students were doing together. We may also guess that this type of practice served in many ways to bridge barriers of culture and language, and helped Zen take root in Japan in a particularly vital way.[11]

Another fascinating example from about five hundred years earlier appears in the *Gateless Barrier*. In case 40, "Kicking Over the Water Jar," is this famous episode:

When Venerable Weishan was still in Baizhang's congregation, he served as a cook. Baizhang wanted to choose a successor for Mount Dawei. He invited the head monk to announce to the assembly that anyone who could go beyond the patterns [of the world] could go to be the Chan Master at Mount Dawei.

Baizhang, in front of everyone, took out a water jar, set it on the ground, and asked, "If you don't call it a water jar, what would you call it?"

The head monk was the first to stand up and said, "You cannot call it a tree stump."

Baizhang turned to Weishan. Weishan just kicked over the water jar and left.

Baizhang laughed and said, "The head monk just lost the mountain." Then he dispatched Weishan to open a monastery at Dawei (see p. 277).[12]

There is much to penetrate in this case as it is. However, there is actually something more to it—a well-known prologue—that was not included in the *Gateless Barrier*. Before the test of the water jar was made, there was a first test: the candidates were each made to simply walk forward a few steps and clear their throat. In this Weishan was also judged the winner, and only the head monk's protests led to the second, final test of the water jar.[13]

What can be observed from the manner of someone's walking and clearing his throat that would be relevant to choosing the abbot of a new monastery? This may seem puzzling to the casual reader, but to a practitioner familiar with the methods of Rinzai Zen training, particularly practices centered on the navel center that transform the manner and depth of one's breathing and movement, the answer is quite clear. To observe someone taking a few steps; to see the posture, movement, and gaze; and to hear the clearing of the throat or the chanting of a few syllables from the sūtras are indeed enough to discern the depth of someone's embodied practice, cultivated energetic vitality, and fruition of meditative absorption. These are the kinds of things that Rinzai Zen teachers still constantly observe as they guide their students.

Of course, consciously trying to move and speak according to one's notions of how a Zen practitioner should appear would miss the point entirely. Such affectation is not uncommon, especially among beginning students, and reveals an attachment to appearances and forms. Subtle shifts in the functioning of body and mind result from long practice and reveal to a trained eye one's inner transformation. These are not things that can be faked.

To sum up: the yogic spirituality of Zen must be understood as a spirituality of the entire body-mind—the whole human being—rather than the mind alone. Zen practice takes place by means of, not in spite of, our bodies. It transforms and manifests within one's entire embodied existence, not simply the mind.

None of this should be surprising. Given the Buddhist analysis of the human situation, and particularly the manner in which sentient beings arise—body and mind—as serial phenomena driven by a causal continuity of delusion stretching back infinitely through the chain of endless rebirths, only practice addressing the totality of one's embodied existence could be considered most effective at cutting the roots of ignorance. A primarily intellectual or conceptual approach simply does not have the power to cut these roots deeply, and in a lasting manner.

There is well-known oral instruction in Zen driving home precisely that point: you cannot wash off blood with blood. Trying to change one's deluded mind with that same mind alone is so difficult as to be futile. But yogic practice, encompassing the whole human being, is a different approach.

With this understanding you may be able to appreciate what *kufū* entails. The word itself can generally refer to any creative, inventive, and skillful effort. But in Rinzai training, it refers to this use of one's whole existence within practice, in the manner required to penetrate the essence of Zen: an intensely energetic undertaking involving the practitioner's entire being. *Kōan* practice, too, is done with one's whole existence, within one's flesh and bones, not solely with the intellect. This does not mean that one must have a particular physical ability, condition, or skill to practice but that the totality of one's embodied being, and all one's conditions however seemingly ideal or difficult, are to be accepted and creatively encompassed within the field of practice. This is *kōan kufū*.

I often speak on this subject and imagine that it must all sound surprising and odd, especially to those accustomed to view Zen mainly as a kind of philosophy or solely through an academic lens. But again, unless we actually enter the gate of Zen practice with our own bodies, put ourselves under the guidance of a qualified teacher, receive the lineage oral instructions, and come to some fruition of awakening, we should not presume there is any way to grasp that to which Zen points. It is only with the transformation of one's own body-mind that the significance of the Zen path is finally understood.

Let us now briefly examine the second topic mentioned earlier: the all-important container within which Rinzai Zen *kōan* practice is accomplished. This is the face-to-face encounter with the Zen master, called *sanzen*.

SANZEN: ENTERING THE FIELD OF BLESSINGS

Sanzen may be translated as "going to" or "visiting" (a Zen teacher) for Zen practice. It thus refers to a mutual participation of teacher and student in the unfolding of Zen: a joint exploration of the teachings. When used generally, the term can simply refer to the commitment to study under a teacher. For example, it is not uncommon in Rinzai Zen circles to say that someone is "doing *sanzen*" with a teacher, meaning that the person has formally been accepted as that master's student.

Zen emphasizes the absolute necessity of practicing under a teacher's guidance. Though one can study Buddhist teachings and even begin to practice basic meditation independently, it will be necessary at some point to find a master upon whom to rely. In the Rinzai view, this is affirmed in the first two of the famous four lines describing Zen that have been attributed to Bodhidharma, the fifth–sixth century Indian monk who transmitted the Zen teachings to China: "A separate transmission outside the scriptures / Not dependent upon words and letters."

Far from implying that Zen is somehow antiscripture or anti-intellectual, these lines reveal that Zen practice is actualized primarily within human relationship rather than through the study of texts. Only within a relationship with a qualified master can the lifeblood of Zen be communicated in the manner called "mind to mind transmission" (J. *isshin denshin*).

That being said, *sanzen* has a second, more specific meaning. This is the actual formal encounter with one's master (commonly also called *dokusan*, "going alone" to the teacher), a frequent occurrence especially within Rinzai monastic life. This is the one indispensable practice of Rinzai Zen, regardless of whether the practitioner is ordained or lay, living in a monastery or in the everyday world. Facing their teachers alone in the *sanzen* room—up to three times daily during periods of intensive retreat—Rinzai Zen students are challenged to dynamically reveal whatever realization they have attained. The teacher will use various means to shatter the student's obstructions and foster conditions for wisdom to arise.

This is easy enough to understand according to the surface meaning. But the hidden aspects of *sanzen* further clarify the embodied Rinzai Zen approach. I call them hidden only because they are not commonly known to outsiders; they are not secret at all to those who have trained under a genuine teacher. But these are the essential aspects of *sanzen* that must be recognized to understand the Rinzai Zen path in general, and its approach to *kōans* in particular.

Let us turn to the third of Bodhidharma's four lines in which the actual method of Zen is described: "Direct pointing at the human mind." This is commonly thought to be a general description of Zen as a tradition pointing out one's intrinsic wisdom, that is, the fact that what we call buddha is not found apart from our own minds. But if that were the full extent of it there would be no reason to say so, since all Mahāyāna Buddhism can be said to share that intent in some manner. In fact, "direct pointing at the human mind" in Zen refers to something more: the various means mentioned above that teachers use to shatter their students' obstructions and facilitate their conditions so that they may arrive at awakening. From this standpoint, the primary initial task of all Zen teachers is to bring the student, by whatever means necessary, through the gate of awakening. In other words: "direct pointing" is not just a general description of Zen but refers to the activity of Zen teachers. And in Rinzai Zen practice, *sanzen* is the main place where this activity is wielded to great effect.

Of course, just entering the gate of awakening is not the end of direct pointing, or of *sanzen*. Thereafter, the purpose of *sanzen* for the student is to polish the sword of wisdom that has been only roughly forged. The teacher must prescribe whatever medicine of practice is required, however bitter, to cause the student to course along the lifelong postawakening path of progressive transcendence—revisiting, integrating, and embodying awakening, causing all actions of body, speech, and mind to accord with it and arrive at the final place of great freedom. A famous phrase describes the task of the teacher: "pulling out nails and knocking out wedges." As Hakuin explained: "Nails are the *sūtras* and commentaries implanted by the Teaching Schools, wedges the *satori* [awakening] implanted by Zen teachers. All must be extracted."[14] Indeed, for our practice to arrive at its fullest fruition, we must extract even the wedges of attachment to awakening itself, setting ourselves upon a path of simultaneously seeking "deeper attainment above . . . while helping other sentient beings below."[15] But it is in *sanzen* that such truths are endlessly clarified, and the student corrected whenever deviations occur, or a shred of self-satisfaction arises.

Perhaps most obviously, a teacher will make use of various actions and words—bodily and verbal means of direct pointing—to cause the student to arrive at a new way of seeing. For example, a Zen teacher may strike or shout at a student, with the result that the student arrives suddenly at awakening, or a student arrive at awakening upon hearing the teacher utter a direct and pithy comment. These kinds of things can seem puzzling. But while the mind is in in the state of meditative absorption, some sharp sound, action, or cutting word can deeply penetrate, causing a small shock, immediately after which our deluded manner of seeing momentarily lessens or even collapses. There are many examples in Zen records, and *kōan* literature especially preserves them. Case 1 of the *Gateless Barrier* is among the most famous. But it is important when considering them to grasp the kind of inner function just described. If we fail to do this, we will tend to create solely intellectual, and mostly misleading, theories about what is going on and how to practice.

Though it is not customary to speak of one's own experiences much, one anecdote may illustrate the power of such actions and words of direct pointing. When young, while deeply practicing with the first *kōan* assigned, I found myself within a state of meditative absorption such that I could barely function. Though I was still engaged in daily activities, my appearance and movement must have been bizarre, perhaps something like that of a wide-eyed zombie shambling about. Inwardly, I was trying with all my might to seamlessly hold the *kōan* with my whole body-mind, allowing not even a moment's lapse. By doing so, I had entered the kind of *samādhi* that is completely still and white, as Hakuin said, "like a huge plain of ice extending ten thousand miles."[16]

Naturally, my teacher observed all of this. He asked me what I was doing. With some effort I was able to reply, "I'm working on the *kōan*." He paused for a moment, and then exclaimed sharply with a fierce glare: "What you're looking for is *nothing special!*"

Those two words—"nothing special"—came from deep within his body and carried a certain piercing quality that Zen practitioners come to recognize well.[17] They completely penetrated my mind in an odd manner, and I felt at once as if something had shattered and a great weight had fallen from my shoulders. The desperate nature of my practice, so hungry to break through the *kōan* and arrive at a resolution to my spiritual search, seemed to dissipate like fog in sunlight, and I felt a soothing relaxation. Thereafter redoubling my efforts, I was able to finally penetrate the *kōan* early the next morning upon suddenly awakening from a deep slumber.

This episode was quite revealing in many ways, and I still experience some feeling of awe when recalling it. But the main point is that it was the keen eye of my teacher, his impeccable timing, and his sharp words of direct pointing—carrying a power arising from his own long years of embodied practice—that served to sever my obstructions. This reveals something of what students experience in *sanzen*.

Aside from physical and verbal means, there is a third, crucial category of direct pointing making use of what we may call *extraordinary* means, involving factors that underlie and give power to all the activities of a genuine teacher. To discuss this, we must understand the Japanese word *ba*, which literally means "place" or "field," the locale where something happens. It is the same character pronounced *jo* in the well-known Japanese word *dojo* ("place of the Way," a training hall). But in *sanzen*, *ba* refers more specifically to the proximity of a deeply awakened person and the effects or influences that can manifest within that space.

Practitioners have long recognized that in the presence of an accomplished teacher one's body-mind can be more easily and spontaneously transformed, opening up the possibility of insight in a particularly effective manner. Much as a vibrating guitar string causes sympathetic vibration in an adjacent string, the teacher's subtle influence can produce change within the student, even to the point that the student may experience something of the teacher's state of mind. To enter the teacher's *ba*, then, is essentially to encounter the blessing stream of their lineage. A teacher who powerfully manifests this is displaying the unique energetic vitality (J. *kiai*) of the lineage that has transformed teachers and students in turn, like strings vibrating one another, down through generations. In this quite real sense, entering the *sanzen* room means that one encounters all those lineage ancestors, back to the Buddha himself.

This field manifests and sustains its power to transform through the teacher's *samādhi* power (J. *jōriki*), a profound state of meditative absorption unified with the clear upwelling of wisdom and bodily integration through long training of the kind discussed. It results from the vitality, *kiai*, that radiates from the teacher. When all of these things are present within a Zen teacher—profound meditative absorption, some degree of embodied realization of wisdom, and the brilliant, surging energy that arises when the body-mind is balanced in its functioning—then their presence itself becomes an extraordinary place of awakening. The skillful means of direct pointing spontaneously employed may then be described as *myō*: wondrous, miraculous.

When encountering such a teacher in *sanzen* students commonly find that their habitual fixations and spinning discursive thoughts lessen. Students may suddenly reach a state of clarity or even be unable to speak. Their surroundings may appear oddly bright or even white in appearance, or colors appear unusually vivid and pure: common signs of entering into a kind of *samādhi*. They may feel, as I did in the anecdote shared earlier, that long-held burdens drop away or that a great weight has been lifted. It is not uncommon for such effects to endure for a while even after leaving the teacher's presence, lending added strength and dimension to one's practice.

Truly, it is not too much to say that the entire course of the Rinzai Zen path, and the inheritance of Rinzai lineages within each generation, pivot upon this crucial practice of encounter. *Sanzen* is not only something that creates conditions for the initial awakening but also the place where the postawakening path—the exhaustive effort to seamlessly embody wisdom, for which *kōan* practice can be so effectively employed—is empowered. This empowerment is through the teacher's manifestation of the very state that the student must attain; in effect, it is a kind of modeling that the student can and must "catch."

We may go so far as to say that Rinzai Zen without face-to-face *sanzen* is not truly Rinzai Zen at all. And naturally, if during *sanzen* the teacher is not manifesting meditative absorption and the fruition of embodied awakening, or lacks a sufficiently clear eye to guide the student, then it is not truly *sanzen* either: it becomes only a kind of dress-up play, or at best simply an everyday conversation. Yet where this thread of embodied realization is present and conditions are correct, *sanzen* is an unmatched tool by means of which to decisively cut through obstructions and make rapid progress on the path. Entering again and again into the presence of the teacher, in a process that is likened to smelting impurities out of gold ore or forging and polishing metal to become a peerless blade, allows the student to gradually resonate with the qualities of the lineage. This living energetic transmission accompanies and gives life to orally transmitted practice knowledge, connecting human beings from one generation to the next. This is what is actually meant by "dharma transmission" (J. *denpō*) in Rinzai Zen. *Sanzen* is the means by which the student is woven into the tapestry of the lineage.

The last of Bodhidharma's four lines sums up the result of "direct pointing at the human mind" and affirms the purpose of the subsequent life-long practice that has been stressed: "Seeing one's nature [*kenshō*], becoming buddha." Indeed, entering the gate of awakening due to meeting with the skillful direct pointing activity of the teacher in *sanzen*—and one's profound aspiration to liberate all beings—reveals the true Zen path of "becoming buddha" in a stunning manner. Clarifying, deepening, refining, and bodily integrating the wisdom of awakening over many years through creative *kufū*, the student discovers a new life.

Now we are finally ready to examine case 1 of the *Gateless Barrier* and see what it reveals about Rinzai Zen *kōan* practice. Regarding the overall structure of practice, including categories of *kōans* and their specific functions within each Rinzai lineage's curriculum, for example, students will become familiar with five such categories most commonly enumerated: *hōsshin* (S. *dharmakāya*) *kōans*, that is, *kōans* of direct pointing to awakening; *kikan* (dynamic action) *kōans*, stressing the functioning and free manifestation of wisdom within the world of everyday phenomena; *gonsen* (explication of words) *kōans*, by means of which the student must learn to express with words that which is inexpressible, within the *samādhi* of language; the *hachi nantō* (eight difficult to pass) *kōans*, which further polish awakening, challenge attachment to it, and stress the endless upwelling of compassion that drives forward one's ascending path; and the *goi jūjūkin* ("five ranks and ten grave precepts") *kōans*, which reveal an overarching structure to one's training, including hidden practices for the seamless embodiment of awakening, and affirm the Buddhist precepts to be not only guidelines for behavior but also signposts pointing out awakening itself. The monk and scholar Victor Sōgen Hori has written perhaps the best English-language guide to the structure and function of Rinzai *kōan* practice including these categories.[18]

For our purposes here, though, it is enough to understand that case 1 of the *Gateless Barrier* functions as a *hosshin kōan*: a means for the student to pass the all-important gate of awakening. As such, it is typically one of the first *kōans* assigned to students, also called a *shokan* (first barrier) *kōan*. It absolutely requires the student to grasp this manner of whole-being practice called *kufū*.

PRACTICING WITH *KŌANS*: MUMON'S KIND ADVICE

Here is the first *kōan* in the *Gateless Barrier*: "A monk asked Zhaozhou, "Does a dog have buddha nature or not?" Zhaozhou said, '*Wu!*'"

Wumen's Comment:

To study Chan, you must pass through the barrier of our lineage masters. To realize wondrous awakening, you must exhaust the ways of the [deluded] mind. If you do not pass through the barrier of the lineage masters and do not exhaust the ways of the mind, then all that you do would amount to being a spirit haunting the forests and fields.

But tell me, what is this barrier of the lineage masters? It is just this single word, *Wu*, which is also the gate of Chan—the gateless barrier of Chan. If you can pass through it, you will not only see Zhaozhou in person but will also be able to walk together hand in hand with all the generations of lineage masters, to see through the same eyes as they do and hear through the same ears as they do. Wouldn't that be delightful? Do any of you want to pass through this barrier?

Arouse a mass of doubt throughout your whole being, extending through your 360 bones and your 84,000 pores, as you come to grips with the word *Wu*. Bring it up and keep your attention on it day and night. Don't construe [this *Wu*] as void or nothingness, and don't understand it in terms of having or not having. It is as if you had swallowed a red-hot iron ball that you cannot spit out—extinguishing all the erroneous knowledge and experiences. In time you will become ripe, and your practice will become pervasive and whole. Like a mute who has a dream, only you would know it for yourself.

Suddenly, [awakening] bursts forth, astonishing heaven and shaking the earth. It is like snatching General Guan Yu's sword into your own hands— slaying both buddhas and lineage masters as you meet them. On this shore of birth and death, you are free. You roam and play in *samādhi* in the midst of the six paths and four types of birth in all existence.

Still, how will you take up [Zhaozhou's *Wu*]? With all of your life force to bring forth the word *Wu*. If you can do this without interruption, then, like a dharma lamp, it takes only a single spark to [suddenly] light it up! (see pp. 251-252)

Though endless theories have been put forth regarding Rinzai Zen *kōan* practice by modern authors, it is through these words of Mumon that the way of *kōan kufū* can be known. Let us examine them more closely, again with reference to oral instruction preserved in Rinzai Zen lineages. Below, I continue changing some Chinese words and names to the Japanese ones familiar to Rinzai Zen practitioners: *Wu* to *Mu*, Wumen to Mumon, Zhaozhou to Jōshū, and Guan Yu to Kan'u.

"Arouse a mass of doubt throughout your whole being, extending through your 360 bones and your 84,000 pores, as you come to grips with the word *Mu*."

In this single sentence, Mumon reveals the essential import of *kufū*, the wholly yogic approach discussed. The words "come to grips" well convey a sense of what *kufū* requires: having received the *kōan* from the master, one begins an exhaustive, creative, and bodily grappling with the word *Mu* in meditative absorption, with a committed spirit willing even to abandon life in this effort. We are motivated not only by a fervent desire to awaken and get to the root of our pressing existential angst but also by a profound recognition of the suffering of all beings: the aspiration to fulfill our bodhisattva vows to aid others. The words "extending through your 360 bones and your 84,000 pores" mean that this very body—the whole pile of flesh and bones, infirm and transient, shot through with suffering and arising due to karma—is nevertheless the vehicle for accomplishing liberation and must be completely permeated with the *kōan*. Using the entire body-mind, sparing no energy, opens the path.

"Bring it up and keep your attention on it day and night. Don't construe [this *Mu*] as void or nothingness, and don't understand it in terms of having or not having."

Here the practitioner's task is further laid out. Activating the whole body-mind and directing attention to this single word *Mu* within the *samādhi* of practice, we must strive until we hold it seamlessly day and night. We do not mull *Mu* over, analyzing its meaning or puzzling out some answer to the *kōan*, having been warned not to intellectually see *Mu* as a teaching of emptiness or fall into our usual dualistic fixation by analyzing it in terms of have or have not, existence or nonexistence. It is not the dog but our own self-reification and self-grasping that is the concern.

As mentioned earlier, Rinzai teachings clarify that meditators must gather the vital currents of the body with the breath at the navel center in order to enter rapidly into meditative absorption. This is the basis for oral instructions commonly given in *sanzan* to "put *Mu* in your belly (that is, at the *tanden*) and work on it there," to "feel the *kōan* penetrate all the way to the tips of your fingers and toes," and to "breathe the *kōan* with your whole body." One's body must become, it is said, something like an incense burner, within which the *kōan* smolders with a heat that radiates to fill this physical frame.

The transmitted method of Rinzai Zen breath cultivation focused on the navel center is called *tanden soku* (*soku* in Japanese means "breath" or "respiration"). By means of a particular body usage engaging the diaphragm, pelvic floor, and anal sphincter, one learns to breathe in a manner that seals some portion of the breath continuously within the body. The practitioner's lower trunk and especially lower abdomen—the area called the *hara* in Japanese—exhibit a slight distension or roundness that does not rise and fall with each cycle of respiration but *remains full throughout*. With this, it may be seen during meditation that the duration of each breath greatly increases with practice. The exhalation phase especially will increase in length, eventually becoming extremely long and fine.[19] Though initially requiring detailed instruction from a qualified teacher and a degree of conscious effort, after some years of practice this manner of breathing becomes unconscious and subtly constant.

There are several interesting effects of *tanden soku*. Breathing centered seamlessly and without dissipation upon the area of the navel causes the gathering of vital currents there in an unusually effective and rapid manner. As Hakuin wrote in "Idle Talk on a Night Boat" (Yasen Kanna): "Before you even realize it, all your primal *ki* will concentrate in your lower body, filling the space from the lower back and legs down to the arches of the feet. The abdomen below the navel will become taut and distended—as taut and full as a leather kickball that has not been used in a game."[20]

With this, meditative absorption of unusual clarity and subtlety manifests. An increased physical vitality, useful for enduring exhaustive practice, is also generated. Eventually the vital currents may be felt to overflow from the navel center and radiate throughout the entire body, enlivening both the strength and the depth of one's practice. Advanced practitioners gain the ability to maintain *tanden soku* not only while sitting in the posture of meditation but in all daily activities, to the point that it becomes effortless and manifests even in sleep.[21] Thus, the mind—unified with the body by means of the breath—may be extended seamlessly into all of life.

But most importantly for understanding *kōan* practice: when one holds the *kōan*, the single word *Mu*, within a sustained bodily *samādhi* by means of *tanden soku*, one experiences that *it too permeates the body* in a remarkable and subtle way. The effort to hold the *kōan* without gap "day and night" in the manner Mumon urges, encompassing one's whole somatic awareness, is thus accomplished physically, without falling into intellectualization. In other words: one does not contemplate the *kōan* with the mind alone but rather unifies body and mind with it. This is what is truly meant by "extending through your 360 bones and your 84,000 pores." When accomplished, it will be, as Mumon writes, "as if you had swallowed a red-hot iron ball that you cannot spit out—extinguishing all the erroneous knowledge and experiences." The teacher in *sanzen* guides the student throughout this process, observing its fruition and advising as needed.

This is often described as a practice of focusing upon the *kōan* in order to "become one with" it. Such language is all right in the beginning. But to frame things in such a way and leave it at that can lead one to fall into a mistaken mode of practice. Mumon's next words are valuable in this regard: "In time you will become ripe, and your practice will become pervasive and whole. Like a mute who has a dream, only you would know it for yourself."

The words "pervasive and whole" further point out what seamlessly unifying oneself with the single word of the *kōan* in this bodily manner really entails. It is a subtle but crucial point: though meditation is commonly described as an exercise of focus or concentration upon some object to the point that we feel we have joined with it, we should learn that such an understanding is inherently dualistic. It is a way of conceptualizing practice that, if clung to, can reinforce rather than dissolve fundamental delusion.

To clarify this, I use the example of another meditation method: the well-known practice of breath counting (J. *sūsokukan*). This extremely useful practice is commonly assigned as a foundational method before *kōan* practice is taken up. To do it, one sits in the meditation posture and counts exhalations from one to ten, returns to one, and repeats the count. Instruction is usually to place one's attention intently upon the breath, count with single-minded focus, and return to the count whenever distracted. By doing so, the mind's habit of fixating upon sensations, thoughts, emotions, and other phenomena of any kind can be gradually lessened and an extremely stable, nonabiding state realized. This is easy enough to understand.

But actually, this is a beginner's way to describe the method of breath counting, and we must pass beyond it. Even the words "breath counting" are misleading from the start, because if the practitioner sets up the breath as a kind of object to be focused upon by the mind, then right there arises the usual habit of dualistic seeing: the reified "I," the subject observing objects, that is at the root of our delusion. Beginning practitioners often lack one-pointed concentration of any sort and may engage in a false breath-counting practice something like this: observing the breath as an object, occasionally wandering to fixate upon other objects of attention (thoughts, feelings, or any of the other endless phenomena that arise seemingly inside or outside our minds and bodies), and occasionally even standing mentally apart to watch *ourselves* as we watch the breath, all the while judging whether or not we are doing it well. Such experiences are familiar to all beginning meditators. Yet they are very far from a true unification with the practice method.

It is actually better to say, instead of counting the breath, that we should *breathe the count*. That, in fact, is the oral instruction given for the method. Though it is a small change in wording, try to feel the difference in meaning. To *breathe the count*—with one's whole being, not watching anything in particular, not ruminating, not observing any one thing to the exclusion of others—simply and wholeheartedly, with each exhalation as if it were one's last, breathing the number utterly and completely: this is the manner of practice in which there is no one counting, no object counted, and only a seamlessness devoid of identity or location.

We do commonly say about this breath-counting method—as with *kōan* practice—that we must become one with the count, unify with it, or hold it. But this is possibly misleading language. In the true practice, there are no such reifications from the start. There is no subject or object set up from the beginning, and so nothing at all to unify. The count encompasses all with each breath, and within that state we cannot even say with certainty that there is a count, or an "all," since to do so would be to fall again into the habit of reifying ourselves as an observer apart from the count. We should recognize that the bodily method of practice enables us to avoid such pitfalls.

This may not be easy for nonpractitioners to understand. But the breath counting is the way we practice with—that is, *kufū*—the single word of the *kōan*. Breathing it with our whole beings as Mumon urges, inwardly reciting *"Mu"* while exhaling long with the whole body, and bringing all the intensity of energy we can muster to the practice moment by moment, we feel that all is swallowed within the nonabiding *samādhi* of the *kōan*. Though this single word *Mu* is not absent, we cannot say where it is. As there is nothing that is apart from *Mu*, we cannot say there is this *Mu* at all. That is, we do not arrive merely at some experience of transcending the dualism of subject and object but at a transcendence of dual and nondual.

This is the meaning behind Mumon's words that practice will become "pervasive and whole." This is the true "union" or "joining" meant by the word *yoga*. And it is what is truly meant by holding, unifying oneself with, or becoming one with the *kōan*. Indeed, it is difficult to express, like "the dream of a mute." But under the teacher's constant watchful eye in *sanzen*, the student can be guided to it.

To sum up: Rinzai *kōan* practice, founded upon the method of entering profound bodily *samādhi* by means of the gathering of the vital currents at the *tanden*, thereby causing the *kōan* to permeate the entire body-mind, is not for the purpose of developing laser-like focus upon a meditation object (though we may describe it as a one-pointed nondistraction) or having a psychological experience of joining with something (though we do enter a seamless unity). The most we can say is that in the fruition of practice, there is no thing that is *not* the practice. If we can arrive at such a place, though it takes time and effort, then we arrive at the ripeness Mumon describes. That unified state, in which even the word "oneness" no longer makes sense, is what Ōmori Sōgen Roshi points to with his practice instructions:

> For instance, in the case of the *kōan* of "*Mu*," we should try to be one with it as we inhale and exhale properly, saying to ourselves, "*Mu*." This is exactly what we do when we count the frequency of our respiration in *susokukan*. It is the right way of solving the *kōan* of "*Mu*." In time, we will become used to this way of solving the *kōan* of "*Mu*," and even when we are asleep, we will concentrate on the *kōan* in accord with our respiration. Thus, we will naturally be prompted to become one with all things both inside and outside ourselves.[22]

Everyone's conditions are different, and we cannot say for sure when it will happen. But as oral instruction clarifies, a practitioner who enters the *kōan* using the whole body-mind is like an apple that matures slowly and almost imperceptibly on the branch, until one day without warning it suddenly falls. At such a time, it may be the direct pointing activity of the teacher in *sanzen* that shatters the profound *kōan* absorption, leading to a breakthrough. It is also possible that some random occurrence will serve. Mumon well describes the experience: "Suddenly, [awakening] bursts forth, astonishing heaven and shaking the earth. It is like snatching General Kan'u's sword into your own hands—slaying both buddhas and lineage masters as you meet them. On this shore of birth and death, you are free. You roam and play in *samādhi* in the midst of the six paths and four types of birth in all existence."

How perfectly this conveys the joy, surging vitality, and utter freedom experienced when one clearly arrives at *kenshō*, the awakening to one's true nature. Smashing through this barrier of the lineage masters is like casting open the dark and stifling cargo hold of a ship so that a fresh ocean breeze sweeps through. All phenomena are seen to be nothing other than the face of one's own nature. *Samādhi* is known as the essence of liberative wisdom (*prajña*); wisdom is revealed as the free functioning of *samādhi*. We can see that our bodhisattva aspiration to aid all beings— now affirmed and greatly increased, along with our faith in the path— guides us unerringly.

Entering the *sanzen* room, where we are required to express our realization and have long been accustomed to the master's disapproval, now there is no hesitation at all. For the first time, we understand that there was no "answer" to the *kōan*: all that was necessary was to grasp Jōshū's state as our own. We realize finally the real function of the *kōan* method: not to puzzle out some meaning from the anecdotes of the old masters but to experientially grasp their profoundly illuminated minds.

Mumon did not speak poetically when he said that this barrier has been set up to allow us to "walk together hand in hand with all the generations of lineage masters, to see through the same eyes as they do and hear through the same ears as they do." It is a quite literal, and immensely kind, statement.

With awakening confirmed and clarified by the teacher, and taking it as the basis and compass, the student may embark joyfully upon the post-awakening practice of liberation. Entering the *sanzen* room again and again, enduring continued forging from teachers and penetrating yet more *kōans*, we shed patterns of habitual ignorance accumulated from beginningless time as if casting aside old, dirty clothes. This very body-mind, embodying the wisdom of awakening, becomes itself buddha.

"Still, how will you take up [Jōshū's *Mu*]? With all of your life force to bring forth the word *Mu*. If you can do this without interruption, then, like a dharma lamp, it takes only a single spark to [suddenly] light it up!"

Mumon reminds us again how to do it: use your whole being, your whole existence, your entire body, all of your life force, your unsparing effort—and just take up this single word. When the student actualizes the seamless practice to which he points, in time the all-encompassing *samādhi* will shatter and the lamp of wisdom flame to life. We will then be able to exclaim in the traditional way: "The buddhas and lineage masters have not deceived me!"

There are many aspects of *kōan* practice not addressed here, and of course many other practices used in Rinzai Zen that are not centered on *kōans*. But I sincerely hope this has provided some grasp of the most essential points of the method andunderstanding of how *kōans* in texts like the *Gateless Barrier* are more than interesting or mysterious stories.

How remarkable is this spiritual training that has been bequeathed to us: striking directly at the heart of delusion, effected by means of direct pointing, accomplished through "this lump of red flesh" (the body), and revealing a path to buddhahood within this very life.

It is the custom in Rinzai Zen monasteries for students to recite each morning the names of all the masters within the lineage carried by the abbot. During the ceremony, the abbot will offer incense and prostrate three times to each grouping of lineage ancestors: those from India, China, and Japan. With the arrival of Rinzai Zen lineages in many nations, how wonderful it will be decades or centuries hence if more rounds of incense offerings and prostrations will be required for new generations of lineage holders in many places across the world. And perhaps there will be new collections of *kōans*, with new casts of characters and new stories.

We may pray that such a happy result comes to be. But regardless, there is no doubt that the *Gateless Barrier* will remain a treasured text within Rinzai Zen, as it has been for centuries: illuminating the path for practitioners and allowing us, even today, to meet the ancient masters for ourselves.

NOTES

1. The Sanskrit word *śramaṇa* refers to an ascetic, one who exerts effort in spiritual seeking. The *śramanic* streams of Indian religious development have long existed in relationship (though not without tension) with the Brahmanic or Vedic streams, and many of the concepts familiar to us from modern Hinduism may be traced to it. Buddhism and Jainism are major *śramanic* traditions.

2. *Tanden* (C. *dantian*) may be translated literally as "elixir field," and the navel center is specifically called the *kikai* ("energy-sea") *tanden*. It is beyond our scope to thoroughly investigate the role of various *tanden*, which, like the *cakras* found in

Hindu and Buddhist tantra, have been much interpreted and reinterpreted in various traditions, including modern New Age teachings. From a practitioner's standpoint, however, we may generally describe these as foci of psycho-physical cultivation that produce known and beneficial effects. There is some possibility that anatomical structures may be related to such centers; for example, it has been theorized that the navel center is related to the enteric nervous system, or to the abdominal aorta.

3. From a canon that Ōmori Roshi (1904–1994) composed for Chozen-ji, a temple he founded in Hawaii.

4. *Shōbōgenzō*, "Treasury of the True Dharma Eye," is the collection of discourses for which Dōgen (1200–1253) is perhaps now best known.

5. Hubert Nearman, trans., *Shobogenzo, The Treasure House of the Eye of the True Teaching: A Trainee's Translation of Great Master Dogen's Spiritual Masterpiece* (Mount Shasta, CA: Shasta Abbey Press, 2007), 486.

6. Giō Shōnin (1217–1281). After arriving in Japan accompanying his teacher Lanxi Daolong (J. Rankei Dōryū; 1213–1278) he went on to serve as abbot of Kennin-ji in Kyoto and Kencho-ji in Kamakura.

7. Koan here refers not to *kōan* practice, but to a period within the Kamakura era stretching from February 1278 through April 1288.

8. The Kamakura-era general Hōjō Tokimune (1251–1284). He is counted among the greatest of the early Japanese students and patrons of Zen. The Chan master Wuxue Zuyuan (J. Mugaku Sogen; 1226–1286), called Bukkō Kokushi, emigrated to Japan from China in 1279 at Tokimune's invitation. Bukkō founded Engaku-ji in Kamakura.

9. This is a famous episode, occurring as the Mongols threatened to attack Japan. Bukkō asked Tokimune how he would meet them, and Tokimune replied with a ferocious shout revealing the depth of his energetic power. In Zen this shout is called the *katsu* or *katzu* (words that also approximate the syllables shouted).

10. Trevor Leggett, trans., *The Warrior Koans: Early Zen in Japan* (New York: Arkana, 1985), 153–154.

11. Much has been said regarding Zen in Japan as "the religion of the samurai," something that is largely a myth. But here we can see that the meeting of cultured medieval Chinese masters with rather unrefined members of the Japanese warrior class did, in fact, involve some commonalities. And there are even today similarities in the training of body, breath, and mind found within Rinzai Zen practice and traditional Japanese martial disciplines.

12. See case 40 in appendix 1, xxx .

13. See Ōmori Sōgen, *An Introduction to Zen Training*, trans. Dogen Hosokawa and Roy Yoshimoto (Boston: Tuttle, 2002), 51–52.

14. Norman Waddell, trans., *Complete Poison Blossoms from a Thicket of Thorn: The Zen Records of Hakuin* (Berkeley, CA: Counterpoint Press, 2017), 94. "Teaching Schools" refers to Buddhist traditions focused upon textual study, but lacking the dynamic means of awakening found in Zen. *Satori*, "to understand," is a word used interchangeably with *kenshō* in Rinzai practice.

15. Waddell, *Complete Poison Blossoms from a Thicket of Thorn*, 206. Hakuin's image of simultaneously progressing upward toward liberation while reaching downward to aid others is found in many places in Mahāyāna and Zen teaching: the manifestation of genuine realization is described as a unity of wisdom and compassion.

16. Phillip B. Yampolsky, trans., *The Zen Master Hakuin: Selected Writings* (New York: Columbia University Press, 1971), 144.

17. Like the *katsu* shout, this penetrating quality is recognized as something connected to cultivation of the tanden.

18. See the introduction to Victor Sōgen Hori, *Zen Sand: The Book of Capping Phrases for Koan Practice* (Honolulu: University of Hawai'i Press, 2010).

19. Experienced practitioners using this method in meditation may breathe only two to four times per minute. The average for resting adults is twelve or more.

20. Norman Waddell, trans., *Hakuin's Precious Mirror Cave: A Zen Miscellany* (Berkeley, CA: Counterpoint Press, 2009), 92. "Yasen Kanna" (Idle Talk on a Night Boat) is among the most famous texts in which Hakuin describes such methods of cultivation, and it saw wide popular distribution even in his day; the quote here is from its preface. "Not yet used in a game" means that the stuffed leather ball is new, and thus still firm and round.

21. The great twentieth-century Japanese master Ōmori Sōgen Roshi was in a coma near the end of his life. One of my teachers who visited him reported that, even in that unconscious state, he continued breathing in this manner. This is a remarkable example of how deeply such cultivation can be accomplished.

22. Ōmori, *An Introduction to Zen Training*, 48–49.

{ 10 }

ON *KŌAN* TRAINING

Jan Chozen Bays

KŌAN (C. *gong'an*) literally means "public case." For thousands of years courts of law have kept records of judicial decisions, which were available to the public. These records serve as precedents to educate and guide people in the future, to help maintain a lineage of wise and compassionate rulers, and to prevent the damage that self-centered usurpers or imposters might cause. In Chan practice, and later in Zen practice, *kōans* or *gong'ans* have served a similar function: to test, deepen, and document the clarity of a student's spiritual understanding and prevent the dilution of the lineage and its teachings. The student's understanding cannot be kept secret. It is tested in the presence of the master, often in the presence of the entire assembly of ordained, and ultimately in their public lives.

I am writing from the perspective of a Zen practitioner of almost five decades, not as a Buddhist scholar. I completed the *kōan* curriculum of Taizan Maezumi Roshi (1931–1995) with supplemental study under Rinzai master Shodo Harada Roshi (b. 1940). Maezumi Roshi studied with and received *inka* (full transmission and permission to teach) from both Koryu Osaka Roshi (1901–1985), a lay Rinzai teacher, and Hakuun Yatsutani Roshi (1885–1973), a Sōtō priest who, like his teacher, Daiun Sogaku Harada Roshi (1871–1961), studied under both Sōtō and Rinzai teachers. Maezumi Roshi's aspiration, perhaps passed down from his dharma grandfather, was to open serious practice to laypeople as well as the ordained and to synthesize the best aspects of the teachings and practices of both the Sōtō lineage (meditation as an expression of intrinsic awakening) and the Rinzai lineage (*kōan* study as a way to experience for oneself that intrinsic awakening).

As a teacher in a Japanese Zen lineage, I shall use the Japanese pronunciation of words and names rather than their original Chinese pronunciation. Below I describe the purpose and process of *kōan* training in that lineage, as well as different types of *kōans*, using cases in the *Gateless Barrier* as examples. *Kōan* training can become a lifelong practice. Its variety permits it to take any shape and to cover any situation. Once undertaken, it is not something from which one escapes or ever graduates.

There is an important difference between studying *kōans* and *kōan* training. I use "studying *kōans*" to refer to a practice of the discursive mind, intellectual study and discussion of *kōans* in books, classes, or "*kōan* salons." "*Kōan* training" refers to the ten- to twenty-year process of one-on-one, face-to-face work with *kōans* in the poison cave of a qualified and experienced teacher who has been sanctioned by a previous *kōan* master. Study of *kōans* is to *kōan* training as reading a cookbook is to cooking yourself on a skewer. What is the skewer? The *kōan*, and your desire to awaken.

Kōans are a mysterious and diabolical device for drilling down through layers of delusion and confusion, personal strategies, and karmic tangles to arrive at an *experience* (not an idea) of a stunningly simple and fundamental truth. The experience is for transforming, not for collecting. As Chan master Zhongfeng Mingpen (1263–1323) wrote, "It cannot be understood by logic; it cannot be transmitted in words; it cannot be explained in writing; it cannot be measured by reason. . . . They [*kōans*] are certainly not intended to be used merely to increase one's lore and provide topics for idle conversation."[1] In short, *kōans* are an entryway into our new experience of who we truly are and a test of the clarity and depth of that experience. Koans ask us to let go of our limited idea of a self-centered identity and plunge into the myriad aspects of our true existence.

BREAKTHROUGH *KŌANS* AND THE OTHER "SIDE" OF REALITY

Kōan training begins with taking up an initial *kōan*, often called a "breakthrough *kōan*." A breakthrough *kōan* works as a catalyst for a realization, often sudden, that in addition to conventional reality there is another aspect of existence that permeates everything but is ordinarily undetected. This "other half of reality" has been called by many names over the centuries, such as true nature, original nature, natural mind, essential nature, buddha nature, the great mystery, and the absolute (in contrast to the relative world). There are different names in other religious traditions for this experience, which is considered beyond description. It has been called awakening, realization, transcendence, revelation, illumination, *kenshō* in Japan, and *jianxing* in China.

People may have had a glimpse of this other aspect of reality. We call these glimpses "peak moments," when everything seems to slow down or stop, our mind switches from constant thinking to pure awareness, colors and sounds become more vivid, and all is right with the world. This could occur when you are running and break through the discomfort of harsh breathing and feet impacting the path to an experience of pure flow. It could occur when you are looking at a beautiful sunset or the infinite expanse of stars at night or when you are present for a birth or a death. Peak experiences are usually brief; we marvel and move on. *Kenshō* (sudden insight) experiences are more substantial openings into the transcendent, but they can be transient too, if meditation practice and work with a teacher do not continue.

Just as peak experiences cannot be created by the rational mind, so *kōans* cannot be "solved" by rational thinking. The student must learn to concentrate and clear the mind of extraneous thought, holding the *kōan* as a constant question. In frequent face-to-face meetings with the teacher, who demands an answer but rejects all answers thrown up by the rational mind, the *kōan* soon becomes a burning question that is irreversibly lodged in the body-mind. One author compared it to a time bomb ticking away underneath the everyday activity of our individual life and work. It bides its time, waiting for the mind to be at utter rest. Not a single human thought.

Often it is after months or years of concentrated, single-minded meditation that a breakthrough occurs. Often it is a seemingly trivial event—the sound of a pebble hitting bamboo, the subtle click of a key laid on a table in a dark room, the sight of plum blossoms, the snuffing out of a candle, a shout, or the sudden blow of the master's stick—that triggers a profound turning, throwing the student into the realm of the absolute. The experience rises through the body, and it may take a while before the mind realizes that something has happened. Consider case 28 of the *Gateless Barrier*, in which Deshan experienced *kenshō* when the flame in the paper lantern was suddenly blown out:

Once when Deshan was getting instructions from Longtan, he stayed on into the night. Longtan said, "It's late; why don't you go?" Deshan said goodbye and lifted up the curtain to go. He saw that it was dark outside, so he turned back and said, "It is dark outside."

Longtan then lit a paper lantern and handed it to Deshan. As Deshan was about to take it, Longtan blew the candle out! At that moment, Deshan suddenly had an insight. He then bowed to Longtan, who said, "What principle have you seen?" Deshan said, "From this day forward, I will no longer doubt your tongues [i.e., words]."

The next day, Longtan went up to the teaching hall and said, "Among you, there's a fellow with teeth like swords and a mouth like a bowl full of blood. Strike him a blow, and he shall never turn back. In the future, he will go to the summit of a solitary peak and establish our path there."

Deshan then went in front of the teaching hall with all of his commentaries and annotations [on the *Diamond Sūtra*]. Holding up a torch, he exclaimed, "Exhausting all the sublime theories is nothing more than placing a single hair in the vastness of space. Investigating the workings of the world is like throwing a single drop of water into a great abyss." He then burned his commentaries and annotations, paid homage [to Longtan], and bid farewell. (see pp. 269-270)

In the Zen/Chan literature this opening has been described as "When the mysterious pivot turns."[2] This means that we pivot 180 degrees, away from our customary, limited, and one-sided view of who we are, lonely and defective individuals who are basically unsafe in a world of suffering. Our mind opens wide, to an entirely different understanding and experience that we are simultaneously one tiny part and the whole of all existence, which has no beginning or end, no where or when, and from which all individual existences continually emerge, then exist briefly, and back into which they disappear.

This pivotal event is like suddenly being turned inside out from an "in" where "you" are a small, painfully finite, and separate being, a tiny spark in the vast scheme of time, into an "out" that is beyond life and death, infinite, and eternal. For some, this experience is completely disorienting, and they may require grounding through physical activity like washing dishes, cleaning toilets, or digging in the garden. For others, it is like returning to a home they once knew. They exclaim, "How could I have forgotten this?"

You never know what will trigger this explosion. You never know what piece of the delusion of I, me, and mine it will take out. *Kōan* work is like psychic surgery. After it is over, the surface is intact, but something deep and dis-eased inside has been removed.

Kōans are not a problem that can be solved with the intellectual mind. They bypass the mind in order to solve the problem of you. *Kōan* work is a lifetime process. To say that you have "finished *kōans*" is not accurate. You don't ever finish one of the old *kōans*.

BREAKTHROUGH KŌANS

The classic first breakthrough *kōans* are these:

Wu or *Mu.*
What is the sound of one hand?
What is your original face before your grandparents were born?
Who (or what) am I?

Many *kōans* involve stories of an encounter between a student and a Zen (Chan) master. Each *kōan* has an essential turning point called the *huatou* (J. *wato*). As the student grapples with a *kōan*, they must reduce it to one or a few essential words that can bore in and take relentless hold. The Japanese Zen master Hakuin asked, "Two hands clap and there is sound, but what is the sound of one hand?" "What is the sound of one hand?" becomes "What is the sound of one?" and then "What is the sound?" and then "What?" until listener and sound merge.

In case 1 of the *Gateless Barrier* the turning point is the word *Mu* (C. *Wu*; E. No): "A monk asked Zhaozhou, 'Does a dog have buddha nature or not?' Zhaoshou said, 'Wu!'"

Wumen's Comment:

To study Chan, you must pass through the barrier of our lineage masters. To realize wondrous awakening, you must exhaust the ways of the [deluded] mind. If you do not pass through the barrier of the lineage masters and do not exhaust the ways of the mind, then all that you do would amount to being a spirit haunting the forests and fields.

But tell me, what is this barrier of the lineage masters? It is just this single word, "Wu," which is also the gate of Chan—the gateless barrier of Chan. If you can pass through it, not only will you see Zhaozhou in person, but you will be able to walk together hand in hand with all the generations of lineage masters, to see through the same eyes as they do, and to hear through the same ears as they do. Wouldn't that be delightful? Do any of you want to pass through this barrier? (see p. 251)

What is happening in this *kōan*? The monk has heard their teacher, Zhaozhou, saying that buddha nature pervades the whole universe and includes all existence, without exception. Perhaps, as the monk is pondering this, they see a pitiful stray temple dog, a mangy, smelly, flea-ridden cur, ribs showing, with scars from fighting. The monk cannot believe that this dog could possibly be part of the eternal wisdom and compassion of the beautiful, shining, golden Buddha on the altar.

For weeks, even years, the monk has been pondering this apparent paradox. The question will not leave their heart. How could this miserable, suffering, half-dead creature be part of the boundless peace and joy that is described as our true nature? This nagging question expands to include the many imperfections of the monk themself, and the entire chaotic and imperfect world.

Many *kōans* are accounts of a critical encounter between a student and their master. Sometimes a *kōan* begins with the phrase, "A monk in all earnestness asked. . . ." This means that the monk has been seized by an existential question that will not let them fully rest until it is "solved." What the *kōans* don't tell you is that years of meditation practice and deep questioning lie behind the stated question.

Although we talk about "working on *Mu*," this is not what actually happens. We work at "working on *Mu*" until we are able to let go and let *Mu* work on *us* penetrating every breath, every footstep, every blink, every touch, every sound. Raindrops falling *Mu, Mu, Mu*. Crows calling *Mu, Mu, Mu*. Hands pick up *Mu* and spoon *Mu* into *Mu*. When our awareness is completely filled with *Mu*, when thoughts are replaced with *Mu*, then the habitual flow of energy reverses. Usually our energy is directed inward toward self-protection, a defense mechanism arising from fear. This fear is carried by anxious, obsessive thoughts and emotions, which reinforce the experience of the small constructed self as core of being. In this habitual mode our life energy is only occasionally directed outward. Even then, too often it is directed outward in defense, in response to perceived threats. When we give ourselves completely over to *Mu*, the awareness of a self that needs protecting disappears, and the energy is able to reverse and flow in its natural direction, which is outward and generous. There is nothing to protect and nothing to protect from.

At first you do have to work, and in a way and harder than you have ever worked before. This unaccustomed inner work can be quite tiring. You have to diligently and continuously strive to settle the mind, but without any judgment of self or other. As Wumen says in his comment on the *Mu kōan*, "To realize wondrous awakening, you must exhaust the ways of the [deluded] mind." This is accomplished in stages. You begin with a busy, complicated mind and continually return to *Mu*, substituting *Mu* for each thought that arises, as soon as you catch it. At first you only catch thoughts when they have been going on for some time and have branched many times. Later you are able to catch a thought as it is arising, before it takes shape as inner words.

After many days of intensely focused meditation on *Mu* you may have periods of pure awareness, when no thoughts even make the effort to arise. Ultimately these periods expand, until *awareness of being aware disappears*. When the witness vanishes, time also vanishes. This is the realm in which cause and effect are one and everything is present, all places and times. This is the realm of *Mu*. Thus, the mind goes from complicated mind to simplified mind, to unified mind, to pure awareness, to no mind. This we call original mind or mind essence. Although it is vivid beyond previous experience, that does not mean that our awareness of it is always vivid. Although it is eternal, that does not mean that our awareness of it is eternal. It cannot be, because of the truth of constant change. All states of mind arise, persist for a time, and fade away.

You hear or read about "beating yourself against the iron wall of *Mu*" or as Wumen says, *Mu* being "[like] a red-hot iron ball that you can't spit out or swallow down." For most Western students these descriptions are dualistic and mischief making. They arouse an effort in the mind that involves willpower and conquering, judging, and comparing. These all add layers of thinking, emoting, and reacting to the utter simplicity and accessibility of *Mu*. *Mu* is not something outside us that we must beat upon and finally get inside of. We can't get inside it because *it has forever been us*. It is closer than our tongue, breath, or beating heart. It moves in and out freely, regardless of our awareness or our ignorance of it. *Mu* is not a destination because it permeates every place and everything. In fact, there is no way to get away from it, even when you die. Isn't that comforting? It is never anywhere else than here. And yet it eludes us. Isn't that frustrating?

We begin practice because we heed the call of *Mu*. *Mu* calls to us continually, asking to be brought into the light of our awareness. Working on this elusive *Mu* is like working on making shy forest animals come to you. You must sit as still as a rock, forgetting that you have a human body. You must withdraw your human personality, become an intention so pure that you drop all wanting, for if the wild and original ones detect any pushing, they will not advance. Your body must become an unmoving rock or an upright tree, your breath a breeze, your mind without a single human thought, only wide open in pure awareness. Then something emerges—utterly simple and fantastically complex, very familiar, known to you from ancient times and yet, during your life, almost always hidden.

CHECKING *KŌANS*

Although the breakthrough experience from the first *kōan* is beyond words, the teacher can immediately recognize that this transformation has taken place. When the protective armor of thoughts, emotions, and strategies that surrounds the small self drops away, the energy of the universe can flow freely. This energy can be felt in the private interview room. There is a childlike sense of wonder and joy and a hunger to go deeper. To prevent this initial opening experience from being confiscated and co-opted by the rational mind, the teacher immediately throws out questions that can only be answered if the student plunges back into original mind. These are called "checking *kōans*." Examples include: "How old is *Mu*?" "What color is *Mu*?" "What is the source of *Mu*?" "Stop the sound of a distant temple bell." "A thousand mountains are covered with snow. Why is one peak not white?" "How can you rescue a man who fell into a thousand-foot-deep well, without using a rope?"[3]

Some traditions employ a set of one to two hundred "checking" *kōans* designed to keep the doors open to the initial experience of the transcendent and to clean out the murky corners where the light of realization did not penetrate. *Kōans* are a test of the clarity and depth of our new experience of who we truly are. Can we let go of our limited idea of a self-centered identity and open again to the myriad aspects of our true existence?

To see into these checking *kōans*, the student must repeatedly dive back into the realm of original mind. It is as if the student has traveled to a foreign country and the teacher calls them up to ask, "What do you see as you look around? What are the inhabitants like? Is time different there? What about suffering there?"

A *kōan* may even ask a student to look back at their breakthrough experience. Sei Kenko (C. Zhao Qingxian, 1008–1084), the famous Song layman and official, composed a verse as he was enlightened upon hearing thunder:

Sitting in the room in absolute silence
Mind source unmoved, filled like still water.
The striking of thunder has opened the gate of the head's crown
Beginningless self-nature has been awakened.[4]

Which line is most important? Present it.[5]

Is just sitting down and starting on the path or attaining the condition of an unmoving, transparent mind most important? Is the sound or touch that triggers awakening most important? What about our life after awakening? Could we single out one bit of the billions of causes and conditions that lead to this transcendent moment in our life and call it the most important?

FEAR AND PITFALLS IN *KŌAN* TRAINING

The following *kōan* speaks to the fear many students encounter as their practice continues and intimations of an impending breakthrough occur. The rational mind keeps clinging, like a frightened little person hanging on to the thin top of a hundred-foot swaying bamboo pole, afraid of letting go of reality as they know it and plunging into a dark abyss, unknown territory where the discriminating mind and the constructed self are not in charge.

Case 46: A Step Beyond the Hundred-Foot Pole

Venerable Shishuang said, "How to take a step beyond the hundred-foot pole? Another ancient worthy said, 'Although the person sitting on top of the hundred-foot pole has found an entry [into the practice], it is still not real. At the top of the hundred-foot pole you must step forward and expose the full body of reality throughout the worlds in the ten directions!'"

Wumen's Comment:

If you are able to take a step forward, then you will be able to flip your body around and see that there is no place that is unholy! Even though it is like this, still, how to take a step beyond the hundred-foot pole? Eh? (see p. 281)

Kōans do not have one "correct" answer. If taken in earnest, they continue to open up new insights throughout one's life. For example, this *kōan* can point to the common observation that a student who has had a first opening will cling to that experience and try to replicate it. This is impossible, as the swiftly flowing waters of impermanence are always in charge. We must continually let go.

Other *kōans* speak of "sitting on top of an icy peak," when a student clings to the cold, impartial aspect of the experience of infinity and time-lessness. The "real world" is seen as an annoyance, an impediment to one's holy state and purity of mind. This can happen even after a week of silent retreat, when students are reluctant to go home and face the demands of their family or work. They are tempted to go into a dark closet to reclaim the perfect equanimity and detachment they experienced during the retreat. Wumen's comment on this *kōan* speaks to the sacred aspect of every bit of life: "There is no place that is unholy!"

Kōan training must be based on three foundations. The first is living an ethical life, in accord with the Buddhist precepts. If we do not, our mind and heart remain clouded. For example, if you have told one lie, you must remember to whom you told it. If the lie is discovered, you may need to cover it up with a second lie, and so on. Even if no one discovers the lie, your heart-mind is aware of and unsettled by it. The second foundation is *samādhi*, the serenity of a profoundly concentrated and settled heart-mind. Deep *samādhi* helps open access to the third foundation, *prajñā* or wis-dom. When the mind is at peace, illuminating insights can arise from the ever-flowing river of truth called *prajñāpāramitā*, wisdom beyond wis-dom. As Chan master Hongzhi (1091–1157) wrote, it is important that these three aspects are balanced. "But if illumination neglects serenity, then aggressiveness appears. . . . Certifying and dialoguing, they respond to each other appropriately. But if serenity neglects illumination, murki-ness leads to wasted dharma."[6]

COLLECTIONS OF *KŌANS*

Once the door into another aspect of reality opens, practice with subse-quent *kōans* can begin. In the Chinese and Korean traditions, a student may be given one *kōan* for life, returning to it for ever-deepening refine-ment and realization.

In the Japanese tradition the student who has had initial *kenshō* and passed through the gates of the first one to two hundred checking *kōans* then undertakes several more years of training with hundreds of *kōans* contained in several collections: The *Gateless Gate*, the *Blue Cliff Record*, the *Record of Serenity*, a record of the enlightenment experiences of the Zen ancestors called *The Transmission of the Light*. In some Zen lineages the student must then elucidate the "Five Ranks," five poems that describe the interplay of the realm of the everyday and the realm of the transcen-dent and that also describe the stages on the path of *kōan* training. For example, the First Rank, the relative within the absolute, is the realization that all of existence is permeated by fundamental emptiness and ultimate peace. As mentioned earlier, this experience that can become a trap, a state that the student clings to. The Second Rank is the experience of more constancy in perceiving the absolute within daily activities and happenings, but not being able to manifest it in all aspects of life.

The last undertaking in this *kōan* curriculum is a nuanced exploration of the Sixteen Bodhisattva Precepts, or guidelines for ethical living. For example, the student will explore the subtle aspects of the first Grave Precept, not to kill. At the basic level, our aspiration is to avoid any form of killing, but as we look more deeply, we realize that our very life depends upon many forms of killing. Even a vegan kills and eats plants. Other people draw the line at cage-free eggs or free-range meat. To prevent malaria we kill mosquitos, and we are likely to kill earthworms as we dig in our garden or moths as we drive at night. Harmful microbes that invade our body are killed by our vigilant white blood cells, and so on. Taking another look, we recognize the need for expedient means such as taking antibiotics to cure pneumonia or medication to kill internal parasites. We may see that when we get angry at a child, we kill their happiness. And as we probe deeper, we may see that experienced from the realm of the absolute, life and death are a continuous manifestation of the undivided One.

Again and again, *kōan* training will reveal that the habit of dualistic thinking is still alive, and the student is asked in hundreds of ways whether true nature includes everyone and everything, old and young, male and female, human and animal, devil and angel, being born and dying, animate and inanimate. Does the tree in the garden outside the window have true nature? If so, if the essential nature of the tree is the same as your essential nature, how would you demonstrate it? Demonstration, not discussion, is required at first to keep the rational mind from co-opting the experience.

Case 37: The Cypress in the Courtyard

Once, when a monk asked Zhaozhou, "What is the meaning of ancestor [Bodhidharma] coming from the West?" Zhaozhou said, "The cypress tree in the courtyard." (see p. 275)

Some *kōans* go even further and ask us to discern and demonstrate without hesitation the essential nature of things we call disgusting.

Case 21: Yunmen's Dried Shitstick

When a monk asked Yunmen, "What is buddha?" Yunmen said, "A dried shitstick." (see p. 265)[7]

Kōans are a test of the clarity and depth of our new experience of who we are. Over and over they demand that we let go of living through our limited self-centered identity and plunge into the myriad aspects of our true existence. Because our original nature transcends the prejudices and limitations of gender, a man student might be given a *kōan* about a woman and a woman student a *kōan* about a man. A classic one is: "That young boy/girl over there, is he/she the older or younger brother/sister?" Without speaking, how would you demonstrate your understanding of that question?

Some *kōans* force us out of the realm of our limited human body-mind and into the realm of pure activity.

Case 8: Xizhong Makes a Carriage

Master Yue'an asked a monk, "Xizhong makes carriages with wheels of a hundred spokes. Yet, dismantle the two parts, the front and the back of the carriage, and remove the axle, then what will the carriage be?

Wumen's Comment:

If you can directly understand, your eyes will be like shooting stars. Such an occasion is like a flash of lightning.

The Verse:

When the axle of the wheel turns,
Even the expert is deluded.
The four directions plus above and below,
South is to the north, as east is to the west. (see pp. 256-257)

The mention of removing the axle is interesting. The word for suffering in Pāli is *dukkha*. It has its origin in the word for friction, like the friction caused by an axle hole that is not centered. What is the cause of the friction we experience in life? What happens when our "axle" and everything attached to it are removed? Remember, in Zen training, the essential point of this *kōan* must be demonstrated, not discussed.

Some *kōans* point to our tendency to become distracted by events around us and by our own mind habits and to fall back asleep, forgetting what a *kōan* has revealed or removed about who we truly are. Wumen pointed this out in the poem for case 8 above. "When the axel of the wheel turns/Even the expert is deluded."

Case 12: Rui Calls the Host

Every day, Master Ruiyan would call to himself, "Host!" Then he would answer himself, "Yes?" Then he would say, "Be wakeful! Be alert!" "I will." "From now on, don't fall for people's deceptions." "No, never!"

Wumen's Comment:

Old man Ruiyan is both the buyer and the seller, creating all sorts of façades of gods and demons. Why use them? One who calls, one who answers. One who is awake, one who doesn't fall for deceptions. If you recognize him, you are still not right. If you try to imitate him, you're holding wild fox views.

The Verse:

People studying the Way do not know the real,
Because they only accept their old discriminating consciousness as
    themselves,
Which is the root of birth and death since endless *kalpas*.
Fools call this the "original person." (see p. 259)

After you demonstrate your experience of the essence of this *kōan* to the satisfaction of the teacher, you might be asked, "Is Wumen's comment praising Ruiyan or pointing out his mistake?" or "Why does he say that fools call this the 'original person'?" Or "Who is the host?" "Who is the guest?" This *kōan* foreshadows later work on the Five Ranks.

CONTRADICTORY *KŌANS*

Sometimes Zen masters will seem to contradict themselves. In the following two cases Nanquan seems to say that our mind is not the way to awakening.

Case 27: Not the Mind, Not the Buddha

A monk asked Nanquan, "Is there a teaching that has not yet been told to people?"

Nanquan said, "There is." The monk asked, "What is that teaching that has not yet been told to people?" Nanquan replied, "It is not mind, not buddha, not a single thing!" (see p. 269)

Case 34: Wisdom Is Not the Way

Nanquan said, "The mind is not buddha. Wisdom is not the Way." (see p. 274)

However, in this next case he seems to contradict himself, asserting that the ordinary mind is the Way. Or does he?

Case 19: Ordinary Mind Is the Path

When Zhaozhou asked Nanquan, "What is the Way?" Nanquan said, "The ordinary mind is the Way."

Zhaozhou said, "Can one strive for it or not?" Nanquan said, "When you strive for it, it recedes."

Zhaozhou said, "If we don't try, how do we know it is the Way?"

Nanquan said, "The Way is not something known or not known. Knowing is false perception. Not knowing is just being oblivious. If you truly arrive on the Way that is free from doubt, [you would realize that] it is vast like open space, through and through. How is it possible to impose affirmation and denial?"

At these words, Zhaozhou was greatly awakened.

Wumen's Comment:

Nanquan was questioned by Zhaozhou, and he cracked like scattering tiles and melting ice—unable to provide any explanation. Even though Zhaozhou did awaken, he still had to investigate thirty more years.

The Verse:

Spring blossoms hundreds of flowers, and autumn the moon.
Summer brings in cool breezes, as does winter the snow.

If your heart is free from hangups,
Then it is the splendid season in the human world! (see pp. 263-264)

What kind of "ordinary mind" is Nanquan talking about? The mind that is full of thoughts? The mind of innocent babies? The mind that over time is at first ordinary, then with awakening extraordinary, and then ordinary again, as the specialness of the awakened mind fades and it becomes one's natural way of being? When Wumen says in the verse that your heart must be free of hangups, is that an extraordinary or truly ordinary state?

The Northern Song dynasty Chan master Qingyuan Weixin (ca. thirteenth century) wrote about the transition from ordinary to extraordinary back to ordinary. "Thirty years ago, before this old monk had begun to practice Chan, I saw mountains as mountains and rivers as rivers. Then later on I came face to face with a teacher and made some headway, and I saw that mountains are not mountains and rivers are not rivers. But now, having reached a place of rest, I once again see that mountains are just mountains and rivers are just rivers."[8] Is the second "ordinary" the same as the first? The Japanese Zen master Dōgen (1200–1253) wrote a *waka* poem about the second "ordinary."

Colors of the mountains,
Streams in the valleys,
All in one, one in all
The voice and body
Of my Shakyamuni Buddha.[9]

A *KŌAN* ABOUT KARMA

Some *kōans* strike deep into the heart of spiritual practice, asking a fundamental human question. Does our practice—including awakening—actually make a difference in our lives and in the lives of others, or are we just slaves to chains of cause and effect? Can we somehow step out of the beginningless karmic chain that led to our birth and provokes us into harmful thoughts and emotions?

In Christianity there is a similar question. Is everything that happens predetermined, known and decided by God? When we are born, is it already determined which people will be saved or not, or go to heaven or hell after death? Or does how we live our life matter? And if our choices matter, then why do good people suffer and evil people prosper?[10] This question is asked in an American folk hymn that explains we will understand this dilemma "farther along," as the old man in the next *kōan* did.

> Tempted and tried will oft' me to wonder
> Why it should be thus all the day long;
> While there are others living about us,
> Never molested, though in the wrong.[11]

In case 2 of the *Gateless Barrier*, a Zen teacher who apparently answered the question about karma wrong endured centuries of karmic retribution as a result:

Every time Baizhang taught, there was an old man who followed the congregation to listen to dharma talks. When the congregation dispersed, so would the old man. Unexpectedly, one day this elderly man stayed behind, so Baizhang approached him. "Who is it that stands before me?"

The old man said, "I'm actually not human. In the time of the ancient Buddha Kaśyapa, when I was dwelling here on this very mountain, a student asked me, 'Does a person of great practice still fall into cause and effect or not?' I replied that he does not fall into cause and effect. As a consequence, I have been condemned as a fox for five hundred rebirths. I now ask you, Master, for a turning phrase so as to release me from being a wild fox."

Then he asked, "Does a person of great practice still fall into cause and effect or not?"

Baizhang said, "He does not evade cause and effect."

At these words, the old man was greatly awakened. He bowed in reverence and said, "I have now shed this fox's body behind the other side of the mountain. Please, Master, give me a funeral service fit for a dead monk."

Baizhang ordered the rector to pound the gavel to summon the assembly and announced to them, "After we eat, we shall hold a funeral for a dead monk." The congregation was puzzled and began to discuss the matter among themselves. They went to the infirmary, but there was no one sick there. They wondered why Baizhang was acting like this.

After their meal, Baizhang led the congregation to a cliff on the other side of the mountain, where he used his cane and dragged out the body of a dead fox from a crevice in the rocks. They then formally cremated the body as would be done for a monk.

That night, Baizhang ascended to the dharma hall and related the full story of what had happened. Huangbo then asked, "One wrong reply and this old man was condemned as a fox for five hundred rebirths. If his reply had been correct, then what?"

Baizhang said, "Come here and I'll tell you." Huangbo then went up and gave Baizhang a good slap in the face. Baizhang clapped his hands and laughed and said, "I knew the [Western] barbarian's beard was red, but didn't know that red was the beard of the barbarian!"

The Verse:

Not falling, not evading,
Two faces of a single [divinatory] die.
Not evading, not falling,
Tens of thousands of errors! (see pp. 252-253)

What happens if a person believes themselves to be beyond cause and effect? What is the difference between "not falling into cause and effect" and "not evading cause and effect"? Zen master Dōgen commented on this *kōan*, "[An enlightened person] does not ignore cause and effect."[12]

DIFFICULT OR *NANTŌ KŌANS* AND THE ROLE OF THE STUDENT

There is something that still must be seen and taken care of. Some *kōans* point to this remaining work and are considered especially "difficult" to see into and to be "passed" (J. *nantō*) or affirmed by the master. Working with these *kōans* and the barriers that a teacher throws up against a glib answer can be a tough test. Here is a *nantō kōan* in the *Gateless Barrier*:

Case 38: A Water Buffalo Passing Through a Window Frame

Wuzu said, "It is like a water buffalo passing through a window frame. Its horns and hooves have all passed through. Why can't the tail pass through?"

Wumen's Comment:

If you can be turned upside down to obtain the eye [of awakening] and to provide a turning word, then you will be able to repay the four kinds of gratitude above and offer sustenance to those in the three lower realms below. If you cannot, then take care of this tail!

The Verse:

Passing through, it falls into a pit.
Turning back, it dies.
This tail
Is indeed very strange. (see p. 276)

As we work on a *nantō kōan*, or let it work on us, we must use all the sensitivity, refinement, and flexibility learned during many years of meditation and *kōan* training, and all the insights and experiences that have arisen in the opening of heart-mind that occurs during *kenshō* events, to ponder deeply. What have we "passed through" during years of *kōan* training? What is the large body or small tail that keeps getting us stuck? What is the "pit" that we can fall into as our understanding deepens and our personal suffering dissipates? What is "turning back" and what then dies?

The difficult-to-pass *kōans* or *nantō kōans* are important because, even after years of practice, we still have obscurations or karmic conditions that prevent deepening practice and further awakening. Zen literature describes the essential requirements for *kenshō* or seeing into true reality as great determination, great doubt or wonderment, and great faith. Great determination means never giving up, absorbing yourself into the *kōan* and the *kōan* into you, until the two fuse. Great doubt or wonderment means that a palpable mass of questioning becomes the engine for complete absorption in the *kōan* and dropping the self. Great faith means never giving up in the certainty that you, like all the ancestors and dharma students of the past, are intrinsically enlightened, and the most important work you can do is to uncover your birthright and live its mandate.

It can be acutely disappointing to feel that you have grasped the essence of a *kōan*, to wholeheartedly demonstrate that essence in a private interview (*dokusan* or *sanzen*), and to have the teacher bark, "No! Work on it some more!" and immediately ring the bell that dismisses you without discussion or argument. Or even worse, laugh out loud and ring you out. You return to the meditation cushion either with more determination to see through the veil that covers true reality or with reactivity and sulking, fuming internally, "I know I saw through this *kōan*!"

But eventually you settle down again, clear your mind, and dive back into the *kōan*. And if you do, you discover after several rejections that the teacher was right; there was more to see and experience. It is frustrating to fall into the same trap repeatedly, into self-view, one-sided view. If you start musing, "I think I have this *kōan* thing figured out," then the very next time you try a presentation that worked with the last *kōan*, you will be rung out. *Kōan* training whips you back and forth between the relative and the absolute, part and whole, emptiness and endless manifestations, self and no self, clarity and confusion, success and failure. Wherever you are unclear, the *kōan* will find you out.

THE TEACHER'S ROLE IN ONGOING *KŌAN* TRAINING

The teacher's role is to keep encouraging and goading the student, so they do not give up before they have plunged into the awakened mind. The teacher's other role is to continue their own practice and realization. Because the teacher knows that there are billions of causes and effects that create each moment, and that they themselves are only a tiny part of all the billions of causes and effects (that become causes) that impinge upon any moment, they can be both patient and unrelenting in not accepting superficial answers. The teacher has faith that even if a student disappears, once the desire to be awakened has been recognized and kindled, that fire will never go out. It may manifest and compel a student back to practice in a year, or in twenty years, or in another lifetime.

The teacher usually assigns a breakthrough *kōan* to the student and encourages them to become completely absorbed in the question. Absorbed means having the *kōan* always present, bringing it up many times a day, and focusing on it for hours each day during silent retreats. For example, the student might keep asking internally, "What is *Mu*? What is *Mu*?" as they wake up, as they look in the mirror, and as they are falling asleep. During the day, as they see, hear, and touch things, they question earnestly, "Is this *Mu*?"

The student must come to private interviews frequently, demonstrate their understanding, and face the disappointment of dismissal. The teacher may ring them out of the room, allow them to go on to the next *kōan*, or review the essence or more subtle points of the *kōan*. This could happen again and again over days, months, or years. Because the teacher knows for certain that everyone has—is the manifestation of—true, pure, original buddha nature, they continue to push and prod, kindly encourage, and laughingly dismiss. The teacher must be patient and supportive and also unrelentingly demanding in not accepting superficial answers.

One awakening experience is just that, one awakening experience. If a student continues with *kōan* training after an initial *kenshō* or breakthrough, the teacher's role is to ensure that their understanding is continuously clarified. A lifetime of earnest practice will contain many small but key insights as well as larger, more transformative openings. Zen Master Hakuin wrote:

> I devoted myself to Introspective Meditation, practicing it over and over on my own. In less than three years—without recourse to medicine, acupuncture or moxacautery—the illnesses that had been plaguing me for years cleared up by themselves. What is more, during that period I experienced the immense joy of great *satori* six or seven times, boring through and penetrating to the root of all those hard-to-believe, hard-to-penetrate, hard-to-grasp, and hard-to-enter *kōans* that I had never before been able to get my teeth into at all. I attained countless small *satoris* as well, which sent me waltzing about waving my hands in the air in mindless dance.[13]

Eventually *kōan* practice will compel the student to become facile at moving between the relative world (of earning money, supporting family, deadlines, debt, shopping, keeping up on the news and latest fashions, and endless decisions) and the realm of the absolute (the eternal, peaceful, boundless aspect of existence that pervades everything). Ultimately the student must fuse these two aspects so that action flows from clarity of body-heart-mind unhindered, appropriate to the situation, the time, the place, the people, and the amount. And "ultimately" may take decades of sincere practice, or maybe lifetimes.

What is our experience of life when we are not impeded by the burdens of past and future and can release the endless strategies the constructed self has created to keep us safe, loved, and successful? Master Hongzhi writes, "Multitasking amid chaos, manifesting in places of encounter . . . Adapting to changes and transforming freely . . . your role will be fulfilled—without you being trapped with the need for respect and honor."[14]

Just as everyone has had glimpses of the absolute through what we call peak moments, everyone has had temporary experiences of what we might call "flow," when the thinking mind is not involved and the appropriate response comes by itself. A very common example is how your hand moves to catch a pencil rolling off a table. You don't think, *Oh, that pencil is about to fall, I better catch it.* Or how your eyelids blink when you hear a sharp sound. As we continue in dharma practice and the obscuration and hesitation caused by the continuous self-preserving activity of the mind move aside, our attention turns outward and our actions become more and more like this, a completely natural response to a need.

Words are inadequate to describe this state. Poetic attempts include, "The body being empty, the arms are in activity," "The ruler stays in the kingdom, the general goes beyond the frontiers," "Dignified without relying on others and radiant beyond doubt . . . the energy turns around and transforms all estrangement. Passing through the world responding to situations, illumination is without striving and functions without leaving traces," and "all gates are wide open, through the open gates are the byways of playful wandering. Dwelling in peace and forgetting hardship, let go of adornments and become genuine."[15]

Each *kōan* has many layers, and one answer is only one answer. Anyone who has worked their way through hundreds of *kōans* and become a teacher, now doing *kōan* training with their own students, has discovered that there were aspects to many *kōans* that they did not perceive when they were themselves students and "passed" a *kōan* given by their own teachers. This is a truly humbling realization. Hopefully it inspires all teachers to continue deepening and clarifying their own understanding.

NOTES

1. John Daido Loori, ed., *Sitting with Koans* (Boston: Wisdom, 2006), 13.
2. Taigen Dan Leighton, trans., *Cultivating the Empty Field: The Silent Illumination of Zen Master Hongzhi* (North Clarendon, VT: Tuttle, 2000), 69.
3. From a collection of preliminary or checking questions used in the lineage of Osaka Koryu Roshi. Copies are not published but pass privately from teacher to disciple. See Barry Kaigen McMahon, *The Evolution of the White Plum: A Short and Incomplete History of Its Founders and Their Practice*, https://whiteplum.org/user_uploads/Evolution of the White Plum.pdf, 11.
4. For the poem in Chinese, see *Fofa jintang bian* (*The Golden Medicinal Decoction of the Buddhadharma*), compiled by Daizong Xintai (1327–1415), X. 1628, 87.422a 02–16. This work consists of the biographies and sayings of 398 Dharma protectors and lay Buddhist believers, including emperors, officials, and famous literati from the time of the Buddha down to the late Yuan dynasty.
5. McMahon, *The Evolution of the White Plum*, 11.
6. Leighton, *Cultivating the Empty Field*, 67–68.
7. Before toilet paper was invented, small sticks, or any other things out in nature, were used for wiping after a bowel movement.
8. Northern Song dynasty Chan master Qingyuan Weixin (Ja: Seigen Ishin). For an alternative translation, see Abe Masao in *Zen and Western Thought*, ed. William R. LaFleur (Honolulu, University of Hawaii Press, 1985), 4. See Robert Sharf's discussion of Qingyuan Weixin's comment about mountains and rivers in chapter 4.
9. Steven Heine trans., *The Zen Poetry of Dogen: Verses from the Mountain of Eternal Peace* (New York: Dharma Communications, 2004), 39.
10. Existential questions do not depend upon a conventional religious foundation. "What is the meaning of my life?" "What is the source of human suffering and is

there a cure for it?" (This was the kōan that compelled the Buddha to leave his palace.)

11. From the hymn "Farther Along," by W. B. Stevens. https://hymnary.org/text /tempted_and_tried_were_oft_made_to_wonde.

12. Gudo Nishijima and Chodo Cross, trans., *Master Dogen's Shobogenzo Book 4* (Charleston, SC: BookSurge, LLC, 2006), 167–168 and note 15. Also, Kazuaki Tana-hashi, trans., *Treasury of the True Dharma Eye: Zen Master Dogen's Shobo Genzo* (Boston: Shambhala, 2010), 852–853.

13. Norman Waddell, trans., *Wild Ivy: The Spiritual Autobiography of Zen Master Hakuin* (Boston: Shambhala, 1999), 108–109.

14. Guo Gu, *Silent Illumination: A Chan Buddhist Path to Natural Awakening* (Boul-der, CO: Shambhala, 2021), 109.

15. Leighton, *Cultivating*, 68, 38, 70.

THE *GATELESS BARRIER*

Translated by Jimmy Yu

PREFACE BY CHENG XUN

[0292a27] IF the Way has no barriers, then everyone in the world should be able to enter. If the Way has a barrier, then master [Wumen] is not qualified to be a teacher. [For me] to impose a few notes as a preface is like putting on a bamboo hat over another bamboo hat. To insist that this old fellow praise [Wumen] is like trying to squeeze sap out of dry bamboo. A book of written whines is not worth my time to [make an effort to even] throw it away. Throw it out and don't let even a drop of [this sap] fall onto the world such that even [the great general Xiang Yu's (232–202)] horse Wuzhui, who is able to gallop a thousand miles, cannot catch it.[1]

First year of the Shaoding era [1228], last day of the seventh month. Written by Cheng Xun (1197–1241), sobriquet Xi'an.[2]

DEDICATION TO THE THRONE

[0292b03] On the fifth day of the first month of the second year of the Shaoding era [1229], I respectfully observe the Imperial Birthday. On the fifth day of the twelfth month of last year, [Your Majesty's] subject the monk [Wumen] Huikai had printed and circulated [a collection of] forty-eight cases citing the awakening stories of the buddhas and ancestors [of the Chan tradition]. I dedicate this to extending the longevity of Your Majesty [Lizong, 1205–1264]: May you live ten thousand years, and ten thousand times ten thousand years! May Your Imperial Majesty's sage

luminosity equal that of the sun and moon, and may your farseeing plans extend to Heaven and Earth. People from the eight directions will sing of Your Sovereign's righteousness, and all in the four seas will rejoice in your effortless and civilizing influence.

[0292b08] Respectfully spoken by Huikai, the monk and subject of Your Majesty, who served as the abbot and transmitter of the dharma at the Baoen Youci Chan Monastery [founded by] the merit of the Empress Ciyi (1144–1200).

MASTER WUMEN'S PREFACE

[0292b12] The heart of the Buddha's words is the principle; the gateless is the dharma gate. Since it is gateless, how can you pass through it? Surely you have read the saying, "That which comes in through the gate is not the family jewels; that which can be gained from conditions is subject to change and decay." To say this is to stir up waves where there is no wind; it's like gouging out an ulcer in healthy flesh. Even worse is to get stuck on words and phrases in the conceptual understanding. Like trying to strike the moon with a stick or scratch an itch from outside the boot. What use is there?

In the summer of 1228, I, Huikai, was head of the congregation at Longxiang at Dongjia. The patch-robed ones asked for instruction, so I took the public cases of the people of old to use as a tile to knock on the gate [of Chan]. I extemporaneously guided students according to their potential. My remarks were transcribed and on the spur of the moment made into a collection of forty-eight cases, not arranged in the order I gave them. The whole collection is called the *Gateless Barrier*.

If you are a person who is fearless of danger or death, you will enter directly at a single stroke. Fearsome monsters cannot hold you back, and even the Chan ancestors of India and China can only beg for their lives as they look to your amazing presence. But if you hesitate, it will be like watching through a window as horse and rider go by—in a blink of an eye it is already gone.

VERSE:

The Great Way has no gate.
[Yet] there are thousands of paths.

If you can pass through this barrier,
You walk alone through heaven and earth.

THE *GATELESS BARRIER*

Compiled and edited by disciple Miyan Zongshao

[292C22] CASE 1: ZHAOZHOU'S DOG

A monk asked Zhaozhou, "Does a dog have buddha nature or not?" Zhao-shou said, "Wu!"[3]

WUMEN'S COMMENT:

To study Chan, you must pass through the barrier of our lineage masters. To realize wondrous awakening, you must exhaust the ways of the [deluded] mind. If you do not pass through the barrier of the lineage masters and do not exhaust the ways of the mind, then all that you do would amount to being a spirit haunting the forests and fields.

But tell me, what is this barrier of the lineage masters? It is just this single word, "Wu," which is also the gate of Chan—the gateless barrier of Chan. If you can pass through it, not only will you see Zhaozhou in person, but you will be able to walk together hand in hand with all the generations of lineage masters, to see through the same eyes as they do, and to hear through the same ears as they do. Wouldn't that be delightful? Do any of you want to pass through this barrier?

Arouse a mass of wonderment throughout your whole being, extending through your 360 bones and your 84,000 pores, as you come to grips with the word "Wu." Bring it up and keep your attention on it day and night. Don't construe [this Wu] as voidness or nothingness, and don't understand it in terms of having or lacking. It is as if you have swallowed a red-hot iron ball that you cannot spit out—extinguishing all the erroneous knowledge and experiences. In time, you will become ripe, and your practice will become pervasive as a whole. Like a mute who has a dream, only you would know it for yourself.

Suddenly, [awakening] bursts forth, astonishing the heaven and shaking the earth. It is like snatching General Guan Yu's sword into your own hands—slaying both buddhas and lineage masters as you meet them. On this shore of birth and death, you are free. You roam and play in *samādhi* in the midst of the six paths and four types of births in all existence.

Still, how will you take up [Zhaozhou's Wu]? With all of your life force to bring forth the word "Wu." If you can do this without interruption, then like a dharma lamp, it takes only a single spark to [suddenly] light it up!

VERSE:

A dog, the buddha nature—
The truth manifests in full.
As soon as there is having or lacking,
You would be harmed, and life would be lost.

[293a15] CASE 2: BAIZHANG AND THE WILD FOX

Every time Baizhang taught,[4] there was an old man who followed the congregation to listen to dharma talks. When the congregation dispersed, so would the old man. Unexpectedly, one day this elderly man stayed behind, so Baizhang approached him: "Who is it that stands before me?"

The old man said, "I'm actually not human. In the time of the ancient Buddha Kaśyapa, when I was dwelling here on this very mountain, a student asked me, 'Does a person of great practice still fall into cause and effect or not?' I replied that he does not fall into cause and effect. As a consequence, I have been condemned as a fox for five hundred rebirths. I now ask you, Master, for a turning phrase so as to release me from being a wild fox."

Then he asked, "Does a person of great practice still fall into cause and effect or not?"

Baizhang said, "He does not evade cause and effect."

At these words, the old man was greatly awakened. He bowed in reverence and said, "I have now shed this fox's body behind the other side of the mountain. Please, Master, give me a funeral service fit for a dead monk."

Baizhang ordered the rector to pound the gavel to summon the assembly and announced to them, "After we eat, we shall hold a funeral for a dead monk." The congregation was puzzled and began to discuss the matter among themselves. They went to the infirmary, but there was no one sick there. They wondered why Baizhang was acting like this.

After their meal, Baizhang led the congregation to a cliff on the other side of the mountain, where he used his cane and dragged out the body of a dead fox from a crevice in the rocks. They then formally cremated the body as they would for a monk.

That night, Baizhang ascended to the dharma hall and related the full story of what had happened. Huangbo then asked,[5] "One wrong reply and this old man was condemned as a fox for five hundred rebirths. If his reply had been correct, then what?"

Baizhang said, "Come here and I'll tell you." Huangbo then went up and gave Baizhang a good slap in the face. Baizhang clapped his hands and laughed and said, "I knew the [Western] barbarian's beard was red but didn't know that red was the beard of the barbarian!"[6]

WUMEN'S COMMENT:

"Not falling into cause and effect"—why was he condemned as a wild fox? "Not evading cause and effect"—why was he released from the fox's body? If you have the eyes of insight, then you will know why, long ago on Mount Baizhang, the old man won for himself five hundred remarkable lifetimes.

THE VERSE:

Not falling, not evading,
Two faces of a single [divinatory] dice.
Not evading, not falling,
Tens of thousands of errors!

[293b10] CASE 3: JUZHI HOLDS UP A FINGER

Whenever he was questioned, Venerable Juzhi would hold up a finger.[7] Later, one of the boys in the congregation was asked by an outsider, a visitor to the monastery, "What is the essential teaching of Juzhi, your master?" The boy also held up a finger.

When Juzhi heard about this, he took a knife and cut off the boy's finger. As the boy ran out howling in pain, Juzhi called him back. When the boy looked back, Juzhi held up a finger. The boy had a sudden insight.

When Juzhi was about to die, he told his congregation, "I got Tianlong's one-finger Chan and have used it my whole life without exhausting it." As his words ended, he died.

WUMEN'S COMMENT:

Juzhi and the boy were not enlightened by the finger. If you can see into this, then Tianlong, Juzhi, the boy, and you yourself are all strung through on the same string.

THE VERSE:

Juzhi made a fool of old Tianlong.
Holding up the sharp blade alone to test the boy,
Like the Great Spirit Julin who lifts his hand effortlessly
And splits apart the great ridges of Mount Hua.

[293b23] CASE 4: THE BARBARIAN HAS NO BEARD

Huo'an said, "Why does the barbarian from the West have no beard?"

WUMEN'S COMMENT:

Investigation must be genuine investigation. Awakening must be authentic awakening. For this, you must see the barbarian in person. But when I say, "see in person," it has already become dualistic.

THE VERSE:

In front of fools,
We must not speak of dreams.
"The barbarian with no beard"
Adds confusion to utter clarity.

[293c01] CASE 5: XIANGYAN'S MAN IS UP IN A TREE

Master Xiangyan said,[8] "It is like a man being up in a tree hanging onto a branch by his teeth, with his hands and feet not touching the tree branches at all. Beneath the tree there is someone who asks about the meaning of [Bodhidharma] coming from the West. If this man does not reply, he is evading the questioner's question. If he does reply, he perishes. At such a moment, how could he answer?"

WUMEN'S COMMENT:

Even if you have eloquence that flows like a river, it is totally useless here. Even if you can preach the whole great [Buddhist] canon of the teachings, that, too, is useless. If you can give an apt, appropriate answer, you bring back to life what before was a dead end, and you put to death what before was your life's path. If you cannot answer, you must wait until Maitreya comes and ask him.

THE VERSE:

Xiangyan is blabbering nonsense;
His venomous poison is inexhaustible.
Making the mouths of patch-robed monks go mute,
His whole body is squirting demon eyes.

[293c12] CASE 6: THE WORLD-HONORED ONE
HOLDS UP A FLOWER

At an assembly on Vulture Peak, the World-Honored One held up a flower and showed it to the assembly. At that moment, everyone in the assembly was silent except Mahākāśyapa,[9] who broke into a smile.

The World-Honored One said, "I have the treasury of the true dharma eye, the wondrous mind of *nirvāṇa*, the true form of no-form, the subtle and wondrous gate to the dharma, the special transmission outside the teaching, not established on words and language. I now entrust it to Mahākāśyapa."

WUMEN'S COMMENT:

The golden-faced Gautama behaved as if no one [was capable among his assembly]. He turned the noble into the lowly and sold dog meat and advertised it as mutton, proclaiming it marvelous. If the whole assembly had smiled, how would the Buddha have passed on the treasury of the true dharma eye? If Mahākāśyapa had not smiled, how would the Buddha have transmitted the treasury of the true dharma eye? If you say that the treasury of the true dharma eye can be transmitted, then the old golden-faced man would just be deceiving villagers. If you say that it cannot be transmitted, then why did he approve of Mahākāśyapa?

THE VERSE:

Holding up the flower—
The fox's tail has already revealed.
Kāśyapa's smile—
Humans and devas are all bewildered!

[293c26] CASE 7: ZHAOZHOU'S "WASH THE BOWL!"

A monk asked Zhaozhou, "I have just entered this monastery. I beg for your instructions, teacher."

Zhaozhou replied, "Have you eaten porridge yet?"
The monk said, "Yes, I have eaten."
Zhaozhou said, "Then go wash your bowl!"
The monk had an insight.

WUMEN'S COMMENT:

Opening his mouth, Zhaozhou shows his liver and reveals his heart and guts. This monk had not truly listened [to Zhaozhou's words], calling a bell a jar.

THE VERSE:

Because it was so extremely clear,
It took so long to come to realization.
If you knew that candlelight is made up of fire,
Then the rice would have been cooked long ago.

[294a06] CASE 8: XIZHONG MAKES A CARRIAGE

Master Yue'an[10] asked a monk, "Xizhong makes carriages[11] with wheels of a hundred spokes. Yet, dismantle the two parts, the front and the back of the carriage, and remove the axle, then what will the carriage be?

WUMEN'S COMMENT:

If you can directly understand, your eyes will be like shooting stars. Such an occasion is like a flash of lightning.

THE VERSE:

When the axle of the wheel turns,
Even the expert is deluded.
The four directions plus above and below,
South is to the north, as east is to the west.

[294a14] CASE 9: GREAT PENETRATING AND SUPREME WISDOM

A monk asked Master Rang of Xingyang,[12] "The Buddha of Great Penetrating and Supreme Wisdom[13] sat at the site of enlightenment for ten *kalpas*,[14] but buddhadharma did not appear to him. How was it that he did not achieve the Buddha Way?"

Master Rang replied, "This question is most appropriate."

The monk said, "Since he sat at the site of enlightenment for ten eons or *kalpas*, why did he not achieve the Buddha Way?"

Rang said, "Because he did not."

WUMEN'S COMMENT:

You may know the old barbarian, but you are not allowed to understand him. If an ordinary person knows, he becomes a sage. If a sage understands, he becomes an ordinary person.

THE VERSE:

Putting the body at ease is not as good as putting the mind to rest.
If you can put to rest the mind, the body will not be worrisome.
If you can put to rest both body and mind,
What need is there for nobility when you're already a god?

[294a24] CASE 10: THE DESTITUTE QINGSHUI

A monk named Qingshui asked of Master Caoshan,[15] "I am poor and destitute. I beg you, Master, relieve my distress."

Caoshan called out, "Ācārya Shui!"[16]

Qingshui responded, immediately, "Yes!"

Caoshan said, "You have already drunk three bowls of our family Qing-yuan's homebrewed wine, and yet you still say you haven't wet your lips!"

WUMEN'S COMMENT:

Qingshui misses the occasion. What was he thinking? Caoshan with the eye [of wisdom] profoundly discerns the potential of those who come to learn. Nevertheless, tell me, how is it that Ācārya Qingshui has drunk the wine?

THE VERSE:

Destitute like Fan Dan,[17]
But with the spirit of Xiang Yu,[18]
Though he has no way to earn a livelihood,[19]
He dares to contend with the richest of them [i.e., Shi Chong].

[294b05] CASE 11: ZHAOZHOU DISCERNS THE HERMITS

Zhaozhou went to a hermit's place and asked,[20] "Have you got it? Have you got it?" The hermit held up his fist. Zhaozhou said, "Shallow water is not a place to dock a ship." And he left.

Zhaozhou went to another hermit's place and asked, "Have you got it? Have you got it?" The hermit also held up his fist. Zhaozhou said, "Able to give and take; capable to kill and save." He paid his respect.

WUMEN'S COMMENT:

Both raised their fists. Why is one affirmed and the other denied? Tell me: Where is the fault? If you can utter a turning word here, then you can see that Zhaozhou's tongue has no bone in it.[21] He can hold up and put down with great freedom. While this is so, these two hermits have also exposed Zhaozhou; they saw right through him. If you say that one hermit was better than the other, you do not have the eye to investigate and learn. If you say that there is no better or worse, you also do not have the eye to investigate and learn.

THE VERSE:

An eye like shooting star.
A response swift as lightning.
A knife that kills.
A sword that brings life.

[294b18] CASE 12: RUI CALLS THE HOST

Every day, Master Ruiyan would call to himself, "Host!" Then he would answer himself, "Yes?" Then he would say, "Be wakeful! Be alert!" "I will." "From now on, don't fall for people's deceptions." "No, never!"

WUMEN'S COMMENT:

Old man Ruiyan is both the buyer and the seller, creating all sorts of façades of gods and demons. Why use them? One who calls, one who answers. One who is awake, one who doesn't fall for deceptions. If you recognize him, you are still not right. If you try to imitate him, you're holding wild fox views.[22]

THE VERSE:

People studying the Way do not know the real,
Because they only accept their old discriminating consciousness[23] as
    themselves,
Which is the root of birth and death since endless *kalpas*.
Fools call this the "original person."

[294b28] CASE 13: DESHAN
CARRIES HIS BOWL

One day Deshan[24] left the hall carrying his eating bowl. Xuefeng said,[25] "The bell and drum have not sounded yet; where are you taking your bowl, old man?" Deshan heard it and returned to the abbot's quarter.

Xuefeng described this to Yantou.[26] Yantou said, "Deshan, who is supposedly great, does not understand the last word."

When Deshan heard about this, he sent his attendant to fetch Yantou and asked him, "So you don't approve of me?" Yantou secretly whispered his intentions to Deshan. Deshan heard it and left it at that.

The next day when Deshan went up to the teacher's seat, sure enough, the way he taught was not the same as usual. In front of the monks' hall, Yantou clapped his hands and laughed loudly. He said, "This old man does have the last word. From now on, no one in the world will be able to cope with him."

WUMEN'S COMMENT:

As for the last word, neither Yantou nor Deshan could ever have dreamed of it. Examine this closely for the sake of posterity. Those two are like puppets at a makeshift show.

THE VERSE:

If you recognize the first word,
Then you will know the last word.
Last and first
Are not *the* word.

[294c12] CASE 14: NANQUAN KILLS A CAT

Master Nanquan[27] saw that the monks from the eastern and western quarters were arguing over a cat, so he held it up and said, "If any of you can say something about it, you save the cat. If you cannot say anything, it will be killed." No one in the assembly could reply, so Nanquan killed the cat.

That evening, Zhaozhou returned from a trip outside the monastery. Nanquan recounted the story to him. Zhaozhou then took off his sandals, put them on top of his head, and walked out. Nanquan said, "If you had been there, the cat would have been saved."

WUMEN'S COMMENT:

Now, tell me, when Zhaozhou put his sandals on top of his head, what did he mean? If you can utter a turning word[28] here and now, then you will see Nanquan did not carry out the imperative in vain. Otherwise, danger!

THE VERSE:

If Zhaozhou had been there,
He would have carried out this imperative in reverse:
He would have snatched the knife away,
And Nanquan would be begging for his life.

[294C23] CASE 15: DONGSHAN'S
THREE ROUNDS OF BLOWS

When Dongshan[29] came to study with Yunmen, Yunmen asked him, "Where have you just come from?"

Dongshan said, "Chadu." Yunmen asked, "Where did you spend the summer?"

Dongshan said, "At Baoci Monastery in Hunan Province."

Yunmen asked again, "When did you leave there?"

Dongshan said, "The twenty-fifth day of the eighth month."

Yunmen said, finally, "Today I give you three rounds of blows!"

The next day Dongshan went back to ask about this. "Yesterday you bestowed on me three rounds of blows, but I do not know where I was wrong."

Yunmen said, "You rice-bag! You've been through Jiangxi and Hunan Provinces, and you go about it like this?"

At this, Dongshan was greatly awakened.

WUMEN'S COMMENT:

At that moment, Yunmen immediately gave Dongshan the fundamental provisions and enabled him to come to life through another road so that the family would not be lonely and vacant.

Dongshan spent the night in the sea of affirmation and denial. When morning came, he went again to Yunmen, who again exposed him thoroughly. Then and there Dongshan was directly awakened, and he was not impetuous by nature.

So I ask all of you, did Dongshan deserve the three rounds of blows or not? If you say he did, then all the grasses and trees and thickets and forests deserve them. If you say that he did not deserve them, then Yunmen becomes a liar. Only if you can understand clearly here are you able to share the same breath as Dongshan.

THE VERSE:

The lion teaches its cub the secret.
When the cubs jump up, the lioness kicks them down.
For no reason, she gives a blow over the head.
The first arrow only nicked him, but the second went deep.

[295a11] CASE 16: THE SOUND OF THE BELL; THE SEVEN-PIECE ROBE

Yunmen said [to his assembly of monks], "The world is so vast and wide—why do you put on your seven-piece robe at the sound of the bell?"

WUMEN'S COMMENT:

All who learn Chan and study the Way must avoid following sound and pursuing form. Even so, awakening to the Way by hearing sound or illuminating your mind from seeing form is quite ordinary. Little do you know, patch-robed monks ride on sound and hover over form, and yet with each circumstance illuminating [this great matter] and taking up each and every wondrous opportunity. But even so, tell me, does the sound come to the ear, or does the ear reach out to the sound? Even if sound and silence are both forgotten, when you reach this point, how do you understand words? If you use your ears to hear, it will be difficult to understand. But if you listen to sound with your eyes, you would be on intimate terms with reality.

THE VERSE:

If you understand, all are one and the same;
If you do not understand, there are thousands of differences and
    distinctions.
If you do not understand, all are one and the same;
If you understand, there are thousands of differences and distinctions.

[295a23] CASE 17: THE NATIONAL TEACHER'S THREE CALLS

The national teacher[30] called his attendant three times, and each time the attendant responded. The national teacher said, "I thought I wronged you, but actually, it is you who have wronged me."

WUMEN'S COMMENT:

With the national teacher's three calls, his tongue fell to the ground.[31] The attendant's[32] three responses, the radiant lights harmonizing with one another. The national teacher was old and lonely; he pressed the ox's head down to make it eat grass. But the attendant would have none of it; delicious food does not suit one who is already full. But tell me, where was he wrong? When the country is at peace, talented men are esteemed. When the family is wealthy, the youngsters are pampered.

THE VERSE:

He makes people wear iron fetters with no openings,
Incriminating his descendants so none can be at ease.
If one wants to prop open our gate and support the family,
One must climb barefooted up the mountain of knives!

[295b04] CASE 18: DONGSHAN'S THREE CATTIES OF FLAX

One time when a monk asked Dongshan,[33] "What is buddha?" Dongshan responded, "Three catties[34] of flax."

WUMEN'S COMMENT:

Old man Dongshan had learned a bit of oyster Chan:[35] As soon as he opens his shell, he shows his liver and guts. Nevertheless, tell me, where or how do you see Dongshan?

THE VERSE:

The abrupt utterance of "Three catties of flax!"
These words are close to the truth, but the intention is even closer.
Those who talk about yes or no, affirm or deny,
Are just yes and no people.

[295b13] CASE 19: ORDINARY MIND IS THE WAY

When Zhaozhou asked Nanquan, "What is the Way?" Nanquan said, "The ordinary mind is the Way."

Zhaozhou said, "Can one strive for it or not?" Nanquan said, "When you strive for it, it recedes."

Zhaozhou said, "If we don't try, how do we know it is the Way?"

Nanquan said, "The Way is not something known or not known. Knowing is false perception. Not knowing is just being oblivious. If you truly arrive on the Way that is free from doubt, [you would realize that] it is vast like open space, through and through. How is it possible to impose affirmation and denial?"

At these words, Zhaozhou was greatly awakened.

WUMEN'S COMMENT:

Nanquan was questioned by Zhaozhou, and he cracked like scattering tiles and melting ice—unable to provide any explanation. Even though Zhaozhou did awaken, he still had to investigate thirty more years.

THE VERSE:

Spring blossoms myriad flowers, and autumn the moon.
Summer brings in cool breezes, winter the snow.
A heart freed from hangups—
A splendid season in this world!

[295b25] CASE 20: A PERSON OF GREAT POWER

Master Songyuan[36] said, "Why can't a person of great strength lift his own foot?"

"[Because] he speaks, without using his tongue," he continued.

WUMEN'S COMMENT:

It must be said that Songyuan spills his guts, but no one takes up his challenge. But should there be one, let that person come to my place for a good, thorough beating. Why so? "If you want to authenticate genuine gold, observe it in fire."

THE VERSE:

Lifting a foot, he kicks over the fragrant ocean.
Lowering his head, he sees the four meditation heavens.[37]
One whole body—ungraspable.
Please supply the next line of this verse.

[295c05] CASE 21: YUNMEN'S DRIED SHITSTICK

When a monk asked Yunmen, "What is buddha?" Yunmen said, "A dried shitstick."[38]

WUMEN'S COMMENT:

It can be said that Yunmen was too poor to prepare even a simple meal and too busy to write a composition. In response, he took a shitstick and propped open the gate [of our school]. The rise and fall of the buddhadharma can be witnessed here.

THE VERSE:

Like a flash of lightning,
Or sparks struck from flint,
In the blink of an eye,
It is already gone!

[295c12] CASE 22: MAHĀKĀŚYAPA'S TEMPLE FLAGPOLE

Ānanda[39] asked Mahākāśyapa, "Besides the golden robe, what else did the Buddha transmit to you?"

Mahākāśyapa yelled, "Ānanda!" Ānanda replied, "Yes?" Mahākāśyapa said, "Take down the temple flagpole at the front gate."

WUMEN'S COMMENT:

If you can utter a turning word here, then you will personally realize that the assembly on Vulture Peak[40] has yet dispersed. If this were not so, then why is it that, since antiquity until now, Vipaśyin Buddha[41] still could not realize the sublime even though he had long set his heart on it?

THE VERSE:

The question is not as intimate as the answer.
Whose eyes have strengthened from this [truth]?
The elder calls, the younger responds—the family's shame is fully exposed.
A spring outside of the realms of *yin* and *yang*.[42]

[295C22] CASE 23: NOT THINKING OF GOOD OR BAD

The sixth ancestral master[43] was chased by Ming all the way to Mount Dayu. The ancestor saw Ming coming, so he placed the robe and bowl down on a rock and said, "This robe symbolizes entrustment [of the dharma]. How can it be taken by force? Take it if you want it."

Ming tried to pick it up, but it was as immovable as a mountain. Ming hesitated and became frightened. He retorted, "I came for the dharma—not the robe. Please teach me, postulant."

The ancestor said, "Not thinking of good, not thinking of bad, at just this moment, what is your original face?" At this, Ming was greatly awakened. His whole body was dripping with sweat; in tears, he bowed in reverence and asked, "Is there any other significance beyond this secret teaching and meaning?"

The ancestor said, "What I have just told you is not a secret. If you revert the light and illuminate on your own [original] face, what is secret is right there."

Ming said, "Though I followed along in the congregation at Huangmei,[44] I've never had insight into myself. Today, I received your instructions and had an opening, like a person drinking water who knows for himself whether it is cold or warm. I shall regard you as my teacher, postulant."

The sixth ancestral master said, "If this is so, then both you and I take Huangmei as our teacher. Let us protect and uphold this [teaching]."

WUMEN'S COMMENT:

Regarding the sixth ancestor, his actions came from a state of emergency. In his grandmotherly kindness, he peeled a fresh litchi fruit, removed the pit, and then placed it in your mouth. All you have to do is swallow it!

THE VERSE:

It cannot be described or pictured;
Nor can it be praised enough, so quit your struggle.
The original face has never been concealed.
Even if the world becomes extinct, it cannot be destroyed.

[296a12] CASE 24: APART FROM WORDS

A monk asked Fengxue, "Words and silence imply *li* and *wei*.[45] How can one penetrate and be free from both without error?"
Fengxue replied:

"Reminiscing about Jiangnan in March,
Where the partridges sing
Is where the hundred flowers emit fragrance."[46]

WUMEN'S COMMENT:

Fengxue's activity functions like lightning. When there is a path, he [immediately] walks it. But why does he not cut off the tongue of the former [poet Du Fu]? If you gain intimacy here, then you will naturally find a way out. Put aside the *samādhi* of eloquence—say something about it!

THE VERSE:

Without disclosing the most potent phrase,[47]
Even before speaking, it is already resolved.
The more one rambles on,
The greater the bewilderment.[48]

[296a21] CASE 25: THE ONE FROM THE THIRD
SEAT PREACHES THE DHARMA

Master Yangshan dreamed that he arrived at Maitreya's palace and sat on the third seat. One of the venerable ones there beat the gavel and announced, "Today, the one on the third seat will preach the dharma." Yangshan then got up, beat the gavel, and said, "The Mahāyāna teaching is apart from the four propositions and cuts off the one hundred negations.[49] Listen carefully, listen carefully!"

WUMEN'S COMMENT:

Tell me, did he preach the dharma or not? To open his mouth is to fail; to shut his mouth is to lose. Neither opening nor keeping it shut, he is still as far apart [from the truth] as 180 thousand miles!

THE VERSE:

Under clear, broad daylight
This guy is dreaming of talking in his dream!
Conjuring up all kinds of bizarre and strange things
To deceive the congregation.

[296b01] CASE 26: TWO MONKS
ROLLED UP BLINDS

A monk came forth and requested a teaching before the midday meal, and the great master Fayan of Qingliang[50] [Temple] gestured with his finger at the blinds. At that, two monks went up to roll them up. Fayan responded, "One succeeds, the other fails."

WUMEN'S COMMENT:

Tell me, who has succeeded and who has failed? If you can obtain the eye [of awakening], you will perceive how Fayan himself failed! That being said, don't try to fathom this in terms of success and failure.

THE VERSE:

Rolling it up: the great space is utterly clear and bright;
But this open spaciousness does not accord with our tradition.
When even emptiness is let go of,
Then not even the slightest breeze passes through [the blinds].

[296b10] CASE 27: NOT THE MIND, NOT THE BUDDHA

A monk asked Nanquan, "Is there a teaching that has not yet been told to people?"
Nanquan said, "There is."
The monk asked, "What is that teaching that has not yet been told to people?"
Nanquan replied, "It is not mind, not buddha, not a single thing!"

WUMEN'S COMMENT:

With this [last] question, Nanquan completely gave away all his family treasures. Not an insignificant loss!

THE VERSE:

Repeated admonitions harm one's virtue.
Wordlessness is truly efficacious.
Even if the oceans should change,
I would never tell you!

[296b19] CASE 28: LONG HAVE WE HEARD OF LONGTAN

Once when Deshan was getting instructions from Longtan,[51] he stayed on into the night. Longtan said, "It's late; why don't you go?" Deshan said goodbye and lifted up the curtain to go. He saw that it was dark outside, so he turned back and said, "It is dark outside."
Longtan then lit a paper lantern and handed it to Deshan. As Deshan was about to take it, Longtan blew the candle out! At that moment, Deshan suddenly had an insight. He then bowed to Longtan, who said, "What principle have you seen?" Deshan said, "From this day forward, I will no longer doubt your tongues [i.e., words]."

The next day, Longtan went up to the teaching hall and said, "Among you, there's a fellow with teeth like swords and a mouth like a bowl full of blood. Strike him a blow, and he shall never turn back. In the future, he will go to the summit of a solitary peak and establish our path there."

Deshan then went in front of the teaching hall with all of his commentaries and annotations [on the *Diamond Sūtra*]. Holding up a torch, he exclaimed, "Exhausting all the sublime theories is nothing more than placing a single hair in the vastness of space. Investigating the workings of the world is like throwing a single drop of water into a great abyss." He then burned his commentaries and annotations, paid homage [to Longtan], and bid farewell.

WUMEN'S COMMENT:

Before Deshan passed through the barrier, his heart had been burning with zeal, and his tongue was very sharp. He traveled south, with the intent to wipe out "the special transmission outside of the scripture" teaching [i.e., Chan teaching].

When he reached Lizhou, he told an old woman selling refreshments by the road that he wanted to buy some dessert to eat. The old woman asked him, "What are those writings that you have in your cart, virtuous one?" Deshan said, "That's my commentary and annotation on the *Diamond Sūtra*." The old woman said, "Ahh . . . Doesn't it say in the *Diamond Sūtra* that the past mind cannot be found; the present mind cannot be found; and the future mind cannot be found? Which mind do you wish to refresh, virtuous one?"

When Deshan heard this question, his mouth remained shut, unable to answer. Yet he was still unwilling to die under the old woman's words. He asked her, "Are there any Chan teachers around here?" The old woman said, "Yes. About five miles from here lives Chan Master Longtan."

By the time he got to Longtan, Deshan was a defeated man. We could say that his former words did not match his later sayings. Longtan was like a mother who, out of love, does not perceive the ugliness of her child. When Longtan saw that Deshan still had a bit of live coal left in him, he doused him over the head with dirty water, putting it out completely. Examining this story impartially, it is rather funny!

THE VERSE:

It is better to see him face to face than to hear of his fame.
Yet, seeing him face to face is not better than hearing of his fame.
Even though Longtan saved [Deshan's] nose,
He blinded his eyes!

[296c17] CASE 29: NOT THE WIND, NOT THE FLAG

Once, the sixth ancestor [Huineng] saw the temple flag fluttering in the wind and two monks arguing with each other about it. One said, "The wind was blowing." "The flag was moving," said the other. They argued back and forth without reaching the truth. The ancestor told them, "It is not the flag moving, and it is not the wind moving. It is your mind that's moving." The two monks were startled.

WUMEN'S COMMENT:

It is neither the flag moving, nor the wind, nor the mind that's moving! Where will you see the ancestor? If you can perceive this truth intimately here, then you will realize that the two monks paid for iron but instead got gold. The ancestor could not refrain from laughing, and so this farce.

THE VERSE:

Wind, flag, the mind moving—
These offences are exposed with a single indictment!
Although they know how to open their mouths,
They do not know that their words have failed.[52]

[296c27] CASE 30: MIND IS BUDDHA

When Damei asked, "What is buddha?" Mazu said, "This mind is buddha."

WUMEN'S COMMENT:

If you can directly grasp this meaning, then you will be wearing buddha's robe, eating buddha's food, speaking buddha's words, and carrying out buddha's practices. You will be buddha. Even though this is the way it is, Damei has misled a lot of people, based on a wrong measurement of standard. One should know that just by saying the word "buddha" you should wash your mouth for three days! If you are a genuine person, upon hearing someone say that mind is buddha, you should cover up your ears and just walk away.

THE VERSE:

Stop seeking after it
Under the clear blue sky in broad daylight.
Asking how is it [that mind is buddha],
Is like holding onto stolen goods and claiming you're innocent!

[297a08] CASE 31: ZHAOZHOU EXPOSES THE OLD GRANNY

A monk asked an old granny, "Which way is the road to Mount Tai?" The old granny said, "Straight ahead." When the monk started walking [toward the direction] three or five steps, the old granny said, "Yet another fine monk goes off like that!"

Later, the monk brought this up to Zhaozhou, who said, "Wait until I go and check out this old granny for you." The next day Zhaozhou went to the old granny and asked the exact same question. Her answer was the same as before.

When Zhaozhou returned, he gathered his congregation and said, "I've exposed the old granny of Mount Tai for you all."

WUMEN'S COMMENT:

The old granny only knew how to sit within her headquarter tent and launch her stratagem to catch the thieves. She did not know that old man Zhaozhou was good at creeping into her tent and menacing her fortress. Furthermore, he did not have the outward marks of a great man. Examining them, both had transgressed. But tell me, what is it that is exposed by Zhaozhou in the old granny?

THE VERSE:

The questions were the same,
And so were the answers.
Sand is mixed in the rice;
Thorns are hidden in the mud.

[297a21] CASE 32: AN OUTSIDER QUESTIONS THE BUDDHA

An outer-path practitioner asked the World-Honored One, "I do not ask for [that which is expressed through] words, nor I do not ask for [that which is expressed through] the wordless!" The World-Honored One sat in his seat.

The outsider exclaimed in praise, "The great merciful and compassionate World-Honored One has dispelled the clouds of delusion in me and enabled me to enter [the Way]." Then he prostrated with great reverence and left.

Later, Ānanda asked the Buddha, "What did that outer-path realize for him to praise you and leave?"

The World-Honored One replied, "A good horse moves when he sees the shadow of a whip."

WUMEN'S COMMENT:

Ānanda was the Buddha's disciple, yet his understanding was inferior to that of the outer-path. Tell me, how far apart is the outer-path's [understanding] compared to that of the Buddha's disciple?

THE VERSE:

Walking on the sword's edge,
Running up an icy hill,
Without steps or stages,
Hanging from a cliff—let go!

[297b03] CASE 33: NOT MIND, NOT BUDDHA

Once when a monk asked, "What is buddha?" Mazu said, "Not mind, not buddha."

WUMEN'S COMMENT:

If you can see into the truth of this, your task of Chan investigation and training will be complete.

THE VERSE:

When you meet a swordsman on the road, show him your sword.
If you do not meet a poet, do not display your verses.
If you meet someone, say only three-tenths of what you mean.[53]
You should not convey the whole of it.

[297b09] CASE 34: WISDOM IS NOT THE WAY

Nanquan said, "The mind is not buddha. Wisdom is not the Way."

WUMEN'S COMMENT:

We could say that Nanquan, though an old man, had no shame. As soon as he opens his stinking mouth, he exposes the family's ugliness to the outside world. Even so, few appreciate his benevolence.

THE VERSE:

The sky clears; the sun emerges.
The rain falls; the ground is wet.
Exhausting his sentiments, he explains everything.
Yet I'm still afraid people won't believe him.

[297b16] CASE 35: LADY QIAN'S SPIRIT DIVIDED

Wuzu[54] asked a monk, "Lady Qian's spirit has divided; which is the real person?"[55]

WUMEN'S COMMENT:

If you can awaken to the real person here, then you realize that both leaving and entering the shell of worldly existence is like sojourning in a traveler's inn.

If you cannot awaken to the real person here, don't go running around in confusion. When the physical elements that constitute your body suddenly disperse, you will be flailing around miserably like a crab dropped into boiling water. When that time comes, don't say I didn't warn you.

THE VERSE:

Clouds and moon are the same,
Streams and mountains are different.
Myriad blessings, countless fortunes!
Are they one and two?

[297b25] CASE 36: IF YOU MEET A PERSON
WHO HAS REACHED THE WAY

Master Wuzu said, "If on the road you meet people who have fulfilled the Way, greet them with neither words nor silence. Tell me, how will you respond?"

WUMEN'S COMMENT:

Right here, if you can respond intimately, it would indeed be delightful. If you cannot, then see to it that in all situations you're observant.

THE VERSE:

If on the road you meet people who have fulfilled the Way,
Don't greet them with words or silence.
Hold their jaw and give a nice blow on the side of the face.
If they can appreciate this directly, then they know [the Way].

[297c04] CASE 37: THE CYPRESS
IN THE COURTYARD

Once, when a monk asked Zhaozhou, "What is the meaning of ancestor [Bodhidharma][56] coming from the West?" Zhaozhou said, "The cypress tree in the courtyard."

WUMEN'S COMMENT:

If you can intimately perceive Zhaozhou's answer, then there is no Śākyamuni before and no Maitreya after.[57]

THE VERSE:

Words cannot reveal it.
Speech does not rise up to the occasion.
Those who pursue words will perish.
Those obstructed by phrases are deluded.

[297c12] CASE 38: A WATER BUFFALO PASSING THROUGH A WINDOW FRAME

Wuzu said, "It is like a water buffalo passing through a window frame. Its horns and hooves have all passed through. Why can't the tail pass through?"

WUMEN'S COMMENT:

If you can be turned upside down to obtain the eye [of awakening] and to provide a turning word, then you will be able to repay the four kinds of gratitude above and offer sustenance to those in the three lower realms below. If you cannot, then take care of this tail!

THE VERSE:

Passing through, it falls into a pit.
Turning back, it dies.
This tail
Is indeed very strange!

[297c21] CASE 39: YUNMEN'S "YOUR WORDS FAIL"

A monk asked Yunmen [about the poem], "The brilliant and quiescent luminosity pervades everywhere, [like sands in the] Ganges."[58] Before the sentence was finished, Yunmen interrupted, "Are these not the words of the scholar Zhang Zhuo?" The monk replied, "Yes." Yunmen said, "Failed!"

Later, Sixin[59] picked this case up, "How did the monk's words fail?"

WUMEN'S COMMENT:

If in this case you can perceive the lofty and perilous workings of Yunmen, and understand why the monk's words have failed, then you are fit to be a teacher of humans and gods.[60] If you are not clear about this, then you cannot even save yourself.

THE VERSE:

Dropping a fishhook in a gushing stream;
The greedy [fish] got caught.
As soon as it opened its mouth,
Life is lost!

[298a02] CASE 40: KICKING OVER THE WATER JAR

When Venerable Weishan was still in Baizhang's congregation, he served as a cook. Baizhang wanted to choose a successor for Mount Dawei. He invited the head monk to announce to the assembly that anyone who could go beyond the patterns [of the world] could go to be the Chan Master at Mount Dawei.

Baizhang, in front of everyone, took out a water jar, set it on the ground, and asked, "If you don't call it a water jar, what would you call it?"

The head monk was the first to stand up and said, "You cannot call it a tree stump."

Baizhang turned to Weishan. Weishan just kicked over the water jar and left.

Baizhang laughed and said, "The head monk just lost the mountain." Then he dispatched Weishan to open a monastery at Dawei.

WUMEN'S COMMENT:

Weishan was brave on this occasion, but even he could not jump out of Baizhang's trap. Just examine the outcome: he picks up a difficult task and gives up the easy. Why? He managed to take off his cloth headband to put an iron cangue on his own shoulders.

THE VERSE:

Flinging the water scoop and the ladle,
he suddenly severs complications and circularities.
Even Baizhang's multibarrier gate cannot hold him back.
The tip of his foot creates countless buddhas.

[298a15] CASE 41: BODHIDHARMA PACIFIES THE MIND

Bodhidharma sat facing a wall. The second ancestor stood in the snow and cut off his arm, saying, "Your disciple's mind is not at peace. Please, teacher, pacify my mind!"

Bodhidharma said, "Bring me your mind, and I'll pacify it for you."

The second ancestor replied, "When I search for my mind, it cannot be found."

At that point, Bodhidharma said, "I've already pacified it!"

WUMEN'S COMMENT:

This gap-toothed old barbarian sailed thousands of miles specially to come to China. This can be considered stirring waves when there is no wind. At last, he accepted a single disciple, but even he was one whose six faculties are incomplete!

Alas, Xie Sanlang was illiterate![61]

THE VERSE:

Coming from the West, [Bodhidharma] directly points to *this*.
An affair initiated by [the Buddha's] instructions.
The one who stirs up a ruckus in Chan forests
Is, after all, you!

[298a25] CASE 42: THE GIRL COMES OUT OF *SAMĀDHI*

Once the World-Honored One [told the story of Devarāja Buddha] and Mañjuśrī wanted to go to his buddha land, where all the buddhas were gathering to collect the essential sūtras, [but Mañjuśrī was forbidden]. When he arrived, all the buddhas had already returned to their own abode, except a girl [named Depart from Consciousness], who remained sitting in *samādhi* near [Devarāja] Buddha.

Mañjuśrī asked [Devarāja] Buddha, "How is it that a girl is here and even sitting next to you but I may not?"

The Buddha told Mañjuśrī, "Bring that girl out of *samādhi* and ask her yourself."

Mañjuśrī circumambulated around her three times and snapped his fingers [which didn't wake her up]; then he took her up to the brahma heaven, exhausting all of his spiritual powers without being able to bring her out [of *samādhi*].

The World-Honored One, Devarāja, said, "Even hundreds of thousands of Mañjuśrīs would not be able to bring this girl out of her *samādhi*. Below, past 1,200,000,000 Ganges Rivers of buddha lands, there is a bodhisattva called Great Bodhisattva Ignorance[62] who can bring this girl out of *samādhi*."

In that instant, Bodhisattva Ignorance emerged from the ground and made obeisance to the World-Honored One, who directed him to snap his fingers. The girl came out of her *samādhi*.[63]

WUMEN'S COMMENT:

Old man Śākyamuni staged this comedy; the inferior would not be able to appreciate it. What is more, Mañjuśrī is the teacher of seven buddhas, so why couldn't he bring the girl out of *samādhi*? Bodhisattva Ignorance was only a bodhisattva of the first *bhūmi*. Why then could he bring her out? If you can perceive this intimately, then this frantic consciousness of karma is precisely the great *samādhi* of the dragon kings.

THE VERSE:

Whether able or unable to bring [her] out,
They [i.e., Mañjuśrī, Ignorance, and the girl] are already free.
A façade of a god or a mask of a demon—
[Mañjuśrī's] defeat is indeed remarkable!

[298b14] CASE 43: SHOUSHAN'S BAMBOO STICK

Master Shoushan held up a bamboo stick and showed it to the assembly saying, "If you call it a stick, you oppose it. If you don't call it a stick, you deny it. Tell me, all of you, how would you call it?"

WUMEN'S COMMENT:

If you call it a stick, you oppose it. If you do not call it a stick, you deny it. You cannot say anything, and you cannot say nothing. Speak! Speak!

THE VERSE:

Holding up a bamboo stick
To mandate the killing or the giving of life.
Where affirming or denying are interfused,
[Even] the buddhas and ancestral masters beg for their lives.

[298b23] CASE 44: BAJIAO'S STAFF

Venerable Bajiao taught the assembly, "If you have a staff, I will give you a staff. If you have no staff, I will take your staff away."

WUMEN'S COMMENT:

It helps you cross the river over a collapsed bridge and helps you return to your own village on a moonless night. If you call it a staff, you shoot straight to hell like an arrow.

THE VERSE:

Everyone, everywhere, deep and shallow—
All within your palm.
Propping up heaven and supporting the earth—
The winds of truth flow everywhere!

[298C02] CASE 45: WHO IS IT?

Ancestor Yan[64] of East Mountain said, "Even Śākyamuni and Maitreya are slaves to this person. Tell me, who is it?"

WUMEN'S COMMENT:

If you can see this person clearly, it is like meeting your own father at a crossroads; you don't have to ask anyone else whether it is him or not.

THE VERSE:

Don't shoot someone else's bow;
Don't ride someone else's horse;
Don't judge someone else's mistakes;
Don't inquire into somebody else's business.

[298C11] CASE 46: A STEP BEYOND THE HUNDRED-FOOT POLE

Venerable Shishuang said, "How to take a step beyond the hundred-foot pole? Another ancient worthy said, 'Although the person sitting on top of the hundred-foot pole has found an entry [into the practice], it is still not real. At the top of the hundred-foot pole you must step forward and expose the full body of reality throughout the worlds in the ten directions!'"

WUMEN'S COMMENT:

If you are able to take a step forward, then you will be able to flip your body around and see that there is no place that is unholy! Even though it is like this, still, how to take a step beyond the hundred-foot pole? Eh?

THE VERSE:

Those who blind their eyes on their foreheads
Mistake the markers on a scale.
Though they throw away their bodies to relinquish their life
[This would still be] the blind leading a crowd of blind people!

[298c20] CASE 47: TUṢITA'S THREE BARRIERS

Master Congyue[65] of Tuṣita Monastery established three barriers to question students: "Pushing aside the weeds to investigate the mysterious is only for the purpose of seeing the [self-]nature. Right now, where is this nature? If you see your self-nature, you are liberated from birth and death. Yet, when the light of your eyes goes out, how will you be liberated? If you are liberated from birth and death, you will know where you will go [after you die]. When the four elements disperse, where will you go?"

WUMEN'S COMMENT:

If you can respond to these three turning words, then you can be your own master wherever you go and engage with the conditions without losing sight of the principle. If you cannot, then you would be like a person who gobbles down food—even though it is easy to be satiated this way, only by chewing food finely will it keep hunger away.

THE VERSE:

A single moment thoroughly reveals countless *kalpas*.
All the countless *kalpas* are just this moment.
If right now you see through this single moment,
This seeing through is [to see though] the one who sees.

[299a01] CASE 48: QIANFENG'S ONE PATH

A monk asked Venerable Qianfeng:[66] "The Bhagavāns[67] of the ten directions have but one path to *nirvāṇa*. Where does this one path begin?"

Qianfeng picked up his staff and drew a line and said, "Right here!"

Later, a monk asked Yunmen for instructions about this. Yunmen picked up his fan and said, "This fan leaps up to the thirty-third heaven and taps Indra on the nose. When it falls in the Eastern Sea, it strikes a carp and great rain pours down."

WUMEN'S COMMENT:

One of them walks on the bottom of the deepest sea, winnowing dust and stirring up dirt. The other stands on the peak of the highest mountain, raising foaming waves to the sky. Holding fast, letting go—each extends a hand to support and to defend the vehicle of our school. But they are like two children charging at each other and colliding. Surely, no one in the world can stand up to them. But observing them with the correct eye [of wisdom], neither of the two great elders know where the path begins.

THE VERSE:

Before even taking a step, you have already arrived.
Prior to moving your tongue, you've already spoken.
Even if you can grasp every opportunity [and respond] before it occurs,
You should know that there is a better way.

[299a15] POSTSCRIPT BY WUMEN

The extemporaneous conditions of the buddhas and ancestors have all been collected here as individual cases. There is no excess of words—I lift off your cranium to reveal your eye [of awakening] so that you can take them up directly and not seek it outside yourself. If you are a person of integrity, then as soon as you hear them mentioned, you will know where these stories land. There is ultimately no gateway for you to enter, nor gradual steps for you to ascend. Freely swing your arms as you walk right through the gateway without asking the border guard. Haven't you heard the words of Xuansha [Shibei (835–908)]? "Gateless is the gate of liberation; no-mind is the mind of those of the Way." Moreover, Baiyun said, "Even though you know it is just so as it is, why can't you pass through it?" Even these words are like rubbing red clay on cow's milk. But if you can manage to pass through the *Gateless Barrier*, you would make a fool out of me. If you cannot pass through the *Gateless Barrier*, then you have let yourself down. As it is said, the mind of *nirvāṇa* is easy to have insight into, but the wisdom of discernment is hard to clarify. If you can be clear about the wisdom of discernment, families and nations will be at peace in their own accord.

Dated the first year of the Shaoding era [1228], five days before the end of the summer retreat. By the monk Wumen Huikai, eighth-generation descendant of Yangqi [Fanghui (992–1049)].

[299a28] CHAN ADMONITION BY WUMEN

Conforming to rules and observing regulations is to tether yourself without a rope. Acting freely without restraint is just being an outer-path heretic or a demon. Holding onto a mind and settling it to a state of quiescence is the perverse Chan of silent illumination.[68] Indulging in desires and being oblivious to circumstances is to plunge into the depth of an abyss. Being wakeful and alert without negligence is to chain yourself to a lock and to wear a yoke [around your neck]. Thinking of good or evil, you create heaven and hell. Holding to views of buddha or dharma is to be held by two iron mountains.[69] Being aware as soon as thoughts arise is just being a conniving spirit. Being persistent in *samādhi* practice is to craft up a ghostly abode. Advancing, you are deluded about the principle. Retreating, you are opposed to the truth. Neither advancing nor retreating, you are simply a breathing corpse. Tell me, how would you practice? Exert yourself so that you resolve [this matter[70]] in this life! Don't put yourself through the misery of an eternal eon.

NOTES

1. This translation is based on the version in the Taishō Buddhist canon, with the preface and postscript dated to 1228, in the CBETA. The Taishō edition, however, is a reprint that dates to 1405 found in Kōonji Zen Temple on Mount Tosotsu in Tokyo, Japan. I have translated only Wumen Huikai's collection, excluding the various appendixes by subsequent practitioners included in the Kōonji edition. The following annotations provide only basic historical and philosophical context so that readers may appreciate the cases' significance and nuance. All dates for figures mentioned in the cases can be found in the character glossary at the end of the book. I have not provided annotations on all the figures, only those with available historical data. My annotations also highlight the lineage affiliations among them when available. For a modern commentary to the cases, please consult my book, *Passing through the Gateless Barrier: Kōan Practice for Real Life* (Boulder, CO: Shambhala, 2016) under my sobriquet Guo Gu. An appendix to this volume contains a survey of English translations of the *Gateless Barrier*, for those who wish to compare other translations.

2. Chen Xun (1197–1241) received the highest civil service examination degree as "a palace graduate" (*jinshi*) in 1217. He was a high-level official who held many posts around the Southern Song region, including being the local magistrate of Jiaxing Prefecture in Zhejiang Province and eventually becoming the assistant

minister in the Ministry of Personnel (*libu*) at the imperial palace, the highest of six ministries in the central government. His parents were students of Chan master Fozhao Deguang (1121–1203), who was a dharma heir of Dahui Zong'gao (1089–1163) and later became the national teacher-preceptor of Emperor Xiaozong (1127–1194). The parents prayed for a son and consulted Fozhao, who prognosticated Chen Xun's birth. After the latter's birth, his parents brought their son to him and, seeing the auspicious appearance of the infant and having dreamed of him as a former venerable, Fozhao gave him the sobriquet Xi'an, which means "Practice at the Cloister." See the section on "Buddhism" in the *Synthesis of Books and Illustrations Past and Present* (C. *Gujin tushu jicheng*) as extrapolated into X. 1661: 88.502b01–05.

3. Zhaozhou Congshen (778–897) was one of the most renowned Chan masters of the Tang period. His toponym Zhaozhou derives from the Zhaozhou region in Hebei Province, where he spent much of his later teaching career. His primary teacher was Chan master Nanquan Puyuan (748–835), a successor of Mazu Daoyi (709–788). For more stories connected with the life of Zhaozhou, see Guo Gu, *Passing through the Gateless Barrier*, 74–75, and James Green, ed. and trans., *The Recorded Sayings of Zen Master Joshu* (Boulder, CO: Shambhala, 1998). There is quite a bit of scholarship on Mazu; for example, see Mario Poceski, *The Records of Mazu and the Making of Classical Chan Literature* (Oxford; New York: Oxford University Press, 2015).

4. Baizhang Huaihai (749–814) was a Chan master of the Tang dynasty and a dharma heir of Mazu Daoyi. Baizhang taught on Mount Baizhang (whence Huaihai derived his toponym) and, according to traditional normative accounts, established the first Chan code of monastic regulations known as the "Pure Rules of Baizhang" (C. *Baizhang Qinggui*).

5. Huangbo Xiyun (d. 850) was a Chan master of the Tang dynasty. A disciple of Chan master Baizhang Huaihai, he later became a high-profile Chan master connected with the powerful minister of state Pei Xiu (787–860) and began to reside on a local mountain that he renamed Mount Huangbo, whence he acquired his toponym. He was also the teacher of Linji Yixuan (d. 866), the founder of the Linji (J. Rinzai) school of Chan.

6. The common usage of "barbarian" (*hu*) in Chinese premodern literature reveals the ethnocentricity of the Han Chinese as the people of the "central kingdom" as opposed to people of peripheral regions, who were viewed as foreign and uncivilized—despite the fact that the Chinese had absorbed plentiful cultural and religious influences from Central Asia and India. As Chinese literary tradition flowered during the Southern Song period, the society's apprehension of foreignness also grew. The contentious relationship between the literary tradition, especially the circulation of vernacular stories, and the formation of Han cultural identity sometimes led to a representation of foreignness under the guise of monstrosity. The Song society's xenophobia and the greatest oscillation between tolerance of and aversion to foreignness occurred when it was forced to navigate between the Jurchen and Mongolian conquests of "China." In Chan Buddhism, however, "barbarian" is generally a Chinese euphemism for the Buddha or anyone from the West, such as Bodhidharma, the supposed first ancestral master of the Chan tradition in China. In the *Gateless Barrier*, the term *hu* as barbarian appears in cases 2, 4, 9, and 41.

7. Jinhua Juzhi (810–880) was a contemporary of some of the great Chan masters of that time, for example, Linji Yixuan. His teacher was Hangzhou Tianlong (770–850). Tianlong's teacher was Damei Fachang (752–839), the subject of case 30. Fachang's teacher was Mazu Daoyi. These are all important Chan luminaries in Chan history.

8. Xiangyan Zhixian (d. 898) was a Chan master in the Weiyang school of the Chan tradition. He was a student of Baizhang and Yangshan Huiji (807–883). He dwelled for a long time at Mount Xiangyan, whence he derived his toponym. After having left Yangshan to practice on his own, one day, while he was sweeping outside of his hut, he experienced great awakening from hearing the crisp sound of a tile or pebble hitting the bamboo.

9. Mahākāśyapa was one of the Buddha's ten great arhat disciples, foremost in asceticism. The story of him receiving the dharma transmission from the Buddha in this case, as argued by Albert Welter in this volume, cemented Mahākāśyapa as the first Indian ancestor of the Chan school.

10. Yue'an Shanguo (1079–1152) was Wumen Huikai's great-grandmaster and a contemporary of the famous Chan master Dahui Zong'gao (1089–1163).

11. According to ancient Chinese historical records such as the *Spring and Autumn Annals* (C. *Chunqiu*), the oldest and the only surviving type of chronicles from the early Eastern Zhou period (770–221 BCE) and among the *Five Confucian Classics*, Ren Xizhong is the legendary horse-cart inventor who lived in the third century BCE.

12. Master Rang here refers to Chan master Xingyang Qingrang (910–980), who was a Chan master of the Weiyang school and disciple of a Korean Chan master who taught in China, Bajiao Huiqing. He was in turn the grand disciple of Yangshan Huiji mentioned in note 8 above.

13. The Buddha of Great Penetrating and Supreme Wisdom is Mahābhijñā-jñānābhibhū Buddha. He is featured in chapter 7 of the *Lotus Sūtra*. For an English translation of the *Lotus Sūtra*, see Leon Hurvitz, *Scripture of the Lotus Blossom of the Fine Dharma* (New York: Columbia University Press, 1976; rev. ed., 2009).

14. *Kalpa* is a Sanskrit word for "eon" or "age"; it is a unit of measurement for cosmological time. In essence, it is a period between the creation and re-creation of a world or universe. *Kalpas* are distinguished according to their general characteristics and lengths. For example, a "great *kalpa*" (or *mahākalpa*) is divided into the four lesser "inconceivable *kalpas*," or phases, which are the formation, existence, destruction, and nonexistence of a universe. Each of these four *kalpas* of the universe is subdivided into twenty *antara-kalpas*. In the *Lotus Sūtra*, it is said that this Buddha realized buddhahood after ten *antara-kalpas*, or ten minor *kalpas*.

15. Caoshan Benji (840–901) was the heir of Dongshan Liangjie (807–869). He taught at Mount Heyu in Fuzhou (present-day Jiangxi province) and later renamed the mountain Mount Cao (or Caoshan) after the sixth ancestor Huineng's (638–713) own residence of Mount Caoxi. Caoshan's line of Chan came to be known as Caodong (J. Sōtō), which is derived eponymously from the first Sinograph in both Caoshan's and Dongshan's names.

16. *Ācārya* is an honorific Indian Buddhist title for a preceptor, teacher, or exemplar. Calling Quingshui by this title suggests that he may have already been a dharma

or Chan teacher. Moreover, stating that he has already drank the "wine" (i.e., teach-ings) of Qingyuan Xingsi (671–741), a disciple of the sixth ancestor Huineng and the progenitor of the Caodong line of Chan, suggests that he must have been a teacher within the Caodong line of Chan.

17. Fan Dan (112–185) was a famous but poor Han dynasty man. He lived humbly and frugally but became a cultural hero through his filiality and diligence. Legend has it that he married the daughter of the richest man in town, Shi Chong. They lived happily and raised a family. Shi Chong had disowned his daughter before they got married and hadn't seen her since. Later, when Shi Chong found out that Fan Dan and his daughter were earning a good living and had become wealthy, he set out to visit them. Shi Chong was quite impressed and was embarrassed at the same time, because he had previously scorned Fan Dan. But as luck would have it, a year later, Fan Dan and his wife lost everything they had by helping victims of a natu-ral disaster. They were still happy, even though they were now again living in pov-erty. His story can be found in the *History of Later Han* (Hou Hanshu), which covers theHan dynasty from 6 to 189 CE, a period known as the Later or Eastern Han.

18. Xiang Yu (232–202 BCE), a great general of the late Qin dynasty, was another cul-tural hero. He had won many difficult battles. The significance of Wumen's con-necting Fan Dan with Xiang Yu in his verse comment is that Qingshui also claimed to be destitute, yet through intense practice, he had great power like General Xiang Yu. Although Fan Dan had no way of earning even the simplest livelihood, he dared to contend with the richest man in the city, Shi Chong, and asked to marry his daughter; similarly, although Qingshui was destitute, he dared to challenge Chan master Caoshan.

19. "Earn a livelihood" (*huoji*) literally means plans for living, as in earning a living through work or skills. The meaning here is that Qingshui perceived his own state as destitute, unable to earn a living or have any livelihood. Caoshan responds, using the story of Fan Dan and Shi Chong, with a statement that richness is already within him.

20. This period when Zhaozhou traveled to visit many hermits corresponds to one of the greatest Buddhist persecutions in China, the Huichang persecution of Bud-dhism, between 841 and 845. This affected many of the doctrinal schools of Chi-nese Buddhism to such an extent that they never really recovered; see Edwin O. Reischauer, *Ennin's Travels in T'ang China* (New York: Ronald Press, 1955), 217–271. It was supposedly the time when many Chan masters and practitioners fled to the mountains to become hermits or gathered to rebuild their Chan communi-ties. Linji, Deshan, and other Chan luminaries included in the *Gateless Barrier* lived through this period.

21. "Tongue has no bone in it" (*shetou wugu*) is a popular Chan expression for that which is obviously true: sentient beings are already awakened; no one is binding anyone to *saṃsāra*. In this context, it means that Zhaozhou is not discriminating between the hermits—there is no better or worse, gaining or lacking, success or failure, right or wrong.

22. "Wild-fox views" is a Chan expression for charlatan Chan practitioners who deceive others. In premodern Chinese popular imagination, foxes are ambivalent spirits and marginal shape shifters; see Steven Heine, *Shifting Shape, Shaping Text: Phi-losophy and Folklore in Fox Koan* (Honolulu: University of Hawaii Press, 2000) and

Xiaofei Kang, *The Cult of the Fox: Power, Gender, and Popular Religion in Late Imperial* (New York: Columbia University Press, 2006).

23. This term "discriminating consciousness" (*shishen*) can have a range of meanings, from mind to consciousness to soul or spirit, depending on context. In this context for a general Chan audience, it may simply refer to that which continues after death. This popular usage was apparently in circulation beginning in the third century and continued to refer to the spirit's survival of death in the fifth and sixth centuries; see Michael Radich, "A 'Prehistory' to Chinese Debates on the Survival of Death by the Spirit, with a Focus on the Term *Shishen / Shenshi*." *Journal of Chinese Religions* 44, no. 2 (2016): 105–126.

24. Deshan Xuanjian (782–865) was a Chan master of the Tang dynasty known for his "blows" when receiving students. He first studied the scriptures and the *vinaya* and became famous as a teacher of the *Diamond Sūtra*. According to his hagiography, he was determined to defeat the Chan masters of the south with his knowledge of the *sūtra*, but on his way, in Lizhou (present-day Hunan Province), Deshan was rendered speechless by the following question from an old granny, a student of Longtan Chongxin (ca. 753–852). For the full story of the exchange, see Guo Gu, *Passing through the Gateless Barrier*, 120–121.

25. Xuefeng Yicun (822–908) was the kitchen monk. He first studied directly with Chan master Dongshan Liangjie (807–869) and had gained some understanding, but the latter told him, "Your causes and conditions are not here. Go see Deshan." So Xuefeng went to Deshan's congregation and practiced there. He later became a great Chan master and taught at Mount Xuefeng in Fujian Province. In 882, Emperor Xizong (r. 873–888) bestowed upon him the title Great Master Zhenjue (Authentic Awakening) and the purple robe, the highest honor for any Buddhist monk. He is the master of Yunmen Wenyan (864–949), founder of the Yunmen line of Chan Buddhism.

26. Yantou Quanhuo (828–887) was a fellow student of Deshan along with Xuefeng Yicun. He was also the teacher of Ruiyan (ca. 820–933), the protagonist of the previous case 12. He later became an important Chan master residing in the Henan Province on Mount Yantou. At the time of this exchange, Yantou was already awakened, and he worked with Deshan to set a trap for Xuefeng to help him realize awakening.

27. Nanquan Puyuan (748–835) studied with Mazu Daoyi (709–788) and eventually became one of his dharma heirs. In 795, he began his longtime residence on Mount Nanquan (in present-day Anhui Province), whence he acquired his toponym. He remained on the mountain for thirty years, where he devoted himself to teaching his students. Among his immediate disciples, Zhaozhou Congshen (778–897) is most famous.

28. A "turning word" (*zhuanyu*) refers to a Chan pivotal utterance that functions as a catalyst that transforms delusion to awakening in the practitioner.

29. Dongshan Shouchu (910–990) was an heir to Yunmen Wenyan (864–949). He later became a Chan master in the Yunmen line and taught during the beginning of the Northern Song period (960–1127).

30. The national teacher or preceptor (C. *guoshi*) here refers to Chan master Nanyang Huizhong (675–775), a dharma heir of the sixth ancestor Huineng (638–713). National teacher or preceptor was a title conferred by the emperor to eminent monks in premodern China, and there could be more than one at any given time.

During the Tang dynasty, many renowned monks were appointed as *guoshi*, including Fazang (643–712), Chengguan (738–839), and Nanyang Huizhong.

31. "Tongue fell to the ground" (*shetou duodi*) is a Chan expression for a kind-hearted, grandmotherly teacher who talks so much to benefit students. It is as if the tongue falls off from talking so much.

32. The attendant in this case refers to Danyuan Yingzhen (ca. 765–864), the first teacher of Yangshan Huiji when the latter was only a novice before moving on to becoming the successor of Weishan Lingyou (771–853).

33. "Dongshan" here refers to the protagonist of case 15, Dongshan Shouchu.

34. A catty in ancient China is about 1.5 pounds of weight.

35. "Oyster (or clam) Chan" (*bang'ge chan*) is a Chan expression for revealing the truth, as is, plainly and directly. Therefore, the following line says that as soon as the shell is opened, the guts and liver are exposed, meaning nothing is hidden.

36. Songyuan Chongyue (1132–1202) was a Southern Song dynasty Linji Chan master—the only contemporary master of Wumen to be included in his *Gateless Barrier*, which shows Wumen's respect for him. When Songyuan died at the age of seventy-one, Wumen was only in his twenties, at the peak of his practice.

37. The four meditation or *dhyāna* heavens refer to four spheres one could be born into, corresponding to the levels of meditative absorption, all of which belong to the realm of form in Buddhist cosmology.

38. A shitstick (*gan shijue*) is an ad hoc tool used to clean the toilet area, usually a bamboo stick shaped like a shovel.

39. Ānanda was Śākyamuni Buddha's cousin, known for his exceptional memory. For example, he was accredited as the reciter of all the teachings for posterity after the Buddha had passed away. He was also Śākyamuni's personal attendant and the one who appealed to Śākyamuni, on behalf of the women, to institute a *bhikṣunī* (nun) lineage.

40. Vulture Peak or Gṛdhrakūṭa-parvata was supposedly a mountain located near Rājagṛha in the ancient Indian state of Magadha. Several *sūtras* were delivered by the Śākyamuni Buddha there, such as the *Lotus Sūtra*.

41. The Vipaśyin Buddha is the first of the seven buddhas of the past mentioned in the collection of early scriptures, *Āgamas* and *Nikāyas*.

42. Since in Chinese cosmology everything is made up of a combination of *yin* and *yang*, this expression refers to something that is beyond this world. The "spring" in the sentence suggests liveliness and life.

43. The sixth ancestral master refers to Huineng, the most important Chan master in China. A lot has been written about him; see, for example, John Jorgensen, *Inventing Hui-neng the Sixth Patriarch: Hagiography and Biography in Early Ch'an*, Sinica Leidensia, 68 (Leiden: Brill, 2005).

44. "Huangmei" here is the mountain site where the fifth ancestral Chan master Daman Hongren (602–675) taught. Thus, Ming is referring to Hongren through his toponym, a common way of addressing a Chan master.

45. The words *li* and *wei* come from a philosophical treatise by the fifth-century Buddhist master Sengzhao (384–414), a student of Kumārajīva (344–413), the great translator who accurately and eloquently rendered many Buddhist works into Chinese. In this treatise, Sengzhao (384–414) used indigenous Chinese philosophical notions to convey the Buddhist teaching in the way he understood it. The word *li* refers to the *li* graph, the sixty-fourth hexagram of the

Yijing or *The Book of Changes* (commonly known in English as the *I Ching*), an ancient divination text. *Li* symbolizes ultimate truth, transcendence, essence, and subjectivity. *Wei* means subtlety; it also refers to the manifold manifestations or functions of the *li*. "*Li* and *wei*" is thus a Chinese way of describing the world through opposites. Setting up *li* and *wei* here assumes that essence and appearance, root and branches, ultimate and conventional realities, words and silence, are separate from each other.

46. Not getting caught up in this duality himself, Fengxue simply cites a famous poem by Du Fu (712–770) that any Chinese person would have known. The poem was composed after Du Fu visited the southern Yangtze River (that is, Jiangnan) during a beautiful springtime in March.

47. "Phrase" (*ju*) in Chan refers to the most potent phrase (*ju*) that embodies awakening. Here, "potent" is a rendering of *gufeng*. Thus, this first sentence means: without disclosing or using any potent words of awakening—instead, just some ordinary poetic expression.

48. This verse is actually attributed to Chan master Yunmen Wenyan (864–949), founder of the Yunmen school of Chan and particularly known for his terse responses to questions. By quoting this verse verbatim, Wumen is just replicating how Fengxue replies to the monk in the story—both don't bother to come up with their own original reply and instead cite someone else's poem. In this sense, they neither reply nor not reply, yet a reply is given as a response to how to transcend "Words and silence," "*li* and *wei*." Yunmen's original poetic verse can be found in *Essential Collection of the Lamp Connections within the [Chan] Tradition* (C. *Liandeng huiyao*), compiled in 1189 by Huiweng Wuming in the Southern Song; see X. 1557: 79.207b18–19.

49. The "four propositions and the one hundred negations" is a stock expression in Chan texts describing the various philosophical propositions about existence and nonexistence. For example, "the four propositions," also known as the *tetralemma*, refers to classical Indian logic and rhetoric regarding any proposition through four possibilities as existent, nonexistent, both existent and nonexistent, and neither existent nor nonexistent. This is distinct from most Western logical traditions, which consider only two propositions: true or false. The Buddhist philosopher Nāgārjuna (second–third c.) uses this *tetralemma* to deconstruct all philosophical arguments of his opponents in his treatise, *The Middle Way* (S. *Mūlamadhyamakakārikā*). For more information, see Jay L. Garfield and Graham Priest, "Nāgārjuna and the Limits of Thought," *Philosophy East and West* 53, no. 1 (2003): 1–21.

50. Fayan Wenyi (885–958), who resided in Qingliang Temple, was the purported founder of the Fayan line of Chan Buddhism. Fayan first visited the Chan master Changqing Huiling (854–932); later, while staying at the monastery Dizang Temple on Mount Shi (present-day Fujian Province), he met Luohan Guichen (867–928) and eventually became his disciple. Later, Fayan arrived in Linchuan (present-day Jiangxi Province) where he was invited by the steward to serve as abbot of the monastery of Chongshou Temple. Admired by the local ruler, Fayan was again invited to be the abbot of Bao'en monastery in Jinling (present-day Jiangsu Province). He later moved to the monastery of Qingliang Temple in Shengzhou (present-day Jiangsu Province), which flourished under his guidance and the support of the ruler of the state of Wuye. The case must have taken place there.

51. Longtan Chongxin (ca. 753–852), as shown in this case, is the teacher of the famous Deshan Xuanjian featured in case 13. This present case is the occasion when Deshan realized awakening. There were historical internal Chan debates about the lineage affiliation of Longtan, because his teacher was Tianhuang Daowu (748–807), and there were supposedly two masters with the same name. One was Tianhuang Daowu, a descendant from Shitou Xiqian (701–791), and the other was Tianwang Daowu, a descendant from Mazu Daoyi's line. The debate arose from sectarian affiliations, because proponents of the Linji faction wanted Deshan to be in their line, but Tianhuang Daowu belonged to the Caodong line. Modern historians corroborated that there was, in fact, no such historical person Tianwang Daowu.

52. Using judiciary language, Wumen passes judgment on and criminalizes all three people involved in this story: the two monks arguing and Huineng as well. Why? They all relied on words and language; thus, all committed the same offense and can be exposed with a single indictment. So while they all can open their mouth, their words all fail to express the ultimate.

53. This expression, "If you meet someone, say only three-tenths of what you mean," from the Southern Song period, was made popular by Zhu Xi (1130–1200) in *Zhuzi yulei* (Thematic discourses of Master Zhu). Zhu uses it in a derogatory way, criticizing this popular expression as being insincere. However, in Chan discourses it conveys something positive; one should allow students of Chan to discover the truth themselves instead of telling the truth through words, which always fail to convey reality.

54. Wuzu Fayan (1024–1104) first studied Yogācāra philosophy in his home province, but later went south and studied under Huilin Zongben (1020–1099), Fushan Fayuan (991–1067), and Baiyun Shouduan (1025–1072). Fayan eventually became Baiyun's disciple and inherited his Linji lineage. After staying at various monasteries in Anhui Province, Fayan moved to Mount Wuzu (also known as East Mountain) in Hubei Province, where he acquired his toponym. The mountain itself received its name, Wuzu (fifth patriarch), from its most famous past resident, the fifth ancestral master of Chan, Hongren (601–674). Mount Wuzu thus became an important center for the Linji lineage, and it was where Fayan taught his famous disciples Yuanwu Keqin (1062–1135), the teacher of Dahui Zong'gao.

55. This *gong'an* derives from a famous tenth-century Tang dynasty novel, *Lihun Ji*, or *Record of the Divided Spirit*, a best seller of its time. The story involves two lovers, one of whom is "Woman Qian" in this case, Zhang Qian. She was very beautiful from an early age and had a very handsome playmate, her cousin, Wang Zhou. Zhang Qian had an older sister who died at a young age, so the father invested all of his love in the younger daughter. Wang Zhou and Zhang Qian lived close to each other and always played together. The father once commented, "You two are such soulmates; when you grow up and get married, that will be a real blessing." But when she came of age, he arranged for her to marry someone else. Heartbroken, she fell into a coma. Miraculously in her coma, she fled with her cousin Wang Zhou and created a family together with two children. When they returned to her hometown, the two Qians met each other, one in bed in a coma and one who had a life with Wang Zhou, and they merged into one. See Chen Yuanyou, *Lihun ji* (Record of the Divided Spirit), *Longwei mishu*, vol. 6, *Baibu congshu jicheng*, no. 32 (Taibei: Yiwen chubanshe, 1968).

56. Bodhidharma is purportedly an Indian (or perhaps Central Asian) emigré monk, the putative "founder" of the school of Chan. According to received sources, Bodhidharma was born as the third prince of a South Indian kingdom. Little is known about his youth, but he is believed to have arrived in China sometime during the late fourth or early fifth century.

57. Maitreya, "The Benevolent One," is the name of the next buddha to come.

58. The monk begins his question by citing the first line of Zhang Zhuo's (ca. ninth c.) poem of awakening and was interrupted by Yunmen. The poem in its entirety is:

> The brilliant and quiescent luminosity pervades everywhere [like sands in the] Ganges.
> Both the ordinary and the holy are endowed with the essence in my abode.
> When a single thought is not born, the essence is completely revealed.
> But with the slightest stirring of the six senses, this essence is blocked by clouds.
> To cut off vexations is to increase your illness.
> To aspire toward true suchness itself is in error.
> [Simply] adapt to worldly conditions without obstructions.
> *Nirvāṇa*, birth and death flowers in the sky!

59. Sixin Wuxin (1043–1116) was a Northern Song dynasty master belonging to the Huanglong branch of Linji Chan.

60. A "teacher of humans and gods" (*rentian weishi*) is one of the ten epithets of any buddha.

61. Xie Sanlang refers to the famous Chan master Xuansha Shibei (835–908). Xie was his lay surname; Sanlang was his nickname. San means the "third," as he was the third son in his lay family. Lang just means "boy." He was an illiterate fisherman but later resolved to become a monk and practiced Chan under various teachers, ending up finally with Xuefeng Yicun (see case 13). He became awakened by accidentally smashing his toe on a mountain trail. When he reported this to Xuefeng, he said, "Bodhidharma never came to China; Huike never went to India!" This is an allusion to his awakening statement. Later he settled on Mount Xuansha, which became his toponym.

62. This story comes from the *Scripture of the Collected Essentials of All Buddhas* (*Zhufo yaoji jing*), translated by Dharmarakṣa (239–316).; see T. 810, 17. The bodhisattva who called the girl out of *samādhi* is Sarvanīvaraṇaviṣkambhin Bodhisattva (C. Qizhuyingai pusa), meaning "Remover of Hindrances Bodhisattva." The *Gateless Barrier* changed the name to "Bodhisattva Ignorance" as a contrast to Mañjuśrī, the bodhisattva of "wisdom," to exaggerate the paradox of Mañjuśrī's inability to call the girl out of *samādhi*.

63. This story can also be found in the *Scripture of the Collected Essentials of All Buddhas* (*Zhufo yaoji jing*). See Natasha Heller's discussion of this story in this volume.

64. This refers to Wuzu Fayan; see note 54.

65. Doushuai Congyue (1044–1091) was a Northern Song Chan master in the Huanglong branch of the Linji line and a dharma heir to Chan master Baofeng Kewen (1025–1102). His secular name was Xiong. He studied widely after having left home at fifteen and receiving full ordination at sixteen. Under Kewen, he realized

awakening and moved to Doushuai yuan (temple), where he acquired his top-onym, in modern day Nanchang in Jiangxi province. He was the teacher of the leading intellectual of his day by any definition, a prominent lay Buddhist, and a statesman, Zhang Shangyin (1043–1122).

66. Very little is known of this ninth-century master, except that he was the dharma heir of Dongshan Liangjie (807–869).

67. Bhagavān is one of the ten epithets of a buddha, usually rendered "World-Honored One."

68. Silent illumination or *mozhao* was a poetic term coined by Chan master Hongzhi Zhengjue (1091–1157) during the Southern Song to describe awakening and its response to the world. However, Dahui used it as a derogatory criticism for a form of passivity that was apparently prevalent during his time. Many Chan masters, including but not limited to Dahui's own teacher, Yuanwu Keqin (1063–1135), used this metaphor to describe the necessary process of eradicating discriminations; see Jimmy Yu, "The Polemics of Passivity and Yuanwu's Usage of It," *The Journal of Chinese Buddhist Studies* 36 (2023), 31–71. Here Wumen is simply following Dahui's (erroneous) criticism.

69. In Buddhist cosmo-geography, each universe is encircled by a range of iron moun-tains (Skt. *cakravāla*), the center of which is Mount Sumeru.

70. Literally, "revolve in this life" means resolving the matter of birth and death or *saṃsāra*, i.e., awakening to *nirvāṇa*.

A SURVEY OF ENGLISH TRANSLATIONS OF THE *GATELESS BARRIER*

THERE ARE fourteen English translations of the *Gateless Barrier* (C. *Wumen guan*) to date, excluding those self-published and available without having been formally reviewed by publishers. Because the *Gateless Barrier* is not only a premodern literary work but also a "living text" made popular by translators and teachers in the Japanese Zen tradition in the twentieth century, most of these English translations were done for Zen practitioners. Perhaps because of this, many translations are loose, conveying only the general gist of the text without bringing forth the nuances of the original Chinese or drawing out the Buddhist allusions. The English translation in this volume has benefited from the best of these earlier translations but also aims for clarity, consistency, accessibility, and scholarly accuracy.

Translating Chinese is difficult. Nuances and allusions are easily missed, unless the translator is also fluent in Chinese classics. All translations come to us already (implicitly) theorized and interpreted, mediated by linguistic and cultural determinants. Some translations make explicit their hermeneutical agendas, which re-create the original Chinese text by reflecting the particular cultural norms of the English language set in a specific social context at a specific historical time. Other translations implicitly mask their agenda with literalism, which compromises the context of the original. Translation necessarily represents a balance and negotiation between several competing aims. It is not a science but an interpretive art; and the translator must rely more on flexibility of judgment and a sense of balanced values than on adherence to fixed rules or personal preferences. Under the best of circumstances, the translation leaves the translator discontented because the intent of fidelity to the original text is much more than literalism. Under the worst conditions, the translation bears little resemblance to the original and ends up being a free imitation.

Kumārajīva (344–413), one of the greatest translators of Buddhist texts, commented to his student Huirui (355–439) about translating beautiful Sanskrit *gāthās* (poetic verses) into Chinese: "Even though the general meaning of the translated verses is similar [to the original], it is like chewed up food being fed to others. While the intent is never to lose the flavor, chewed-up food inevitably tastes like emesis."[1] Kumārajīva was privileging the beauty of Sanskrit over Chinese. His comment is not to diminish the merit or the creative process of translation. After all, he and his team translated 384 volumes of texts. Rather, his comment should serve as an admonition for translators not to "chew up the food" too much with unnecessary interpolations or mistranslations, even though it is impossible to avoid chewing up the original and spitting it out in a different language.

Part of the issue with "chewing up the food" too much is the tendency to read into and translate a text through a particular doctrinal or sectarian interpretation. As Stephen Teiser has noted, some Buddhologists tend to read a text through "a specific sect" with "distinctive beliefs" so the text becomes swallowed up by that particular tradition.[2] Many of the fourteen translations of the *Gateless Barrier* reviewed below stem from the vantage point of Japanese Rinzai Zen, and in that sense may be understood as having been swallowed up by that particular tradition. For example, privileging "oneness" of subject and object as point of reference for awakening is very distinct among many Zen teachings, so this shows up in many translations—even though such language is absent in the original Chinese.

All the translations have their strengths and weaknesses—depending on which "model" the translator is leaning toward—instrumentalist or hermeneutical.[3] There can be as many translations as there are interpretants, but when the idiosyncratic agendas come through too strongly, the translation becomes problematic. Below, I provide an evaluation of the quality of these fourteen translations for teaching purposes. My criteria are heuristic—only my attempts at striking a balance of competing aims.

Stylistic fluency and clarity, devoid of clumsy locutions, awkward or hard-to-understand neologisms, exoticisms, and the other flaws that often arise from overlabored and overliteral adherence to the original text: Such overliteralness, however, need not always spring from scholarly caution, for there is another varietyliberately cultivated by certain translators in the hope of enhancing the quaintness and color of their work. A good translation, in my opinion, would translate colorfully only what is authentically intended to be colorful in the original; for the rest, it would use more sober language. And if, having done this, the translator still believes the literal wording to be important, endnotes are always available to convey the significance of the terms. As Kumārajīva's statement shows, in many cases the aesthetic qualities of the original are impossible to convey in another language. So the translator must judiciously translate in a different linguistic medium with different standards.

Consistency of technical vocabulary whenever possible: The Chinese language is often evocative and nuanced, so bringing out the sense of a term according to context may require a flexible approach. If consistency becomes unfeasible despite all efforts, it is then the translator's duty to call this fact to readers' attention.

Accuracy, not necessarily of lexicon meaning—vital though such accuracy is—but also fidelity to the flavor and tone in which the original is written: A merely literal translation of the original Chinese does not always achieve its purpose. Humor, sarcasm, or some highly charged emotional and intellectual overtones (e.g., allusions to ancient Chinese texts or idioms) in the original Chinese, for example, should be conveyed appropriately. In my humble opinion, a good translation is attuned to the literary nature of the original and aims to reproduce as nearly as possible the Chinese reader's experience of the feel of the text. Of course, some terms are impossible to render fully (e.g., *yin* and *yang*, *samādhi*, *nirvāna*); in those cases, it may be best to transliterate, not translate, them. The *Gateless Barrier* is a wonderfully terse text, full of irony, paradoxes, and sarcastic humor. Fidelity to the tone of the *Gateless Barrier* should outweigh all other considerations, for the greatness of this work rests in its complexity.

The reviews below are arranged chronologically, showing the progression of improvements or lack thereof. Readers are encouraged to compare the highlighted passages against the translation offered in this volume.

Senzaki, Nyogen, and Paul Reps. "The Gateless Gate." Originally published in 1934 by John Murray, Los Angeles, and later included in Paul Reps and Nyogen Senzaki's popular anthology *Zen Flesh, Zen Bones*. Tokyo: Tuttle, 1957.

This is the earliest attempt at translating the *Gateless Barrier* into the English language from the Japanese Zen perspective. It became widely popular with the countercultural Beatniks of the postwar period, whose fascination with Zen was largely stimulated by the prolific writings of D. T. Suzuki and Alan Watts Zen. Some of the glosses reflect a peculiar early twentieth-century Western understanding of Zen, using phrases such as "oneness of subjectivity and objectivity" or "ego" that do not actually appear in the original Chinese. This translation renders all Chinese figures in the Japanese pronunciation and does not provide any annotations or comments.

Ogata Sōhaku. *Zen for the West*. London: Rider & Company, 1959.

This is the second English translation of the *Gateless Barrier* by a Japanese Zen teacher and scholar for English-speaking Zen practitioners. Again, all Chinese figures are rendered in the Japanese pronunciation, and it does not provide any annotations or comments. The English reads a bit awkwardly, the translation does not capture the nuances of the Chinese, and sometimes it misreads minor Chinese syntax. For example, in case 36, the last two lines of the verse are terse, without specifically identifying a subject in the sentence—often the case with classical Chinese. Wumen says if you meet people who have fulfilled the Way, then "Hold their jaw and give a nice blow on the side of the face. If they can appreciate this directly, then they know [the Way]." Ogata renders these lines as "Feeling a slap in the face, you will wake up to comprehension (of the truth)." This changes the meaning, syntactically; the subject is intended to be those who have fulfilled the Way, not the reader. There are several other places where the glosses miss the original Chinese grammar.

Blyth, R. H. *Zen and Zen Classics, Volume Four: MUMONKAN*. Tokyo: Hokuseido Press, 1966.

This good translation provides both the original Chinese and the English rendering. Interested readers can examine how terms and expressions are actually translated. All Chinese figures are still rendered in the Japanese pronunciation. Blyth also offers his comments, making this the first volume in any Western language to include such commentary. For the most part, Blyth is able to highlight the nuances of the terms and Buddhist scriptural allusions. Although his translation is good, he occasionally offers "creative" renderings for terms or ideas that are absent in the Chinese. For example, *huoji* or "livelihood" in case 10 is translated as "commercial system"; *liao* or "put to rest" is rendered as "one" or "oneness of body and mind" in case 9's verse; and "life" or *ming* is translated as "soul" in the verse of case 46. Sometimes Blyth inserts, in square brackets, words that not only are unnecessary but also encourage erroneous associations.

For example, in the first line of the verse in case 46, instead of rendering in a straightforward manner "eyes" or *yan*, Blyth renders it as "the [third] eye." What does the third eye have to do with Zen awakening or Buddhism?

Shibayama, Zenkei, and Sumiko Kudo. *Zen Comments on the Mumonkan*. New York and Ontario: Mentor Books, 1974.

This is one of the finest translations in English, withstanding the test of time and surpassing even the most recently published translations. It provides all Chinese figures and terms in the Japanese pronunciation only, clearly targeting English-reading Zen practitioners. It picks up on all the literary and Buddhist scriptural allusions, and even though there are no endnotes or annotations in the text, Shibayama's comments bring out all the nuances of the cases. The very minor mistranslations do not detract from the main thrust. Nevertheless, the subtleties of the Chinese could have been brought forth more clearly. For example, Kudo omits the last few characters of one of the lines in Wumen's comment to case 13 and renders the line "If I examine it carefully." Yet the last few characters actually explain why Wumen provides his comments and should be rendered, "Examine this closely *for the sake of posterity*." Also, with regard to the verse in case 36, Wumen says that if you meet people who have fulfilled the Way, then give them a good punch in the face; Kudo then renders the following line, "Get it at once, get it immediately!" But this phrasing makes the reader the subject and turns the sentence into a command. Syntactically, the subject is those who have fulfilled the Way, so it should be read "If *they* can appreciate this directly [i.e., the punch in the face], then they know [the Way]." Perhaps the change in syntax of the classical Chinese was intentional. These minor issues probably do not matter for Western Zen practitioners, unless they are interested in conveying the full range of implications of the text and staying true to Wumen's words.

Sekida, Katsuki. *Two Zen Classics: The Gateless Gate and the Blue Cliff Record*. Boulder, CO: Shambhala, 2005. Originally published by Weatherhill in 1977.

This translation is popular among Western Japanese Zen practitioners. All Chinese figures and terms are given in the Japanese pronunciation. There are few annotations or notes, which allows the *kōans* to stand alone. In this volume, the *Gateless Barrier* is translated first, followed by the *Blue Cliff Record*, even though the latter was published earlier by about a hundred years. This is because, in the Japanese *kōan* curriculum, the *Gateless*

Barrier is worked through first before the *Blue Cliff Record*. The brevity of Sekida's translation and annotation is useful for practitioners, so they are not influenced by too many ideas in the commentaries. The English is smooth, and it is a good translation. But it contains the same issues of earlier Japanese Zen translations. For example, rendering the last line of Wumen's comments in case 13 before the verse, Sekida has "They are both like puppets on the shelf" (the exact phrasing by Shibayama), which makes it seem like puppets are just placed on some shelf, lying stagnant. The Chinese actually means, "Those two are like puppets at a makeshift show," meaning that they're *in* a show that's happening now. The bantering between Yantou and Deshan is just a farce, performed on the fly, atop a "prop" (the character for prop here is *peng*, which is used in a makeshift puppet show). The prop is the whole story; the performance is Yantou's skillful means and Deshan's willingness to go along with it for the benefit of Xuefeng—and by extension, all those who are reading this case now. Mistranslations like this may not obscure the main points of the *gong'ans* or *kōans*, but a more accurate translation would amplify the skillfulness and liveliness of Chan interactions and Wumen's assessment of them.

Yamada, Kōun. *The Gateless Gate: The Classic Book of Zen Koans.* Somerville, MA: Wisdom, 2004. Originally published by Center Publications, 1979.

This is one of the key translations on which many subsequent English versions are based. The English reads smoothly, thanks to Yamada's English-speaking students. Again, all Chinese figures are rendered in the Japanese pronunciation because this translation (and the comments), like its predecessors, are intended for Western Zen practitioners. This translation carries a particular flavor, sometimes at the expense of the zing of the original. For example, in the verse (and comments) of case 16, Yamada emphasizes "oneness" as the enlightened view. But the original Chinese presents oneness and difference as a paradox—neither is correct. In fact, Yamada consistently emphasizes oneness throughout his translation and comments; in cases 29, 30, 37, and 39, Zen awakening is explicitly defined as oneness. Perhaps this penchant reflects the sensibilities or terminology of the Zen lineage to which he belongs, but for a practitioner of Chinese Chan, the concept of oneness merely refers to a unified state in which self-grasping is still present, so this state must be shattered. Awakening in buddhadharma is neither oneness nor nothingness, and thus the emphasis on the term "oneness" seems a poor translation choice. Perhaps this is a case where a translation is swallowed up by a particular sectarian tradition. Also, in some instances, ideas and words have been inserted into the English that are absent in the Chinese. For example, in the last sentence of the verse in case 24, Yamada has "You should be ashamed of yourself," which carries a punitive tone. But the original is simply "The greater the bewilderment"—meaning, the more one rambles on with words, the more confusing it is. In the last line of the verse in case 48, Yamada has "You must know there is still the all-surpassing hole," which is a very literal reading of the word "hole" (*qiao*). What is an "all-surpassing hole"? This is a case in which a literal reading confuses more than it clarifies. *Qiao* also means "method," "way," or "essence." Thus, the last line should be more simply understood as, "You should know that there is a better way."

Seung Sahn. *The Barrier That Has No Gate.* Los Angeles: Before Thought Publications, 2010. Originally published 1983.

This is an in-house publication of the *Gateless Barrier* prepared by students of Sŏn Master Seung Sahn, founder of the Kwan Um School of Zen, for their use. The purported translator, Paul Lynch, took the earlier translation done by a group of Seung Sahn's students and published it. The translation is bilingual, offering a line-by-line comparison of the Chinese and English, but the English is actually quite loose and interpretive and is influenced by earlier translations by Japanese Zen teachers. The last line of Wumen's comments in case 13, for example, is just one place where it replicates errors made by Yamada, Seikida, and Shibayama, as well as other English translations on which they are based. (See my comments regarding Low's rendering.) The footnotes, which supposedly provide context for the cases, are not always well researched. For example, a footnote identifies "Dongshan" in case 15 as Dongshan Liangjie, but it should be Dongshan Shouchu, the disciple of Yunmen. The translation is accompanied by Seung Sahn's brief comments, and there seems to be a disjunct between the two. Yet Seung Sahn succinctly identifies the potential *huatous*, or critical questions, embedded within each *gong'an*, which is excellent and something that the prior translations do not offer. This is, no doubt, because the practice methods of Korean Sŏn are much closer to the Chinese Chan approach of working with *huatous* as a method of meditation.

Aitken, Robert. *The Gateless Barrier: The Wu-Men Kuan (Mumonkan).* Berkeley, CA: North Point Press, 1991.

This translation relied on the previously published versions by Yamada and Sekida. It also benefited from the version provided by Shibayama-Kudo and even Ogata. Cases 1, 2, and 23 in this volume, however, are by Norman Waddell. His translations of cases 1 and 2, especially the verses, do not reflect the original source material from Wumen. He inserts sentences that are absent in the original. It is unclear where the extra passages came from or whether he was relying on some other text. The rest of Aitken's translation appears to be a polished rendering of the earlier translations referenced above. For example, Wumen's comment in case 13 replicates Ogata's 1959 translation about "Punch and Judy in a booth" instead of rendering that passage "like puppets on the shelf," as did Shibayama and Sekida. Elsewhere he mostly follows the version by Yamada. One change he did make is to render the Chinese names into the now obsolete Wade-Giles transliteration instead of giving the Japanese pronunciation of Chinese names. This is the first Japanese Zen–influenced translation to do this. Aitken's commentary is useful for Zen practitioners, offering new clarity to the earlier translations on which it is based.

Cleary, Thomas. *No Barrier: Unlocking the Zen Koan: A New Translation of the Zen Classic "Wumenguan" (Mumonkan)*. New York: Bantam, 1993.

This is a creative translation that reads very smoothly. It also uses the updated pinyin system of rendering the Chinese names. And it is clearly targeting Western practitioners, with the aim of "unlocking" the inner logic of the *gong'ans*. Privileging accessibility over accuracy, meaning over technicality, Cleary rids the *Gateless Barrier* of all Chinese literary and Buddhist allusions. In doing so, he makes the cases simpler, but at the expense of nuances in the original. For example, he renders the first two lines of case 10's verse as "Poor as the poorest, brave as the bravest" where, being true to the Chinese, it should be "Destitute like Fan Dan, but with the spirit of Xiang Yu." I am certain that Cleary knew of these ancient Chinese figures, but he opted to delete them. Ordinary English readers probably do not need to know who Fan Dan or Xiang Yu were,, if they are only interested in the main gist of the story. But those who wish to understand the text in its cultural context would not be served by such a deletion. There are also minor mistranslations of terms, but they do not detract from Cleary's intended purpose for this book. Clearly, his aim is *not* to provide yet another translation of the *Gateless Barrier* but to offer a new interpretation of and insight into the text. Cleary also supplements Wumen's verses, adding (unfortunately uncited) verse comments to each of the same *gong'ans* from different Chan masters throughout history, but it does not make the meaning clearer for general readers. To those unfamiliar with *gong'an* language, the added verses are just as obtuse as those from Wumen. For seasoned Zen practitioners, however, these verses may offer insights from different perspectives and elicit new understandings.

Low, Albert. *The World a Gateway: Commentaries on the Mumonkan.* Boston: Charles Tuttle, 1995.

This is a translation derived from the version used in the Zen community of Roshi Philip Kapleau, which was prepared in consultation with the versions by R. H. Blyth and Zenkei Shibayama. But Low must have also consulted the versions by Shibayama, Sekida, and Yamada, because many of the phrasings (and mistranslations) are nearly exactly the same. For example, Low copied the exact English phrasing of these earlier translations in the last line of Wumen's comments in case 13, "They are both like puppets on the shelf" (see my review of Sekida above). There are other similarities. Low appears to have relied not on an ability to read Chinese or Japanese—as far as I'm aware, he was not fluent in either language—but on his years of practicing and teaching Zen. All personal names are given in their Japanese pronunciation. That said, this translation reads well, and his comments would be helpful for Zen practitioners.

Cleary, Jonathan Christopher. *Wumen's Gate.* In *Three Chan Classics: The Recorded Sayings of Linji, Wumen's Gate, and The Faith-Mind Maxim.* Berkeley, CA: Bukkyo Dendo Kyokai and Numata Center for Buddhist Translation and Research, 1999.

This is a very good translation that reads smoothly and captures most of the literary and Buddhist scriptural allusions. It also uses the preferred pinyin system of rendering the Chinese names. It was probably intended for both general readers and Zen practitioners. There are, however, some places where Buddhist stock phrases or literary expressions are missed. For example, case 25 refers to the "four propositions and one hundred negations," which is a technical Buddhist expression. J. C. Cleary renders it "all the permutations of propositional logic." The word "free" (*ziyou*) in the poetic verse of case 42 is strangely rendered "on your own." A couple of lines down in the same verse, "remarkable" (*fengliu*) is rendered as "flowing wind," which makes the English incomprehensible. This term also appears at the end of Wumen's comments to case 2, before the verse. *Fengliu* is an expression for something admirable, outstanding, exuberant, or remarkable. Thus, this last line in case 42 should read, "[Mañjuśrī's] defeat is indeed remarkable," highlighting the paradox that although he could not bring a girl out of *samādhi*, a low-level bodhisattva could. There are other places where the Chinese vernacular expressions are missed or rendered literally, making the resultant English somewhat incomprehensible. But Cleary does not seem to have worked off of earlier Japanese Zen translations because the mistranslations he made are different than those of Shibayama, Sekida, and Yamada.

Addiss, Stephen. *The Gateless Barrier.* In *Zen Sourcebook: Traditional Documents from China, Korea, and Japan.* Ed. Stephen Addiss, Stanley Lombardo, Judith Roitman, Paula Arai. Indianapolis: Hackett, 2008.

This is a literal translation of the *Gateless Barrier* that reads smoothly in English. Unfortunately, it misses many literary allusions and Buddhist technical expressions that would have been obvious to the Chinese reader. Such references are important not only to help the reader appreciate the richness of the text but also to make it usable. Wumen's comments are curiously not translated, only the original cases and his verses. The translation also omits the prefaces and postscripts to the *Gateless Barrier* and uses the now obsolete Wade-Giles system of rendering the Chinese names. The translator seems not to have consulted earlier translations; he offers no footnotes, endnotes, and commentary on the cases. With the mistranslations and omissions, this version is not particularly useful for practitioners or readers of Zen texts; it may leave readers to conclude that the *Gateless Barrier* is just a cryptic Zen text.

Guo Gu. *Passing through the Gateless Barrier: Koan Practice for Real Life.* Boulder, CO: Shambhala, 2016.

This is my first translation (under the moniker Guo Gu); all Chinese names are rendered using the pinyin system. It is a decent rendering of the text that balances accuracy and accessibility for Chan and Zen practitioners, and there are plenty of endnotes to contextualize all the literary and scriptural allusions. It also offers a concordance in the appendix of all Chinese names and terms in Japanese. Its usefulness, however, rests not in the translation but in the comments, which redress many of the Japanese Zen interpretations of the *Gateless Barrier* and present the paradoxes in the *gong'ans* as situations relatable to daily life, pointing out the ways in which people create vexations for themselves. This translation is not without errors. For example, I also rendered *fengliu* in cases 2 and 42 as "flowing with the wind"—opting to be literal in the translation and unpack its deeper, premodern meaning in my comments. Also, in the last line of the verse for case 9, I mistranslated *fenghou* as "sanction and assist," but it should be simply rendered as "nobility." These and several other mistakes are corrected in my new, revised translation offered in this volume, with additional annotations in the endnotes to bring out the nuances of the original.

Hinton, David. *No-Gate Gateway: The Original Wu-Men Kuan*. Boulder, CO: Shambhala, 2018.

Although Hinton's translation has been appreciated for its poetic and imaginative approach to the text, it is both overly literal in some places and inadequately straightforward in others. For example, he adopts the (erroneous) early twentieth-century practice of translating the names of mythological beings literally and applies them to the names of real, historical Chan masters. Thus, Chan master Zhaozhou is now rendered "Visitation Land" and Chan master Baizhang is "Hundred-Elder Mountain." This rendering reads like stereotyped exonyms for Native Americans (e.g., Chief Black Bear, Brother Eagle Eye) and introduces an unnecessary exoticism that does not reflect how Chan practitioners would refer to historical Chan masters. In other places, however, he strays from the literal meaning of the text and renders phrases in ways that do not reflect the original Chinese. In case 2, for example, where an old man responding to Baizhang says, "I'm actually not human," Hinton translates the response as "Someone. No one. Not a human being." This rendering misses the basic Chinese grammar of the sentence, which has a straightforward A (i.e., "I am") = B (i.e., "not human") construction. The translation also employs the obsolete Wade-Giles system. Perhaps the greatest flaw is its seeming bias toward viewing the *Gateless Barrier* as a Daoist, rather than Buddhist, work (claiming in the introduction that Wumen's primary concern was to return Chan to its "Taoist dwelling" and that Chan is actually a form of "Taoist thought"). His translation choices push toward pre-Buddhist, "Daoist" associations of a term, rather than presenting the Buddhist meaning in its historical context. Hinton's interpretation also emphasizes the pictographic associations of characters, regardless of how Wumen or his audience would have understood the words. There may be value in this version as an imaginative work, but because of the overly quaint and quirky translation choices and agenda to filter everything through a (Western romanticized) "Daoist" lens, it is perhaps not the best choice for readers of Buddhist literature nor Zen practitioners wanting to further their insight into the *Gateless Barrier* as Wumen had intended.

NOTES

1. See the biography of Kumārajīva in the *Chu sanzang ji* (Collection of Notes on the Translation of the Tripiṭaka) by Sengyou (445–518). T. 2145: 55.101c11–13. T. 2145: 55.101c11–13.

2. See Stephen F. Teiser, "Perspectives on Readings of the Heart Sutra: The Perfection of Wisdom and the Fear of Buddhism," in *Ways with Words: Writing about Reading Texts from Early China*, ed. Pauline Yu et al., 130–45 (Berkeley: University of California Press, 2000).

3. There are generally two dominant models of translation based on distinct theories of language. One approach can be called "instrumental." On the empiricist assumption that language is direct expression or reference, the instrumental model treats translation as the reproduction or transfer of an invariant which the source text contains or causes, typically described as its form, its meaning, or its effect. The other approach can be called "hermeneutic." On the materialist assumption that language is creation thickly mediated by linguistic and cultural determinants, the hermeneutic model treats translation as an interpretation of the source text whose form, meaning, and effect are seen as variable, subject to inevitable transformation during the translating process. For a full discussion and critique of both models, see Lawrence Venuti, "Genealogies of Translation Theory: Jerome," in *The Translation Studies Reader*, 3rd ed., ed. Lawrence Venuti, 483–502 (London; New York: Routledge, 2012; first published 2000). Other chapters in this volume, by George Steiner and Kwame Anthony Appiah, are also worth reading.

CROSS-REFERENCE TO CITATIONS OF THE
GATELESS BARRIER

T HE CHART below shows page ranges cited for English translations of the *Gateless Barrier* as compared to my translation in this volume, which is used as the standard for the chapters. Other translations in this chart are the 1974 version by Zenkei Shibayama (translated by Sumiko Kudo); the 1991 version by Robert Aitken; and the 2005 revised version by Katsuki Sekida that originally came out in 1977. All these in their original publication include commentaries on the cases. My own comments on the cases appear in Guo Gu, *Passing through the Gateless Barrier*. These English translations are selected based on their accuracy and nuance. The last column of this chart provides the citation of the original Chinese version from *Taishō* no. 2005.

Case Numbers	Page References in This Book	Shibayama 1974 Trans. Page	Aitken 1991 Trans. Page	Sekida 2005 Trans. Page	*Taishō* No. 2005. Vol. 48 Page
1	251–252	19	24	42	292c22
2	252–253	33	50	49	293a15
3	253–254	43	69	56	293b10
4	254	50	81	61	293b23
5	254–255	54	90	63	293c01
6	255–256	59	106	70	293c12
7	256	69	123	75	293c26
8	256–257	74	136	79	294a06
9	257	79	145	82	294a14

(*continued*)

Case Numbers	Page References in This Book	Shibayama 1974 Trans. Page	Aitken 1991 Trans. Page	Sekida 2005 Trans. Page	*Taishō* No. 2005. Vol. 48 Page
10	257–258	84	159	85	294a24
11	258–259	88	171	89	294b05
12	259	93	182	92	294b18
13	259–260	101	198	97	294b28
14	260–261	109	209	103	294c12
15	261–262	116	222	109	294c23
16	262	125	237	116	295a11
17	262–263	132	251	122	295a23
18	263	139	264	128	295b04
19	263–264	145	277	132	295b13
20	264–265	153	289	136	295b25
21	265	160	299	140	295c05
22	265–266	164	308	143	295c12
23	266–267	172	319	148	295c22
24	267	181	336	155	296a12
25	268	188	345	159	296a21
26	268–269	194	358	165	296b01
27	269	202	368	169	296b10
28	269–271	207	381	172	296b19
29	271	215	395	179	296c17
30	271–272	220	405	182	296c27
31	272–273	229	416	186	297a08
32	273	235	425	190	297a21
33	273–274	241	437	193	297b03
34	274	246	446	195	297b09
35	274–275	250	456	197	297b16
36	275	259	472	202	297b25
37	275–276	265	483	205	297c04
38	276	272	494	209	297c12
39	276–277	280	503	212	297c21
40	277–278	286	516	216	298a02
41	278	292	529	221	298a15
42	279	300	545	227	298a25
43	280	306	558	232	298b14
44	280	310	566	235	298b23
45	281	314	575	238	298c02
46	281	318	583	240	298c11
47	282	323	594	246	298c20
48	282–283	333	604	252	299a01

CHARACTER GLOSSARY

CHINESE PRONUNCIATIONS of personal names in the *Gateless Barrier* are given first, with their life dates in parentheses, followed by the Japanese pronunciations for readers more familiar with the Japanese Zen tradition. The numbers next to them, in round brackets, refer to the specific *Gateless Barrier* cases in which they appear. All other Asian technical terms and titles of texts mentioned in this book are indicated by (S), (C), (K), and (J) for Sanskrit, Chinese, Korean, and Japanese.

A

A'nan; Ānanda 阿難; Anan (22)

B

ba 場 (J)
Baiyun Shouduan 白雲守端 (1025–1072); Hakuun Shutan
Baizhang Huaihai 百丈懷海 (720–814); Hyakujō Ekai (2, 40)
Bajiao Huiquing 芭蕉慧清 (880–950); Bashō Esei (44)
bang'ge chan 蚌蛤禪 (C)
Baochi Xuanzong 寶持玄總 (ca. seventeenth c.)
Bao'en Chan Monastery 報恩禪寺
Baofeng Kewen 寶峰克文 (1025–1102); Hōbō Kokumon

Baofeng Yunan Zhenjing chanshi zhu Jinling Baoning yulu 寶峰雲庵真淨禪
師住金陵報寧語錄 (C)

Baolin 寶林 (C)

biexing 別行 (C)

Biyan lu 碧巖錄 (C); *Hekigan roku* (J)

Bodhidharma (S). *See* Putidamo

Bukkō Kokushi 仏光国師 (1226–1286)

buli wenzi 不立文字 (C)

bu zheng 不正 (C)

C

Caodong 曹洞 (C); Sōtō (J)

Caoshan Benji 曹山本寂 (840–901); Sōzan Honjaku (10)

Caoxi Baolin zhuan 曹溪寶林傳

Chan 禪 (C); Sŏn (K); Zen (J)

Changsha Jingcen 長沙景岑 (788–868); Chōsha Keishin (46)

Chanlin sengbaozhuan 禪林僧寶傳 (C)

Chanyuan qinggui 禪苑清規 (C)

Chanyuan zhu zhuji duxu 禪源諸詮集都序 (C)

Chanzong songku lianzhu ji 禪宗頌古聯珠集 (C)

Chanzong songku lianzhu tongji 禪宗頌古聯珠通集 (C)

Chanzong songgu lianzhu tongji xulu 禅宗颂古联珠通集叙录 (C)

Chengguan 澄觀 (738–839); Chōkan

Chen Xuanyou 陳玄祐 (d.u., active eighth c.)

Chen Xun 陳塤 (1197–1241) (preface)

Chin'gak Hyesim 眞覺慧諶 (1178–1234) (K)

Chiri, Mount 智異山 (K)

Ch'oe Ch'unghŏn 崔忠獻 (1149–1219) (K)

Ch'oe U 崔瑀 (1166–1249) (K)

Chogye 曹溪 (K)

Chŏndŭng 傳燈 (K)

Ch'ongjijong 摠持宗 (K)

Ch'ongnamjong 摠南宗 (K)

Ch'ŏnt'ae 天台 (K)

Chuanxin fayao 傳心法要 (C)

Chunpeng Dugu 淳朋獨孤 (1259–1336) (C)

chuanfa 傳法 (C); *denpō* (J)

Chunqiu 春秋 (C)

Congrong lu 從容錄 (C); *Shōyō roku* (J)

D

Dabanniepan jing 大般涅槃經 (C)

Dachuan Puji 大川普濟 (1179–1253) (C)

Dafan tianwang wenfo jueyi jing 大梵天王問佛決疑經

Dahui Pujue Chanshi pushuo 大慧普覺禪師普說 (C)

Dahui Pujue chanshi yulu 大慧普覺禪師語錄 (C)

Dahui Zong'gao 大慧宗杲 (1089–1163); Daie Sōkō

dahuoi 大活 (C)

daigo 代語 (J)

Daitokuji 大德寺 (J)

Daitō Kokushi 大燈国師 (1283–1338) (J)

Daizong Xintai 岱宗心泰 (1327–1415) (C)

Damei Fachang 大梅法常 (752–839); Daibai Hōjō (30)

Danyuan Yingzhen 耽源應真 (ca. 765–864) Tangen Ōshin (17)

dao 道 (C)

Daosheng 道生 (C)

daoxue 道學 (C)

Daoyuan 道原 (C)

Daozhen 道臻 (1014–1093) (C)

dashi 大事 (C)

dasi 大死 (C)

dawu 大悟 (C)

dayi 大疑 (C)

Dayu Shouzhi 大愚守芝 (d.u.) (C)

daxiu daxie 大休大歇 (C)

Dazang jing 大藏經 (C); *Daizōkyō* (J)

da zhangfu 大丈夫 (C)

de pianyi 得便宜 (C)

denglu 燈錄 (C)

Deshan Xuanjian 德山宣鑑 (782–865); Tokusan Senkan (13, 28)

dian 點 (C)

dianxin 點心 (C)

Dōgen Kigen 道元希玄 (1200–1253) (J)

dōjō 道場 (J)

dokusan 獨參 (J)

Dong, Mount 洞山 (C)

Dongguo 東郭 (d.u.)

Dongjia [region] 東嘉 (C)

Donglin si 東林寺 (C)

Dongshan Liangjie 洞山良价 (807–869); Tōzan Ryōkai

Dongshan Shouchu 洞山守初 (910–990); Tōzan Shusho (15, 18)

Dongshan Daowei 洞山道微 (d.u.) (C)

Dongshan Qingbing 洞山清稟 (d.u.) (C)

Doushuai Congyue 兜率從悅 (1044–1091); Shinjaku Jūetsu (47)

Doushuai yuan 兜率院 (C)

Duanji Chanshi 斷際禪師. *See* Huangbo Xiyun

Du Fu 杜甫 (712–770); Toho (24)

Du Mu 杜牧 (803–852); Toboku (5)

Dushun 杜順 (557–640) (C)

E

Emperor Daigo 醍醐天皇 (885–930) (J)

Emperor Nakamikado 中御門天皇 (1702–1737) (J)

Enkei Soyū 遠溪祖雄 (1286–1344) (J)

F

Fan Dan 范丹 (112–185); Hantan (10)

Fayan Wenyi 法眼文益 (885–958); Hōgen Buneki (26)

fayin 法印 (C)

Faying 法應 (ca. thirteenth c.); Hōō

Fazang 法藏 (643–712); Hōzō

Fengxue Yanzhao 風穴延沼 (897–973); Fuketsu Ensho (24)

Fenyang Shanzhao 汾陽善昭 (947–1024) (C)

Feng Zizhen 馮子振 (1253–1348) (C)

fenghou 封侯 (C)

fengliu 風流 (C)

foguo 佛國 (C)

Foguo Keqin chanshi xinyao 佛果克勤禪師心要 (C)

Fozhao Deguang 佛照德光 (1121–1203); Busshō Tokkō

Fozu tongcan ji 佛祖同參集 (C)

Furong Daokai 芙蓉道楷 (1043–1118); Fuyō Dōkai
Fushan Fayuan 浮山法遠 (991–1067); Fuzan Hōon

G

gan shijue 乾屎橛 (C)

Gaofeng Yuanmiao 高峰原妙 (1238–1295); Kōhō Genmyō

Genjū Stream 幻住派 (J)

Genkō shakusho 元亨釈書 (J)

Giō Shōnin 義翁紹仁 (1217–1281) (J)

goi jūjūkin 五位十重禁 (J)

gong'an 公案 (C); *kōan* (J)

gonsen 言詮 (J)

Gorokushō 語録抄 (J)

Gozan 五山 (J)

guan 關 (C)

guangdeng 廣燈 (C)

Guangjiao Cloister 廣教院 (C)

Guangzhige 廣智歌 (C)

gufeng 風骨 (C)

Guisheng 歸省 (C)

Gujin tushu jicheng 古今圖書集成 (C)

Guifeng Zongmi 圭峰宗密 (780–841); Keihō Shūmitsu

guze 古則 (C)

Guzun su yulu 古尊宿語錄 (C)

Guzun suyu yao 古尊宿語要 (C)

H

ha 派 (J)

hachi nantō 八難透 (J)

Hakuin Ekaku 白隠慧鶴 (1685–1768) (J)

Han Feizi 韓非子 (C)

Hangzhou 杭州 (C)

Hangzhou Tianlong 杭州天龍 (770–850); Kōshū Tenryū

hanhui 寒灰 (C)

hara 腹 (J)

Heze Shenghui 荷澤神會 (684–758); Kataku Jinne

Hōjō Tokimune 北条時宗 (1268–1284) (J)

Hōkyōji 宝鏡寺 (J)

Hongfu Ziwen 洪福子文 (d.u.)

Hongren 弘忍 (601–674); Kōnin

Hongwu nanzang 洪武南藏 (C)

Hongzhi Zhengjue 宏智正覺 (1091–1157); Tendō Shōgaku

Hongzhou Chan 洪州禪 (C)

hōsshin 法參 (J)

Hōtō kakushi hōgo 法燈国師法語 (J)

Hou Hanshu 後漢書 (C)

hu 胡 (C)

Huai Chanshi 懷禪師 (C)

Huai chanshi lu 懷禪師錄 (C)

Huangbo Xiyun 黃檗希運 (d. 850); Ōbaku Kiun

Huangbo duanji chanshi wanling lu 黃檗斷際禪師宛陵錄

Huanglong Huinan 黃龍慧南 (1002–1069); Ōryū Enan

huatou 話頭 (C); *wato* (J)

Huayan 華嚴 (C)

Huike 慧可. *See* Shenguang Huike (C)

Huilin Zongben 慧林宗本 (1020–1099); Erin Sōhon

Huineng 惠能 (638–713); Enō (23, 29)

Huirui 慧叡 (355–439) (C)

Huitang Zuxin 晦堂祖心 (1025–1100) (C)

Huo'an Shiti 或菴師體 (1108–1179); Wakuan Shitai (4)

huoji 活計 (C)

Huqiu Shaolong 虎丘紹隆 (1077–1136); Kukyū Jōryū

huoju 活句 (C)

hwadu 話頭 (K)

Hwanam Honsu 幻庵混修 (1320–1392) (K)

Hyakunijussoku 百二十則 (J)

Hyeam Sangch'ong 慧庵尙聰 (d.u.) (K)

Hyesim 慧諶 (1178–1234) (K)

I

ichinen 一念 (J)

ishin denshin 以心伝心 (J)

J

jakugo 着語 (J)

Jiandeng xinhua 剪燈新話 (C)

Jiangxi 江西 (C)

Jiangxi Mazu Daoyi chanshi yulu 江西馬祖道一禪師語錄

jianxing 見性 (C)

jianxing chengfo 見性成佛 (C)

Jianzhi Sengcan 鑑智僧璨 (d. 606); Kanchi Sōsan

Jianzhong Jingguo xudeng lu 建中靖國續燈錄 (C)

jiaochan yi zhi 教禪一致 (C)

jiaowai biechuan 教外別傳 (C)

jiaowai biexing 教外別行 (C)

Jiatai pudeng lu 嘉泰普燈錄 (C)

Jiatai pudeng lu zongmulu 嘉泰普燈錄總目錄 (C)

Jingde chuandeng lu 景德傳燈錄 (C)

Jingang jing 金剛經 (C)

jinshi 進士 (C)

Jingjie 淨戒 (d.u.) (C)

Jingshan Xiling 徑山希陵 (1247–1322) (C)

Jingyin Chansi 淨因禪寺 (C)

Jinhua Juzhi 金華俱胝 (810–880?); Gutei Chikan (3)

jishō zanmai 自證三昧 (J)

Jiumoluoshi 鳩摩羅什 (344–413)

jiyuan wenda 機緣問答 (C); *kien mondō* (J)

Jōgon 浄厳 (J)

jōriki 定力 (J)

ju 句 (C)

Juefan Huihong 覺範慧洪 (1071–1128) (C)

K

kafū 家風 (J)

Kaihua si [monastery] 開化寺 (C)

Kaihua Xingming 開化行明 (932–1001) (C)

kan 勘 (C)

kanguo 勘過 (C)

kankin 看經 (C)

kanhua 看話 (C)

Kanhwa kyŏrŭi ron 看話決疑論 (K)

kanpo 勘破 (C)

katsu 喝 (J)

kenshō 見性 (J)

ki 気 (J)

kiai 氣合 (J)

kikan 機關 (J)

Kikigakishō 聞書抄 (J)

kirigami 切紙 (J)

Kitano Tenjin engi 北野天神縁起 (J)

kōan 公案 (J)

Koan [historical period] 弘安 (1278–1288) (J)

kōan kufū 公案工夫 (J)

kōan shitsunai 公案室内 (J)

Kokan Shiren 虎関師錬 (1278–1347) (J)

Koshiroku 故紙録 (J)

kuden 口伝 (J)

kufū 工夫 (J)

Kūkai 空海 (774–835) (J)

Kumārajīva (S). *See* Jiumoluoshi

kumu 枯木 (C)

kushū 句集 (J)

Kye ch'osim hagin mun 誡初心學入門 (K)

Kyo 教 (K)

kyōgen 狂言 (J)

Kyŏngguk taejŏn (K) 經國大典 (K)

Kyŏngje yukchŏn (K) 經濟六典 (K)

L

Langya Huijue 瑯琊慧覺 (d.u.)

Lanxi Daolong 蘭渓道隆 (1213–1278) (C); Rankei Dōryū

Leian Zhengshou 雷庵正受 (1147–1209) (C)

leishu 類書 (C)

li 理 (C)

li 離 (C)

Liandeng huiyao 聯燈會要 (C)

liao 了 (C)

libu 吏部 (C)

Lidai fabao ji 歷代法寶記 (C)

Lihun ji 離魂記 (C)

Li Langzhong 李郎中 (d.u.)

Lin'an 臨安 (C)

Linji 臨濟 (C); Rinzai (J)

Linji lu 臨濟錄 (C)

Linji Yixuan 臨濟義玄 (d. 866); Rinzai Gigen (21, 24)

Linjian lu 林間録 (C)

Liuzu dashi fabao tanjing 六祖大師法寶壇經 (C)

Li Wenhe 李文和 or Li Zunxu 李遵勗 (988–1038)

liyi 離意 (C)

Liyi ruren 離意女人 (*sūtra* character) (42)

Li Zunxu 李遵勗 (988–1038)

Longtan Chongxin 龍潭崇信 (ca. 753–852); Ryōtan Sūshin (28)

Longxiang si [monastery] 龍翔 (C)

Lu Jiyi 呂機宜

Luohan Guichen 羅漢桂琛 (867–928); Rakan Keijin

luo pianyi 落便宜 (C)

Lu, Mount 廬山 (C)

Luo Zhixian 羅知縣 (d.u.)

M

Ma Fang 馬防 (C)

Mahākāśyapa (S). *See* Mohejiaye

Maitreya (S). *See* Mile

Mangming pusa 罔明菩薩 (*sūtra* character); Momyō bosatsu (42)

Mañjuśrī (S). *See* Wenshu

Mazu Daoyi 馬祖道一 (709–788); Baso Doitsu (19, 30, 33)

meguru めぐる (J)

Miaodao 妙道 (d.u., active twelfth c.)

Mile 彌勒 (*sūtra* character); Miroku (25, 45)

ming 命 (C)

missan 密參 (J)

Miyan Zongshao 彌衍宗紹 (d.u.); Yaen Sosho (preface)

Mohejiaye 摩訶迦葉; Makakashō (6, 22)

mondō 問答 (J)

monsan 門參 (J)

mozhao 默照 (C); *mokushō* (J)

Mugai Nyodai 無外如大 (1223–1298) (J)

Mugaku Sogen 無学祖元. *See* Bukkō Kokushi (J)

Muhak Chach'o 無學自超 (1327–1405) (K)

Muhon Kakushin 無本覚心 (1207–1298) (J)

Mumonkan shō 無門関鈔 (J)

Musō Soseki 夢窓疎石 (1275–1351) (J)

myō 妙 (J)

Myōan Eisai 明菴栄西 (1141–1215) (J)

N

Nāgārjuna (second–third c.) (S)

Namsanjong 南山宗 (K)

Nanquan Puyuan 南泉普願 (748–835); Nansen Fugan (14, 19, 27, 34)

nantō 難透 (J)

Nanyang heshang dunjiao jietuo chanmen zhiliaoxing tanyu 南陽和上頓教
解脱禪門直了性壇語 (C)

Nanyang Huizhong 南陽慧忠 (675–775); Nanyō Echū (17)

Nanyuan shan (Mount) 南源山 (C)

*Nanzong dunjiao zuishangcheng mohe bore boluomi liuzu Huineng dashi
yu Shouzhou Dafan si shifa tanjing* 南宗頓教最上大乘摩訶般若波羅蜜經
六祖惠能大師於韶州大梵寺施法壇經 (C)

Naong Hyegǔn 懶翁惠勤 (1320–1376) (K)

nenbutsu 念仏 (J)

nüren 女人 (C)

O

Ōmori Sōgen 大森曹玄 (1904–1994) (J)

P

Pei Xiu 裴休 (787–860)

peng 棚 (C)

pingchang xin shi dao 平常心是道 (C)

Pojo Chinul 普照知訥 (1158–1210) (K)

pozi 婆子 (C)

Puli chanyuan 普利禪院 (C)

Puhui 普會 (ca. fourteenth c.)

Putidamo 菩提達磨 (ca. sixth c.); Daruma (41)
Princess Rishū 理秀女王 (1725–1764) (J)

Q

qiannü lihun 倩女離魂 (C)
qiao 毃 (C)
Qingbing 清稟 (d.u.) (C)
qinggui 清規 (C)
Qingshui 清稅 (d.u.): Seizei (10)
Qingyuan Weixin 青原惟信 (ca. thirteenth c.) (C)
Qingyuan Xingsi 青原行思 (671–741); Seigen Gyōshi
Qizhuyingai pusa 棄諸陰蓋菩薩 (C)
Qu You 瞿佑 (1341–1427)

R

Rentian baojian 人天寶鑑 (C)
Rentian yanmu 人天眼目 (C)
Ren Xizhong 任奚仲 (ca. 3 BCE); Nin Keichū (8)
Rinka 林下 (J)
Rongqing Qingxuan 隆慶慶閑 (1027–1082) (C)
roshi 老師 (J)
ruding 入定 (C)
rushi 入室 (C)
Ruzhou 汝州 (C)
Ruiyan Shiyan 瑞巖師彥 (ca. 820–933); Zuigan Shigen (12)
ryū 流 (J)
Ryūkōji 龍興寺 (J)

S

Saichō 最澄 (767–822) (J)
Śākyamuni (S). *See* Shijiamouni
sanmitsu 三密 (J)
sanzen 参禅 (J)
Sarvanīvaraṇaviṣkambhin Bodhisattva. *See* Wangming pusa
satori 悟り (J)

Sei Kenko (J) or Zhao Qingxian 趙清獻 (1008–1084) (C)

Sengcan 僧璨. *See* Jianzhi Sengcan (C)

Sengliang 僧亮 (d.u.) (C)

Sengzhao 僧肇 (384–414?); Sōjō

shangtang 上堂 (C)

Shaozhou 邵州 (C)

Shenguang Huike 神光慧可 (487–593); Shinkō Eka (41)

shenshi 神識 (C)

Shenxiu 神修 (d.u.) (C)

shetou duodi 舌頭墮地 (C)

shetou wugu 舌頭無骨 (C)

shi 事

Shiji 實際 (d.u.); Jissai (3)

Shijiamouni 釋迦牟尼; Shakamuni (32, 42, 45)

Shin bukkyō 新仏教 (J)

shin fukatoku 心不可得 (C)

Shingon School 真言宗 (J)

shishen 識神 (C)

Shishuang Chuyuan 石霜楚圓 (986–1039); Sekisō Soen (46)

Shitou Xiqian 石頭希遷 (701–791); Sekitō Kisen

Shōbōgenzō 正法眼藏 (J)

shokan 初關 (J)

Shōmono 抄物 (J)

Shōnan kattō roku 湘南葛藤錄 (J)

Shoushan Shengnian 首山省念 (926–993); Shūzan Shōnen (43)

shujō 拄杖 (J)

shū 宗 (J)

Shūhō Myōchō 宗峰妙超 (1283–1338) (J)

siju 死句 (C)

Sixin Wuxin 死心悟新 (1043–1116); Shinshin Goshim (39)

Sŏn 禪 (K)

Song gaoseng zhuan 宋高僧傳 (C)

songgu 頌古 (C)

Songyuan Chongyue 松源崇嶽 (1132–1202); Shōgen Sūgaku (20)

Sŏnmun yŏmsong jip 禪門拈頌集 (K)

Sŏnwŏn Monastery 禪源寺 (K)

sōrin 叢林 (J)

Sōtō School 曹洞宗 (J)

Sugawara no Michizane 菅原道真 (845–903) (J)

sūsokukan 数息観 (J)

Susŏn Monastery 修禪寺 (K)

T

Tachibana no Someko 橘染子 (1667–1705) (J)

Taiping guangji 太平廣記 (C)

Tamjin 曇眞 (d.u.) (K)

tanxuan shuomiao 談玄說妙 (C)

tanden 丹田 (J)

tanden soku 丹田息 (J)

Tanxiu 曇秀 (d.u., active eleventh c.) (C)

T'anyŏn 坦然 (1070–1159) (K)

Tendai school 天台宗 (J)

Tianhuang Daowu 天皇道悟 (748–807); Tennō Dogō

Tiansheng guangdeng lu 天聖廣燈錄 (C)

Tiantai 天台 (C); J. Tendai

Tiantai Zhiyi 天台智顗 (538–597) (C)

Tiantong Yunxiu 天童雲岫 (1242–1324); Tendō Unshū

Tianwang 天王 (C)

Tianwang rulai 天王如來 (C)

Tori no sorane 鳥のそら音 (J)

U

Ŭich'ŏn 義天 (1055–1101) (K)

Ungan 雲巌 (d.u) (J)

Upper Tianzhu Monastery 上天竺寺 (C)

W

waka 和歌 (J)

Wanan Daoyan 卍庵道顔 (1094–1164) (C)

Wangming dashi 罔明大士; Momyo dashi (42)

Wanling 宛陵

wanxing 萬行 (C)

Wang Zhou 王宙 (Tang dynasty fictional figure) (35)

Wansong Xingxiu 萬松行秀 (1166–1246); Banshō Gyōshū

wei 微 (C)

Weishan Lingyou 溈山靈祐 (771–853); Isan Reiyū (40)

Wenshu 文殊 (C); Monju (J) (42)

Wenzhou [city] 温州

wenzi Chan 文字禪 (C)

wu 無 (C); *mu* (J)

Wudeng quanshu 五燈全書 (C)

Wudeng huiyuan 五燈會元 (C)

Wujia zhengzong zan 五家正宗贊 (C)

Wumen guan 無門關 (C); *Mumonkan* (J)

Wumen Huikai (1183–1260); Mumon Ekai (preface; 1–48)

wunian 無念 (C)

Wushi Jiechen (1080–1148) (C)

Wutai shan 五臺山 (C)

Wuyue 吳越 (C)

wuxiang 無相 (C)

wuzhu 無住 (C)

Wuzhu 無住 (714–774) (C)

Wuzhun Shifan 無準師範 (1177–1249); Bujun Shiban

Wuzhuo Miaozong 無著妙總 (1095–1170) (C)

Wuzu Fayan 五祖法演 (1018–1104); Goso Hōen (35, 36, 38, 45)

X

Xi'an 習菴. *See* Chen Xun

Xiangyan Zhixian 香嚴智閑 (d. 898); Kyōgen Chikan (5)

Xiang Yu 項羽 (232–202 BCE); Kōu (10)

Xiaozong (1127–1194) 孝宗

Xie Sanlang 謝三郎. *See* Xuansha Shibei; Sha Sanrō (41)

xin 心 (C)

xin buzhu fa; dao ji liudong 心不住法，道即通流 (C)

Xingming. *See* Kaihua Xingming

Xingyang Qingrang 興陽清讓 (910–980); Kōyō Seijō (9)

Xiong 熊 (C)

Xisou Shaotan 希叟紹曇 (d.u.)

xiuzhu 朽株 (C)

Xuanjue 玄覺 (d.u.; Northern Song period)

Xuansha Shibei 玄沙師備 (835–908); Gensha Shibi (41)

Xuanzang 玄奘 (602–664)

Xuanzong 宣宗 (846–859)

Xu chuandeng lu 續傳燈錄 (C)

Xuedou Chongxian 雪竇重顯 (980–1052); Setchō Jūken

Xuefeng Yicun 雪峰義存 (822–908); Seppō Gison (13)

Xu guzunsu yuyao 續古尊宿語要 (C)

Y

Yanagisawa Yoshiyasu 柳沢吉保 (1658–1714) (J)

yang 陽 (C)

Yangqi Fanghui 楊岐方會 (992–1049); Yōgi Hōe (postscript)

Yangshan Huiji 仰山慧寂 (807–883); Kyōzan Ejaku (25)

Yang Yi 楊億 (974–1020)

Yantou Quanhuo 巖頭全豁 (828–887); Gantō Zenkatsu (13)

Yasen kanna 夜船閒話 (J)

Yijing 易經 (C)

yin 陰 (C)

yinian wannian 一念萬年 (C)

yiqing 疑情 (C)

Yi Sŏnggye 李成桂 (1335–1408) (K)

Yongming Monastery 永明寺 (C)

Yongming Yanshou 永明延壽 (905–976); J. Yōmyō Enju

youguo 有過 (C)

Yuanwu Foguo chanshi yulu 圓悟佛國禪師語錄 (C)

Yuanwu Keqin 圜悟克勤 (1063–1135); Engo Kokugon

Yuanzhou 袁州 (C)

Yue'an Shanguo 月庵善果 (1079–1152); Getsuan Zenka (8)

Yuelin Shiguan 月林師觀 (1143–1217); Gatsurin Shikan

Yuezhou 越州 (C)

Yuezhou Qianfeng 越州乾峯 (d.u.); Esshū kempō (48)

Yuhang 餘杭 (C)

yulu 語錄 (C)

Yunan Zhenjing heshang xingzhuang 雲庵真淨和尚行狀 (C)

Yungai Shouzhi 雲蓋守智 (d.u.)

Yunmen Wenyan 雲門文偃 (864–949); Ummon Bun'en (15, 16, 21, 39, 48)

Yushan zhu 郁山主 (eleventh c.) (C)

Z

Zanning 贊寧 (919–1001)

zazen 坐禅 (J)

zenji 禪師 (J)

Zhang Jiucheng 張九成 (1092–1159)

Zhang Qian 張倩 (Tang fictional figure); Cho Jo (35)

Zhang Wujin 張無盡, a.k.a. Zhang Shangying 張商英 (1043–1121)

Zhang Yi 張鎰 (d. 783) (C)

Zhang Zhuo 張拙 (ca. ninth c.); Cho Setsu (39)

Zhantang Wenzhun 湛堂文準 (1061–1115); Tandō Monjun

zhaopo 照破 (C)

Zhaojue Changcong 照覺常聰 (1025–1091)

Zhaozhou Congshen 趙州從諗 (778–897); Jōshū Jūshin (1, 7, 11, 14, 19, 31, 37)

zhende 真底 (C)

zhen shizi er 真師子兒 (C)

Zhengfa yanzang 正法眼藏 (C); *shōbōgenzō* (J)

Zhenhui Yuanlian 真慧元璉 (951–1036) (C)

Zhenjing Kewen 真淨克文 (1025–1102)

zhizhi renxin 直指人心 (C)

Zhongfeng Mingben 中峰明本 (1263–1323); Chūhō Myōhon

zhuan 轉 (C); *ten* (J)

zhuanyu 轉語 (C)

Zhuangzi 莊子 (d.u.)

Zhufo yaoji jing 諸佛要集經 (C)

Zhu Xi 朱熹 (C)

zhuzhao bikong 築著鼻孔 (C)

Zhuzi yulei 朱子語類 (C)

ziyou 自由 (C)

Zongmen tongyao ji 宗門統要集 (C)

Zongmen wuku 宗門武庫 (C)

Zongmi. *See* Guifeng Zongmi

zuochou weiwo 坐籌帷幄 (C)

Zutang ji 祖堂集 (C)

Zuting shiyuan 祖庭事苑 (C)

BIBLIOGRAPHY

COLLECTIONS

Taishō shinshū daizōkyō 大正新修大藏經 (85 vols., ed. and comp. Takakusu Junjiro 高楠 順次郎, Watanabe Kaigyoku 渡邊海旭, et al., Tokyo: Taisho Issaikyo Kanko Kai, 1924– 1934), compiled on the basis of the Koryŏ Canon and collated against the Song, Yuan, and Ming versions, with reference to the Shōsoin 正倉院 collection, the Chongning Canon, the Pilu Canon (kept in the Library of the Ministry of the Impe- rial Household 宮內省 Kunai-shō), and the early manuscripts found in Dunhuang. Reprint, Taibei: Xinwenfeng chuban gongsi, 1974. Abbreviated as T., followed by the work number, volume number (and when appropriate page number and the registry column: a, b, or c).

Dainihon zokuzōkyō 大日本續藏經 (150 vols., ed. Nankano Tatsue, Kyoto: Zōkyō shoin, 1905–1912), compiled on the basis of the *Ōbaku Daizōkyō* 黃檗大藏. Reprint, *Wanzi xuzang jing* or *Manji-zōkyō* 卍 字續藏經, 150 vols., Taiwan: Xinwenfeng chubangongsi, 1968–1970. Abbreviated as X., followed by the work number, volume number (and when appropriate page number and the registry column: a, b, or c).

Gujin tushu jicheng 古今圖書集成 (*Synthesis of Books and Illustrations Past and Present*) by Chen, Menglei 陳夢雷 (b. 1651) et al. Biography of Chen Xun 陳塤 (1197–1241) is found in X. 1661, 88:502b01–05.

PRIMARY SOURCES

Biyan lu 碧巖錄 (*Blue Cliff Record*) by Xuedou Chongxian 雪竇重顯 and Yuanwu Keqin 圓悟克勤. T. 2003, 48.

Chanyuan zhu zhuji duxu 禪源諸詮集都序 (Preface to the Collection of Chan Sources) by Zongmi 宗密. T. 2015, 48.

Chanzong songku lianzhu tongji 禪宗頌古聯珠通集 (Comprehensive Anthology of the String of Pearls Verse Commentaries on Old Cases of the Chan Lineage), completed in 1318 by Puhui 普會 (ca. 14th c.). 40 fascicles. X. 1295:65.

Chanzong wumen guan 禪宗無門關 (Gateless Barrier of the Chan Lineage) by Wumen Huikai 無門慧開. T. 2004, 48.

Chen, Yuanyou 陳元祐. *Lihun ji* 離魂記 (Record of the Divided Spirit). *Longwei mishu* 龍威秘, vol 6. *Baibu congshu jicheng* 百部叢書集成, no. 32. Taibei: Yiwen chubanshe, 1968.

Chu sanzang ji 出三藏記集 (Collection of Notes on the Translation of the Tripiṭaka) by Sengyou 僧祐 (445–518). T. 2145, 55.

Congrong lu 從容錄 (Record of Serenity). Hongzhi Zhengjue 宏智正覺 and Wansong Xingxiu 萬松行秀. T. no. 2004, 48.

Dahui Pujue chanshi yulu 大慧普覺禪師語錄 (Discourse Record of Chan Master Dahui Pujue). T. 1998A, 47.

Dōgen Kigen. *Shobogenzo: The Treasure House of the Eye of the True Teaching: A Trainee's Translation of Great Master Dogen's Spiritual Masterpiece*. Trans. Hubert Nearman. Mt. Shasta, CA: Shasta Abbey Press, 2017.

Fofa jintang bian 佛法金湯編 (The Golden Medicinal Decoction of the Buddhadharma) by Daizong Xintai 岱宗心泰 (1327–1415). X.no. 1628, 87.

Foguo Yuanwu chanshi Biyanlu 佛果圜悟禪師碧巖 (The Blue Cliff Record of Chan Master Foguo Yuanwu). T. 2003, 48.

Hakuin Ekaku. *Complete Poison Blossoms from a Thicket of Thorn: The Zen Records of Hakuin*. Trans. Norman Waddell. Berkeley: Counterpoint Press, 2017.

——. *Hakuin's Precious Mirror Cave: A Zen Miscellany*. Trans. Norman Waddell. Berkeley: Counterpoint Press, 2009.

——. *The Zen Master Hakuin: Selected Writings*. Trans. Phillip B. Yampolsky. New York: Columbia University Press, 1971.

Huangboshan duanji chanshi wanling lu 黃檗斷際禪師宛陵錄 (Wanling Record of Chan Master Duanji from Mt. Huangbo), by Pei Xiu 裴休 (797–870). T. 2012b, 48.

Jiangxi Mazu Daoyi chanshi yulu 江西馬祖道一禪師語錄 (Discourse Record of Chan Master Mazu Daoyi of Jiangxi [Province]). X. 1321, 69.

Jingde chuandeng lu 景德傳燈錄 (Transmission of the Lamp Record in the Jingde Era) compiled by Yang Yi 楊億 (974–1020). T. 2076, 51.

Liandeng huiyao 聯燈會要 (Essential Collection of the Lamp Connections within the [Chan] Tradition). 30 fascicles. Compiled in 1189 by Huiweng Wuming 晦翁悟明 (d.u.). X. 1557, 79.

Li Jingde 黎靖德, ed. *Zhuzi yulei* 朱子語類 (Thematic Discourses of Master Zhu). Published in 1270. Reprinted in *Lixue congshu* 理學叢書 (Compendium on Neo-Confucianism). Compiled by Wang Xingxian 王星賢, vol. 83: 2146. Beijing: Zhonghua shuju, 1985.

Liuzu dashi fabao tanjing 六祖法寶壇經 (Platform Sūtra of the Great Sixth Ancestral Master). T. 2008, 48.

Song gaoseng zhuan 宋高僧傳 (Biographies of Eminent Monks Compiled in the Song Dynasty). Zanning. T. 2061.

Sŏnmun yŏmsong chip 禪門拈頌集 (Collection of Prose and Verse Comments on Cases of the Sŏn School) by Chin'gak Hyesim 眞覺慧諶. Han'guk Pulgyo chŏnsŏ 韓國佛教全書, vol. 5, ed. Tongguk taehaekkyo Ha'guk Pulgyo chŏnsŏ p'yŏnch'an wiwŏnhoe 東國大學校韓國佛教全書編纂委員會, 1–923. Seoul: Tongguk taehakkyo, 1994.

Taiping guangji 太平廣記 (Extensive Gleanings from the Era of Great Harmony) by Li Fang 李昉 et al., comps. Beijing: Zhonghua shuju, 1961.

Tiansheng guangdeng lu 天聖廣燈錄 (Tiansheng Extensive Record of the Flame) by Li Zunxu 李遵勗 (988–1038). X. 1553, 78.

Zhufo yaoji jing 諸佛要集經 (Scripture of the Collected Essentials of All Buddhas) by Dharmarakṣa (Zhu fahu 竺法護; 239–316). T. 810, 17.

Zuting shiyuan 祖庭事苑 (Collections of Topics from the Garden of the Patriarchs) by Mu'an Shanqing 睦庵善卿 (ca. 1050–1108) in 1108. X. 1261, 64.

SECONDARY SOURCES

Abe Masao. "God, Emptiness, and Ethics." *Buddhist-Christian Studies* 3 (1983): 53–60.

Abe Masao and William R. LaFleur. *Zen and Western Thought*. Honolulu: University of Hawai'i Press, 1985.

Abé, Ryūichi. "Revisiting the Dragon Princess: Her Role in Medieval Engi Stories and Their Implications in Reading the Lotus Sutra." *Japanese Journal of Religious Studies* 42, no. 1 (2015): 27–70.

Adamek, Wendi L. *The Mystique of Transmission: On an Early Chan History and Its Contexts*. New York: Columbia University Press, 2007.

——. "Revisiting Questions about Female Disciples in the *Lidai fabao ji* (Record of the Dharma-Treasure through the Generations)." *Pacific World: Third Series* 18 (2016): 57–65.

——. "Transmitting Notions of Transmission." In *Readings of the* Platform Sūtra, ed. Morten Schütter and Stephen F. Teiser, 109–33. New York: Columbia University Press, 2012.

Ahn, Juhn Y. *Buddhas and Ancestors: Religion and Wealth in Fourteenth-Century Korea*. Studies of the Weatherhead East Asian Institute Series at Columbia University and the Korean Studies of the Henry M. Jackson School of International Studies. Seattle: University of Washington Press, 2018.

——. "Hakuin." In *The Dao Companion to Japanese Buddhist Philosophy*, ed. Gereon Kopf, 511–535. Dordrecht: Springer, 2019.

——. "Have a Korean Lineage and Transmit a Chinese One Too: Lineage Practices in Seon Buddhism," *Journal of Chan Buddhism* 1 (2019): 1–32.

——. "Pure Rules and Public Monasteries in Korea." *Approaches to Chan/Sŏn/Zen Studies: Chinese Chan Buddhism and Its Spread throughout East Asia*, ed. Albert Welter, Steven Heine, and Jin Y. Park, 215–237. Albany: State University of New York Press, 2022.

——. "Who Has the Last Word in Chan? Secrecy, Transmission, and Reading During the Northern Song Dynasty," *Journal of Chinese Religions* 37 (2009): 1–72.

Ahn, Juhn Y., trans. *Gongan Collections I*, Collected Works of Korean Buddhism, vol. 7–1. Seoul: Jogye Order of Korean Buddhism, 2012.

Allen, Sarah M. *Shifting Stories: History, Gossip, and Lore in Narratives from Tang Dynasty China*. Cambridge, MA: Harvard University Press, 2014.

Andō Yoshinori 安藤嘉則. "Chūsei Zenshū no kōan Zen nitsuite" 中世禅宗の公案禅について, *Komazawa Joshi Daigaku Kenkyū Kiyō* 駒沢女子大学研究紀要 7 (2000): 12–24.

Balkwill, Stephanie. "Disappearing and Disappeared Daughters in Medieval Chinese Buddhism: *Sūtras* on Sex Transformation and an Intervention into Their Transmission History." *History of Religions* 60, no. 4 (June 2021): 255–286.

Bareau, Andre. 1993. "The List of the Asamskrta-dharma According to Asanga." In Alex Wayman, and Rāma Karaṇa Śarmā, eds., *Researches in Indian and Buddhist Philosophy: Essays in Honour of Professor Alex Wayman*. Delhi: Motilal Banarsidass, 269–308.

Barrett, T. H. "How Important is Mount Wutai? Sacred Space in a Zen Mirror." In *The Transnational Cult of Wutai: Historical and Cultural Perspectives*, ed. Susan Andrews, Jinhua Chen, and Guang Kuan, 238–252. Leiden: Brill, 2021.

Blair, Heather. "Mothers of the Buddhas: 'The Sutra on Transforming Women into Buddhas' (Bussetsu Tennyo Jōbutsu Kyō)." *Monumenta Nipponica* 71, no. 2 (2016): 263–293.

Bodiford, William M. *Sōtō Zen in Medieval Japan*. Honolulu: University of Hawai'i Press, 1993.

Bol, Peter. "The 'Localist Turn' and 'Local Identity' in Later Imperial China." *Late Imperial China* 24 (2003): 1–51.

——. "Neo-Confucianism and Local Society, Twelfth to Sixteenth Century: A Case Study." In *The Song-Yuan-Ming Transition in Chinese History*, ed. Paul Jakov Smith, Richard von Glahn, et al. 241–283. Cambridge. MA: Harvard University Asia Center; 2003.

——. *Neo-Confucianism in History*. Cambridge, MA: Harvard University Asia Center, 2008.

Borrell, Ari. "Ko-wu or Kung-an? Practice, Realization, and Teaching in the Thought of Chang Chiu-ch'eng." In *Buddhism in the Sung*, ed. Peter N. Gregory and Daniel A. Getz Jr, 62–108. Honolulu: University of Hawai'i Press, 1999.

Broughton, Jeffrey. *Zongmi on Chan*. New York: Columbia University Press, 2009.

Broughton, Jeffrey L., ed. and trans. with Elise Yoko Watanabe. *The Letters of Master Dahui Pujue*. Oxford: Oxford University Press, 2017.

Buswell, Robert. "The 'Short-cut' Approach of K'an-hua Meditation: The Evolution of a Practical Subitism in Chinese Ch'an Buddhism." In *Sudden and Gradual Approaches to Enlightenment in Chinese Thought*, ed. Peter N. Gregory, 321–377. Honolulu: University of Hawai'i Press, 1987.

Buswell, Robert, trans. *The Collected Works of Chinul*. Honolulu: University of Hawai'i Press, 1983.

Carey, Conán Dean. "In Hell the One Without Sin Is Lord." *Sino-Platonic Papers* 109 (2000): 1–60.

Carter, Thomas Francis. *The Invention of Printing in China and Its Spread Westward*. New York: The Ronald Press, 1955.

Cass, Victoria. *Dangerous Women: Warriors, Grannies, and Geishas of the Ming*. Lanham, MD: Rowman & Littlefield, 1999.

Chŏng Sua 정수아. "Hyejo kuksa Tamjin kwa 'Chŏnginsu:' Puk-Song Sŏnp'ung ŭi suyong kwa Koryŏ chunggi Sŏnjong ŭi puhŭng ŭl chungsimŭro 혜조국사 담진과 '정인수:' 북송 선풍의 수용과 고려 중기 선종의 부흥을 중심으로" In *Hanguk sahak nonch'ong: Yi Ki-baek sŏngsaeng kohŭi kinyŏm*, vol. 1, ed. Yi Ki-baek sŏngsaeng kohŭi kinyŏmhoe, 616–639. Seoul: Ilchogak, 1994.

Cleary, Thomas, trans. *Book of Serenity*. Hudson, NY: Lindisfarne Press, 1988.

Cleary, Thomas, and J. C. Cleary, trans. *The Blue Cliff Record*. Boston: Shambhala, rpt. 2005.

Collcutt, Martin. "Zen and the Gozan." In *The Cambridge History of Japan*, vol. 3, ed. Kozo Yamamura, 583–652. Cambridge: Cambridge University Press, 1990.

Cook, Francis H. *Hua-yen Buddhism: The Jewel Net of Indra*. University Park: Pennsylvania State University Press, 1977.

Darnton, Robert. "History of Reading." In *New Perspectives on Historical Writing*, ed. Peter Burke, 140–167. University Park: Penn State University Press, 1991.

Davin, Didier. *"Mumonkan" no Shusse Sugoroku: Kikashita Zen no Seiten* 『無門関』の出世双六: 帰化した禅の聖典. Tokyo: Heibonsha, 2020.

Deal, William E., and Brian Douglas Ruppert. *A Cultural History of Japanese Buddhism*. Chichester: Wiley Blackwell, 2015.

Deguchi, Yasuo, Jay L. Garfield, and Graham Priest. "The Way of the Dialetheist: Contradictions in Buddhism." *Philosophy East and West* 58, no. 3 (2008): 395–402.

Deguchi, Yasuo, Jay L. Garfield, and Graham Priest. "Does a Table Have Buddha-Nature?: A Moment of Yes and No. Answer! But Not in Words or Signs! A Response to Mark Siderits." *Philosophy East and West* 63, no. 3 (2013): 387–398.

Deguchi, Yasuo, Jay L. Garfield, and Graham Priest. "How We Think Mādhyamikas Think: A Response To Tom Tillemans." *Philosophy East and West* 63, no. 3 (2013): 426–435.

Deguchi, Yasuo, Jay L. Garfield, Graham Priest, and Robert H. Sharf. *What Can't Be Said: Contradiction and Paradox in East Asian Thought*. Oxford: Oxford University Press, 2021.

Drott, Edward R. *Buddhism and the Transformation of Old Age in Medieval Japan*. Honolulu: University of Hawai'i Press, 2016.

Dumoulin, Heinrich. *Zen Buddhism: A History, Volume 1: India and China*. New York: Macmillan, 1988.

Faure, Bernard. "From Bodhidharma to Daruma: The Hidden Life of a Zen Patriarch." *Japan Review* 23, no. 23 (2011): 45–71.

——. *The Rhetoric of Immediacy: A Cultural Critique of Chan/Zen Buddhism*. Princeton, NJ: Princeton University Press, 1991.

Fister, Patricia. "Commemorating Life and Death: The Memorial Culture Surrounding the Rinzai Zen Nun Mugai Nyodai." In *Women, Rites, and Ritual Objects in Premodern Japan*, ed. Karen M. Gerhart, 269–303. Leiden: Brill, 2018.

Foulk, T. Griffith. "The Spread of Chan (Zen) Buddhism," In *The Spread of Buddhism*, ed. Ann Heirman and Stephan Peter Bumbacher, 433–456. Leiden: Brill, 2007.

——. "The Form and Function of Koan Literature: A Historical Overview." In *The Kōan: Texts and Contexts in Zen Buddhism*, ed. Steven Heine and Dale S. Wright, 15–45. Oxford: Oxford University Press, 2000.

Foulk, T. Griffith, and Robert H. Sharf. "On the Ritual Use of Ch'an Portraiture in Medieval China." *Cahiers d'Extrême-Asie* 7 (1993): 149–219.

Fuller, Michael A. *Drifting among Rivers and Lakes: Southern Song Dynasty Poetry and the Problem of Literary History*. Cambridge, MA: Harvard University Press, 2013.

Garfield, Jay L. *The Fundamental Wisdom of the Middle Way: Nāgārjuna's Mūlamadhyamakakārikā*. Oxford: Oxford University Press, 1995.

Garfield, Jay L. and Graham Priest, "Nāgārjuna and the Limits of Thought." *Philosophy East and West* 53, no. 1 (2003): 1–21.

Gethin, Rupert. *Foundations of Buddhism*. Oxford: Oxford University Press, 1998.

Gimello, Robert M. "Mārga and Culture: Learning, Letters, and Liberation in Northern Sung Ch'an." In *Paths to Liberation: The Mārga and Its Transformations in Buddhist Thought*, ed. Robert E. Buswell Jr. and Robert M. Gimello, 371–437. Honolulu: University of Hawai'i Press, 1992.

Grant, Beata. "Da Zhangfu: The Gendered Rhetoric of Heroism and Equality in Seventeenth-Century Chan Buddhist *Discourse Records*." *Nan Nü* 10 (2009): 177–211.

Grant, Beata, trans. *Zen Echoes: Classic Kōans with Verse Commentaries by Three Female Chan Masters*. Boston; Wisdom, 2017.

Green, James. *The Recorded Sayings of Zen Master Joshu*. Boulder, CO: Shambhala, 1998.

Gregory, Peter N. *Tsung-mi and the Sinification of Buddhism*. Kuroda Institute, Studies in East Asian Buddhism, 16. Honolulu: University of Hawai'i Press, 2002.

Gregory, Peter N., and Daniel A. Getz Jr., eds. *Buddhism in the Sung*. Honolulu: University of Hawai'i Press 1999.

Guo Gu, trans. and comm. *Passing through the Gateless Barrier, Kōan Practice for Real Life*. Boulder, CO: Shambhala, 2016.

Harrison, Paul. "*Vajracchedikā Prajñāpāramitā*: A New English Translation of the Sanskrit Text Based on Two Manuscripts from Greater Gandhāra." In *Manuscripts in the Schøyen Collection*, vol. 3, ed. Jens Braarvig, Paul Harrison, Jens-Uwe Hartmann, Kazunobu Matsuda, and Lore Sander, 133–159. Oslo: Hermes Publishing, 2006.

Harrison, Paul. "Resetting the Diamond: Reflections on Kumārajīva's Chinese Translation of the *Vajracchedikā ('Diamond Sūtra')*." *Journal of Historical and Philological Studies of China's Western Regions* 3 (Beijing Science Press, 2010): 233–248.

Haskel, Peter. "Bankei and His World." PhD diss. Columbia University, 1988.

Heine, Steven. *Chan Rhetoric of Uncertainty in the Blue Cliff Record*. Oxford University Press, 2016.

——. *Like Cats and Dogs: Contesting the Mu Kōan*. New York: Oxford University Press, 2014.

——. *Opening a Mountain Kōans of the Zen Masters*. Oxford: Oxford University Press, 2002.

——. *Shifting Shape, Shaping Text: Philosophy and Folklore in Fox Koan*. Honolulu: University of Hawai'i Press, 2000.

——. "Thy Rod and Thy Staff They Discomfort Me: Zen Staffs as Implements of Instruction." In *Zen and Material Culture*, ed. Steven Heine, and Pamela D. Winfield, 1–36. New York: Oxford University Press, 2017.

——. "Visions, Divisions, Revisions: The Encounter between Iconoclasm and Supernaturalism in Kōan Cases about Mount Wu-t'ai." In *The Kōan: Texts and Contexts in Zen Buddhism*, ed. Steven Heine and Dale Wright, 137–167. New York: Oxford University Press, 2000.

——. *The Zen Poetry of Dogen: Verses from the Mountain of Eternal Peace*. Boston: Tuttle, 1997; rpt. New York: Dharma Communications, 2004.

Heine, Steven, and Douglas Berger. *Zen Kōans*. Honolulu: University of Hawai'i Press, 2014.

Heller, Natasha. *Illusory Abiding: The Cultural Construction of the Chan Monk Zhongfeng Mingben*. Cambridge, MA: Harvard University Asia Center, Harvard East Asian Monographs, 2014.

Hori, Victor Sōgen. *Zen Sand: The Book of Capping Phrases for Koan Practice*. Honolulu: University of Hawai'i Press, 2010.

Hsieh, Daniel. *Love and Women in Early Chinese Fiction*. Hong Kong: Chinese University Press, 2008.

Hsieh, Ding-hwa E. "Images of Women in Ch'an Buddhist Literature of the Sung Period." In *Buddhism in the Sung*, ed. Peter N. Gregory and Daniel A. Getz Jr., 148–187. Honolulu: University of Hawai'i Press, 1999.

Hurvitz, Leon. *Scripture of the Lotus Blossom of the Fine Dharma (The Lotus Sūtra)*. Translated from the Chinese of Kumārajīva. Records of Civilization: Sources and Studies 94, Translations from the Asian Classics. New York: Columbia University Press, 1976; rev. ed., 2009.

Hu Shih 胡適. *Shenhui heshang yiji—fu Hu xiansheng zuihou de yanjiu* 神會和尚遺集—附 胡先生最後的研究. Taibei: Hu Shi jinian guan, 1968.

Hymes, Robert. *Statesmen and Gentlemen: The Elite of Fu-chou, Chiang-hsi, in Northern and Southern Sung*. Cambridge: Cambridge University Press, 1986.

Iriya Yoshitaka 入矢義高. *Denshin hōyō: Enryōroku, Zen no goroku* 伝心法要: 宛陵錄. 禪の語錄, vol. 8. Tokyo: Chikuma shobō, 1969.

Ishikawa, Rikizan. "Transmission of Kirigami (Secret Initiation Documents): A Sōtō Practice in Medieval Japan." In *The Kōan Texts and Contexts in Zen Buddhism*, ed. Steven Heine and Dale S. Wright, 233–243. New York: Oxford University Press, 2000.

Ishii Shūdo. "Daie goroku no kisoteki kenkyū (jo)." *Komazawa daigaku bukkyō gakubu kenkyū kiyō* 31 (1973): 283–292.

——. "Kung-an Ch'an and the Tsung-men t'ung-yao chi," Trans. Albert Welter. In *The Kōan: Texts and Contexts in Zen Buddhism*, ed. Steven Heine and Dale S. Wright, 110–136. New York: Oxford University Press, 2000.

——. *Sōdai Zenshū shi no kenkyū: Chūgoku Sōtōshū to Dōgen Zen* 宋代禅宗史の研究: 中国 曹洞宗と道元禅 (Gakujutsu sōsho Zen Bukkyō). Tōkyō: Daitō Shuppansha, 1987.

——. "The *Wu-men kuan* (J. Mumonkan): The Formation, Propagation, and Characteristics of a Classic Zen Kōan Text." Trans. Albert Welter. In *The Zen Canon: Understanding the Classic Texts*, ed. Steven Heine and Dale S. Wright, 207–244. New York: Oxford University Press, 2004.

Jorgensen, John. "The Figure of Huineng." In *Readings of the Platform Sūtra*, ed. Morten Schütter and Stephen F. Teiser, 25–52. New York: Columbia University Press, 2012.

——. *Inventing Hui-neng, the Sixth Patriarch: Hagiography and Biography in Early Ch'an*. Sinica Leidensia, 68. Leiden: Brill, 2005.

Jorgensen, John, trans. *Seon Dialogues*, Collected Works of Korean Buddhism, vol. 8. Seoul: Jogye Order of Korean Buddhism, 2012.

Josephson, Jason Ānanda. *The Invention of Religion in Japan*. Chicago: University of Chicago Press, 2012.

Kamata Shigeo 鎌田茂雄, ed. *Zengen shosenshū tojo, Zen no goroku* 禪源諸詮集都序: 禪の 語録, vol. 9. Tokyo: Chikuma shobō, 1971.

Kang, Xiaofei. *The Cult of the Fox: Power, Gender, and Popular Religion in Late Imperial*. New York: Columbia University Press, 2006.

Kawamura Kōdō et al., eds. *Collected Works of Zen Master Dōgen (Dōgen Zenji zenshū*, 道元禅師全集). Tokyo: Shunjūsha, 1998–1993.

Kirchner, Thomas Yuho, and Ruth Fuller Sasaki, eds. and trans. *The Record of Linji*. Honolulu: University of Hawai'i, 2008.

Kohn, Livia. *Introducing Daoism*. New York: Routledge, 2008.

Kraft, Kenneth. *Eloquent Zen: Daitō and Early Japanese Zen*. Honolulu: University of Hawai'i Press, 1992.

Kyŏngguk taejŏn. Repr. Keijō: Chōsen Sōtokufu, Chūsūin, 1934.

Lau, D. C. *Lao Tzu Tao Te Ching*. New York: Penguin, 1963.

Leggett, Trevor, trans. *The Warrior Koans: Early Zen in Japan*. New York: Arkana, 1985.

Leighton, Taigen Dan, trans. *Cultivating the Empty Field: The Silent Illumination of Zen Master Hongzhi*. North Clarendon, VT: Tuttle, 2000.

Leitch, Donovan P. "There Is a Mountain." Recorded 1967 Epic Records, 45 rpm vinyl.

Levering, Miriam. "Ch'an Enlightenment for Laymen: Ta-hui and the New Religious Culture of the Sung." Cambridge, MA: Harvard University Press, 1978.

——. "Dahui Zonggao (1089–1163): The Image Created by His Stories about Himself and by His Teaching Style." In *Zen Masters*, ed. Steven Heine and Dale S. Wright, 91–115. Oxford: Oxford University Press, 2010.

——. "Dahui Zonggao and Zhang Shangying: The Importance of a Scholar in the Education of a Song Chan Master." *Journal of Song-Yuan Studies* no. 30 (2000): 115–139.

——. "The Dragon Girl and the Abbess of Mo-shan: Gender and Status in the Ch'an Buddhist Tradition." *Journal of the International Association of Buddhist Studies*, 5 no.1 (1982): 9–35.

——. "Lin-Chi (Rinzai) Ch'an and Gender: The Rhetoric of Equality and the Rhetoric of Heroism." In *Buddhism, Sexuality, and Gender*, ed. José Ignacio Cabézon, 137–156. Albany: State University of New York Press, 1992.

——. "Miao-tao and Her Teacher Ta-hui." In *Buddhism in the Sung*, ed. Peter N. Gregory and Daniel A. Getz Jr., 188–219. Honolulu: University of Hawai'i Press, 1999.

Loori, John Daido, ed. *Sitting with Kōans*. Boston: Wisdom, 2006.

McMahon, Barry Kaigen. *The Evolution of the White Plum: A Short and Incomplete History of Its Founders and Their Practice*. Accessed March 2023. https://whiteplum.org/user_uploads/Evolution of the White Plum.pdf.

McRae, John. "The Antecedents of Encounter Dialogue in Chinese Ch'an Buddhism." In *The Kōan: Texts and Contexts in Zen Buddhism*, ed. Steven Heine and Dale S. Wright, 46–74. New York: Oxford University Press, 2000.

——. "Encounter Dialogue and the Transformation of the Spiritual Path in Chinese Ch'an." In *Paths to Liberation: The Mārga and Its Transformations in Buddhist Thought*, ed. Robert E. Buswell Jr. and Robert M. Gimello, 339–370. Honolulu: University of Hawai'i Press, 1992.

——. *The Platform Sūtra of the Sixth Patriarch*. Honolulu: University of Hawai'i Press, 2000.

Meeks, Lori R. *Hokkeji and the Reemergence of Female Monastic Orders in Premodern Japan*. Honolulu: University of Hawai'i Press, 2010.

Miura, Isshū, and Ruth Fuller Sasaki. *Zen Dust: The History of the Koan and Koan Study in Rinzai (Lin-Chi) Zen*. New York: Harcourt, Brace & World, 1966.

Mohr, Michel. "Emerging from Nonduality: Kōan Practice in the Rinzai Tradition since Hakuin." In *The Kōan Texts and Contexts in Zen Buddhism*, ed. Steven Heine and Dale S. Wright, 244–279. New York: Oxford University Press, 2000.

Nattier, Jan. "Gender and Hierarchy in the *Lotus Sūtra*." In *Readings of the Lotus Sūtra*, ed. Stephen F. Teiser and Jacqueline I. Stone, 83–106. New York: Columbia University Press, 2009.

Nishijima, Gudo, and Chodo Cross, trans. *Master Dogen's Shobogenzo Book 4*. Charleston, SC: BookSurge, 2006.

Ōmori, Sōgen. *An Introduction to Zen Training*. Trans. Dogen Hosokawa and Roy Yoshimoto. Boston: Tuttle, 2002.

Ōtani, Setsuko 大谷節子. "Kyōgen Shujō to Mumonkan dai yonjūyon soku 'Bashō Shujō'" 狂言「拄杖」と『無門関』第四四則「芭蕉拄杖」. *Seijō Kokubungaku Ronshū* 成城國文學論集 41 (2019): 5–25.

Overmeire, Ben Van. "Reading Chan Encounter Dialogue during the Song Dynasty: The *Record of Linji*, the *Lotus Sutra*, and the Sinification of Buddhism." *Buddhist-Christian Studies* 37 (2017): 209–221.

Poceski, Mario. "Killing Cats and Other Imaginary Happenings: Milieus and Features of Chan Exegesis." In *Communities of Memory and Interpretation: Reimagining and Reinventing the Past in East Asian Buddhism*, ed. Mario Poceski, 111–144. Freiberg: Projekt Verlag, 2017.

——. *The Records of Mazu and the Making of Classical Chan Literature*. Oxford: Oxford University Press, 2015.

Radich, Michael. "A 'Prehistory' to Chinese Debates on the Survival of Death by the Spirit, with a Focus on the Term *Shishen* 識神 / *Shenshi* 神識." *Journal of Chinese Religions* 44, no. 2 (2016): 105–126.

Reischauer, Edwin O. *Ennin's Travels in T'ang China*. New York: Ronald Press, 1955.

Riggs, David E. "The Rekindling of a Tradition: Menzan Zuihō and the Reform of Japanese Sōtō Zen in the Tokugawa Era." PhD diss., University of California, Los Angeles, 2002.

Sadler, A. L., and Paul S. Atkins, eds. *Japanese Plays: Classic Noh, kyogen and Kabuki Works*. Tokyo: Tuttle, 2010.

Sanvido, Marta. "On the Verge of Damnation and Buddhahood. Motherhood, Female Corporeality, and Koan in Sōtō Zen." *Japanese Journal of Religious Studies* 49, no. 2 (2023): 1–47.

Sasaki, Ruth F., trans. *The Recorded Sayings of Chan Master Lin-Chi Hui-chao of Chen Prefecture*. Kyoto: The Institute for Zen Studies, 1975.

Scheid, Bernhard, and Mark Teeuwen, eds. *The Culture of Secrecy in Japanese Religion*. London: Taylor and Francis, 2015.

Schlütter, Morten. *How Zen Became Zen: The Dispute over Enlightenment and the Formation of Chan Buddhism in Song-Dynasty China*. Honolulu: University of Hawai'i Press, 2008.

——. *Readings of the Platform Sutra*. New York: Columbia University Press, 2012.

Sharf, Robert. "How to Think with Chan *Gong'ans*." In *Thinking with Cases: Specialized Knowledge in Chinese Cultural History*, ed. Charlotte Furth, Judith Zeitlin, and Hsiung Ping-chen, 205–243. Honolulu: University of Hawai'i Press, 2007.

——. "Is *Nirvāṇa* the Same as Insentience? Chinese Struggles with an Indian Buddhist Ideal." In *India in the Chinese Imagination: Myth, Religion, and Thought*, ed. John Kieschnick and Meir Shahar, 141–170. Philadelphia: University of Pennsylvania Press, 2014.

——. "Ritual." In *Critical Terms for the Study of Buddhism*, ed. Donald S. Lopez Jr., 245–269. Chicago: University of Chicago Press, 2005.

Shimauchi, Keiji 島内景二. *Shin'yaku "Tori no sorane:" Genroku no josei shisōka, Iizuka Someko, Zen ni idomu* 心訳「鳥の空音」: 元禄の女性思想家, 飯塚染子, 禅に挑む. Tokyo: Kasama Shoin, 2013.

Shultz, Edward J. *Generals and Scholars: Military Rule in Medieval Korea*. Honolulu: University of Hawai'i Press, 2000.

Siderits, Mark. "Does a Table Have Buddha-Nature?" *Philosophy East and West* 63, no. 3 (2013): 373–386.

Stevens, W. B. "Farther Along." Accessed March 6, 2012, https://hymnary.org/text/tempted_and_tried_were_oft_made_to_wonde.

Stone, Jacqueline I. *Original Enlightenment and the Transformation of Medieval Japanese Buddhism*. Honolulu: University of Hawai'i Press, 1999.

Sueki, Fumihiko 末木文美士. "Tachibana no Someko no Zen Rikai" 橘染子の禅理解. In *Ejima Yasunori Hakushi Tsuitō Ronshū: Kū to Jitsuzai* 江島惠教博士追悼論集·空と実在, ed. Ejima Yasunori Hakushi Tsuitō Ronshū Kankōkai 江島惠教博士追悼論集刊行会, 593–606. Tokyo: Shunjūsha, 2001.

Suzuki, D. T. *Essays in Zen Buddhism*, First Series. London and New York: Rider, 1926.

Swanson, Paul L. *Foundations of T'ien T'ai Philosophy: The Flowering of the Two Truths Theory in Chinese Buddhism*. Berkeley: Asian Humanities Press, 1989.

Takeshita Ruggeri, Anna 竹下ルッジェリ·アンナ. "Jendā ni taisuru Edo jidai no Rinzai shū: Hakuin Zenji wo chūshin ni" ジェンダーに対する江戸時代の臨済宗: 白隠禅師を中心として. *Kenkyū johō* 研究所報 31 (2021): 12–25.

Tanahashi, Kazuaki, trans. *The Treasury of the True Dharma Eye*. Boulder, CO: Shambhala, 2010.

Teiser, Stephen F. "Perspectives on Readings of the Heart Sutra: The Perfection of Wisdom and the Fear of Buddhism." In *Ways with Words: Writing about Reading Texts from Early China*, ed. Pauline Yu et al., 130–145. Berkeley: University of California Press, 2000.

Teiser, Stephen F., and Jacqueline I. Stone, eds. *Readings of the Lotus Sūtra*. Columbia Readings of Buddhist Literature. New York: Columbia University Press, 2009.

ter Haar, Barend J., and Maghiel van Crevel, eds. *Knowledge and Text Production in an Age of Print: China, 900–1400*. Leiden: Brill, 2011.

Tillemans, Tom J. F. "How do Mādhyamikas Think? Notes on Jay Garfield, Graham Priest, and Paraconsistency." In *Pointing at the Moon: Buddhism, Logic, Analytic Philosophy*, ed. Mario D'Amato, Jay L. Garfield, Tom J. F. Tillemans, 83–100. Oxford: Oxford University Press, 2009.

Tillemans, Tom J. F. "'How Do Mādhyamikas Think?' Revisited." *Philosophy East and West* 63, no. 3 (2013): 417–425.

Tōdai goroku kenkyū han 唐代語録研究班, ed. *Jinne no goroku: dango* 神会の語録: 檀語. Kyoto: Zen bunka kenkyūjo (Hanazono University), 2006.

Tongguk taehaekkyo Ha'guk Pulgyo chŏnsŏ p'yŏnch'an wiwŏnhoe 東國大學校韓國佛教全書編纂委員會, ed., *Han'guk Pulgyo chŏnsŏ* 韓國佛教全書, 13 vols. Seoul: Tongguk taehakkyo, 1994.

Vallor, Molly. *Not Seeing Snow: Musō Soseki and Medieval Japanese Zen*. Leiden: Brill, 2019.

Van Overmeire, Ben. "Reading Chan Encounter Dialogue during the Song Dynasty: The Record of Linji, the Lotus Sutra, and the Sinification of Buddhism." *Buddhist-Christian Studies* 37 (2017): 209–221.

Venuti, Lawrence. "Genealogies of Translation Theory: Jerome." In *The Translation Studies Reader*. Third Edition, ed. Lawrence Venuti, 483–502. New York: Routledge, 2012.

Waddell, Norman, trans. *Wild Ivy: The Spiritual Autobiography of Zen Master Hakuin*. Boston: Shambhala, 1999.

——. *The Essential Teachings of Zen Master Hakuin: A Translation of the Sokkō Roku Kaien Fusetsu*. Boston: Shambhala, 1994.

Watson, Burton. "Han Feizi (d. 233 BCE): Two Passages." In *Classical Chinese Literature*, vol. 1, ed. John Minford and Joseph S. M. Lau, 224–225. New York: Columbia University Press, 2000.

———. *The Lotus Sutra*. New York: Columbia University Press, 1993.

Welter, Albert. *The Administration of Buddhism in China: A Study and Translation of Zanning and his Topical Compendium of the Buddhist Order in China*. Amherst, NY: Cambria Press, 2018.

———. "Mahākāśyapa's Smile: Silent Transmission and the Kung-an (*kōan*) Tradition." In *The Kōan: Text and Context in Zen Buddhism*, ed. Steven Heine and Dale Wright, 75–109. New York: Oxford University Press, 2000.

———. *Yongming Yanshou's Conception of Chan in the Zongjing lu: A Special Transmission within the Scriptures*. Oxford: Oxford University Press, 2011.

Wang, Youru. *Linguistic Strategies in Daoist Zhuangzi and Chan Buddhism: The Other Way of Speaking*. Routledge, 2003.

Yampolsky, Philip B., trans. *The Platform Sutra of the Sixth Patriarch: The Text of the Tun-huang Manuscript*. New York: Columbia University Press, 2012.

———. "Hattō Kokushi's Dharma Talks." *Cahiers d'Extrême-Asie* 7, no. 1 (1993): 249–265.

Yanagida, Seizan 柳田聖山, and Shiina Kōyū 椎名宏雄, eds. *Zengaku tenseki sōkan* 禅学典籍叢刊, vol. 9. Kyoto: Rinsen Shoten, 1999.

Yanagida, Seizan 柳田聖山. *Daruma no goroku: Ninyū shigyōron* 達摩の語錄:〈二入四行論〉. Chikuma Shobō, Tōkyō, 1996.

———. *Shoki zenshū shisho no kenkyū* 初期禪宗史書の研究. Kyoto: Hozōkan, 1967.

———. *Sōzō ichin Hōrinden: Dentō gyokuei shū* 宋藏遺珍宝林伝: 伝灯玉英集. Zengaku sōsho no. 5. Kyōto-shi: Chūbun Shuppansha, 1983.

———. "Zenseki kaidai 禅籍解題." In *Zenke goroku* 禅家語録, vol. 2, ed. Nishitani Keiji and Yanagida Seizan, 445–514. Tokyo: Chikuma shobō, 1974.

Yifa, trans. *The Origins of Buddhist Monastic Codes in China: An Annotated Translation and Study of the Chanyuan qinggui*. Honolulu: University of Hawaii Press, 2002.

Yoshizawa, Katsuhiro 芳澤勝弘, ed. *Hakuin Zenji hōgo zenshū* 白隠禅師法語全集. Kyoto: Zen Bunka Kenkyūjo, 1999.

Yu, Chun-fang. "Ta-hui Tsung-kao and Koan Chan." *Journal of Chinese Philosophy* 6 (1979): 211–235.

Yu, Jimmy. "The Polemics of Passivity and Yuanwu's Usage of It." *The Journal of Chinese Buddhist Studies* 36 (2023): 31–71.

———. *Reimagining Chan Buddhism: Sheng Yen and the Creation of the Dharma Drum Lineage*. Routledge, 2022.

Zhang Changhong 張昌紅. "Chanzong songgu lianzhu tongji xulu 《禅宗颂古联珠通集》叙录." *Xin shiji tushuguan* 新世纪图书馆 1 (2013): 58–59.

Ziporyn, Brook. *Evil And/or/as the Good: Omnicentrism, Intersubjectivity, and Value Paradox in Tiantai Buddhist Thought*. Cambridge, MA: Harvard University Press, 2000.

CONTRIBUTORS

Juhn Ahn is associate professor in the Department of Asian Languages and Cultures, University of Michigan, where he teaches Buddhism and the history of Korea. He is the author of *Buddhas and Ancestors* (University of Washington Press, 2018), and his current research topics include the history of reading habits and the development of new soteriological techniques in Song dynasty Chan Buddhism; the economic history of the Koryŏ dynasty; and the cultural history of wealth and weather and monastic economy during the Chosŏn period.

Jan Chozen Bays is the Zen teacher at Great Vow Monastery and Zen Community of Oregon, as well as a pediatrician with a specialty in cases of child abuse. She is the author of six books, most recently *Mindful Medicine: 40 Simple Practices to Help Healthcare Professionals Heal Burnout and Reconnect to Purpose* (Shambhala, 2022) and *The Vow-Powered Life: A Simple Method for Living with Purpose* (Shambhala, 2016). She began studying Zen in 1973 under Maezumi Roshi, who gave her dharma transmission in 1983. Since the death of Maezumi in 1995 she has continued her training with Shodo Harada Roshi, a Rinzai Zen teacher and the abbot of Sogen-ji monastery in Japan.

Steven Heine is professor of religious studies and history as well as director of Asian Studies, Florida International University. He specializes in East Asian and comparative religions, Japanese Buddhism and intellectual history, Buddhist studies, and religion and social sciences. He is the author or editor of more than two dozen books, including *Wisdom Within Words: An Annotated Translation of Dōgen's Chinese-Style Poetry* (Oxford, 2022); and *From Chinese Chan to Japanese Zen: A Remarkable Century of Transmission and Transformation* (Oxford, 2017).

Natasha Heller is associate professor in the Department of Religious Studies, University of Virginia, where she teaches Chinese Buddhism in the contexts of cultural and intellectual history in the premodern (tenth through fourteenth c.) and the contemporary era. She is the author of *Illusory Abiding: The Cultural Construction of the Chan Monk Zhongfeng Mingben* (Harvard, 2014). Her current book project concerns picture books published by Buddhist organizations in Taiwan, and how such children's fiction not only teaches young people about the Buddhist tradition but also addresses how to relate to clergy, family members, and society.

Meido Moore is the abbot of Korinji Monastery in Wisconsin and the guiding teacher of The Rinzai Zen Community. He is the author of *The Rinzai Zen Way: A Guide to Practice* and *Hidden Zen: Practices for Sudden Awakening and Embodied Realization* (Shambhala, 2018 and 2020). He began Zen practice in 1988 and trained under three teachers in the line of the Rinzai master Ōmori Sōgen Roshi. He has been a lineage holder since 2008.

Jin Y. Park is professor in the Department of Philosophy and Religion, American University. She specializes in East Asian Buddhism, Buddhist and comparative ethics, intercultural philosophy, and modern Korean philosophy. Her research focuses on gender, violence, politics of discrimination, and narrative philosophy. Marginality has been a consistent theme in her scholarship, which deals with the marginalization of non-Western philosophy as well as of women's philosophy. She is the author, translator, editor, or coeditor of a number of books including *Approaches to Chan/Sŏn/Zen Buddhism* (State University of New York, 2022), *New Perspectives in Modern Korean Buddhism* (State University of New York, 2022), *Women and Buddhist Philosophy* (University of Hawai'i, 2017) and *Reflections of a Zen Buddhist Nun* (University of Hawai'i, 2014).

Marta Sanvido is a Glorisun Research Fellow in East Asian Buddhism at the Asien-Afrika-Institut of the University of Hamburg in Germany. Her research interests lie at the intersection of different types of knowledge emerging from Zen medieval and early modern secret textual corpuses. Her first book project traced the intellectual history of medieval and early modern Sōtō school, focusing on the development of different Sōtō Zen branches and their connection with the broader context of the Japanese cultural milieu as depicted in secret manuals and accounts exchanged from the fourteenth to the eighteenth centuries. Shedding light on the dynamics of secrecy in premodern Japan, she explores a wide variety of sources such as secret texts, literary works, mythological narratives, and historical records.

Robert H. Sharf is professor in the Department of East Asian Languages and Cultures, University of California, Berkeley, where he teaches medieval Chinese Buddhism (especially Chan/Zen Buddhism) and publishes in the areas of Japanese Buddhism, Buddhist modernism, Buddhist art, ritual studies, Asian philosophy, and methodological issues in the study of religion. He is the author of *Coming to Terms with Chinese Buddhism: A Reading of the Treasure Store Treatise* (University of Hawai'i, 2002) and close to thirty articles and book chapters, most recently "The Curious Case of the Conscious Corpse: A Medieval Buddhist Thought Experiment" (Springer, 2023).

Albert Welter is professor in the Department of East Asian Studies, University of Arizona, where he teaches Chinese Buddhism, particularly on the transition from the late Tang (ninth century) to the Song dynasty (tenth through thirteenth centuries); he has also published in the area of Japanese Buddhism. He is the author of several books, the most recent ones are: *The Future of China's Past: Reflections on the Meaning of China's Rise* (State University of New York, 2023) and *A Tale of Two Stūpas: Histories of Hangzhou Relic Veneration through Two of Its Most Enduring Monuments* (Oxford, 2022). His is currently involved in the Hangzhou Region Buddhist Culture Project, supported by the Khyentse Foundation, in conjunction with Zhejiang University, the Hangzhou Academy of Social Sciences, and the Hangzhou Buddhist Academy.

Jimmy Yu is professor in the Department of Religion, Florida State University, where he teaches Chinese Buddhism and East Asian religious traditions, with an emphasis on the history of the body in Chinese religions, Buddhist material culture, and Chan/Zen Buddhism within the broader contexts of the premodern (fifteenth through seventeenth c.) and contemporary eras. He is the author of *Sanctity and Self-Inflicted Violence in*

Chinese Religions, 1500–1700 (Oxford, 2012) and *Reimagining Chan Buddhism: Sheng Yen and the Creation of the Dharma Drum Lineage of Chan* (Routledge, 2022). He is also a Chan teacher and founder of the Tallahassee Chan Center. In that capacity, he has published several books, including *Passing through the Gateless Barrier* (Shambhala, 2016).

INDEX

Printed in the USA
CPSIA information can be obtained
at www.ICGtesting.com
JSHW022018061124
73104JS00001B/1

9 780231 207379